A History of Modern Lebanon

A History of Korean Literature

A History of Modern Lebanon

FAWWAZ TRABOULSI

Pluto Press

LONDON • ANN ARBOR, MI

First published 2007 by Pluto Press
345 Archway Road, London N6 5AA
and 839 Greene Street, Ann Arbor, MI 48106

www.plutobooks.com

British Library Cataloguing in Publication Data
A catalogue record for this book is available from the British Library

Hardback
ISBN-13   978 0 7453 2438 8
ISBN-10   0 7453 2438 X

Paperback
ISBN-13   978 0 7453 2437 1
ISBN-10   0 7453 2437 1

Library of Congress Cataloging in Publication Data applied for

10   9   8   7   6   5   4   3

Designed and produced for Pluto Press by
Chase Publishing Services Ltd, Fortescue, Sidmouth, EX10 9QG, England
Typeset from disk by Stanford DTP Services, Northampton, England
Printed and bound in the European Union by
Antony Rowe Ltd, Chippenham and Eastbourne, England

Contents

LIST OF MAPS

Preface

An updated history of modern Lebanon is long overdue as the last such attempt dates from the mid-1960s. Much has happened since and a lot of new historical material has been uncovered and researched. The last civil war (1975–90) was the occasion for a wealth of intellectual production on Lebanon in a variety of fields. Some are remarkable path-breaking works. Nevertheless, the modern history of Lebanon is still full of serious gaps, especially concerning the post-Independence period. On the other hand, researchers have extensively drawn upon European government archives, leaving important primary sources untapped. The Ottoman archives, for one, have been recently organised and made accessible to the public. Unfortunately, the results of most of the research on this vast stock are not yet available for use. Other, more recent, untapped primary sources have been strangely ignored, such as the US State Department Archives. Nevertheless, a number of secondary sources in Arabic, French and English have made precious contributions to the study of different periods of Lebanese history and various aspects of Lebanese life. I am referring here to the works of `Abd al-Rahim Abu Husayn, Albert Hourani, Engin Akarli, Leila Fawaz, Irene Gendzier, Michael Johnson, Kamal Salibi, Meir Zamir, Carolyn Gates, Theodor Hanf, Georges Corm, Wajih Kawtharani, Selim Nasr, Ahmad Beydoun, Samir Kassir, Marwan Buheiry, Mas`ud Dhahir, Waddah Sharara, Eyal Zisser, and others. Their contributions have enriched the present volume in many ways.

Two distinctive features have had a significant impact on the shaping of modern Lebanon: its sizeable Christian population, on the one hand, and the country's long exposure to the West, on the other. Their combined effect largely accounts for the main themes around which Lebanon's modern history is articulated: first, a political system based on the institutionalisation of religious sects ('sectarianism'); second, an outward-looking liberal economic system based on the service sector; and third, a problematic relation to its regional setting. Though my approach to the history of Lebanon will be mainly chronological, events and developments will be related and analysed in the light of these three themes.

The relationship between external and internal factors acquires crucial importance in a country of Lebanon's size and exposure. As many writings have tended to emphasise external factors and external interpretations of its historical events, the present work will emphasise the often-neglected and obscured internal factors.

Writings on Lebanon, and perception of Lebanon, have often sacrificed economic and social history in favour of an exclusively political perspective. In order to avoid this political fixation and bring out the underlying economic and social factors that have also shaped Lebanon's development, a political-economy approach is likely to contribute to a more comprehensive historiography.

Religious and identitarian discourses greatly colour the writings on Lebanon. The reduction of the identity of the Lebanese to one unique form of identity – their sectarian affiliation – is too simplistic and reductionist an approach to an extremely complex situation. Politicised religious sects are treated here as historical products, rather than ahistorical essences rooted in religious differences or as mere political entities. Sects in Lebanon are a perfect example of the way pre-capitalist formations are recycled to play new roles in a peripheral capitalist economy. They constitute multifunctional forms of identification and solidarity that came to permeate all aspects of Lebanon's life with a specific mode of articulation between the struggle for power, on the one hand, and socio-economic structures and interests, on the other. Two major functions of sects are often neglected: first, their role as enlarged clientelist networks designed to resist the inequalities of the market and compete for its benefits and for the appropriation of social wealth and services of the state, and second, their long-standing habit of enlisting outside help in their struggle for power or for sheer survival.

State–society relations in Lebanon have long been strained owing to the combined effects of extreme *laissez-faire* policies and the extensive political, legal and, often, military, autonomy enjoyed by Lebanon's sects. Hence the resilience of the question of state-building, which has acquired a large bearing on Lebanon's national unity, its social cohesion, even the country's very existence.

Finally, culture plays a major role in Lebanese life. The different approaches to the creation of Lebanon, perceptions of its role in the region as well as the representation and justification of its economic, social and political system and its significance as a cultural producer, provider and intermediary for the Arab region will be given the importance they deserve in this survey.

Fawwaz Traboulsi

Acknowledgements

Many people have contributed to making this work possible. Maysoon Sukkarieh and Mirna Mneimneh provided assistance in research and logistics while graduate students at AUB and LAU, respectively. Marlin Dick edited the manuscript in addition to correcting and polishing my English. I am endebted to Alexander Medawar for drawing the maps. The late Samir Kassir read earlier drafts of the manuscript and offered many suggestions. The contribution of this dear friend, comrade and colleague was tragically interrupted by his assassination at the hands of enemies of free speech and of Lebanon's independence. Aziz al-Azmeh, Noam Chomsky, Irene Gendzier, Charles Glass, Tarif Khalidy, Assaf Kfoury and Roger Owen read the manuscript and made useful corrections and comments. Last but not least, Nawal and Jana provided the love and encouragement without which this book would not have seen the light.

To all my thanks, my gratitude and the assurance that I assume sole responsibility for the book's mistakes and shortcomings.

Map 1   Modern Lebanon

Part I

Ottoman Lebanon

1
The Emirate of Mount Lebanon (1523–1842)

> Men resemble their present more than they resemble their fathers.
> Arab proverb, cited in Marc Bloch, *Apologie pour l'histoire*

Lebanon as a polity begins with the Emirate of Mount Lebanon, constituted in the late sixteenth century as an autonomous region inside the Ottoman Empire. The history of this emirate is primarily the history of the integration of the entirety of Mount Lebanon under its authority and its expansion toward surrounding regions of Palestine and the Syrian hinterland. Within the emirate developed a number of distinguishing characteristics that would greatly impact on the structure and developments of Lebanon in modern times: a sizeable Christian numerical majority; an early conversion to production for the market (silk) and to international trade; a long cultural exposure to Europe, and a tradition of intervention by European powers in its internal affairs.

THE *IQTA`* IN MOUNT LEBANON

The Emirate of Mount Lebanon under Ottoman rule was run according to the *iqta`* system, or *iltizam*, which alloted tax-farming rights in mountainous or desert areas to ethnic or tribal chiefs under the control of the Ottoman walis. The holders of the *iqta`*, the *muqata`ji* families, enjoyed varying degrees of autonomy in running the affairs of their *iqta`*s as long as they provided the High Porte with the fixed amount of purses, supplied armed men to the authorities when in need and generally kept order in the regions under their control.

Life in Ottoman Mount Lebanon was characterised by a set of interrelated divisions and conflicts, most of which were shared with similar regions of the Empire. These can be itemised as follows.

First, Ottoman subjects were divided along the religiously based distinction codified in the *millet* system, which etablished a two-tier hierarchy between a higher community, made up of Muslims, and a lower 'protected' community, made up of the 'people of the book',

Christians and Jews. The latter enjoyed a measure of freedom of religious belief and the right to perform their religious rites in return for the payment of a protection tax, the *jizya*. This distinction implied tangible differences in the relations of the two communities in regard to the social division of labour. Generally barred from military/administrative functions, Christians and Jews tended to specialise in commerce, finance and handicrafts. In Mount Lebanon, this uneven social location expressed itself in a Druze community dominated mainly by the tribal-warrior function, and a Christian community dominated mainly by commoners, with a large peasant base. This uneven location would be largely responsible for transforming social and political conflicts into sectarian conflicts.

Second, there was the division between ranking orders (*manasib*) and commoners (`amma*). The former held hereditary titles – emir, muqaddam and sheikh – bestowed upon them by the ruling emir of the Mountain, the Ottoman Wali or the Sultan himself. The holders of *iqta`*, or *muqata`ji* families, controlled political/judiciary power and lived off their extraction of the social surplus through collection of taxes and control over land, all the while benefiting from tax exemptions and privileges. Although `amma* was the generic term for all untitled subjects, the majority of whom were peasants, this lower order also included rich farmers, merchants, artisans and manufacturers. Conflicts arising from the division between the two main orders, mainly concerning taxation and political participation, frequently erupted in commoners' revolts.

Third, conflict between local rulers and the central authorities in Istanbul (the High Porte) was a permanent aspect of Ottoman politics. Local rulers, Turkish walis in the main centres, or tribal chieftains – whether in the highlands of Yemen or in Mount Lebanon – generally controlled a port, trade route or vital produce (coffee, cotton, silk, etc.). When rich enough or strong enough, they would attempt to shake off the authority of Istanbul and stop their payment of taxes, usually exploiting a military reversal of the Ottoman troops or a power struggle in Istanbul. These rebellions and autonomous movements were frequently encouraged and aided by one European power or another.

Fourth, conflicts between *muqata`ji* families, and within each family, competing for power or for the control of an *iltizam* (a tax-farming concession), were a natural aspect of the *iltizam* system. Those conflicts invariably entailed competition over the favours of well-placed people in Istanbul or regional walis (through bribes, gifts or military help). The traditional partisan form in the Arab East was *Qaysi/Yamani* factionalism. In Mount Lebanon, this dichotomy was later transformed into the Junblati–Arsalani cleavage within the Druze community.

Fifth, *muqata`ji* economic power was not limited to tax farming. They controlled land that they leased to peasant share-croppers for a share of the crops. In Mount Lebanon, landlord–peasant relations generated conflicts over rent and land ownership, and frequently erupted out in violent peasant revolts.

FAKHR AL-DIN II, THE MERCHANT EMIR (1590–1633)

At the time of the Ottoman conquest of Syria in 1516, the greater part of the territories that would constitute present-day Lebanon was divided among a number of ethnic/tribal chiefs. The Tanukhs and the Arsalans, both Yemeni tribes, were brought by the Umayyads to defend the Mediterranean shores against Byzantine incursions. They settled on the western approaches of Beirut and later adopted the Druze faith. The `Assafs were the Turkomen Sunni rulers of Kisrawan and Beirut and the Sayfas, the Kurdish Sunni rulers of Tripoli and the north. In the southern Biqa`, the Sunni Shihabs ruled Wadi al-Taym and the Harfush were the Shi`i rulers of Ba`albak and the northern Biqa`. The Ma`ns were a South Arabian warrior tribe that had been invited by the Tanukhs to settle in Ba`aqlin; its chiefs soon became tax farmers of a few villages in the Shuf region.

The early history of Ottoman rule in these parts of Syria was characterised by a series of rebellions, internecine fighting between the ethnic/tribal chiefs and local rulers, alliances and counter-alliances with the Ottoman authorities against the other/s, and frequent invitations to European powers seeking a foothold in the eastern Mediterranean to intervene in the various conflicts.

In 1518, the Ma`ns participated in the rebellion of the Sunni tribal sheikh Muhammad Ibn al-Hanash, in the western Biqa`, aiming at the restoration of the Mamluks. Three Ma`n chiefs were captured in the ensuing Ottoman punitive campaign, many of the rebels were beheaded, villages plundered and women and children taken captive. Not long after, the Ma`ns rallied to the Ottomans to fight the Harfushs, allies of the Safavid rulers of Persia and bitter enemies of the Ottomans. Thus the Ma`n chieftain Fakhr al-Din bin `Uthman bin Mulhim (1516–44) was appointed multazim of the Shuf; he became later emir liwa` or *sanjakbey* of the *Sanjak*s of Sidon–Beirut and Safad (in Palestine).[1] However, the people of Mount Lebanon were soon on the path of revolt again and remained so for long decades to come. They were only pacified in 1585 after a major expedition by Ibrahim Pasha, the governor of Egypt, allegedly related to the theft, along the coastal road to Tripoli, of Egyptian tribute on its way to Istanbul. Qurqumaz Ma`n, emir of the Druze at that time (1544–84), fled from the punitive campaign to the Tyron cave (near Niha), where he died in 1584.

Qurqumaz's son Fakhr al-Din Ma`n (born 1572), known as Fakhr al-Din II, took over after his father's death. In 1590, he was appointed multazim of the Druze mountain by the wali of Damascus, then emir liwa` of the *Sanjak* of Sidon–Beirut. However, Fakhr al-Din joined forces with the Kurdish leader and governor of Aleppo, `Ali Janbulad (later Junblat), as the latter rose in rebellion against the Ottomans in 1605–7. Janbulad was defeated but Fakhr al-Din managed to remain in power thanks to large bribes paid to the wali of Damascus.

`Ali Janbulad's rebellion was backed by Tuscany, the most active European power in the eastern Mediterranean. Catholic missionaries had began their activity among the Maronites of Mount Lebanon, and Mansur `Assaf, the ruler of Kisrawan, had put the Maronites under his protection. He also appointed a Maronite from the Hubaysh family as his *mudabbir* (secretary, adviser and educator of his children). Fakhr al-Din inherited the Tuscan connection from Janbulad, adopted the Khazins of Kisrawan as *mudabbir*s and established close ties with the ruling Medicis of Tuscany, who sent him arms and ammunition. Pope Gregory XIII addressed a letter to the Maronite patriarch requesting that his community side with Fakhr al-Din in future wars.

Periods of rebellion would alternate with periods of service to the Sultanate. When the Sayfas took over Kisrawan and Beirut following the decline of the power of the `Assafs, the governor of Damascus called upon Fakhr al-Din to regain those territories. He enlisted the support of the Harfushs and expelled the Sayfas from Kisrawan and Beirut; he was rewarded by receiving the *Sanjak* of Safad and was charged with keeping its Shi`as and Bedouin inhabitants under control.[2] Strengthened by his alliance with Tuscany, Fakhr al-Din by then had an army of some 30,000 troops and controlled thirty forts in the region. He proceeded to dominate the Hawran plain and the Golan in southern Syria. In 1611 he sent Maronite Bishop Jirjis to conclude an anti-Ottoman alliance with Tuscany and the Holy See. News of the mission reached Istanbul and Ahmad Pasha al-Hafiz, wali of Damascus, was ordered to pacify the Syrian coast. Fakhr al-Din fled just in time to Tuscany with his retinue. He was replaced by his brother Yunis Ma`n who managed to evade the ensuing Ottoman punitive expedition by paying a large indemnity. But the Ma`ns lost their authority over the coast and their status was reduced to that of *iltizam* of the Shuf.

During the five years of his Italian exile, spent mainly in post-Renaissance Florence (1613–18), the Lebanese emir studied life in the Italian city-states. He especially admired the banks, the central treasury, the local judicial system and the organisation of the militia. Although the Medicis were on the decline, Florence's Cosimo II (1590–1621), the Grand Duke of Tuscany, and his suzerain Spanish king Philip III, considered the Arab emir a major asset in their plans to extend their influence to the eastern Mediterranean.

Upon his return in September 1618, Fakhr al-Din set about reaffirming his control over Mount Lebanon and regaining the territories he had lost. This was a time when Sultan Othman II was occupied with consolidating his rule after taking power in a palace coup. By 1621, Fakhr al-Din had taken control of Bsharri and subdued its Maronite muqaddams. Luckily for the Ma`n emir, Othman II was overthrown by the Janissary corps in 1622, just as he was about to launch a campaign against Mount Lebanon. By 1623, Fakhr al-Din had come to control `Akkar from the Sayfas and advanced into Safita and beyond in the Hums and Hama region (Tripoli fell to him later, in 1633). Having achieved full control over Mount Lebanon, Fakhr al-Din moved against the Harfushs and seized the Biqa`. The wali of Damascus, Mustafa Pasha, the Harfushs and the Sayfas joined forces against him but were defeated in November 1623 in the battle of `Anjar, in which Mustapha Pasha was captured. Fakhr al-Din besieged the seat of the Harfush in Ba`albak (which he later entered and destroyed), and had his men loot the Biqa` and plunder its agricultural produce. Finally, he agreed to release the wali of Damascus in return for the restoration of the Palestinian regions of Safad, `Ajlun and Nablus to his authority.[3]

But Fakhr al-Din had gone too far in his expansion and was a threat to Damascus. Moreover, he was seeking military and financial help from the Tuscans for his project to secede totally from Ottoman rule. Then, following their military successes against the Persians in 1629, the Ottomans turned their attention to punishing and controlling the Syrian rebels, Fakhr al-Din at their head. In 1633, Kutshuk Pasha was appointed governor of Damascus with the express task of eliminating the Druze emir. When Kutshuk Pasha's forces moved against Fakhr al-Din, the Tuscans failed to come to his aid and Fakhr al-Din surrendered. He was brought to Istanbul in chains and decapitated on 13 April 1635.

Fakhr al-Din's main economic achievement was the introduction of silk production to Mount Lebanon as a cash product for export to the Italian city-states. For that purpose, he encouraged Christian peasants, who were mainly Maronite, to emigrate from the settled northern parts of Mount Lebanon (especially in Kisrawan) to the Druze-controlled regions, where they engaged in silk cultivation and other agricultural and artisanal occupations considered unworthy by the majority of the Druze.[4] In addition, Druze *muqata`jis* and warrior families began expelling Shi`as from the villages on the frontiers of Druze territory, in the western Biqa` and the Iqlims, and settling Christian peasants in their place.[5] Thus was launched a process that would have a lasting impact on the history of Mount Lebanon, gradually changing the social demography of the southern, Druze part of the area by transforming it into a Christian–Druze 'mixed region' in which the Christians would ultimately become a majority.

Intimately related to his introduction of silk production was the emir's encouragement of foreign merchants to settle in his emirate. For this purpose, he attracted European merchants trading with the Empire by the construction of a traveller's inn for them (Khan al-Faranj) in Sidon. Alhough Sidon remained his capital, Fakhr al-Din selected Beirut as a winter residence, enlarged its port and built a castle and a fort in it. The emir was a silk merchant in his own right. In one instance in 1631 we are told that he sent the Maronite Ibrahim al-Haqallani to Florence with 45 bales of silk. He offered one bale to Cardinal de Medici and sold the remaining 44; the proceeds were deposited in the Monte de Pieta bank in Fakhr al-Din's name and the names of his three sons.

Fakhr al-Din was succeeded by his nephew Mulhim bin Yunus bin Qurqumaz (1635–58), who was appointed by the Ottomans to rule the five *nahies* of the Shuf, in addition to the Gharb, the Jurd, the Matn and Kisrawan. His reign lasted for twenty years. Upon his death those same regions were granted as an *iltizam* to Fakhr al-Din's grandson, Ahmad Ma`n (1658–97) who followed his grandfather's tradition of exploiting Ottoman weakness to seek autonomy. This time it was Ottoman military reversal on the Hungarian front (1683–99) that prompted him to take up arms. Ahmad managed to escape arrest by a punitive campaign and died without a male heir, thus ending the

Ma`n dynasty. Summoned by the Ottomans to elect a new ruler, the Druze *muqata`jis*, meeting in Simqaniyeh, could not agree on one from among themselves and chose Bashir Shihab, a Sunni emir and relative of the Ma`ns from Wadi al-Taym in the southern Biqa`.

THE CENTRALISING POWER OF BASHIR SHIHAB II

During the early periods of Shihab rule (1697–1788) Mount Lebanon was marginalised and the Ottoman pashas of Sidon, Acre and Damascus exercised direct control over Mount Lebanon, playing aspiring Shihabi factions against each other. Bashir I (1697–1707) should be mainly remembered for pursuing Fakhr al-Din's efforts to extend the authority of the Lebanese Emirate to Jabal `Amil and Palestine. The rule of his successor, Haydar Shihab (1707–32), achieved the final victory of the *Qaysi*s, led by the Shihabs, over their *Yamani* challengers, led by the `Alam al-Din family, in the battle of `Ayn Dara in 1711. Haydar extended his control over Bsharri (then ruled by the Shi`i Hamadeh family), Batrun, Jubayl, the Biqa`, and Jabal al-Rihan (the southern Shuf) and reorganised the *muqata`ji* system by redistributing the districts among the chiefs of his victorious faction. Upon Haydar's death began an interlude of Druze internal strife for succession, exploited by the strong rulers of Acre, Dhahir al-`Umar (1750–75) and his successor Ahmad Pasha al-Jazzar (1775–1804), to extend their control over Mount Lebanon.

Bashir Shihab II (1788–1840) took over power with the help of Jazzar, while supported locally by the chief Druze leader Bashir Junblat. Of humble origins, Bashir Shihab began his political life at the court of his cousin Yusuf in Dayr al-Qamar, but soon married Princess Shams, the rich widow of a distant cousin from Hasbaya and stood as a candidate for the emirate. Thus began his long and bloody rise to power, the assassinations of his rivals and the repression of opponents earning him the title of the 'Red Emir'.

In 1797, Bashir played off the Imad and Jumblat clans against the Abu Nakad, who were backing the sons of Emir Yusuf, his rivals for the princedom. Five young Abu Nakads were killed and their house in Dayr al-Qamar looted and burnt. At that time, the Sa`d al-Khuri family formed the first political leadership of Christians in southern Mount Lebanon, hitherto deprived of any form of political representation. Sheikh Sa`d (1722–86) and his son Ghandur had been attached to the service of Emir Yusuf. Sa`d's nephew, Girgis Baz (1768–1807), a Maronite from Dayr al-Qamar, would become the most illustruous of

Christian *mudabbir*s. Regent to Yusuf's sons, Husayn and Sa`d al-Din (governors of the Shuf and of Jubayl), Baz became the real holder of power in the Mountain during the violent struggles for power among the Druze chiefs. His authority was further consolidated by his successful military campaigns to repulse the Hamadehs from Jubayl, subject the Sunni chiefs in `Akkar and Dhunniya and overcome the Ansaris of the Alawite region in northern Syria. Girgis Baz was close to the Maronite Patriarch Tiyan and played a major role in the rise of Christian influence in the emirate. Furthermore, the authority exercised by Baz and Bashir Junblat on their respective communities prefigured the emergence of sectarian leaderships, Maronite and Druze, at the expense of the multi-communitarian *Qaysi–Yamani* factionalism.[6] To crown his struggle for power, Bashir Shihab had Girgis Baz and his brother `Abd al-Ahad assassinated and, in 1807, managed to neutralise the three sons of emir Yusuf by blinding them. Then he turned against the other Druze *muqata`ji*s: the Arsalans, Talhuq, Imads and `Abd al-Malik. Thus, the Maronites were for a time excluded from the post of *mudabbir* to the emir, which was held by a Catholic Christian, while real power shifted to the temporary alliance of the two Bashirs: Bashir Shihab and Bashir Junblat.

The Antiliyas and Lihfid communes

The commoners' tax revolt (`ammiya) of 1820–1 was the first serious affront to the centralising policy of Bashir II, and the *muqata`ji* order in general. Representatives of Christians, Sunnis, Shi`a and Druze, meeting in Mar Iliyas church in Antiliyas, the 'border' between the two parts of Mount Lebanon, vowed 'not to betray one another and to struggle together for the common good'. They demanded tax reductions (Bashir collected nine million piastres in taxes of which he retained five million), the payment of only one combined tax at the end of the silk season and the 'suspension of other injustices'. The revolt of 1820–1 signalled the introduction of commoners into the political life of the emirate and constituted the first challenge to the old modes of political allegiance and alliance. It was opposed by the majority of the Druze and Christian *manasib*, who, though opposed to Bashir II, refused to participate in the revolt under the leadership of Christian commoners. The latter were led by *wakils*, elected delegates of the villages, who were held accountable by the villagers and could be recalled by them. They would play a major role in the destabilisation of the *muqata`ji* system.[7] The ensuing revolt that swept the Shuf, the Matn, Kisrawan, Batrun and Jubayl regions was powerful enough to force Bashir II to seek refuge in Hawran for a year. Upon his return, he ensured the defection of a number of sheikhs and convinced the rebels of the Shuf and the Matn to lay down their arms in return for rich merchants paying their tax dues in their place. But the revolt was rekindled in the northern districts of Kisrawan, Jubayl, Batrun and `Akkar, under the leadership of two intellectuals who had collaborated to write a history of Mount Lebanon: Archbishop Yusuf Istfan (1759–1823), founder and director of the famous Maronite college at `Ayn Waraqa, and the writer Abu Khattar al-`Anturini. Bashir Junblat rallied to the help of the Shihab emir, and their joint forces marched upon the rebels, who engaged in a heroic resistance as they retreated to Lihfid, in the Jubayl highlands, where they led their final battle. `Anturini died from torture in Bashir's prison while Yusuf Istfan was poisoned during a visit to Bashir in his Bayt al-Din palace.

The break between the two Bashirs

Nevertheless, the alliance of the two Bashirs did not long survive the crushing of the commoners' revolt. Their rupture, in 1825, constituted a decisive turning point in the history of the Emirate and a temporary victory for the centralising policy of Bashir Shihab, finally overcoming the last powerful Druze lord. Having mercilessly suppressed the northern Christian commoners, Shihab – now officially declared a convert to Christianity – relied on the numerical power of the Christians in the south to overcome the Druze *muqata`jis*. Junblat opposed him in the name of Muslim Ottoman identity and enticed the Ottomans to move against him as a Christian ruler holding power in the Muslim empire. The regional context of this confrontation was a power struggle between the Ottoman walis of Damascus and Acre: Junblat rallied Damascus to his side, while Shihab remained committed to his alliance with Acre. Finally, Shihab had the wali of that city lure Junblat to Acre where he was arrested and decapitated. With Bashir Junblat out of the way, the Druze *muqata`jis* were dispossessed of their fiefs and a number of them went into exile to Hawran. Of the twelve seigneurial domains in the southern districts, only two remained in the hands of Druze lords. The rest were taken over by Bashir and distributed between his relatives. On the other hand, Bashir drew closer to the Maronite Church, already an impressive economic, social and cultural institution under its new patriarch, Yusuf Hubaysh (1823–45).

Lebanon under Egyptian rule (1831–40)

Muhammad `Ali Pasha, the wali of Egypt, was summoned by Sultan Muhammad II to participate in the military campaign of the Sultanate against the Greek rebellion for independence. Although the Greeks finally achieved their goal, Muhammad `Ali was to be compensated by the Porte. He asked for Syria but was offered Crete; he sent his army, commanded by his son Ibrahim, to take Syria. When the Egyptian troops besieged Acre, Ibrahim Pasha sought Bashir's help. Reluctant at first, Bashir nevertheless put his armed men in the service of the Egyptians in their battles to occupy Tyre, Sidon, Beirut, Tripoli and finally Damascus, as the whole of Syria fell to Egyptian rule. As the Egyptian forces threatened Istanbul, the Porte recognised Ibrahim as ruler of Syria, but started to prepare a counter-offensive, backed by Britain, the fierce enemy of Muhammad `Ali, who enjoyed extensive French support.

In Syria, Ibrahim Pasha followed the policies his father had drawn up for Egypt. He strengthened the administration, tried to fight corruption, set up representative councils in towns and cities, treated Christians and Muslims equally and encouraged industry and international trade. But he was especially interested in Mount Lebanon's sericulture, which he developed, declaring silk imports a state monopoly and establishing one scale for silk for the whole of Mount Lebanon, located in Beirut. For this purpose, Beirut's port was enlarged and the city developed and provided with a council to run its affairs.

Egyptian rule was contested from the beginning by the Druze *manasib*. The 1838 Druze revolt in Hawran led by Shibli al-`Aryan spread to the Biqa`and Wadi al-Taym, and was soon joined by the `Imads and Jumblats. To counter it, Ibrahim Pasha distributed arms to the Christians and asked Bashir to send his son Khalil to lead 4,000 armed Christians in fighting the rebellion. It was the first time that the inhabitants of the Lebanese territories had confronted each other on a sectarian basis. Defeated, the Druze rebels waged their last battle at Shib`a on the slopes of Mount Hermon. The following year, the Shi`a of Jabal `Amil rebelled and were also quelled with the help of Bashir's forces. However, Ibrahim Pasha alienated wider sectors of the population with his exorbitant taxes, forced labour and military conscription. Revolts against him broke out in Palestine, Tripoli and northern Syria. Afraid that the Christians would be encouraged to join the Druze and Muslims in revolt against Egyptian rule, Ibrahim

Pasha asked Bashir to disarm the Christians. That put them on the path of revolt.

The inhabitants of Dayr al-Qamar were summoned to hand over their arms; they refused and rebelled, both Christians and Druze, under the leadership of their Abu Nakad lords. In June 1840, representatives of the Maronites, Druze, Sunnis and Shi`a met in Intiliyas and launched their rebellion against the Egyptians and Bashir. They called for a reduction in tax, and demanded the abolition of the corvée (in the iron mines), the restitution of firearms, the abolition of Bashir's monopoly over soap production, administrative reform, and the representation of religious communities in the council (*diwan*) at Bayt al-Din. This last demand was directly aimed at the authority of the Druze *manasib* and contributed to alienating many of them from the revolt. Though some *muqata`ji* families joined the rebellion in the hope of regaining their privileges, the revolt was mainly organised around popular chiefs, the *sheikhs shabab*, and directed by a council of *wakils* in which the *manasib* sat side by side with the elected commoners. But the church was reluctant to support the uprising, clinging to the Shihab Emirate and taking into consideration France's support for Bashir and Ibrahim Pasha. Patriarch Hubaysh blessed the rebellion two months after its inception as its first wave was defeated by the forces of Bashir and the Egyptian pasha. The second phase was launched in September in support of the foreign military intervention of mid-July. Beirut was bombarded by Ottoman warships, and Ottoman, British and Austrian sea-borne troops landed in Junieh, signalling the end of Egyptian rule in Syria. In October 1840, the Egyptian troops withdrew to Acre and Bashir was arrested and exiled to Malta. Paradoxically, the Christians, the great beneficiaries of the emirate, had nevertheless contributed to its downfall.

The patriarch's programme

The emirate did not long outlast Bashir II. Appointed by the foreign powers, Bashir Milhim Qasim, baptised Bashir III, ruled for no more than 18 months. Returning from exile, the Druze sheikhs tried to regain their domains and power over their Christian subjects and faced the hostility of the new prince as well as the resistance of the Christians. Conflicts over landed property broke out everywhere and dominated the period. The inhabitants of Dayr al-Qamar obstructed the return of the Abu Nakads to their town, while the inhabitants of Jizzin forcibly expelled the agents of the Junblat family from their region. Nevertheless, the Ottoman authorities and the British stood firm in support of Druze property 'rights'.

Although the Christian emirate was now dead, it became transformed into a banner under which many Maronites would rally for decades to come. Patriarch Hubaysh supported Bashir III out of fear of being replaced by a Muslim and made the first serious attempt to unite the community around a common political programme. In October 1840, he addressed a memorandum to the Porte demanding that a Shihab Maronite prince rule Mount Lebanon, that he be appointed for life by the Sultan and be assisted by a Maronite *mudabbir* and 12 councillors representing the different sects, all elected for a period of three years. The prince would exercise his judiciary powers 'according to the Law and after investigation', and torture would be abolished. On the other hand, the right to judge and punish the Maronite clergy would become the exclusive prerogative of the Maronite patriarch, who would have a special representative in Istanbul. The patriarch's memorandum reiterated the demand for a unified land tax and the abolition of the corvée. More importantly, it raised the demand that the Sultanate recognise France's protection of the Maronites. In support of his programme, in March 1841, Hubaysh convened the Maronite notables from all regions of Mount Lebanon, who vowed to remain united 'in Christian love' and renewed their allegiance to the Sultan. In order to assure the unity of the community, the programme established a delicate compromise between its two main social components. While respecting the titles and ranks of the *manasib* 'according to tradition', it called for the nomination of *wakils* for all regions of Mount Lebanon whose task would be to 'reform and educate the people'.[8] Thus the role of this popular representative institution was reversed: rather than represent the people, it should henceforth educate them.

In fact, Hubaysh's programme was a repetition of the main articles of the Ottoman reforms of centralisation and modernisation, the famous *Tanzimat*, promulgated by the Sultan in his famous Edict of Gulhan in November 1839. Nevertheless, Hubaysh's programme, based on the notion of the Christian majority, destabilised the established order in Mount Lebanon. The now-official Christian prince-ruler heralded the end of the Druze Emirate and deprived the Druze *manasib* of their main prerogative, the election of the Prince of Mount Lebanon, reducing Druze representation to a minority in the proposed consultative council. No wonder that the Druze *manasib*, increasingly alienated by Bashir III's hostility, withdrew their support for the Shihab Emirate. In 1841, armed Druze attacked Bashir III in his palace in Dayr al-Qamar. Armed Christians hurried to his defence but were overcome. In response, Hubaysh called for a mass Christian uprising to take power in the south. Significantly, the leadership of the Christian army, stationed in Ba`abda, was divided between sheikhs and *wakils*. The first group feared popular power and believed that the loss of power by the Druze sheikhs in the south would lead to the demise of the Christian sheikhs in the north. However, secret contacts between Christian and Druze sheikhs to form a common front against the commoners were offset by the patriarch, who threatened to excommunicate the sheikhs, later branded as 'traitors' by Tannus al-Shidyaq, a moderate Maronite historian. The fighting in 1841 ended inconclusively but it spelled the death of the emirate. On 13 January 1842, the Porte declared the end of the special status of Mount Lebanon and appointed `Umar Pasha as governor.

INEQUALITY OF ORIGINS TO UNEVEN DEVELOPMENT

The end of Egyptian rule in Syria not only was a military defeat for Muhammad `Ali Pasha, but also had important economic repercussions for the region: the victorious British did not impose free trade on Egypt alone, but on the whole of the Ottoman Empire. In fact the 1840s signalled the entry of the Ottoman Empire into the world market, opening up to European commodities and reducing customs duties to their bare minimum. The direct impact in Mount Lebanon was the transformation of the original uneven social locations of the Druze and Maronite communities into a pattern of uneven socio-economic development. By then, the Christians were constituted into a network of forces that were quickly eroding the Druze-dominated *muqata`ji* system. A brief social mapping of Mount Lebanon on the eve of the second half of the nineteenth century helps provide a clear picture of the major components of this process.

At the basis of the developments of this period lies the effects of the expansion of the Maronites from the extreme north of Mount Lebanon toward the south that had began under Fakhr al-Din II and had been rapidly developing since. This productive and 'settlers' function gave the Christians the right to bear arms and contributed to the creation of an asymmetrical social formation: a Druze bloc, primarily tribal, in which the tributary and military function dominated, and a Christian bloc, with a wide peasant and artisan base and commercial/financial ramifications. There was also a distinction between the status of the Druze and Christian leadership. Salibi rightly notes that while the Maronite *muqata`jis* were tax collectors and quasi-feudal lords over their own co-religionists, the Druze sheikhs were primarily tax farmers and quasi-feudal lords over their Christian subjects. The Druze bloc was characterised by its cohesion, as it coalesced around a single sheikh, a Junblat, elected by all the *manasib* of the Shuf, and whose authority covered the entire community. More importantly, the political and social position enjoyed by the Druze sheikh implied a number of privileges and exemptions for his community. The large domains allotted to the Junblat family by the Porte were generally distributed among the various allied *manasib*, Druze commoners paid less taxes, if any, and the whole Shuf benefited from the revenues collected by the Junblats from their domains outside this region. As early as the commoners' revolts of 1820–1 and 1840, the Christians were complaining about this inequality in the social division of labour and in taxation among the communities. A *zajaliya* (popular poem) by father Yusuf al-Ma`luf complained of the injustice suffered by the Christians, peasant producers who paid taxes and were subject to impositions, while a large number of the Druze, mainly warriors and non-producers, benefited from many exemptions and privileges. This complex asymmetry served as the matrix upon which the sectarian system and sectarian mobilisation were built; both features would long preside over the destinies of Mount Lebanon. The main components of the Christian network were the peasantry, the merchant class and commercial towns, the *mudabbir*s and the clergy.

PEASANTS, MERCHANTS, *MUDABBIRS* AND CLERGY

Sheikhs and peasants

In the principality of Mount Lebanon, the majority of the land was under the joint control of the Maronite Church (whose vast domains were exempted from taxation) and a limited number of big *muqata`ji* families. In the north, the Maronite Khazin and Hubaysh controlled 60 per cent of the lands of Kisrawan and a sizeable part of those of Batrun and Jubayl. In the south, the Junblats held, in addition to their *iqta`* in the Biqa`, most of the Shufs (the lower and upper Shuf in addition to the Bayyadhi Shuf, covering most of the western Biqa`) and the Iqlims (the Iqlims of Jizzin, Tuffah, Rihan and Kharrub) – in total some 100 villages, most of which were inhabited by Christians.[9] The rest of the lands were of two kinds: first, 'territories with an individual structure', as Weulersse calls them, which were individually reclaimed land at the expense of a mountain or a forest, or appropriated in a form of tenant farming that allowed the tenant to own part of the plot of land he had been renting after six, eight or ten years' uninterrupted cultivation of it;[10] and second, the village commons (*musha`*), usually under the control of the *muqata`jis*. Thus, with the exception of a restricted number of small and middle-level agricultural owners, the majority of the inhabitants of Mount Lebanon were landless peasants. This was the section of the population that gave rise to tenant farmers, priests, hermits, agricultural workers, day labourers, artisans, muleteers, lumbermen and so on.

Share-cropping (*sharaka*) governed by yearly contracts constituted the main form of agricultural relations. Rent was paid in kind (a third or a quarter of the product) or in a mixture of rent in kind and monetary rent. Production was carried out inside 'kin-ordered' units in which social labour was allocated on the basis of family ties. Further, villages and towns specialised in different trades and handicrafts, for example, bell production in Bayt Shabab, silk `abayas in Bayt al-Din or Zuq Mikhail and tanning in Zahleh.

Tributary and rent-based relations coexisted with commercial activities, but not without ambivalence. Merchants and middlemen frequently resorted to the *muqata`jis* in order to impose on peasants the delivery of their share of the harvest or the payment of debts. A curious dialectic operated here: the exorbitant political rent imposed by the rulers on the merchants limited their scope of action and reduced their profits, but, on the other hand, the tendency of merchants to commercialise everything weakened the tribute system and increasingly submitted the *muqata`jis* to the whims of merchants and usurers.

As for the peasants, they were submitted to a triple exploitation: tributary, rentier and commercial/usurer. Mikha'il Mashaqqa, an eyewitness of that period, said that 90 per cent of the silk harvest in Mount Lebanon (amounting to 1,500 quintals) was appropriated by the emirs, sheikhs, monasteries, middlemen and Beirut merchants and usurers, leaving to a population of some 300,000 people no more than 10 per cent of the product of their toil.[11]

Politically, this system implied, if not serfdom in the strict European feudal sense, at least very strong political and military ties of dependence that bound the commoners to their lords. In the seigneurial domain (the `*uhda*), commoners were linked to the name of their lords by the *ismiya*. In a much larger context, factionalism (*gharadhiya*) mobilised blocs of seigneurial families and their subjects against other blocs. The inhabitants of Mount Lebanon, as was the case for most of Greater Syria, were divided into two major 'parties': the *Qaysis*, who claimed descent from the north Arabian tribes, and the *Yamanis*, who claimed descent from south Arabia. What was at stake in most of the factional struggles was, of course, the appropriation of the social surplus, the control of trade routes, of `*uhda*s, commercial centres and ports, or some lucrative commodity (coffee, cotton, silk, etc.)[12]

Mudabbirs

The asymmetry of the social formation of Mount Lebanon also entailed new forms of representation and leadership among the Maronites, notably in the regions where the Druze *iqta`* dominated. The *mudabbir* was the intellectual/administrative function through which Christians, being more privileged in clerical and missionary education, achieved social mobility and avoided the many rigid constraints of the *muqata`ji* order. As private secretary, tutor of the children of the emir, sheikh or governor, treasurer and administrator of the domains of his master, the *mudabbir* was a trade based on merit invested in a multiplicity of economic, social and political functions. Initially, this post helped constitute the Maronite *iqta`* in the northern part of the country and also helped in the accumulation of merchant capital, especially among Catholic and Greek Orthodox families.

The Sa`d al-Khuri family, already mentioned in connection with Bashir Shihab, were by no means the only *mudabbirs* in Mount Lebanon. Joseph Qassis and Joseph Diyab served the ruler of Acre, Zhahir al-`Umar. Ibrahim Sabbagh, the Sakroujs and the Mashaqqas, all Greek Catholic, took turns in serving his redoubtable successor, Ahmad Pasha al-Jazzar of Acre. Among them were also Maronite families – the Iddis – or Jewish ones, the Farhis. Ibrahim Mashaqqa, father of Mikha'il, at the apex of his influence under Jazzar, collected taxes from some 300 villages and farms in Jabal `Amil for eight years, before being expropriated and expelled by Jazzar. He took refuge in Dumiyat, Egypt and then went to Dayr al-Qamar, where he served Emir Bashir II as his *mudabbir*. Abu `Assaf Rizq Allah al-Khuri was secretary to `Ali Junblat and managed his properties in Jizzin and Iqlim al-Rihan. His son, Abu Shakir, inherited his father's post at the service of `Ali Junblat's successor, Sa`id.

In addition to its role in socio-economic promotion, the function of *mudabbir* was a hotbed for the production of new leaders and notables, as in the case of the Iddis and the Khuris, and a middle class of functionaries and members of the liberal professions.

Merchants and merchant communes

The rise of a Christian middle class, another effect of the asymmetric social structure, was the product of the extension of commercial production, mainly through sericulture, the differentiation of the peasantry, and the development of commerce, finance and artisan production.

In fact, Mount Lebanon, Syria and Palestine were already economically interdependent thanks to a network of trade exchanges centred on the supply of staples and livestock, the provision of raw materials and the circulation of artisan products. Mount Lebanon imported its cereals and livestock from the Biqa` and the north of *Bilad al-Sham* (the Syrian interior). Nablus, in Palestine, also exported cereals and livestock to Mount Lebanon and furnished Hasbaya with cotton for its looms. In return, Mount Lebanon furnished raw silk to the Damascus weavers. Zahleh merchants exported cereals to Damascus, Beirut and Mount Lebanon and received livestock from nomadic tribes in Iraq and Palestine.

The Christian artisanal/commercial towns lying at the intersection of commercial routes or linking the interior to the exterior were the vital nodes in this network. Progressively, they came to control an ever-expanding space of villages and farms and sap the foundations of *muqata`ji* power on which they depended. The lords – and not only the peasants – become more and more financially dependent on the towns and cities and indebted to their merchants and moneylenders.

In Kisrawan and Jubayl, we observe the rise of rich farmers and merchants/moneylenders investing part of their wealth in land. By the mid-nineteenth century, Zuq Mikha'il, mainly Greek Catholic, possessed 150 to 300 weaving looms and distributed its products on a large scale; it constituted with its sister town Jouniyeh a market for the whole region. `Amshit, on the coast of Jubayl, developed outside *muqata`ji* suzerainty and was associated with the name of the Tubiya Zakhya, the partner of the Asfars, one of the oldest merchant families in Beirut and creditors to the Khazins. Zakhya lent money to peasants at 12 per cent interest and provided silk eggs at double their price, to be repaid in kind in the form of raw silk at half its market price.

He thus appropriated the lands of peasants and farmers and soon became the biggest landowner in the Jubayl region. David Urquhart, who visited Zakhya, estimated his wealth at 5 million piastres and considered him a representative of the 'rising Third Estate'.[13]

Dayr al-Qamar, with 8,000 inhabitants, was the most senior of the Mountain communes. An entrepôt on the route between Sidon, Damascus and the Syrian hinterland since the seventeenth century, it constituted a centre for the collection of raw silk, which its merchants exported to the Italian city-states and then to France starting in the eighteenth century. It was also a centre for weaving 'Arab silk' and cotton and for the manufacture of traditional `abayas, worn by the sheikhs, not to speak of its role as a market for cereals and livestock. As an administrative centre, usually exempt from the payment of taxes, Dayr al-Qamar prospered and reinforced its autonomy under Bashir II, who expropriated its Druze lords, the Abu Nakad, and distributed their property and households among his Christian followers. But the affluence of the Christians had already sapped the authority of the Abu Nakad who were heavily indebted and sold many of their properties to their Christian creditors. And at the end of Bashir's reign, the inhabitants of Dayr al-Qamar already ruled themselves through a 'council of twelve', and had a militia of several hundred armed men at their disposal.[14]

Jizzin was an ancient Shi`i agglomeration, progressively inhabited by Christians; 37 of its 43 villages and farms belonged to the Junblats. Its Christian population benefited from the calamities suffered by their Druze lords to take over their lands, with resulting conflicts over tax arrears, shares of crops and land distribution. These exploded when the Junblats returned from Hawran after the fall of Bashir II, as the inhabitants of Jizzin forcibly expelled the agents of the Junblats from their region.

In the southeastern part of the Biqa`, Rashaya and Hasbaya (some 60 km southwest of Damascus) were two commercial/artisanal enclaves under Druze control. Their Christian subjects progressively came to own the parcels of land they cultivated under the *muqassama*, system of share-cropping, and their wealth became a 'temptation for the Druze, whose villages formed like a circle of fire around the two localities'.[15]

The way the town of Zahleh was constituted is a characteristic example of the beginning of the communes in the domains of the *Iqta*`. Situated on the borders of a tributary of the Litani, with its back to the eastern slopes of Mount Lebanon, the mainly Greek

Catholic town occupied an intermediary position between the Mountain and the Plain, a position that would command its destiny. Originally, Zahleh was a Druze agglomeration of three seigneurial closures (*hawch*) in the domain of the Abil-l-Lama`, Druze lords of the Matn who converted to the Maronite faith during the nineteenth century. Beginning in the mid-eighteenth century, peasants, artisans and shepherds, who were principally Greek Catholic, took refuge in Zahleh from Hawran, the Biqa` and the Matn and were placed under the protection of its Druze lords. Its Christian population soon became a majority and undertook commercial and artisanal activities, in addition to cultivating the lands of the Abi-l-Lama`s while preserving a hierarchical family and tribal structure, inherited from Bedouin society in Hawran. In the nineteenth century, Zahleh was already an important multifunctional commercial centre: for wheat grinding and supply to the Bedouins of the Plain and a cereal market for Mount Lebanon. Its merchants bought cereals from Hawran, Hums and the Qalamun and supplied Damascus with wheat. On the other hand, armed caravans from Zahleh travelled as far as Baghdad and Mosul to buy livestock, horses and wool in order to sell them in Beirut, with which the Biqa` city was progressively linked from the 1840s. The town was also an artisan centre for a prospering textile industry, exporting its products to Hawran, Hums and Nablus (which provided it with cotton and raw wool), in addition to tanning, shoemaking, arms manufacture, tailoring, dyeing, `*arak* distilling and molasses pressing. Under the direction of its 'seven families' of merchant/warriors and landlords, the armed people of Zahleh put themselves at the service of the emirs of the Mountain against their adversaries. This was their means of acceding to greater autonomy vis-à-vis their Abil-l-Lama` overlords and the dominant forces in the Plain: the walis of Damascus, and the Shi`i and Kurdish tribes that imposed their laws and exactions and threatened the security of caravan routes. A durable alliance had linked the people of Zahleh to Bashir II. The town's rich lent him money and the poor fought on his side, in return for which the emir granted the town the right of self-administration. In 1825, the people of Zahleh exploited the conflict between Bashir Shihab II and Bashir Junblat to expel the remaining Druze families in their town.[16]

Beirut, whose economic fortunes had slumped under the Mamluks, prospered under the Egyptians. The town greatly benefited from the political turmoil in the competing ports of Tripoli, Sidon and Acre to become the principal port of Damascus, linked to it by a road that was opened to carriages in 1856. Between 1827 and 1862, the value of goods transiting through Beirut increased 800 per cent. Its population increased more than four times from 6,000 inhabitants in 1830 to 25,000/50,000 in 1860. Its Christian population, which had tripled in twenty years (between 1840 and 1860), had already become half of its population. 'A wealthy class of Christians reside here, whose habits, both as regards dress and the consumption of other luxuries of civilised societies, exceed those of the generality of their countrymen',[17] wrote a British consul.

Raw silk was Beirut's main export, accounting for a quarter of the value of its trade. Between 1840 and 1860, commercial capital in Beirut started to invest in silk reeling. In addition to the Asfar family, Levantine families such as the Sursuq, leading landowners and merchants of silk and staple exporters, settled on Beirut from the mid-eighteenth century; the Bustrus, importers of manufactured products from Manchester, were represented in the city's council under the Egyptians; the Fayyad, Jubayli, Naccache and Pharaon families also rose in social rank in Beirut. In 1840, the Bayhums, creditors to the Druze sheikhs, established the first Sunni Muslim trading house in the city. After 1840, foreign merchants came back in force but commercial leadership had already passed into the hands of the locals.[18] British goods invaded the region from Beirut port and led to the collapse of the traditional textile industry. Merchants strengthened their positions by playing the role of intermediary between foreign traders on the one hand, and the peasants and the domestic market on the other.[19] During these years, interest on money lending to peasants reached 40 per cent; it had not surpassed 20 per cent under the Egyptians. In the city, the representation of the new social interests in Beirut slowly but gradually slipped into the hands of the Maronite Church.

The Maronite Church

By the mid-nineteenth century, the Maronite Church had already become an important player in the political life of Mount Lebanon. Three major factors contributed to this development.

First, the Maronite Church had become an impressive economic force. To begin with, it was the biggest landowner in the region, dominating at least a third of all the lands of Mount Lebanon, with its *waqf*s and some of the richest and largest lands owned by a large network of monastic orders and convents that had come under its control. In addition, the convents performed a number of extra-religious functions: they were artisan centres for a wide variety of jobs like silk reeling, weaving, building and milling, and also housed schools, libraries and centres for copying, printing and bookmaking.[20]

Second, in the 1840s, the patriarchal see was moved from the Qannubin valley in the upper north of the Bsharri region to Bkirki in the heart of Kisrawan, signalling the extension of the church's influence to the southern parts of the country.

Third, as a reflection of the social mobility inside the Maronite community, in 1854, Bulus Mas`ad because the first cleric of commoner descent to be elected patriarch, breaking a long-established tradition of *muqata`ji* family monopoly over the patriarchal seat. His election, opposed by the *manasib* of the north, was acclaimed by popular demonstrations in support of the 'patriarch of justice and equality'. A learned man educated by the Jesuits at the Propaganda School in Rome during the Catholic counter-offensive against Protestantism and the ideals of the French Revolution, the new patriarch was mainly attached to the purity of the Catholic doctrine. He had been the right-hand man of Patriarch Hubaysh when the latter launched his campaign against the 'Protestant heresy'. Mas`ad had all the prerequisites to become a major actor in the events to come.

However, it would take twenty years of travail, blood and tears for the *muqata`ji* system to finally collapse.

2
The Bloody Death of the
Muqata`ji System (1842–1861)

The responsibility for [the war of 1860] does not fall at all on the commoners but all of the responsibility falls on the *muqata`jis*. We should not blame only one party for what it has committed against the other. Had the people of the Iqlim [of Jizzin] won over those of the Shuf, they would have done the same.

Shakir al-Khuri, *Majma' al-Masarrat*

Nobody wins in civil wars. The losers lose, the winners lose.

Druze shaykh Husayn Talhuq on the '1860 events'

The end of the Emirate of Mount Lebanon spelled the death of its *muqata`ji* system. The *Qa'im maqamiya* declared in early 1843 divided Mount Lebanon into two administrative regions, exacerbating the struggle over its identity. It further constituted the context for the Harakat, a series of commoners' uprisings, *muqata`ji* preemptive strikes and civil disorder that lasted from 1841 to 1861, marking the bloody transition from the *muqata`ji* system to peripheral capitalism. The crumbling of the predominantly Druze *muqata`ji* system led to the end of Druze political supremacy over Mount Lebanon and the institutionalisation of the sectarian system of political representation.

THE *QA'IM MAQAMIYA*, A SYSTEM OF DISCORD

The idea of dividing Mount Lebanon between Christians and Druze was a compromise proposed by the Austrian Chancellor Metternich with the British and the Ottomans, who backed the Druze demand for a Muslim governor, and the French, who insisted on the return of the Shihab principality. Druze Emir Ahmad Arsalan was appointed *qa'im maqam* of the mixed southern district and Christian Emir Haydar Ahmad Abi-l-Lama' *qa'im maqam* of the predominantly Christian northern district.[1] Each *qa'im maqam* was to be seconded by two *wakils*, a Druze and a Christian, who exercised judicial and fiscal authority over the members of their respective communities.

Both parties contested the new arrangement. The Maronite Church demanded that the Christians in the *qa'im maqamiya* of the south (now around 60 per cent of the population) be put under the jurisdiction of the Christian *qa'im maqam* of the north, wrenching them definitively from the authority of their Druze chieftains. The Druze, for their part, insisted on their traditional right to rule over the whole of Mount Lebanon. It did not take long before the Ottoman governor alienated both communities, and the Druze chieftain Shibli al-'Aryan once again took the path of revolt in Wadi al-Taym and the Hawran, backed by the 'Imads and the Jumblats. The Christians, invited to join the revolt, did not budge: their condition was the return of the Shihab principality.[2]

The identity of the land

The declaration of the *qa'im maqamiya* triggered a new wave of violence about the Mountain's identity. A memorandum by the people of Zahleh to the French consul, Poujade, in 1843 spelled out the asymmetry between the forces in conflict and the amalgam between communitarian belonging and social status:

We are sure that the Druze attack us only because they are forced to do so by their *muqata`ji*s, even by baton blows. In fact, as long as the leaders enjoy privileges and immunities, Lebanon will never enjoy peace (...) Peace may well be achieved between Druze and Christian peasants but not with their leaders, who will always acquire unacceptable prerogatives over our brothers.[3]

This definition distinguishes between *muqata`ji* and peasant among the Druze, whereas 'Christians' is taken to be a generic term for commoners, all equally subject to the Druze *muqata`ji*s. More importantly, the inhabitants of Zahleh called for a 'return' to what they called 'the Christian origin of the territory' by claiming that the Christians, 'original inhabitants' of Mount Lebanon, had received the Druze when they were expelled from Egypt.[4] This is a curious inversion of historical reality as it was the inhabitants of Zahleh who came from the Upper Matn and the Ba`albak region and were themselves received by the Druze overlords of Zahleh and allowed to inhabit the town![5] In its extreme form, this desire to appropriate the territory culminated in a project to expel the Druze of Mount Lebanon to Hawran, 'the favourite dream of the Maronites since 1840', in the words of a French eyewitness who named the bishop of Beirut, Tubiya 'Awn, as a principal initiator of that project.[6]

Having become a numerical minority in Mount Lebanon, the
Druze were afraid of losing status and power to a Christian majority.
Hence the paradoxes of the new situation: the Christians, a majority
in Mount Lebanon, were nevertheless a minority in the context of
the Ottoman Empire, while the Druze, having become a minority in
what was called not so long ago 'the Druze Mountain', considered
themselves part of an oppressed Islamic majority in the Empire.
The violence of the Druze reaction expressed its fear of a subaltern
majority, increasingly attached to the monetary sectors of the
economy, threatening not only to overthrow the privileged status of a
semi-aristocratic tribal minority, but also to deprive that community
of 'its' territory. This explains both the power of attraction exercised
by the Druze overlords over their co-religionists and the fierce fighting
they engaged in.

Troubled years (1845–58)

The Porte intervened in force in 1845 to end a new round of Druze–
Christian fighting in the mixed districts of the south. In April of that
year, responding to a Druze rally at Mukhtara, a massive Maronite
attack was launched against the fief of the Junblats, destroying a
number of Druze villages in their advance, which was stopped by the
Ottoman troops. But the Druze regained the upper hand, benefiting
from the tacit neutrality of the Ottoman authorities, and many
more Christian villages were destroyed in their turn and exactions
committed upon civilians.

Istanbul dispatched Shekib Effendi to establish order, confirm the
Ottoman occupation of Mount Lebanon and disarm its inhabitants.
Furthermore the Ottoman emissary declared the end of the
intervention of European consuls into the affairs of Mount Lebanon.
That reorganisation of the *qa'im maqamiya*, known as the *règlement*
of Shekib Effendi, should first be remembered as the legalisation
of sectarian political representation in Mount Lebanon. Each *qa'im
maqamiya* was endowed with a council to assist in the collection of
taxes and the administration of justice. Each council, presided over
by a *qa'im maqam*, was composed of 12 members: a councillor and a
judge representing each of the six religious communities: Maronite,
Druze, Greek Orthodox, Greek Catholic, Sunni Muslim and Shi`i
Muslim. As the latter did not have the right to be represented by
a judge, since all of the Sultanate's Muslims were subject to Sunni
jurisdiction, the twelfth member would be the vice-*qa'im maqam*, a
Maronite in the north and a Druze in the south. Both *qa'im maqam*s

were considered Ottoman government officials and subject to the authority of the wali of Sayda, while Jubayl, Zahleh and Dayr al-Qamar were granted the status of autonomous towns and put under an Ottoman governor.

Shekib Effendi's settlement only served to exacerbate rather than resolve the deep crisis of the *muqata`ji* system. Indeed, the councils and *wakils* constituted alternative institutions to *muqata`ji* power, but they by no means had the ability and power to overcome it. While a heavy blow was dealt to the Druze *muqata`jis*, who were theoretically deprived of most of their fiscal and judicial functions, they were nevertheless compensated by the appointment of the heads of the five main Druze *muqata`ji* families as administrators of the five districts of the southern *qa'im maqamiya*, though robbed of any authority over their Christian subjects. A *wakil* would exercise judicial functions and tax collection regarding his co-religionists in each district. The Christian *wakils* in the southern region were to be chosen by the governor, after consultation with the clergy and the notables of the community. In the north, the institutions of the council and the *wakil* were not applied nor were the feudal `*uhdas* reorganised as administrative units: the Ottoman Sultanate recognised sectarian and not social divisions and conflicts. Thus, while the Christian commoners were already represented in the council and held the post of *wakil* in the south, their northern co-religionists were left without any form of political representation, at the mercy of the Khazin and Hubaysh Maronite *muqata`jis* who effectively retained all their political and judicial functions in addition to their privileges, exactions and impositions.

A series of overlapping and complicated conflicts dominated the years that followed. First, inter-*muqata`ji* rivalries arose as the Khazins opposed Bashir Ahmad Abi-l-Lama`, *qa'im maqam* of the north (succeeding Emir Haydar Ahmad Abi-l-Lama`, who died in 1854), and the powerful Druze leader Sa`id Junblat refused to recognise the authority of Amin Arsalan, *qa'im maqam* of the south. The Druze–Ottoman clash on that issue led to a Druze armed revolt in 1852. When the Ottoman troops were defeated in the first round of fighting in Jabal al-Duruz, they enlisted Christians for support, increasingly poisoning sectarian relations.

Second, the *muqata`jis* of all sects not only resisted the Shekib Effendi *règlement* but tried by all means to preserve their declining economic and political power. In 1858 the Ottoman government issued the land code with the intention of creating a peasant-led market economy that would maximise state revenues from taxes. Land registration in Mount Lebanon exacerbated conflict over land ownership and was sabotaged by the *muqata`jis* of both communities, as they had done with the earlier land registration of 1846. Under the pressure of the European consuls, (excepting the French) the Ottoman authorities agreed to defer its implementation.

Third, *muqata`ji*/commoner conflicts raged in the mixed districts where the returnee Druze sheikhs, especially the Abu Nakad and Junblat, demanded that Christian commoners pay their tax arrears and return plots of land seized during the sheikhs' absence. The situation was serious enough for a delegation from Jizzin, led by three clerics, to meet with the Ottoman authorities in Beirut in 1850 and convey the determination of the town's inhabitants to collectively immolate themselves if nothing was done to reduce taxes owed and solve their conflicts with their Junblat overlords concerning land ownership. The Ottoman authorities agreed to slash the taxes to one-third of their initial value but refused to take any measures concerning landed property.

Fourth, in 1857, at least four major merchant towns had finally shaken off *muqata`ji* control and ran their own affairs through elected councils in which merchants, silk producers and middlemen predominated. The towns of `Amshit in Bilad Jubayl and Ghazir in Kisrawan liberated themselves from the Khazins and the Hubaysh respectively. Dayr al-Qamar, the central Christian town in the Shuf, overthrew its Druze overlords, the Abu Nakad, and was run by two elected delegates, one Druze and one Christian. Finally, Zahleh declared itself an independent commune under the leadership of a council of eight notable families, expelled the appointee of *qa'im maqam* Bashir Ahmad and expropriated the rest of the properties of the Abi-l-Lama`. In order to completely free itself from *muqata`ji* control, this Catholic town in the Biqa` requested to be detached from Mount Lebanon altogether. The Ottoman authorities obliged and Zahleh was attached to the *wilaya* of Beirut in the summer of 1859, then to the *wilaya* of Sayda.

Interestingly, these years witnessed considerable social agitation in Europe and in the other Arab provinces of the Ottoman Empire. In the latter, agrarian revolts were mixed with dissent against the *Tanzimat*, social movements and bread riots. An obscure peasant rebellion rocked the `Urqub region in the eastern mountains of Lebanon, leaving 200 people killed. Lattakiya in the north of Syria witnessed a large peasant revolt in 1858. Bread riots erupted in Aleppo and its surrounding region in October 1859. In May of that year, rioters pillaged the houses of the mufti of the city, its chief notable and the Ottoman governor. They also attacked the police chief before looting shops and obliging the authorities and the merchants to distribute free wheat and bread to the population. On 24 and 25 October 1859, a strange reversal of the situation occurred when the rioters suddenly altered their targets and attacked twelve shops owned by Christian merchants, looting and burning them. Riots and acts of violence against foreign merchants and foreigners in general reached as far as the Arabian peninsula, where, in July 1858, an angry populace attacked British merchants in Jidda and invaded the French and British consulates.

These revolts and riots constituted the regional context for the events of the years 1858–60 in Mount Lebanon. The main protagonists were the two parties that suffered most from the *qa'im maqamiya*: the Maronite commoners and peasants of the north and the Druze *muqata`ji*s of the south.[7] The ensuing events and developments can be seen as a commoners' revolt against the *muqata`ji* system, which produced two different types of movements following the uneven social demography of Mount Lebanon: a social revolt of Christian commoners against Christian overlords in the north and a sectarian civil war between Christian commoners and Druze overlords in the southern mixed districts. Indeed, an eyewitness, the American missionary William Thomson, described the war as 'simply a rising of the people against the wishes of the ruling classes, on all sides'.[8]

THE COMMONERS' REVOLT OF KISRAWAN

The opposition of the Khazins' to *qa'im maqam* Bashir Ahmad Abi-l-Lama was the spark that ignited the commoners' revolt against the *iqta`* of Kisrawan. Kisrawan was already the 'weakest link' in the *muqata`ji* system of Mount Lebanon, a microcosm of its contradictions pushed to the point of rupture. The region was dominated by commercial production and dependent on the external market through its main economic activity, sericulture. Its sheikhs, increasingly indebted and their lands parcelled out by inheritance, imposed higher taxes and rents on the peasants, who were over-indebted to silk courtiers, merchants and usurers who lent them money at usurious rates reaching 50 per cent.[9] As early as the 1820s, Gérard de Nerval wrote of those 'emirs of olive and cheese' whose declining economic power was being compensated by a morbid attachment to political and judicial privileges and social distinction at the expense of the commoners.[10] To make matters worse, the years 1856–58 were particularly cruel; a severe winter in 1857 was followed by an exceptional dry season in 1858, when bad harvests and diseases beset the silkworm, olive trees and vineyards. In addition, the silk crisis centred on Lyon reduced silk production in Mount Lebanon by half.

In the conflict between the Khazins and Bashir Ahmad, both parties solicited the backing of the commoners. The latter's demands – lower taxes, revision of rents and participation in the election of governor – were rejected by the sheikhs, focalising popular anger against them. Revolt broke out on Christmas Eve 1858 with a strike against the payment of taxes and rents. After a relatively moderate phase led by Salih Jirjis Sfayr, a notable from the coast and creditor of Bashir Ahmad, the uprising took a more radical turn in mid-January 1859, when a blacksmith from Rayfoun, Tanius Shahin (1815–95), was elected 'first delegate' (*wakil awwal*). In February, Ottoman troops entered Kisrawan and the emissaries of Khurshid Pasha to Shahin tried to convince him to seek Ottoman military help. But Ottoman troops soon withdrew after the intervention of the French consul. The latter visited Ghazir a few weeks later and was received by a massive crowd brandishing the tricolour flag and chanting in support of France. By the summer of 1859 peasants in arms had chased almost all of the Khazin clan, no fewer than 500 persons, out of the region. Shahin, elevated to 'general delegate' (*wakil `amm*) in the fall of that year, moved the revolt headquarters from Zuk Mikayil, on the coast, to Rayfoun in the highlands, a confirmation of the rebellion's radicalisation and of the rise of the peasant element within its ranks.

Kisrawan, liberated from both the sheikhs and the *qa'im maqam*, was under the control of rebel authority for more than two years. A council of some one hundred members, elected directly by the villagers under the presidency of Shahin, ruled by the 'force of popular government' (*'Bi-quwat al-Hukuma al-Jumhuriya'*), imposed new taxes, purchased arms, administered common property, intervened in local conflicts and commanded a militia of some one thousand men. More than half of the council members were small or landless peasants, the rest were comprised of 32 rich or middle-level farmers, ten clergymen and at least three merchants and moneylenders.[11] Among the delegates was Iliyas Habalin, a delegate of the market town of Zuq, known to be an anti-clerical and secular intellectual who publicly defended the ideas of the French Revolution.[12]

The Kisrawan revolt's main demands were equality between sheikhs and commoners; the abolition of the former's political and judicial privileges; the rescinding of additional taxes; the designation of one local governor, to be seconded by two elected commoners; the establishment of a tribunal of sheikhs and commoners to look into conflicts between the two parties; the abolition of extra impositions and injustices such as obligatory gifts (in the form of monetary goods like coffee, tobacco, sugar and soap), *sukhra* (forced labour) and other 'humiliating practices' (*ihtiqarat*) such as discrimination in the port of dress and the obligation to kiss the hand of the sheikhs.

In this sense, the Kisrawan rebels were pioneers in demanding the application of the Ottoman *Tanzimat*, the last edict of which had been promulgated only two years earlier. Their main slogan was inspired by the moving spirit of the Ottoman reform: 'full equality and complete freedom' (*'Taswiya `Umumiya wa Hurriya Kamila'*), to use the terms of Tanius Shahin himself. But Shahin would amalgamate the sectarian with the social by claiming that he received an official pledge from the European powers for the 'liberation of Christians from their servitude'.[13] On the other hand, two criteria were competing among the rebels. One was the criterion of money and wealth, which required that 'status and honor be granted on the basis of wealth and not birth', according to a contemporary eyewitness.[14] This was the demand of the new middle class of merchants, usurers and rich farmers, who wanted free trade and social recognition. The other criterion represented the mainly peasant democratic component, which demanded land and autonomy for the village communes administered by their elected delegates and councils. This elective autonomy was the Christian peasants' way of joining the two aspects of their demands: establishing equality vis-à-vis their Christian *manasib* on the one hand and parity with the Muslim majority within the Ottoman Empire on the other. Hence the crucial importance of the governorship (the *ma'mur*) of the district of Kisrawan that dominated the entire period of the rebellion.

As the revolt gained ground, the rebels introduced the idea of a commoner governor chosen by the Maronite patriarch and finally advanced the idea of a governor directly elected by the people. Tanius Shahin and the majority of the delegates insisted on this latter demand, and the 'general delegate' went on signing petitions in the villages supporting his own claim to the post. All parties to the conflict, local and regional, put forward contradictory demands regarding the famous governorship, yet all were agreed to bar the access of a commoner to that post.

On one occasion, the church did envisage Shahin as *ma'mur*. Father Yuhanna Habib, emissary of the patriarch to Shahin, sent a note to his superior, on 24 October 1859, suggesting that, short of bloodily repressing the revolt, there was no way out but to choose Shahin as governor:

[The appointment of Shahin as *ma'mur*] is the best suggestion for achieving a return to calm, in addition to being most beneficial for the sheikhs. If anybody else becomes *ma'mur*, the sheikhs would not be able to regain their homes or property. But if Shahin is elected, they would be able to return and recuperate their occupied property and their expropriated crops, because the *amigo*, in the post of *ma'mur*, would enrich himself and be inclined toward equity, and divisions would run amock [among the rebels]. Rather than continuing to cook in cauldrons and lending his ear to the ignorants, he would be surrounded by wise men from whom he would draw counsel; and that course would be the best.[15]

However ingenious this suggestion for socially corrupting a rebellion, it was nevertheless rejected by the patriarch.

It was not long before the commoners' revolt gave way to a peasant *jacquerie*, which demanded land distribution and better conditions for tenant farming. Armed peasants confiscated land, harvests and livestock belonging to the sheikhs while tenant farmers cultivated the land of their lords and took over the harvesting of mulberry leaves, silk cocoons, olives, cereals and livestock. Villagers collectively exploited the commons (forests and grazing land), which were traditionally under the control of the sheikhs. Bands of landless peasants – men and women, tenant farmers and unemployed workers from silk-reeling factories – roamed around the area's villages tracking down the Khazins, looting and setting fire to houses, and assaulting and sometimes murdering Khazin families.[16] Scenes of collective drunkenness, characteristic of peasants' uprisings, reached a degree that required the intervention of the patriarch himself, with Shahin, to put an end to them.[17]

Contrary to interpretations that stress the leading role of the Maronite Church in the commoners' revolt, the main concern in Bkiriki appeared to be the unity of the community. When the rebellion broke up, Patriarch Mas`ad was caught between contradictory pressures and interests. Inside the church, members of the lower-ranking clergy had joined the rebel ranks, and some of them were elected village representatives, while influential bishops were violently hostile to the revolt, which they considered a divisive movement. Preeminent among the latter group was Tubiya `Awn, the Maronite bishop of Beirut, who had backed Mas`ad's candidacy for the patriarchal seat. `Awn led the Maronite Youth League and a Committee of Public Safety, composed of Christian merchants and notables who were financing the purchase of arms for the inhabitants of the mixed districts. Yusuf Karam, son of a minor sheikh from Bisharri, was the revolt's fiercest enemy, accusing Shahin of dividing Christian ranks and the patriarch of complicity with the rebel leader.[18] This made it easy for the patriarch to pit him against Shahin. Mas`ad invited Karam to come, at the head of some 200 of his armed men and police the coastal region. Demonstrations that would head toward Bkirki, organised by partisans and opponents of the revolt, symbolised the contradictory pressures exerted on the patriarchal seat. However, Mas`ad refused to take sides. Indeed, the church managed to establish direct links with the towns and villages of Kisrawan and Jubayl, without passing through the *manasib*, and Mas`ad became, in a way, the necessary intermediary for all parties to the conflict. But in its capacity as the biggest landowner in Mount Lebanon, the church was determined to censor the peasant demands for land and better conditions of land tenure. However, there came a time when the church was 'outflanked by the people', to use the term of the Bentivoglio, the French consul in Beirut, and the rebellion directly challenged clerical authority.[19] In brief, the commoners' movement was strong enough not to fall under the control of the church, and the latter was sufficiently opposed to the *muqata`ji* system not to confront the rebellion and cause it to become a millenarian or anti-clerical movement, as often happened with peasant *jacqueries*.

THE 'EVENTS OF 1860'

The fighting in the southern part of Mount Lebanon was initiated by the Druze leadership as a preemptive measure to ward off the possible repercussions of the Kisrawan revolt but, more importantly, to overcome the social and political agitation of their 'own' Christian commoners.

The 'events of 1860', as they were called, reportedly started in August 1859 in Bayt Miri, a village in the 'mixed regions', and spread in the Matn region through a series of assassinations and limited armed confrontations. The winter and spring of 1860 passed without newsworthy events, as the 'silk truce' held. Toward the end of May 1860, fighting resumed with a Druze attack in the Matn. In the Shuf and the Iqlims, neighbouring villages and towns were pitted one against the other. The fighting lasted two months, from the end of May to the end of July. Jizzin was the first Christian town to fall, but this was after an armed detachment of its inhabitants had attacked and burnt Druze farms in the Niha region. Besieged in early June, Dayr al-Qamar negotiated for some three weeks until it finally surrendered, but it was nevertheless attacked, looted and its people massacred. A Druze version claims that the inhabitants of Dayr al-Qamar still possessed 4,000 firearms when the town was taken, which explained the killings inside the town, while Christian sources maintain that the Ottoman authorities had already disarmed the inhabitants in return for assurances of official Ottoman protection and grouped them in the *serail*, where they were attacked. Whatever the case, the conquest of Dayr al-Qamar resulted in a massacre in which an estimated 900 to 2,000 Christians lost their lives. Christians who fled Jizzin and Dayr al-Qamar, and were lucky enough to evade the Druze fighters hunting for Christians on the roads, regrouped in Sayda, which had been neutral in the fighting. Many sought refuge in the Shi`i villages and were put under the protection of the Shi`i notables of Zahrani, Nabatiyeh and Juba`. Other Christian refugees made it to Beirut, whose notables had managed to contain the rising tension between the two warring communities.

On the other slope of the Mountain, Druze fighters, led by `Ali Junblat, descended on Saghbin, the principal Maronite village in the western Biqa`, and occupied it. After having looted, destroyed and burnt Hasbaya and Rashaya, inhabited by Greek Orthodox Christians, they killed 17 Sunni Muslim Shihab princes in Hasbaya, presumably as a punishment for their alliance with the Christians. The Druze forces were then joined by armed men from Hawran and encircled Zahleh, eager to punish its inhabitants for their participation in the campaign of Ibrahim Pasha against Hawran in 1839 and their victory against the Druze in the battle of Shtura in 1841–42. The Catholic capital, victim of its numerous enemies, withstood the Druze offensive alone: its Shi`a allies of Ba`albak had deserted it and Yusuf Karam, who left Kisrawan at the head of 500 armed men to rescue Zahleh, never arrived at his destination.[20] The town, deserted by the majority of its population, was pillaged, burnt and partially destroyed.

Kisrawan and the north did not participate in the war. After an incursion by Tanius Shahin and his rebels into the Matn area, where he was stopped by Ottoman troops, the forces of the revolt limited themselves to patrolling their own territory. The patriarch had opposed the fighting from the beginning, despite pressures upon him by Bishops Abou Rizk, Bustani and `Awn. To alleviate pressures upon him, the Patriarch nonetheless formed an army and put it under the joint command of a Hubaysh sheikh and Tanius Shahin. The latter, called upon to come to the rescue of the Christians of the mixed regions, declared that he was waiting for orders from the patriarch to move his armed men. So was Yusuf Karam. But the orders never came.

Both camps practised 'sectarian cleansing'. In retaliation for the expulsion of their co-religionists from the Shuf and Jizzin by the Druze, the Kisrawanis, under Shahin, expelled the Druze from Antelias – the old demarcation line between the northern and the southern parts of Mount Lebanon – and the Christians would later expel the Druze from the mixed villages of the Matn with the help of French troops. Interestingly, Christians and Druze, all the while fighting each other, profited from the occasion to get rid of Shi`i pockets in 'their' respective territories. In one known instance, Druze fighters invaded the predominantly Shi`i Iqlim al-Tuffah and expelled many of its inhabitants and forced them to flee toward Harat Sayda. On the other hand, the Kisrawanis, led by Shahin, launched an attack on the Jubayl highlands in an attempt to expel the Shi`a of Jubbat al-Munaytra in the direction of the Biqa`. Some Shi`i villages were also plundered in other parts of Jubayl and Kisrawan. However, sectarian cleansing had its economic limits. Soon Sa`id Junblat called upon the Christians of the Shuf and Jizzin to come back: he needed them to work in his domains.

Damascus: an anti-Christian or anti-merchant 'pogrom'?

As the events of 1860 in Lebanon died down, an anti-Christian riot exploded in Damascus. During the last week of July 1860, an angry Damascene mob, driven by a number of the city's notables and enjoying the complicity of the city's Ottoman authorities, killed, looted and burnt in the Christian quarter of Bab Touma. No fewer than 1,000 people died, and many thousands were saved from a similar fate thanks to the intervention of Algerian emir `Abd al-Qadir, whose armed men helped them to safety toward Beirut.

The Damascus riots, situated in their larger context, expressed overlapping predicaments in the Arab regions of the empire: the negative reactions toward the *Tanzimat*, on the one hand, and the economic crisis, on the other. Damascus had led the opposition to the Ottoman reforms of 1839 and 1856, spurred by the fatwa of the city's mufti in rejecting the proclaimed equality between Christians and Muslims. The entire *Tanzimat* were even looked upon as a European and Christian conspiracy against Islam. The marked complicity of the Ottoman authorities of Damascus in the massacre of 1860 was a sure sign of this hostility to the new reforms.

Against a background of soaring prices and a shortage of livestock and cereals, the Christians flourished in business and in the administration of Damascus under Ibrahim Pasha.[21] With numbers estimated in 1860 at about 20,000 out of a population of some 120,000, they were mainly artisans and members of the liberal professions. But they also contained a small number of 'multimillionaire merchants' who 'lent money, with high interest rates, to individuals as well as governments', according to a French eyewitness. Although traditional Damascene trade was still in the hands of Muslim merchants, Christians had come to play an increasingly important role in the economic life of the city and in its foreign trade. Rather than enjoying monopolistic control, they represented an uneven commercial competition to the interests of Muslim merchants in internal trade, and benefited from privileged relations with Europe as importers and representatives of foreign commercial firms. This gives credence to the accusation that Muslim merchants played a role in the incitement to rioting. As for the rioters, research by Shelly Walter on 300 of the accused rioters who passed through the Damascene courts reveals that they were a typical mob mixture, grouping *déclassé* middle-class property owners who had to sell their landed estates to upper-class Christians, impoverished sayyids, military men and artisans, especially those related to the services sector.[22] Significantly, the rioters spared the more socially modest Christian quarter of al-Midan.

Thus, many factors contributed to focusing popular violence against a minority that deployed typical 'victimary signs' (René Girard). The above-mentioned example of the Aleppo riots of the preceding year is significant in that respect: in a few months, the riotous mobs, previously directed against the city's Muslim notables and its Ottoman governor, were diverted against Christian merchants.

The role of foreign powers

The Sultanate viewed the 'events' in Mount Lebanon as a proof of the failure of the *qa'im maqamiya* and an opportunity to re-establish its authority over Mount Lebanon. Beirut's wali, Khurshid Pasha, contented himself with administering the crisis but the Damascus killings projected the 'events of Syria' on the international stage, and the pressure of the European powers prompted the Porte to dispatch Fu'ad Pasha, minister of foreign affairs, to the region. The Ottoman official arrived in Beirut on 18 July and arrested its governor, Khurshid Pasha, and a number of Druze leaders, including Sa`id Junblat. On 28 July he entered Damascus at the head of 4,000 armed men, arrested and executed Ahmad Pasha, the city's governor and military commander, three of his officers and 117 Turkish soldiers and functionaries. Some 400 Damascenes accused of participation in the riots were arrested, 56 were hanged and the rest condemned to prison. Around 40 notables accused of sedition were locked up and sent to Istanbul in chains.

Nevertheless, Emperor Napoleon III insisted on armed intervention in Lebanon. In mid-August 1860, 6,000 French troops landed on the Lebanese coast under the command of General Beaufort d'Hautpoul, who had served for two years under Ibrahim Pasha in Syria. D'Hautpoul had been tasked with varied and contradictory assignments: to cooperate with the Ottoman authorities, restore peace, help the Christians, contribute to the reconstruction of Mount Lebanon and get the silk workers back to work, as well as help create an autonomous Christian enclave in Mount Lebanon. That was not all. Napoleon III, as if eager to confirm Karl Marx's accusation that he was just a farcical repetition of his illustrious relative, envisaged the Lebanon expedition as a reenactment of Bonaparte's Egyptian venture by sending the learned Ernest Renan, with an assignment to investigate the country's Phoenician past, along with the military expedition. Cartographers were sent to draw the first map of Mount Lebanon and its surroundings, which was to serve for future military purposes. Last but not least, d'Hautpoul was also commissioned to buy pure Arab steeds from the Bedouins of the Syrian desert to rejuvenate the French cavalry.

This period saw especially bitter competition between the colonial designs and interests of France and Britain. Britain stuck to its policy of defending the unity of the Ottoman Empire and sought to influence its policies through relations with the Porte rather than encourage secessionist movements at the peripheries. As the Briritsh were primarily exporters of fabrics, rather than importers of raw materials, their main economic interest was to distribute their goods in the Syrian market. Traditionally, they were supportive of the *muqata`ji* system and of the Druze, to whom they sent arms during the fighting. The French meanwhile had to defend French capital invested in sericulture, and needed to rebuild the silk-reeling factories and bring the silk workers back to work. But the French military intervention was being played out within a much more ambitious project. Napoleon III had already launched his dream of an Arab kingdom in Algeria, and he envisaged his intervention in Mount Lebanon as an outlier of his Maghreb project: an Arab kingdom, attached to France, led by its faithful ally, Emir `Abd al-Qadir, whose entity would play the role of a buffer state between Anatolia and the Suez Canal. In France, political parties were divided over the intervention. Catholics, who were pressing for an armed intervention in Italy to save the Vatican from the approaching forces of Italian unity, suspected the Syrian campaign of being a subterfuge for not defending the threatened papacy. Paradoxically, the enthusiastic supporters of the Syrian adventure were the secular parties, foremost among them the Saint-Simonian socialists, nostalgic for a repetition of the Muhammad `Ali experience. They supported `Abd al-Qadir as an enlightened despot who would build railways and roads, and above all the Suez Canal linking Europe to Asia.[23]

THE PAST AS PRESENT

Though the Kisrawani rebels did not participate in the civil war, they still had to pay its costs. They resisted a mere return to the *status-quo ante*. The Ottoman marine imposed an embargo for a number of weeks on the port of Junieh to oblige the rebels to negotiate. On 29 July 1860 the accord was signed with the Khazins, under the patronage of Bishop Tubiya `Awn and an Ottoman emissary, in which the revolt was described as an 'exaggeration of a minor dispute' exploited by 'troublemakers' who were moved by 'suspect goals' against the Ottoman government. The accord stipulated the return of the sheikhs and the restitution of their properties, and obliged the peasants to pay their arrears in rent and taxes. In return, all the commoners got was a promise to put an end to the 'inhuman practices' of the *muqata`ji*s.

An international commision of the consuls of Britain, France, Prussia, Russia and Austria convened in Beirut with the participation of Fu'ad Pasha. It held meetings from 5 October 1860 to 5 March 1861 to supervise the punishment of the accused, reparations and reconstruction and to devise a new social and political status for Mount Lebanon. On 8 December 1860, a legal tribunal was set up in Mukhtara in which 300 people were tried, 25 Druze were sentenced to death and executed; the rest were later reprieved.

On 18 November 1860, Fu'ad Pasha, keen for a quick withdrawal of French troops, appointed Yusuf Karam *qa'im maqam* of the Christians. Karam's first task was to put an end to the Kisrawan revolt. In March 1861, he launched an attack on the headquarters of Tanius Shahin in Rayfoun and set fire to it as Shahin fled to Beirut and put himself under the protection of the French consul. Karam earned the congratulations of Lord Dufferin, the British government representative in the international commission, for having reestablished 'social order'. But no sooner had the *'Règlement organique'* instituting the *Mutasarrifiya* been approved, and the French forces departed, than the first *Mutasarrif*, Dawud Pasha, deposed Karam in May 1861. Majid Shihab, a candidate for the governorate of Mount Lebanon, was named governor of Kisrawan and charged with collecting taxes from a population that had been bled white.

In the final tally, there were only a few dozen victims of the Kisrawan uprising while at least 5,000 perished in the civil conflicts of Mount Lebanon alone, 200 villages were burnt and 100,000 people displaced.

We are told that history does not repeat itself, yet it has a remarkable knack for reactualising past events and scenes. In this sense, the present serves sometimes to elucidate the past. For the contemporary Lebanese who have lived through the wars of 1975–90, a chronicle of the 'events of 1860' would be an occasion to review scenes that seem quite familiar. The trigger events, be they the `Ayn al-Rummaneh bus incident of 13 April 1975 or the 'accident' of the two muleteer boys of Bayt Miri in 1859, always concern a question of the right of passage in a country where traffic is always jammed. The front lines have been the same, passing through Mutayn, or along the Beirut–Damascus road. Sieges have been repeated in Zahleh, Dayr al-Qamar, Jizzin and Damur; inhabitants have fled by sea from the latter on boats sent from Beirut by Bishop `Awn and from Junieh on French vessels, fearing a Druze and Shi`i invasion from the Biqa`.

What can we say about political assassinations, such as the reported attempts on the lives of Tanius Shahin and Patriarch Mas`ad, the two leaders who maintained a measure of independence vis-à-vis external forces? Last but not least, from this past emerges a scene that resumes the founding drama of civil violence in modern Lebanon. Here, born from the sea, like in the myths of old, are the 'enemy brothers' of the chronicler Abikarius:

During the fighting, a Druze got hold of a Christian. They battled and resisted each other and went on fighting until they reached the waterfront from which they fell into the water still exchanging punches and blows. A huge wave unfurled and dragged them into the open sea where they were swallowed up by the tide. The next morning, their corpses were recovered on the beach scrunched up in a tight embrace and gripping each other's hands.[24]

3
Grandeur and Misery of the
Mutasarrifiya (1861–1915)

Happy is he who has but a goat's perch in Mount Lebanon.
Lebanese proverb

The 'Long Peace' (Akerli) that Mount Lebanon enjoyed for more than a half century under the *Mutasarrifiya* was the product of a combination of factors: the economic growth generated by the silk economy; the exportation of the surplus peasant population beyond Mount Lebanon, and the relatively weak intervention by the European powers in the affairs of Mount Lebanon.

Politically, the *Mutasarrifiya*, under a Christian Ottoman administrator, was a compromise between the French-sponsored project for an independent Christian emirate (under a Shihab amir or Yusuf Bey Karam) and the complete submission of Mount Lebanon to Ottoman authority. Accordingly, France withdrew its grandiose plan for an Arab kingdom in favour of what it called its 'catholic experience in the Orient'. Furthermore, the export of the French Revolutionary model was shelved, replaced by the new colonial model, which encouraged provincial and ethnic autonomy in the development of a world division of labour.

However, the salient characteristic of the *Mutasarrifiya* was that its political autonomy inside the Ottoman Empire became the framework for the development of a double economic dependence. Mount Lebanon was economically tied to Beirut and the European market as it relied increasingly on the Syrian interior for the better part of its requirements in cereals and livestock. This double dependence would ultimately erode the foundations of political autonomy itself. Hence, evaluating the *Mutasarrifiya* reveals a dramatic dichotomy in the final balance sheet: its external dependence contributed to Mount Lebanon's economic prosperity and privileged contribution to the Arab cultural renaissance of the mid-nineteenth century, but was also partly responsible for the successive waves of migration

41

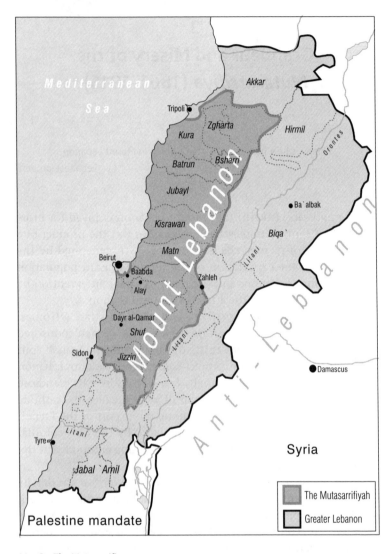

Map 2   The Mutasarrifiya

of its inhabitants to the New World and for the tragic famine of World War I.

The war of 1860 had ended with a Christian military defeat despite the fact that Christians constituted a majority of the population and the biggest fighting force. Divided geographically and socially, they lacked a unifiying leadership and faced a cohesive minority fighting not only to preserve its privileges but also to ensure its survival. Nevertheless, the Christians' military defeat was transformed into a political victory by the intervention of the European powers. Conversely, the Druze military victory could not halt their loss of political and social power, despite British attempts to mitigate the effects of this loss. The Druze defeat led to the collapse of the entire *muqata`ji* order, as the Druze leadership had fought in the name of all *muqata`ji*s to preserve it. The balance of power in the Mountain had been turned upside down: the history of the Druze henceforth would be the history of their struggle to survive as a minority.

A RELATIVE AUTONOMY

The *Règlement organique* of 9 June 1861 granted Mount Lebanon limited autonomy inside the Ottoman Empire, guaranteed by the European powers: France, Great Britain, Austria, Prussia and Russia, later joined by Italy in 1867. The new organisation merged the two *qa'imaqamiya*s of 1841–61 into a *mutasarrifiya*, the first subdivision of a *wilaya*. Zahleh, in the east, which had been part of the *wilaya* of Damascus under the Double *Qa'im maqamiya*, was reintegrated into Mount Lebanon, in addition to parts of the Hirmil district (eastern Biqa`). To the west, the *Mutasarrifiya* extended to the Mediterranean coast with the exception of the main cities, Tripoli, Beirut and Sayda, which remained part of the *wilaya* of Damascus, along with the rest of the Biqa` plain.

The governor of Mount Lebanon was a non-Arab Ottoman Christian who enjoyed wide-ranging executive powers and reported directly to the Porte. An Administrative Council (AC) of 12 elected members enjoyed only consultative powers vis-à-vis the *Mutasarrif*, but was granted the right to veto his decisions on two crucial issues: the intervention of Ottoman troops in the territory of the *Mutasarrifiya* and tax increases. Elections to the AC were held in two stages. Each village would elect a local *sheikh shabab*, who was required to receive official confirmation from the *Mutasarrif*. Then, the *sheikh shabab* of each constituency proceeded to elect the 12 councillors.[1] Initially, the AC councillors were equally divided between Christians and Muslims, two for each of the six major sects (Maronite, Druze, Greek Orthodox, Greek Catholic, Sunni, Shi`i). But the revised *Règlement organique* of 1864 modified this into seven Christians to five Muslims.

Administratively, the territory of the *Mutasarrifiya* was divided into seven districts (*caza*s) governed according to the majoritarian community in each. The only armed force on *Mutasarrifiya* territory was a local police force, the *gendarmerie*, trained and organised by French officers, whose number was set at 1,400 but never reached half this figure. Nevertheless, the *Mutasarrif* – who enjoyed the rank of military ruler with the title of *mushir* – was granted the right to disarm the population.

Taxes collected in Mount Lebanon constituted the basis for the budget, and only the surplus was to be turned over to Istanbul. In the event of a budget deficit, aid was to be provided by the central Ottoman treasury.

The judicial system was vested in courts of first instance and in a court of appeal whose judges were appointed by the *Mutasarrif*, and elected village shaykhs, who also acted as justices of the peace. Finally, the *Règlement* reiterated the formal abolition of the *muqata`ji* system and declared the inhabitants of Mount Lebanon to be equal before the law.

DAWUD PASHA, YUSUF KARAM AND `ABD AL-QADIR

Yusuf Karam's Christian emirate and `Abd al-Qadir's Arab Kingdom were the victims of the *Règlement organique*. In compensation for the part he played in saving thousands of Christian lives in Damascus, `Abd al-Qadir was congratulated and decorated by Europe's rulers and invited to France. In Marseilles, crowds greeted him as 'saint `Abd al-Qadir', and Emperor Napoleon III received him with great pomp at his residence in Saint-Cloud. On his way back to Damascus, the Algerian prince visited Istanbul, where he obtained from the Sultan the release of Damascene notables accused of instigating the anti-Christian massacres of 1860. Retired in his Damascus home, he repeatedly declared his withdrawal from political affairs and spent the rest of his days in pious recollection and Sufi contemplation. He died on 24 May 1883.

Matters were more difficult concerning Yusuf Karam. After the revision of the *Règlement organique* in 1864, Dawud Pasha's term in office was extended for five more years. Dawud took a number of conciliatory measures to appease the Christian opposition in the north: he left the appointment of the Maronite councillors to the church rather than being elected by popular vote, and established the post of a Maronite deputy chairman of the AC unaccounted for in the initial *Règlement*. A month after the renewal of Dawud's mandate, Yusuf Karam was allowed to return from his exile in Istanbul. The armistice between the two men lasted for a year, then in January 1866, Karam launched an armed rebellion. Skirmishes between Karam's armed men and Ottoman troops alternated between Kisrawan and his native Ihdin, and in early 1867, the northern bey decided to march on Bayt al-Din in an attempt to overthrow the *Mutasarrifya*. He was encircled and practically defeated near Bikfaya (in the Matn), but French mediation secured Ottoman approval to transport the rebellious bey to a European exile aboard a French gunship.

After a short stay in France, Karam moved to Algeria, where he was granted land in the Constantine region and was approached to lend his support to the project of settling Lebanese Maronite peasants in Algeria.[2] When the scheme was finally abandoned, Karam returned to France whence he commuted for years between the French capital, Austria, Belgium and Istanbul, repeatedly requesting permission to return to Lebanon, but to no avail. He finally settled in Italy, in 1878, where he spent the rest of his days. He died on 7 April 1889.

COLONIAL TRADE AND SILK PRODUCTION

Yusuf Karam's second rebellion (1864–67) was the last attempt to set up a Christian government in Mount Lebanon. After the rebellion's defeat and the northern leader's exile, Bkirki assumed leadership of the autonomist tendency. In order to resist the pressures of Dawud Pasha (1861–68) and his successor Franco Pasha (1868–73), who had required that the patriarch take an oath of loyalty to them and submit the nomination of bishops for their approval, Mas`ad headed to Istanbul in 1867, where he was cordially received and decorated by the Sultan, to whom he declared his allegiance.

Throughout the *Mutasarrifiya* era, the political life of Mount Lebanon revolved around two poles: Bkirki, the home of the Maronite patriarcate, and Bayt al-Din (later Ba`abda), the headquarters of the *Mutassarrif* and the Administrative Council. The AC soon established itself as the other pole of attraction and representation for the Maronites in the south of Mount Lebanon, as well as those of the north.

At first, France was content to act as mediator between the patriarch and the Ottoman governors, as its main concern was its 'catholic experience' in Mount Lebanon, which it hoped to be a model for the whole Empire. In addition, the postwar reconstruction and economic take-off contributed to tempering the extreme autonomist demands, which had become deprived of any external backing.

Monoculture and emigration

Economically, the *Mutasarrifiya* was primarily an enclave of monoculture and monoproduction of silk at the service of the silk industry of Lyons. Mount Lebanon, from Jizzin and the Shuf to `Akkar, was the centre of silk production, which also covered the Biqa`, Hasbayya and Hums in addition to the *wilaya* of Beirut. No wonder Ducousso speaks of a 'French naturalised' Syrian silk industry and ranks Syria among the 'French sericulture departments'. The Lyons Chamber of Commerce went even further, referring to Syria as a 'colony of Lyons'. Soon, this dependence on the external market transformed Mount Lebanon into an exporting enclave, dominated by Beirut. Half of Mount Lebanon's population were engaged in the silk economy, which generated around a third of its total revenue (the other sources being tobacco and olive oil). In 1867, there were 67 silk-reeling factories, the seven biggest and most modern being French-owned. In 1885, their number had reached 105, with only five French factories, as foreign investment (mainly Lyons-based) moved from the productive sector to the control of sericulture through the market. Some 14,500 workers were employed in the silk-reeling factories,12,000 of whom were women, with an overall majority of Maronites (8,500 Maronite workers compared to 2,500 Greek Catholics, 2,500 Greek Orthodox and around 1,000 Druze). Working conditions were harsh, working hours were long and salaries excessively low. Men's salaries were three times those of women and child labour was employed abundantly, especially girls aged between 7 and 13, not to speak of free labour provided by the orphanages of French missionnaries or local convents.

Sericulture, far from being a 'leading sector' of the economy, developed at the expense of the other sectors, which led to grave consequences. In a principally mountainous region, where cultivated land amounted to no more than 4 per cent of the total surface, thousands of the best plots were devoted to the culture of mulberry trees, which came to cover some 45 per cent of Mount Lebanon's cultivated surface. Sericulture had developed primarily at the expense of cereal culture. The result was the growing dependency of Mount Lebanon on the Biqa` and the Syrian interior (*Bilad al-Sham*) for two-thirds of its needs in cereals and livestock. The rapid regression of subsistence agriculture and the dominance of cash crops were responsible for this grave commercial deficit.[3]

The generalisation of the monetary economy in addition to the persistence of large landed holdings and the church *waqfs* (the Church controlled no less than a third of the total land surface of Mount Lebanon) led a succession of migration waves. The 1860s witnessed a 'baby boom', a frequent postwar phenomenon, which was also encouraged by relative economic prosperity. But the limited growth in cultivable land compared to the rapid population growth was instrumental as a 'push' factor for emigration.[4] Starting in the last quarter of the nineteenth century, the peasant surplus, mainly Maronite Christian, which had previously migrated to the south of Mount Lebanon and the Biqa`, now went overseas. Christian migrants were accompanied by numerous Druze peasants and commoners, silent victims of the failure of the commoners' and peasants' revolts in which they did not even participate. Sericulture, far from halting or even reducing the haemmorhage of human resources, became one of its main causes. Between 1860 and 1914, roughly a third of the inhabitants of Mount Lebanon left the country.[5] Nevertheless, the remittances of the émigrés (some 45 per cent of total revenue) hardly covered the commercial deficit, which also drained the country's gold reserves.

In the beginning, a good portion of those who migrated returned after having gathered enough money to buy a plot of land. But those who owned the land would not sell. 'Thus', wrote Jouplain, 'they were obliged to remain overseas and settle permanently with their families and found new homes. Even the extention of the Church *Waqf* expelled yearly thousands of other Lebanese from their country and still does.'[6] Migration from Mount Lebanon reached such proportions that the Ottoman authorities decided to intervene to control departures and, in any event, peasant movements calling for the distribution of land did not cease. On the eve of the First World War, a peasant movement in the northern part of the Mountain was still calling for the distribution of *waqf* lands among landless peasants. The movement seemed strong enough to alarm a francophile writer, who saw in it a continuation of the 1858–60 commoners' revolts, and he called for the progressive takeover by the state of the church *waqf* in return for fair compensation, the only way to achieve 'gradual change' that would forestall a 'revolution'.[7]

A new social and political force

By the time the *Mutasarrifiya* was set up, Mount Lebanon's demographic composition had definitely shifted in favour of a

Christian, and more specifically Maronite, majority.[8] But it was mainly in the socio-economic fields that the gap was widening between the two communities. First, there was a noticeable transfer of landed property from Druze to Christians. In 1862–63, three-quarters of those who sold land were Druze and two-thirds of those who bought land were Christians.[9] Second, the Maronites were increasingly being anchored in the privileged sectors of the economy – trade, services and sericulture – while the Druze were being marginalised and remained linked to agricultural and artisanal production. Third, this asymmetry between the two communities was further aggravated by political dominance as the Christians now held a majority of seven to five votes in the Administrative Council. To this should be added an internal development inside the Druze community itself in which the strong Junblat leadership was temporarily challenged, after the death of Sa`id Bey Junblat in an Ottoman jail in Beirut in 1861, by the competing leadership of the Arsalans. Deprived of their judicial, fiscal and political privileges, the ex-*muqata`ji*s – the Junblats, Arsalans, Khazins, Hubayshs, Dahdahs, Shihabs, Abi-l-Lam`s and others – were recycled into the administration.[10] Mutassarrif Wassa Pasha (1883–92) recognised that this situation constituted a violation of the official Ottoman policy of the breaking up the *iqta`* system and declared:

We must prove that no family or group will have any privilege or any social status higher than that of the others, and that the nomination to the governing posts should depend, and depend solely, on the criteria of devotion, integrity and competence.[11]

This was easier said than done. Functionaries of commoner origins acceded to administrative posts with great difficulty, while the *Mutasarrifiya* continued to depend for long periods on those ex-lords recycled in the administration and to back the landed owners against peasant demands.

However, the most salient socio-political aspect of life under the *Mutasarrifiya* was the rise of a new social class and political force linked to the development of sericulture, the penetration of colonial capital and emigration. It was composed of members of *mudabbir* families, middle-level landed notables, administrators and members of the liberal professions in addition to merchants and those directly related to the silk economy. But it was also being swelled by the influx of returnee migrants. This socio-political force was 'middle' in both senses: it was situated in between the two orders that underpinned social hierarchy, the sheikhs and the commoners, and it also was localised politically in between the two poles of Mount Lebanon politics: Bkirki and Bayt al-Din. In terms of ideological expression, this group could be considered nationalist and reformist.

The AC was the fortress of that new force. Among its members Habib Pasha al-Sa`d, scion of a family of *mudabbirs* and a big landowner in the `Alay (Aley) region, was the AC's president, while Sa`d Allah Huwayik, representative for Batrun and brother of Patriarch Iliyas Huwayik (elected in 1897), was vice-president and leader of the reformist group. The representatives of Kisrawan were grouped around the anti-Khazin 'Popular Front': Jirjis Zuwayn, elected in 1907 against a Hubaysh candidate backed by the church; Habib al-Bitar and Na`um Bakhus, members of merchant notable families and landowners, and Muhammad al-Haj Hasan, a Shiite commoner. Shadid `Aql, Maronite councillor for the Matn, was the owner of a silk-reeling factory; Iliyas Shuwayri was Greek Orthodox councillor for the Matn, and Sulayman Kin`an was Maronite councillor for Jizzin. To those should be added the specialist functionaries of the judiciary and the bureaux of the *Mutasarrifiya*, the francophone intellectuals such as K.T. Khairallah, Bulus Nujaym (Paul Jouplain), who headed the 'foreign affairs' bureau (external relations), and Bichara Khalil al-Khuri, son of a family of landowning notables and silk-reelers of Rishmaya, whose father was director of the 'Arabic Bureau' (internal affairs).

This new force, united around the AC, and quite independent of the Maronite Church, was constantly wooed by the reformist and centralising *mutasarrifs*. But these AC members were frequently opposed to the *mutasarrif*'s tendency to raise taxation levels, demanding more financial autonomy and greater financial support from Istanbul, while they deplored the old *muqata`ji* families' monopoly of the administrative posts. Ideas of independence, Lebanonese nationalism and reformism germinated among their ranks.

In fact, it was with great difficulty that the *Mutasarrifiya* system filtered the great reforms and transformations that the other regions of the Ottoman Empire were witnessing, especially after the declaration of the Ottoman constitution in 1876. Even when reforms were proposed, they were either blocked or nipped in the bud by the Maronite Church with the backing of France. French politics after 1879 relied more on the Maronite Church than on the *mutasarrif*, while trying to maintain the social and political *status quo*. Although French consul Joseph Sienkiewics was a republican and a secularist he declared that 'France should remain clerical in Lebanon', and his successor in 1881 still considered the Maronite Church as 'the only social force among the Maronites'. On the other hand, the reformist and secular *mutasarrifs*, such as Rustum Pasha (1873–83), tried to reduce the role of clergy and the influence of private religious schools by backing the new notables of the AC against clerical authority. Muzaffar Pasha (1902–7), was engaged in an ambitious project of administrative reform, took measures to reduce Mount Lebanon's dependence on Beirut – by developing the port of Juniyeh and trying to open it to foreign trade – and introduced the secret ballot in elections to the AC. However, all his reforms were undone by his successor, the conservative Yusuf Bey (1907–12).

COLONIAL DESIGNS AND INDEPENDENTIST DEMANDS

The Ottoman defeat in the Russian–Ottoman war of 1877 revived the hopes of independence in Mount Lebanon. But by then Paris and London had begun to envisage the dismemberment of the Ottoman Empire, and their common interest was mainly focused on a comprehensive strategy for the entire region. Upon the request of Paris, the French military attaché in Beirut produced a plan for military intervention in Syria and Palestine using the Lebanese coast and Mount Lebanon as a 'fort' and 'bridgehead' for the occupation of Hawran and the port of Hayfa.[12] In 1902 the advisers to French prime minister Poincaré had envisaged a direct French military occupation of Mount Lebanon, or, at the least, French support for the Maronites to create a 'little France, free, industrious and loyal'.[13]

On the eve of World War I, Mount Lebanon witnessed the most difficult period under the *Mutasarrifiya*. A fall in the revenues of the silk sector and a decline in the taxable population, owing to migration, increased the budget deficit and spurred the AC to act. It demanded financial aid from the central government and permission to open the ports on the coast for international trade so as to use customs duties to increase budget revenue. The AC also reiterated its call for widening its electoral base and increasing its fiscal and executive powers. The reformist struggle of the AC was backed by an emigrant intelligentsia organised by the *Comités libanais* in Beirut, Cairo and Paris. The *Union libanaise* (*al-Ittihad al-Lubnani*), founded in February 1909 in Cairo by Yusuf al-Sawda, Antoine Jumayil and Iskandar `Ammun, echoed the demands of the AC reformists, demanding one electoral college for elections to the AC.[14] In June 1912, K.T. Khairallah, of the Paris *Comité libanais* founded the year before, presented the Quai d'Orsay with a memorandum demanding the limitation of the prerogatives of the *Mutasarrif*, an increase in the number of the AC to 18 members, all elected by universal suffrage, the election of an independent president of the AC with executive powers, the right to open ports on the coast and levy customs duties, and the immediate payment of the three years' arrears by the central government to the *Mutasarrifiya*.[15]

The Quai d'Orsay showed little interest in this memorandum, which did not enjoy the patriarch's approval. As for the Ottoman administration, the defeats in the Balkans forced the Porte to make concessions to the reformists in order to counter French and British influence, which was becoming more and more menacing in Syria. The Protocol of December 1912, a modified version of the *Statuts organiques* of 1861 and of 1864, enlarged the electoral base of the AC and gave it a say in the elaboration of the budget and control over its implementation, allocated an additional Maronite seat to Dayr al-Qamar (but added another Druze seat for the Shuf to compensate the loss of the Jizzin seat finally allotted to the Maronites) and opened the port of Juniyeh to the commerce of Mount Lebanon. This last concession – the only one that could have assured Mount Lebanon some measure of financial autonomy – was aborted by the joint opposition of the Beirut bourgeoisie and French interests. The reforms, associated with the *Mutassarrif* Ohannes Pasha, were a step in the right direction, but they arrived too late. In 1913, Bishara al-Khuri expressed the desires of many inhabitants of Mount Lebanon for a local ruler elected by the local population rather than one appointed by the foreign powers. In addition, Khuri proposed the 'restitution of Lebanon to its natural and historic frontiers' and granting it financial autonomy. In November 1914, the Ottoman Empire entered the war on the side of Germany and annulled the special status granted to Mount Lebanon, which was reincorporated into the Ottoman Empire and governed by a Muslim Ottoman Turk.

In the end, the tragedies of World War I gave new meaning to the demands for the expansion of Mount Lebanon and for its autonomy.

4
Beirut, Capital of Trade and Culture
(1820–1918)

We are like the belly in relation to the other organs of the body, a belly that lives off the work of the hands and legs and is comfortably carried by them.

Salim Bustani, 1872

THE 'DOOR' TO EAST AND WEST

Beirut's phenomenal growth and development in the latter half of the nineteenth century benefited from the two major trends that characterise the late Ottoman period: post-*Tanzimat* modernisation and centralisation processes, and the extensive penetration of European capital in the eastern Arab provinces of the empire. A last attempt by the ailing Ottoman Empire to face up to European colonial domination and dismemberment, the *Tanzimat* produced the opposite of the desired effects as the ambitious infrastructure and modernisation projects inflated Ottoman debt, increased the empire's colonial dependency and ultimately led to its demise. Paradoxically, Beirut benefited greatly from both trends: as a model of late nineteenth-century Ottoman modernism and a base and bridgehead for European control over Syria.

As European colonialism radically changed international trade routes in the era of the second industrial revolution, the Beirut–Damascus axis became the main avenue of international trade in the eastern Mediterranean. In addition to its control over the traditional export of grain from the Syrian hinterland, Beirut's principal export was raw silk, the production of which had achieved a new stimulus and largely expanded under the *Mutasarrifiya*. In return, Beirut's principal imports were cotton fabrics and manufactured goods. Raw silk was exported to France, while most manufactured goods arrived from England, invading the markets of Mount Lebanon and the Syrian interior and contributing to the collapse of traditional handicrafts and local production. As Beirut's trade developed, imports exceeded exports by a factor of three. In 1887, the Ottoman authorities recognised Beirut's role and named it the capital of a new

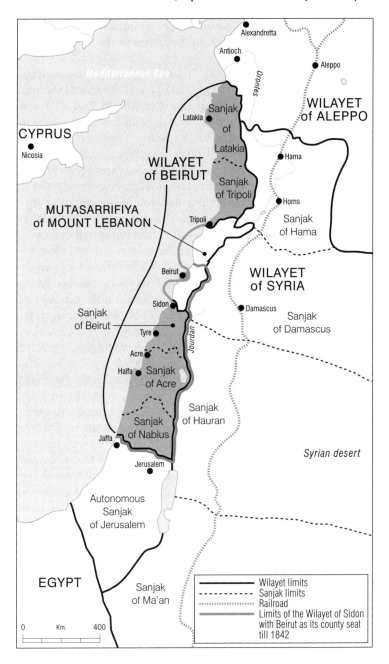

Map 3   The Wilayet of Beirut

Ottoman *wilaya* bearing its name and governing a territory of some 20,000 sq. km, extending from Alexandretta in the north to Acre and Nablus in the south.

In effect, Beirut had already become the economic, judicial, educational and cultural, if not political, capital of Mount Lebanon. The seat of the *Mutasarrifiya* was transferred from Bayt al-Din to Ba`abda to be closer to the new capital. Commercial disputes in Mount Lebanon were heard in the Beirut Commercial Court. Moreover, many consulates, foreign investors and missionaries adopted Beirut as their regional seat or upgraded their representation in the city. Both the silk economy and immigration contributed to the development of Beirut's intermediary role, economic prosperity and dominance over the Mountain. The city became the base for maritime and insurance companies (the latter numbered twenty by the end of the nineteenth century). Its usurers lent villagers the *nawlun* (money to buy their travel tickets) in return for liens on mortgages and exorbitant rates of interest. Its strongmen (*qabadays*) organised the contraband between the *wilaya* and the territory of the *Mutasarrifiya* in addition to the transport of illegal passengers for travel abroad. Beirut banks advanced credit to silk farmers, financed silk manufacture and handled the remittances of émigrés, estimated at one million sterling pounds per year in 1908.[1]

The constitution of Beirut into a separate Ottoman *wilaya* attracted considerable French and European investment, especially in infrastructure and communications. In 1863, a French–Ottoman company, the Compagnie Ottomane de la Route Beyrouth-Damas, finished building a carriage road linking the two cities. The 110 km trip from Beirut to Damascus now took no more than 13 hours. Jacques Thobie described the road as the most lucrative French enterprise in the Ottoman Empire.[2] The first telegraphic link with Europe was established in 1858 and in 1890, the Compagnie impériale des ports, des quais et entrepôts de Beyrouth (with capital of 5 million francs) obtained a 100-year concession for the construction and running of a new harbour, managing customs sheds and the loading and unloading of all goods. When the new harbour started work in 1895, a Franco-Belgian company, the Société ottomane des chemins de fer Damas, Hamah et prolongements (DHP), proceeded to build a railway line between Beirut, Damascus and the Hawran. The first trains ran in 1894–95.

As Beirut's regional economic role grew, competition between British and French interests became more pronounced. While the French monopolised the silk economy, the British dominated the export of manufactured goods and were gaining an edge in insurance, maritime transport and banking. But more important was the scramble of the two colonial powers for control over ports and means of communication (at that time roads and railways). French investment in this sector was greater, estimated at 168.3 million francs in Lebanon, Syria and Palestine. The British, out of favour in Beirut, started work on enlarging the Palestinian port of Hayfa, which was rapidly replacing the traditional port of Acre, and constructing a railway line linking Hayfa to Damascus. Thus began the long-term competition between Hayfa and Beirut to win the role of gateway to the eastern Mediterranean. By the early twentieth century, however, Beirut port had superseded the port of Hayfa and came to handle 75 per cent of the trade of Barr al-Sham.

Perhaps the most eloquent expression of Beirut as a new economic powerhouse is found in an article by Salim Bustani (1848–84) entitled 'Our Position' (1872), which can be considered a 'founding text' on the political economy of 'natural Syria' and its coast in a changing world. 'We have become', he wrote, 'the door from which the West enters the East and the East accedes to the West.' The 'we' refers to 'natural Syria', which occupies the 'centre' of the 'Oriental nation', flanked by Turkey in the north and by Egypt and Tunis in the south. The author recommends that economic activities should exploit this geostrategic position between the West, 'land of civilization and success' and the East, 'a demographically rich territory and a land of wealth and agricultural abundance'. Bustani thus conceived of an economic role for Syria based on agriculture and trade, the latter distributing the products of the former. To legitimise trade as the vocation for the Syrian coast, Bustani makes reference to Phoenicia.[3]

A NEW KIND OF CITY AND SOCIETY

Commenting on the particularity of Beirut's position and role, Albert Hourani has talked about 'a new kind of city, a new kind of urban society with a new kind of relationship with the rural hinterland'. A convergence of factors – migration, rapid urbanisation, the symbiosis between the city and Mount Lebanon, the development of an enterprising indigenous bourgeoisie, and a rapidly growing educational and cultural infrastructure – accounted for much of what made this new city and society.

Beirut's population had already quadrupled in three decades (1830–60). On the eve of the creation of Greater Lebanon in 1920, it had tripled to 120,000 inhabitants. Much of this growth must be attributed to the refugees fleeing civil strife in 1841–45 and the 1860s. They came from Aleppo, Damascus, the Biqa` and, of course, Mount Lebanon. In 1860, some 20,000 had fled from the latter to Beirut. Affluent merchants and skilled artisans from Dayr al-Qamar, Jizzin and Damascus settled in the city and contributed to its economic growth. Later on, more numerous but less affluent migrants flocked there from Mount Lebanon and the neighbouring countryside, seeking employment opportunities. Immigration altered the city's sectarian composition, as most of the newcomers were Christians of all sects who, by the turn of the century, constituted at least 60 per cent of its population.

The absence of strong artisan guilds or unions greatly assisted the unhindered development of Beirut's international trade and services sector.[4] On the other hand, internal migration was an important factor in diversifying the city's economic activities and helped create a plural urban society characterised by fluid social mobility. At the close of the nineteenth century, Beirut had earned its title of the 'jewel in the crown of the Empire', as German Emperor Wilhelm II remarked during his visit in 1898. The city witnessed unprecedented urban development, thanks to the joint effect of ambitious Ottoman infrastructure projects and the efforts of the city's municipality, set up in 1868. The municipal council, which brought together representatives of the city's merchant and notable families with some middle-class professionals, enjoyed considerable powers. It proposed projects of public works to the Sublime Porte, secured funding and supervised their execution. The council also collected taxes, maintained law and order, managed public places, constructed public schools, controlled market prices and took over responsibility for the city's sanitary infrastructure. But most importantly, Beirut's municipal council ultimately became the representative of the city's local interests, as opposed to those of the central government.

The city's centre shifted from the area around the port to the old city, now penetrated by two major streets, one to connect the port to the sugs, the other linking the city's centre, Sahat al-Burj, transformed into a public garden in honour of Sultan `Abd al-Hamid, to Bab Idriss, a southern gate on the city wall. Just outside the city walls rose new official Ottoman buildings, symbols of regenerated Ottoman bureaucratic and military control. The Serail, situated on the eastern flank of the city wall, was built on the location of the old fort constructed by Fakhr al-Din II. It housed local magistrate courts and administrative services. The new infantry barracks – later called the Grand Serail and presently housing the office of the prime minister – and the adjacent military hospital (later the Palace of Justice), were architectural expressions of the new Ottoman military organisation. The barracks dominated Sahat al-Sur and the old city. A clock tower was erected in 1899, the first of its kind in the Arab region, symbolising Ottoman modernism in obvious contrast to mosques, as more traditional symbols of the Ottoman presence.

The city expanded rapidly beyond its walls, which had virtually disappeared by the 1880s. A construction boom raised the price of land by 40 per cent in less than a decade as the city spread toward Nahr Bayrut to the east and Ras Bayrut to the west. By the end of the century, the majority of the city's inhabitants were already living outside the walls. Families of the merchant aristocracy built villas and palaces with Italianate architecture on the hills of Ashrafiya, in the east overlooking the port, while newer bourgeois families moved to Zuqaq al-Bulat and Qantari in the west. New quarters developed further west in Bashura and Musaytiba, middle-class quarters of merchants and civil servants, in addition to the popular neighbourhoods of Basta and Mazra`at al-`Arab. Streets were enlarged and paved. A Belgian company, the Compagnie de Gaz de Beyrouth, which had provided Beirut streets with gas lighting in 1889, obtained the concession to build an electric tramway and provide the city with electric power under the name of Tramways et Eclairage de Beirut (TEB). Opened in 1909, the tramway had five lines. Many of the city's streets were enlarged, paved and cleaned after the municipality imposed street-cleaning taxes on houses, shops and cafés in 1891. Sanitary and health conditions generally improved and the quarantine for maritime visitors was moved from the quarter of Rumayl to a new location further north, near Nahr Bayrut. Adjacent parts of the countryside swelled with newcomers who worked in Beirut but preferred to continue living within the *Mutasarrifiya* in areas that would soon become the city's southern suburbs of Ghubayri, Shiyah and Burj al-Barajina.

New Europeanised suqs developed outside the old city, offering imported manufactured and luxury goods. Beirut's most impressive novelty in this field was the lavish Orozdi Bek department store, part of an Egyptian commercial chain with branches in many cities of Egypt and Bilad al-Sham, located in a Westernised multi-storey building modelled after the Parisian galleries. The old khans were supplanted by no fewer than 17 modern hotels, including the prestigious Hôtel Bassoul in the Zaytuna quarter on the waterfront, later renamed Grand Hôtel d'Orient.

One major factor that explains Beirut's unique position and role as a new city is the development of its indigenous bourgeoisie. Much of the city's role in the colonial economy and the opportunities of wealth and profit it offered were exploited by its merchant class. Ultimately, European entrepreneurs played a smaller role in Beirut as compared to their involvement in other Levantine ports such as Alexandria. Local entrepreneurs imposed themselves as representatives of European companies, as local retailers for European wholesalers, intermediaries in the silk market and brokers for local crops, in addition to their role as usurers. By the time Beirut became a separate *wilaya*, its trade had passed from European to local hands.[5] Its local merchants invested part of their commercial profits in manufacture, especially silk-reeling, and banking.

Inside the city's merchant class, the balance of economic power rapidly tipped in favour of its Christian component. Christian merchants controlled the international import trade, whereas Muslim merchants had to content themselves with trade between the different ports of the Ottoman Empire, the export of agricultural products from the Syrian interior to Europe and the local trade in grain, both in bulk and in retail. Indeed, Christian merchant aristocrats were associated with their Sunni counterparts – the Bayhum, Da`uq, Salam, Tabbara families and others – in big farms, trade and franchise holding companies. But, on the eve of World War I, Christian economic, if not political, interests had become preponderant in the city. Foreign trade, finance and representation of European firms (particularly insurance and maritime companies) were now their semi-exclusive domain. Of the 26 houses engaged in the export of raw silk, only three belonged to Muslim families. The importers of manufactured products, building material and pharmaceutical products were all Christians. There was only one Muslim among the eleven cotton merchants. Local banks were in the hands of Christian families, with the exception of two owned by Jewish families. Christians also dominated the liberal professions. There were only ten Muslim lawyers out of a total of 81 and two Muslim dentists out of a total of 20.[6]

The Christian merchant class was itself undergoing a process of differentiation between an aristocratic and a bourgeois faction. Its older-established merchant aristocracy was mainly composed of Greek Orthodox families, whose activities covered the various *wilaya*s of the empire. The Abella, Sursuq, Bustrus, Trad, Fayyad, Jubayli, Tuwayni and Tabet families arrived in the city in the seventeenth and eighteenth centuries. Originally *mudabbir*s, tax and customs duties collectors, merchants and moneylenders, they appropriated landed property and accumulated capital even before being attracted to the city's commercial and financial possibilities. Almost all of them benefited from the protection of one consulate or another, a privilege granted to Europeans under the famous capitulations.[7]

Though partly engaged in the import trade and finance, the families of the merchant aristocracy remained primarily landowners – in Turkey, Egypt, Syria, and Palestine and, of course, Beirut and Mount Lebanon – and exporters of grain to Europe. Part of their commercial profits was invested in real estate and in modern agricultural projects in the Ammiq marshes (the Biqa`) or the Hula plain (Palestine). Politically, they were closely linked to the Ottoman authorities. Though their Greek Orthodox creed earned them aid and protection by Tsarist Russia, they also enjoyed close relations with Germany and Great Britain (Salim Bustrus was reputed to be a friend of Disraeli). Their matrimonial alliances with the Italian and British aristocracy earned them noble titles.

Parallel to this merchant aristocracy, and sometimes in competition with it, arose a financial, commercial and manufacturing bourgeoisie. Its families were mainly Greek Catholics of Syrian origin and more recent arrivals to the city. They were more closely related to European capital through the silk economy (as exporters of raw silk, moneylenders to peasant producers and silk-reelers), banking activities and the import of European manufactured products. Two associated and related families, Pharaon and Chiha, were typical representatives of this new class. In 1876, Antoine Chiha and his father-in-law Raphael Pharaon invested the big profits they had earned from speculation on raw silk in establishing a commercial and financial society that became the 'Banque Pharaon–Chiha', one of the first indigenous banks in Lebanon. In 1914, the Pharaon–Chiha association had become the biggest silk-reeling firm in the *wilaya* of Beirut, and its commercial branch controlled 12 per cent of the total volume of silk exports from the city. In 1894, it gained a quasi-monopoly on the import of British coal (the main energy source for the silk-reeling firms) transported by their merchant ship, flying the British flag, and kept warehouses in Mersine, Yafa and Beirut.[8]

EDUCATIONAL AND CULTURAL INFRASTRUCTURE

Foreign missionaries, local churches and central and local government authorities competed to provide Beirut with a sizeable and rapidly expanding educational and cultural infrastructure that would support the flowering of a distinctive intellectual climate.

Education provision in Mount Lebanon had long preceded that of Beirut. The Maronite Church, a pioneer in the field, sent student missions to Rome, particularly after the establishment of the Maronite College in the Vatican in 1584, and adopted the establishment of schools for male children as official church policy as early as the Synod of Luwayza in 1736. One such school was the renowned Maronite seminary of `Ayn Waraqa, established in 1789, where the principal intellectuals of the Nahda studied. At about that time, the Greek Catholics established a similar school in `Ayn Traz (the `Alay highlands). The French envisaged their missionary and educational role as a supplementary asset in their competition with the British. As early as 1733, the Jesuits established their institutions in Kisrawan and the north before leaving the country for a relatively long period. Upon their return in 1839, they opened a school in Beirut. Three years later, they had installed a network of institutions in Ghazir, Zahleh, Bikfaya, Ta`nayil, Jizzin, Dayr al-Qamar and Sidon. Meanwhile, in 1834, the Lazarites opened their school at `Ayn Tura, the first to teach in French.

Protestant missionaries, first British then American, started their activities on Lebanese territories in 1810 with a school for boys in Beirut. As`ad Shidyaq, a graduate of `Ayn Waraqa, taught Arabic in that school and became the first Protestant convert. He wrote a letter against the adoration of icons and called for a direct interpretation of the Holy Book by believers. In 1820, the Maronite patriarch Hubaysh, under orders from Rome, launched his attack against Protestant 'heresy', banning any commerce with Protestants under the threat of excommunication. As`ad Shidyaq was arrested and incarcerated in the patriarchal seat at Qannubin (Bisharri), where he died of maltreatment in 1830. Following Shidyaq's arrest, most Protestant missionaries left but returned under Muhammad `Ali, to open a boys' school in Beirut (1835) followed by a school for girls (1837) and later a boarding school for boys (1850). In 1838, they set up their leading Protestant seminary in `Ubay and, two years later, a school for Druze girls in Mount Lebanon. By 1862, the Protestants were running 41 schools with 948 students.

After the 1860s, the tendency was to set up schools or upgrade them in Beirut or move them to the city. College education had begun in 1866 with the founding of the Protestant Syrian American College (later renamed the American University of Beirut). The Jesuits followed suit as they transferred their college from Ghazir (Kisrawan) to Beirut. In 1874–75, a medical school and a faculty for Oriental studies were added, marking the beginning of the Université Saint Joseph.

The Protestant challenge prompted local churches to engage in a new round of school construction in Beirut and Mount Lebanon. The Greek Orthodox built a school in the convent of Balamand near Tripoli (1833) and in Suq al-Gharb (1852). The Catholics founded the Ecole Patriarcale in 1865 and, in 1874, the Maronite bishop of Beirut established the Ecole de la Sagesse.

Lay charitable institutions also contributed their share to this rapid growth of education. In 1878, a group of Sunni notables of Beirut founded Jam`iyat al-Maqasid al-Khayriya al-Islamiya, the Muslim Association for Benevolent Intentions, whose main goal was the spread of education among the city's Muslim youth, as a reaction to missionary schooling. The first Maqasid schools were soon established in Beirut, Tripoli and Sidon. For the Greek Orthodox, Emilie Sursuq established Zahrat al-Ihsan (Flower of Charity) a school for girls in 1880.

Finally, Ottoman public education should not be underrated. Sultan `Abd al-Hamid II had greatly encouraged the construction of public schools. Through the joint efforts of Ottoman walis and the city's municipality, Beirut's public schools grew in number from 153 in 1886 to 359 in 1914.

Beirut also became a centre for printing and publishing. Book publishing in Arabic in the Arab regions of the Empire did not start until after 1727, when the Porte lifted the ban on printing in Arabic. Before then, books in Arabic were produced in Italy and France, although presses in Mount Lebanon had been established at an earlier period. The first known printing press in Mar Quzhayya monastery (in the north) began printing religious books in Syriac script as early as 1610. In 1723, Deacon `Abdalla Zakhir started a new Arabic press in the Greek Catholic monastery of Mar Yuhanna al-Shuwayr, including printing the first book in Arabic in 1734. The Protestants' concern with spreading the Bible in Arabic provided Beirut with its first printing press. In 1834, Eli Smith moved the American Press from Malta to Beirut and donated a new set of elegant Arabic letters. In

1848, the Jesuits followed suit and set up their Catholic Press, and local presses soon followed.

In 1856 the poet and critic Khalil Khuri founded *Hadiqat al-Akhbar*, the first Arabic weekly in Syria. By 1914, there were 168 publications in Beirut alone, ranging from daily and weekly political newspapers to academic and scientific journals. Among them were a dozen women's magazines pioneered by Hind Nawfal's *Al-Fatat* in 1893. One of the leading newspapers was *Lisan al-Hal* (the Spokesman), published by Khalil Sarkis. In addition to *Al-Mashriq* (the Orient), the Jesuit Orientalist journal, we should mention the scientific journal *Al-Muqtataf* founded in 1876 by two students, and later teachers, at the Syrian Protestant College, Ya'qub Sarruf (1852–1927) and Faris Nimr (1860–1952). *Al-Muqtataf*, which was transferred to Cairo in 1883, established itself as a forum of scientific thought, played an important role in the translation of scientific terms and published celebrated polemics on Darwin's theories. To these should be added the role of Lebanese men of letters in the development of Arab journalism in the rest of the Sultanate. Ahmad Faris al-Shidyaq's *Al-Jawa'ib* (the News), published in Istanbul in 1861, is considered the first pan-Arab modern newspaper. It enjoyed a wide distribution and considerable influence in all the capitals of the Arab provinces of the Empire. Intellectuals from Lebanon also played a major role in the development of journalism in Egypt. Jirji Zaydan (1861–1914) founded *Al-Hilal* (the Crescent) and the Taqla brothers Salim (1849–1912) and Bishara (1852–1911) established *Al-Ahram* (the Pyramids), which remain to this day the most influential monthly and daily publications respectively in Egypt.

The first cultural associations in the region saw the light in Beirut. The Syrian Association for the Sciences and Arts, a literary and scientific circle, was founded in 1847 in Beirut by Ibrahim al-Yaziji, Butrus al-Bustani and Mikha'il Mashaqqa, encouraged and influenced by the Protestant missionary and scholar Cornelius Van Dyck. The deliberations of the society, collected and published by Bustani, covered many themes in science, history, rationality, women's rights, the fight against superstition, the history of Beirut and the importance of trade. The society was dissolved, but its members in 1852 and its inner circle founded the Syrian Scientific Association six years later, with a much wider and multi-sectarian audience and a membership of more than 180. There was also the short-lived Oriental Society founded in 1850, whose records have unfortunately disappeared.

Literary salons appeared at that time as well, the most reputed at the initiative of Ibrahim al-Yaziji's wife, Warda.

AL-NAHDA: THE CULTURAL RENAISSANCE

The contribution of Lebanese territories to the renaissance of Arab letters and culture, the *Nahda*, was the product of a singular symbiosis between Beirut and Mount Lebanon in the wider context of the opening of both to Europe and the Syrian interior. While Beirut offered the educational and cultural infrastructure and the urban setting, Mount Lebanon provided the human element and the experience of a dramatic transitional period that witnessed the collapse of the old *muqata`ji* order, amid a bloody civil war. The *Nahda*'s principal actors were recent migrants from Mount Lebanon to Beirut. The city transformed them into a new type of intellectual. They had studied in the Mountain but perfected their education in the city. Almost all had been *mudabbir*s, serving as secretaries and copyists under *muqata`ji*s and rulers. In the city they became educators, translators, journalists or simply writers. Their patrons were sometimes merchant bourgeois who advertised in their newspapers or financed the publication of their books.

Nasif al-Yaziji (1800–71) began his career as a private secretary to Prince Haydar al-Shihabi and Bashir Shihab II. He settled in Beirut around 1840 and came in contact with Protestant missionaries as a tutor in Arabic and later taught at the Syrian Protestant College (the present AUB). He wrote on philosophy, grammar, style, rhetoric and poetry. Among his many essays are a commentary on the great poet al-Mutanabbi (915–955) and a treatise on the *muqata`ji* system in Mount Lebanon. His principal contribution to the *Nahda* is his attempt to emulate classical Arab writers. His son Ibrahim (1847–1906) was a grammarian, man of letters and educator (who taught at the Ecole Patriarchale and the National School in Beirut). Yaziji made a valuable contribution to the modern study of Arabic poetics, and his wide range of interests included music, painting and astronomy. Among his many innovations was the creation of a simplified Arab font, which reduced Arabic character forms from 300 to 60 and contributed to the creation of the Arabic typing-machine. Ibrahim died in exile in Egypt fleeing Ottoman repression.

Butrus al-Bustani (1819–83) was the *Nahda*'s encyclopaedist. The *Mu`allim* (Master) was also a grammarian, educator, journalist, critic and a pioneer in liberal, nationalist and secular thought. He studied in `Ayn Waraqa, the famous Maronite college, and taught at the Protestant seminary in Beirut, then at the Syrian Protestant College. In 1863, Bustani founded the National School in Beirut, the first secular school in the Arab East, with instruction in Arabic, Turkish, French, English, Greek and Latin. He also published the first political bulletin, *Nafir Suriya* (September 1860–April 1861). In 1870, he launched the daily *Al-Janna*, edited by his son Salim, the weekly *Al-Junayna*, edited by his kinsman Sulayman (1856–1925), the translator in verse of Homer's *Iliad*, and the monthly *al-Jinan*.[9] His main contributions, however, are the first modern Arabic dictionary (1870) and a six-volume encyclopaedia (1870–82).

Faris Shidyaq (1805–87) is undoubtedly the most radical and creative of the *Nahda* figures. Born in `Ashqut (in Kisrawan), he lived in Hadath, near Beirut, in a family that suffered greatly from the oppression of the Church and the local feudal leaders. His grandfather, father and brother died as 'martyrs of freedom of thought and inclination', as he was to write later. Faris also studied at `Ayn Waraqa and, upon the death of his father, worked as a copyist of manuscripts yet continued his studies under his elder brother As`ad, whose arrest and death completely changed the course of Faris's life. He broke from the Maronite Church, converted to Protestantism and left the country for an exile from which he never returned. In Cairo, under Muhammad `Ali, he taught Arabic to American Protestant missionaries and studied under the sheikhs of al-Azhar. From 1834 to 1848 Shidyaq was in Malta, where he taught at the American missionary school and edited the publications of the American Press. Later, he spent a decade between England and France during which he assisted Dr Samuel Lee in the translation of the Bible. After a brief stay in Tunis in 1859, invited by its reformist governor, Ahmad Bey, to edit the official *al-Ra'id al-Tunis*, he converted to Islam and went to settle in Istanbul where he spent the remainder of his days. In the Ottoman capital, he worked at the Imperial Press, translated the *Journal of Ottoman Court Orders* into Arabic (1868–76) and founded the newspaper *al-Jawa'ib* in 1861. Man of letters, philologist and grammarian, Faris is the author of two books relating his travels in Europe, *Al-Wasita fi Ma`rifat Ahwal Malta* (Means of Knowing Malta) and *Kashf al-Mukhabba `Ann Funun Urubba* (Unveiling the Hidden in European Arts), both published in 1863. His writings on philology and grammar include a number of dictionaries from French and English into Arabic, *Al-Jasus `ala-l-Qamus* (The Spy on the Dictionary), a monumental critique of Fayruzabadi's classic dictionary and two books on grammar and rhetoric. His masterpiece, *al-Saq `ala-l-Saq* (The Thigh over the Thigh), written and published in Paris in 1855, is considered a founding text of Arab modernity, both in content and form.

Yusuf al-Asir (1815–89) was born in Sidon and stood out as the leading Muslim among the men of the *Nahda*. A graduate of al-Azhar in Cairo, he held the position of judge in Tripoli, mufti in `Akkar and attorney-general in Mount Lebanon under the *Mutasarrifiya*. In addition to a collection of poetry, his writings include a commentary on the Ottoman Code. He was also the founder of the first newspaper in Lebanon (1875) to be published by a Muslim.

A common concern of all the *Nahda* pioneers was to liberate Arabic writing from its torpor and conventional styles. They succeeded brilliantly in prose but much less so in poetry. Undoubtedly the translation of the Bible into Arabic was a landmark in that effort as the process of translation itself contributed to the innovation of Arabic prose. Three translations were produced within a period of fifteen years. The Shidyaq–Lee translation came out first, in 1857, but remained largely unknown. Eli Smith (1801–52) started the project in 1847, assisted by Butrus al-Bustani, and the translation was corrected by Nasif al-Yaziji. After Smith's death, the effort was continued by Cornelius Van Dyck (1818–95), helped by Yusuf al-Asir, and the final version came out in 1865. In 1880, Yaziji produced the Bible translation for the Jesuits. Regardless of the controversies it provoked, the new translation of the Bible would influence generations of writers, among whom Gibran Khalil Gibran, author of *The Prophet*.

Literary renewal did not stop at language. New literary forms appeared under the direct influence of Western literature. Marun Naqqash (1817–55) introduced the theatrical arts. In 1848, he staged the first modern play in Arabic, *Al-Bakhil*, a loose translation of Molière's *L'Avare*. Mikha'il Mashaqqa must be mentioned as a pioneer in the genre of autobiography with his *al-Jawab `ala Iqtirah al-Ahbab* (An Answer to the Enquiry of the Beloved Ones, 1873), while Salim al-Bustani initiated the novel form with his *Al-Huyam fi Jinan al-Sham* (Love in the Gardens of Sham) and *Zannubiya* (Zenobia). Jirji Zaydan wrote the first historical novels evoking glorious or dramatic episodes of Arab–Muslim history along with his classic histories of Arabic literature and Muslim civilisation.

Those men lived through a dramatic transitional period in which the old society was disintegrating, and they were not content to be passive witnesses of its transformations. They were actively engaged in the struggle against the two pillars of the old order: the *muqata'ji* system and the Maronite Church. Equally important in understanding their motives, thought and positions is the decisive impact that the 1860 civil war left on their lives. Many factors account for the conversion of the Maronites Bustani and Shidyaq and the Greek Catholic Mashaqqa to Protestantism and the close association of the Greek Catholic Yazijis with Protestant missionaries. However, their reaction to the Maronite Church and their secular views were certainly contributing factors. However, dissidents from their communities were not all Christians. Amir Muhammad Ibn `Abbas Arsalan, appointed *qa'im maqam* of the Druze in 1858, resigned his post in protest against the horrors of the 1860 war and settled in Beirut, where he devoted himself to literature until the end of his days. He was later to preside over the Scientific Association.

Moreover, those Christian intellectuals did not turn to Christian Europe for inspiration but to the secular Europe of the Enlightenment, of English liberalism and the ideals of the French Revolution of 1789. Freedom of expression, the rule of law, the central role of the individual in society and the state and equality were the underlying themes in their writings. Shidyaq, questioning the arbitrary arrest and incarceration of his brother As`ad by the Maronite patriarch, writes: 'suppose my brother argued and polemized in religious affairs and maintained you were in error, you did not have to kill him for that. You should have refuted his proofs and arguments by words, spoken or written...'[10] Bustani, for his part, emphasised the need for good government (governance) and the respect for laws.

Even so, European concepts were not uncritically assimilated. The attraction of civilisation, progress, democracy and freedom did not hide, in Shidyaq's eyes, the misery of the working populations in mid-nineteenth-century Europe. As much as he admired equality among citizens in England, he was also deeply aware of the rigidity of the country's social hierarchy and was shocked to find out that the condition of the English peasants was no better than that of peasants in Mount Lebanon. He soon discovered that the basis of the peasants' misery in England was the system of land ownership, in which a few thousand families monopolised the majority of cultivable land. Shidyaq was opposed to inherited wealth, sceptical about the idealisation of poverty as propagated by religion; he meditated at length on the way money corrupts human relations and feelings. In Victorian London, where rich and poor quarters coexisted 'as Heaven and Hell would coexist', Shidyaq realised that poverty was at the basis of all social ills: crime, suicide, prostitution of adolescents, abortion, etc. But he discovered that the misery of the many made the happiness of the few: 'How could it be that a thousand human beings, nay two thousands, should labour for the happiness of only one man?' Shidyaq's deep sense of social justice led him to socialism (which he translated into *Ishtirakiyyah* in 1878). Ultimately, he believed that a society of peasants and workers was more reasonable than one exclusively and entirely composed of rich people.

The Lebanese *Nahda* followed the tradition of its Egyptian counterpart in assigning the greatest importance to education as a principal mode of access to modernity and civilisation. However, Shidyaq departs from his colleagues in his emphasis on industrialisation and the value of work and of time, which he linked to the notion of progress. He further warned against reducing modernity and civilisation to living in the cities and speaking a foreign language. 'Education without work, says he, is like a tree without fruits or a river without water.'

The intellectuals of the Lebanese *Nahda* were also pioneers of feminism. Bustani, in his famous 'Allocution on the Education of Women' (1849), argued the case for the education of women perhaps for the first time in the Arab world. But the *mu`allim* essentially envisaged an ideal Oriental woman, educated yet restricted to her household, where her main role was the education of her children. Shidyaq went much further than his contemporaries in calling for complete equality between women and men. He defended women's right to work and to choose their husbands, and supported their equal right to divorce. However, the Lebanese libertarian's most original contribution to women's liberation, in the mid-nineteenth century, was his defence of women's equal right to sexual pleasure, even justifying extra-marital relations!

Finally, the Lebanese *Nahda* was a movement for the national revival of the Arabs. Ibrahim al-Yaziji's poem 'Arabs, arise and awake!' became the rallying call for the early generations of Arab nationalists. However, it was Butrus Bustani who elaborated the notion of homeland (*watan*), although the national space was Syria (present-day Lebanon, Syria and Palestine) whose people was bound by the bonds of a common language, culture and history. In line with the *Nahda*'s passion for scientific concepts, Bustani used the metaphor of the magnet to describe the power of attraction that the homeland exercised on its members.

ARAB DECENTRALISTS AND INDEPENDENTISTS

Beirut harboured one of the earliest manifestations of Arab nationalism, providing it with its cultural ethos. Turbulent developments inside the Ottoman Empire eventually transformed the idea into a movement.

In 1876, the Grand Vizir, Midhat Pasha, backed by Ottoman reformers, deposed Sultan `Abd al-`Aziz, and replaced him with his brother, Sultan `Abd al-Hamid II (1876–1909). The 'Hamidian revolution' marked a turning point in the history of the Ottoman Empire and the destiny of its Arab regions. The Ottoman reformers had envisaged a set of political reforms in order to save the empire from European encroachment. On 23 December of that year, they declared the Ottoman constitution. Known as 'Midhat Pasha's constitution', the new charter confirmed the equality of all the subjects of the empire, guaranteed basic liberties and adopted a constitutional and limited parliamentary regime.

Nationalist agitation in the Arab regions was a direct consequence of developments in Istanbul. In 1877, the project of an independent Arab kingdom, covering the territories of Lebanon, Syria and Palestine, was revived. Encouraged by the outbreak of the Russo-Ottoman war on 18 April 1877, Muslim notables and intellectuals from Syria's major cities and rural centres converged upon Damascus to pay allegiance to `Abd al-Qadir and urge him to lead the movement for the unity of *Bilad al-Sham*.[11] They still conceived of that unity inside the confines of the Ottoman Empire. Significantly, the movement welcomed a new recruit in Yusuf Karam, whose political beliefs had undergone a radical transformation while in exile.

As soon as the regions of the Empire had started to react favourably to the declaration of the constitution, `Abd al-Hamid suspended it under the pretext of the Russo-Ottoman war. Midhat was dismissed and sent to exile. The outcome of the war shifted in favour of the Russians, laying a heavy burden on the empire. According to the treaties of San Stephano and Berlin (March and April 1878) the Ottoman Empire lost territories to Russia, was forced to recognise the independence of Romania and Serbia and to concede additional Ottoman territory to the European powers. `Abd al-Hamid ceded Cyprus to Britain, and the latter encouraged France to occupy Tunisia. More importantly, Britain occupied Egypt in 1882 under the guise of suppressing the `Arabi revolt. In the end, Yusuf Karam was proven right: Britain and France had started planning the dismemberment of the ailing Ottoman Empire. Aware that Istanbul could no longer count on Britain to help preserve the unity of the empire, `Abd al-Hamid II resorted to an internal policy of massive repression and allied himself externally with Germany, the new and rival European imperial power.

When Midhat Pasha was reinstated in 1878 and appointed wali of Syria, a new lease of life was granted to Syrian nationalists. The first clandestine brochures calling for revolt against the Turks and for Arab independence appeared on the walls of Beirut in 1881 and 1882. They were attributed to a secret society founded in 1876 by a dozen Christian intellectuals, mostly former SPC students. However, Midhat's mandate was short-lived. Accused by the central government of seeking to detach the Arab provinces, he was arrested and exiled to Ta'if (in the Arab peninsula) in 1881 and assassinated two years later, probably on the orders of `Abd al-Hamid. Midhat's demise ended the first phase of Arab national agitation. In 1882–83, the 'Arabist' secret society was disbanded and its members, including Sarruf, Nimr and Yaziji, fled to Egypt and many of the pro-`Abd al-Qadir notables and ulemas were confined to their residence or exiled.

To consolidate his rule and combat European designs, `Abd al-Hamid called for Islamic unity, now that Arabs and Muslims constituted the majority of his subjects. If this helped temporarily appease Arab independentist agitation, it nevertheless unleashed a new wave of struggle against Hamidian authoritarianism. The major demands were the return to the constitution, decentralisation and a larger measure of participation for the Arabs in running the affairs of the Sultanate. In 1902, a secret circle calling for constitutional life and the end of Hamidian rule was founded in Damascus. Hamidian repression pushed independentists to transfer their activities outside the Arab provinces. In 1906, a group of Arab students in Istanbul formed the Association for Arab Renaissance (*Jam`iyyat al-Nahda al-`Arabiyya*), calling for reform and wider political Arab participation. In Paris, a group of Christian Lebanese notables and merchants founded the Ottoman League (1908), while Arab Muslim students formed the Young Arab League (*Al-Jam`iya al-`Arabiya al-Fatat*) in 1911. Among them were Muhammad Rustum Haydar and Ghalib Mahmasani from Lebanon, `Awni `Abd al-Hadi from Palestine, Jamil Mardam from Syria, and Rafiq al-Tamimi from Iraq. Their aim was to 'raise the Arab nation to the level of modern nations'. In response to the official policy of Islamisation, which emphasised the historical role of the Arabs in propagating Islam, decentralists demanded equal rights for

Arabs and the officialisation of Arabic, and proclaimed the unity of the Arab regions of the empire. The multi-sectarian decentralists took residence in Cairo, where Rashid Rida, Haqqi al-`Azm, Shibli Shimayil, Iskandar `Ammun and others founded, in 1912, the Ottoman Party for Administrative Decentralisation.

The revolt of the Young Turks in 1909 and the reactivation of the constitution revived nationalist agitation in the Arab provinces. In 1913, the Young Arab Society moved its offices to Beirut and published *Al-Mufid*, edited by `Abd al-Ghani `Uraysi. The most notable of the local movements for reform and decentralisation was the Beirut Reform Movement of 1912–13. In late 1912, 84 Beiruti notables and intellectuals met at the municipality and elected a Preparatory Committee for Reform of 25 members. They demanded the officialisation of Arabic, decentralisation, the extension of the powers of the *wilaya*'s council and the reduction of military service. It was also suggested that the council be formed of 30 elected members, half Muslims and half non-Muslims (13 Christians and two Jews) and control a larger share of the budget revenues – in fact, all except the revenues from customs, post and telegraph and the exemption tax from military service. The reformists further threatened to join the autonomous region of Mount Lebanon in case their demands were not met. But the outcome of Beirut's autonomist demands was no better than that of the Mountain. On 8 April 1913, the CUP declared the movement's demands 'an act of treason against the Ottoman State', dismissed wali Adham *Beyk* for his sympathies toward the city's reformists and appointed Hazim *Beyk* who disbanded the Reform Committee on that same day. The next day, all Beirut papers were bordered in black in sympathetic protest. Three days later, the committee's general assembly, convening in the meeting hall of the Syrian Protestant College, called for a general strike and a memorandum signed by 1,300 of the city's inhabitants (mainly merchants, rentiers, physicians, lawyers and journalists) was addressed to the Porte, objecting to the disbanding of the Reform Committee as unconstitutional. The response came in the form of further repression. The police were ordered to force merchants to open shop, six members of the committee were arrested and accused of instigating the strike, and the two nationalist newspapers, `Uraysi's *Al-Mufid* and Shaykh Ahmad Tabbara's *Al-Ittihad al-`Uthmani*, were closed. Though the detainees were released, the Ottoman authorities appointed a more restricted committee (with considerably fewer Christians). The movement fizzled out.

The apogee of that period was the First Arab Congress in Paris representing the different nationalist tendencies among the elites of the Arab regions. Held from 17 to 23 June 1913 under the auspices of the Ottoman Party for Administrative Decentralisation, the congress was attended by delegates from Syria, Iraq, Palestine, Beirut and Mount Lebanon, in addition to the Lebanese support committees in Paris, Cairo, the United States and Mexico. The Syrian ˈAbd al-Hamid al-Zahrawi presided, and participants demanded Ottoman reform, decentralisation, the recognition of Arabic in the Ottoman parliament and its officialisation in the Arab provinces and the extension of the right for Arab conscripts to serve their terms in their own provinces in time of peace. The congress further supported the programme of the Beirut Reform movement and the increase of the *Mutasarrifiya*'s financial revenues. The dominant mood was set by ˈAbd al-Ghani al-ˈUraysi, who affirmed that Arabs were simultaneously members of a nation with its specific characteristics and Ottoman citizens, and consequently possessed legitimate rights in both capacities. An issue of discord revolved around the demand of some Christian delegates from Mount Lebanon that 'foreign experts and advisers' should assist in carrying out the reforms. The majority of the delegates saw in this proposal an attempt to introduce the idea of enlisting European help against Ottoman rule. That note of discord, which was eventually settled, foreshadowed the later rift between independentists and protectionists.

Although the negotiations with a delegation of the Arab Congress (obtained from CUP members Talˈat Pasha and Jamal Pasha) seemed at first quite promising, they ended up by only allowing the appointment of six Arab notables in the Ottoman senate. In the end, the CUP's abandonment of ˈAbd al-Hamid's policy of Islamic unity, its military dictatorship and Turkish nationalist policies drove Arab nationalists and Lebanese independentists alike to seek independence by force, even with the help of European powers.

THE CATASTROPHIES OF WORLD WAR I

The catastrophies that befell the inhabitants of Beirut and Mount Lebanon during World War I would have a direct impact on later developments. Ottoman repression against the independentist movement in Beirut and the Mountain was particularly harsh. Under the iron hand of Ottoman envoy Jamal Pasha, the 'Butcher', in 1915 and 1916, 33 Lebanese and Arab nationalist activists were sentenced to death before the martial court in `Alay for high treason, accused of connections with the Allies and publicly hanged in Beirut and Damascus.

After the declaration of the war, the terrible Safar Barlik was imposed – a compulsory military service that still today haunts the popular imagination. The exemption tax – set at 44 gold pounds per head – put people at the mercy of the usurers. Ottoman authorities controlled trade, expropriated wheat and livestock, speculated, issued paper money (which it arbitrarily paid as equivalent in value to gold) and imposed a compulsory subscription to war bonds, payable in cash. Most importantly, the war revealed the economic insufficiency of autonomous Mount Lebanon, which depended on overseas trade for over half of its revenues and mostly fulfilled its needs in cereals and livestock with imports from the Biqa` and the Syrian interior. The shortages of the war – aggravated by a locust invasion during the summer of 1915 – and the speculation of the usurers and governors made the territories of the *Mutasarrifiya* and Beirut the hardest hit by famine among all the other Ottoman provinces.

Father Yammin, a Maronite priest from the north, wrote a poignant account of Beirut and Mount Lebanon during the war years in which he describes, in painful details, the ravages of locust, the epidemics – typhus, cholera and leprosy – prostitution and famine. People devoured the meat of dead dogs and camels, and cases of anthropophagy were reported in Beirut, Mount Lebanon, Tripoli and Jabal `Amil. In Beirut, victims of the famine stacked in the streets were collected by municipal carts and dumped into collective graves in the Al-Raml quarter on the city's outskirts. Many were taken for dead and buried alive. Significantly, Yammin refused to follow the tradition of blaming all his country's ills on the Ottomans. He likewise accused rich Lebanese who had become 'devoid of any feeling of tenderness and pity toward their kin'. But his rage was primarily directed against Beirut usurers, who lent money in return for exorbitant interest rates, set at 25 to 50 per cent at the beginning of the war, and raised to 70 to 150 per cent by 1916. Those 'traders in souls', as Yammin called them, had introduced the most cynical methods for robbing people of their properties and belongings.[12]

By the end of the war, an estimated 100,000 inhabitants of Beirut and Mount Lebanon had died of famine.

Part II
State and Society

5
Greater Lebanon: The Dialectics of Attachment and Detachment (1915–1920)

Little Lebanon spells economic death, union with Syria, political death.

Yusuf al-Sawda

Lebanon, in the frontiers defined on 1 September 1920, had never existed before in history. It was a product of the Franco-British colonial partition of the Middle East. Its creation did not imply a return to any 'natural and historical' boundaries, as Lebanese nationalists claimed, nor was it an 'artificial' entity, contrary to Arab nationalist pretences, as it is no more nor less artificial than any of the other eastern Arab states (Syria, Jordan, Palestine or Iraq) created by the partition process. Like the rest of these states, Lebanon's borders were imposed against the will of the majority of its population. Greater Lebanon's creation was mainly determined by the interests of France in dividing and controlling Syria, in the context of the partition of the Arab provinces of the ex-Ottoman Empire between Paris and London. Indeed, many Lebanese Christians had called for territorial expansion and separation from the rest of Syria, under some form or other of French protection or guarantee. But the final product – Greater Lebanon under French mandate – hardly corresponded to the programme of any Lebanese political party.

LEBANON IN THE PARTITION OF THE MIDDLE EAST

As has become widely known, the Sykes–Picot accords of 1916 divided the Arab provinces of the Ottoman Empire into two broadly defined British and French zones, each of which was to exercise direct control over the coasts and retain zones of influence in the hinterland, with the Jerusalem region as an international zone. France's interest in Syria was not new although an expedition funded by the Chambers of Commerce of Lyons and Marseilles was sent during the war to ascertain whether, and to what extent, the region was worth colonising; the

mission's report reached positive conclusions. But there lingered in
the French conception of Syria the idea that Palestine constituted
its southern part while Britain had a strong claim over Palestine as a
buffer zone between Sinai and the Levant to defend the Suez Canal
and the road to India. British interest in the territory that constitutes
present-day Iraq was mainly in its oil fields and the control over the
Gulf, which had become a zone of British influence.

There was of course a marked difference between those colonial
aims and their official justification. In a postwar period dominated by
the right of nations to self-determination, a principle invoked with
equal force by Woodrow Wilson's America and Lenin's Soviet Russia,
the legitimisation was rooted in the age-old minorities policy, focused
on ethnic and religious communities. France justified its claim to
Syria by the necessary defence of the Christian, Druze, `Alawi and
Shi`i minorities, while Britain claimed Palestine in order to create a
'national homeland' for the Jews. The text of the Balfour Declaration
of November 1917 is a striking example of this ethnicisation of the
peoples of the region.[1] Whereas the Jews are assumed to be a people
and a nationality, since the aim was to establish a 'national home'
for them in Palestine, the Arabs, the majority of the inhabitants
of the country, were negatively defined by their non-Jewishness
and reduced to the status of religious communities (Muslim and
Christian) whose only rights were civil and religious, that is, neither
national nor political.

After having occupied Lebanon and overthrown the Arab
government, France's priority was to ensure that it received a mandate
over Greater Syria. Behind the British-supported Arab revolt loomed
the spectre of Britain breaking its Sykes–Picot commitments. An Arab
prince, whose revolt was inspired, advised, financed and armed by
Britain, ruled Damascus, the seat of the Arab government. Ultimately,
the Sykes–Picot agreement was revised and modified according to
recent developments: France dropped any claim to Palestine, and
ceded the Mosul region – originally considered part of Syria – to
Britain in return for a share in the Anglo-Persian Petroleum Company
that had recently discovered oil in that region. In return, France's
control over Syria was legitimised, with British encouragement to try
and find a solution with Faysal.

France's 'Lebanese project' was made subject to that priority. In order
to obtain its mandate over the Syrian territories, France relied mainly
on the Maronite Church, represented by Patriarch Elias Huwayik. But
the elected representatives of Mount Lebanon were giving different

signals. In April 1919, the Administrative Council (AC) unilaterally declared Lebanon's independence, under a 'democratic system' based on the principles of 'liberty, equality and fraternity' and guaranteeing 'the rights of minorities and freedom of belief'. However, at the Paris peace conference a month later, the AC delegation headed by Dawud `Ammun encountered robust pressure by French officials to limit its demands to French protection and territorial expansion.

During the following months, Lebanon's fate was left in the balance as it awaited the outcome of negotiations between France and Emir Faysal. In October 1919, French Prime Minister Clemenceau vaguely promised Patriarch Huwayik the annexation to Mount Lebanon of 'territories in the Biqa`' and 'appropriate ports' under 'an autonomous government and an independent national status'. Negotiations between Clemenceau and Faysal led to a secret accord on the creation of an Arab state in Syria under Faysal, according to which the capital would be Damascus while a French high commissioner would be posted in Aleppo. In return, the prince agreed to resort exclusively to French civil and military advisers, and economic, cultural and military aid, while giving priority to French enterprises in his country's economic projects. On the other hand, Faysal recognised 'Lebanon's independence and territorial integrity under French mandate'. Although the definition of Lebanon's borders was left to the peace congress, it was understood that 'Lebanon' meant Mount Lebanon.

To convince Damascus that the Biqa` was negotiable, French troops kept a modest presence on the Beirut–Damascus road, while the rest of the plain was left in the hands of Faysal's armed partisans. From Ba`albak to Marj`uyun and from Tyre to Tripoli, armed operations were being conducted against French forces. Southern Lebanon had rallied to the Arab cause beginning in late 1918 and received Faysal's personal emissary, the Christian Ilias Dhyb al-Khuri. Kamil al-As`ad, Shiite *za`im* of the south, was declared governor-general of Jabal `Amil, and Riad al-Sulh, son of Rida al-Sulh, the Sunni patron of south Lebanon, governor of Sayda. Riad, who had a law degree from the Université Saint-Joseph in Beirut and the University of Constantinople, had been engaged at an early age in the Arab national struggle against Ottoman rule and condemned in *absentia* to life imprisonment. The southern rebellion was led by Adham Khanjar and Sadik Hamza, whose armed bands attacked French troops stationed in the Christian villages of Judayda (Marji`yun) and `Ayn Ibil. On 24 April 1920, some 600 Shiite notables, ulemas and leaders of armed partisans of the Arab revolt met at the Hujayr Valley Congress to declare Jabal `Amil an 'independent district linked to the Syrian federation'.

On 7 March 1920, the Arab Congress, convened in Damascus, declared the integral independence of Syria and proclaimed Faysal King of Syria. Lebanon was the object of a vague promise to 'take into consideration the national *desiderata* of the Lebanese regarding their country in its borders known before World War I on condition that Lebanon avoid any foreign influence'. Faysal, increasingly criticised by the nationalist opposition for his compromises with France and Britain, finally opted for the arbitration of the International Mandate Commission set up by the Allies to decide the fate of the populations of the Ottoman Empire. Boycotted by the French and the British, only the commission's American members – Chicago businessman Charles Crane and Henry King, president of Oberlin College – arrived in the region in June 1919. The King–Crane commission, as it became known, met delegations from 36 cities and 1,520 villages and received no fewer than 1,863 petitions. Fully 80 per cent of the respondents voted for a united Syria, 74 per cent supported independence and 60 per cent chose a 'democratic and decentralised constitutional monarchy'. In the event of the imposition of a foreign mandate on Syria, 60 per cent opted for an American mandate, a much smaller number for a British mandate and only 14 per cent, mainly Lebanese Maronites, requested a French mandate. A total of 72 per cent of the respondents were opposed to Zionist colonisation and to the separation of Palestine from the rest of the Arab East. In its report to the peace conference in Paris in 1919, the commission recommended a united state for the whole of natural Syria governed by Prince Faysal under one mandatory power. It also emphasised that the Zionist project of unlimited emigration of Jews into Palestine and its final goal, the creation of a Jewish state, required 'serious modifications' and concluded: 'anything else would be tantamount to treason of the Syrian people'. The commission's findings were shelved, however, and a few weeks later, on 26 April 1920, the San Remo conference granted France its mandate over Syria and Lebanon.

Parallel to the Franco-Syrian negotiations, talks had been engaged between Prince Faysal on the one hand, and Patriarch Huwayik and the Administrative Council members on the other. The latter two opposed the independence declaration of the Arab Congress of March 1920. But when the Arab government recognised Lebanon's right to territorial expansion and independence, the majority of the AC members accepted, concluding an agreement with Damascus despite the objection of the patriarch, who was already won over to the idea of the French mandate. On 10 June 1920, a declaration by the AC reiterated the main points of its independence declaration, adding Lebanon's desire to 'live in peace with its neighbours'.

After Clemenceau's fall and the formation of a new government under Millerand, France broke its commitments to Faysal. Nevertheless, on 10 July 1920, eight of the AC's 13 members (the Maronite seat for Kisrawan was vacant) set off to Damascus to sign a joint declaration in which both parties would denounce the French mandate in return for Prince Faysal's recognition of Lebanese independence. The party was then intercepted and arrested by French troops in Sawfar, on the Beirut–Damascus road. The delegation, led by Sa`d Allah Huyawik, vice-president of the council and brother of Patriarch Huwayik, included four Christians (three Maronites and one Greek Orthodox), two Druze and one Shi`a (the Catholic councillor for Zahleh was reportedly delayed by illness from joining the delegation). General Gouraud accused the delegation of planning to accompany Faysal to Europe, through a Palestine port, where they would claim to represent Lebanon and declare the integration of Lebanon to a Syrian kingdom under Faysal. Two days later, on 12 July, Gouraud disbanded the AC and in September of that year, the eight AC members were convicted of corruption, accused of cashing money from Faysal's men and exiled to Corsica.

On 14 July, Gouraud sent Prince Faysal a four-day ultimatum that ordered him to accept the French mandate, French currency, a French military presence on the Rayaq–Aleppo railway and the reduction of the Sheriffian army. First-hand accounts from Damascus relate that Faysal had cabled Gouraud accepting the terms of the ultimatum but the French claimed that the answer came too late. Whatever the case, on 21 July, French troops under General Goybet crossed the Biqa`, occupied Rayaq and moved across the Anti-Lebanon range. On 24 July they defeated the Arab army in Maysalun – led by Minister of Defence Yusuf al-`Azmeh, who was killed in a battle that pitted cavalry against tanks – and marched into Damascus. On the afternoon of the 25th, Gouraud entered the capital of the Arab revolt. Lebanon had served as 'bridgehead' for the occupation of Syria, as the French military planners had proposed more than three decades earlier. The Arab revolt crushed, Faysal fled the country to be declared King of Iraq under British occupation a year later, and his brother `Abd Allah became Emir of Transjordan. Syria was divided into four 'autonomous states': Greater Lebanon, Aleppo, Damascus and the Alawi state. A fifth state of Jabal al-Duruz was added in 1921.

On 1 September 1920, General Gouraud officially declared the creation of Greater Lebanon under French mandate. To the original territory of the *Mutasarrifiya* were annexed the coastal cities of Beirut, Sidon, Tyre and Tripoli, and the four ex-Ottoman *cazas* of Hasbaya, Rashaya, Ba`albak and `Akkar. Its borders were set at Nahr al-Kabir in the north, Palestine in the south, the Mediterranean in the west and the summits of the anti-Lebanon range in the east.

The imposition of French mandate on Lebanon, according to Akarli's apt formula, was the victory of the church of Patriarch Elias Huwayik over the secular Lebanon of his brother Sa`d Allah Huwayik![2] And it was in Maysalun that this secular Lebanon – aspiring for independence – was defeated alongside the troops of the Arab revolt.

ATTACHMENT AND DETACHMENT

Almost all of Greater Lebanon's Muslim population rejected the mandate, opting instead for an independent Arab state and, short of that, for annexation to Syria. The declaration of Greater Lebanon was met with widespread anti-French violence on the coast, Jabal `Amil, the Biqa` and Mount Lebanon. On 24 July, Georges Picot and Admiral Mornet, commander of the naval forces in the eastern Mediterranean, suffered an attempt on their lives in the Shuf, and the house of Habib Pasha al-Sa`d (in Rishmaya, the `Alay region) was burnt and sacked. Between 6 December 1920 and 6 January 1921, 30 Christian villages were attacked in south Lebanon, and in May of the same year, a raid by the inhabitants of Bint Jubayl against the neighbouring Christian village of `Ayn Ibil left some fifty dead. The killing was in retaliation for French officers' reliance on Christian collaborators in the conquest of the south. It took a number of months before the 3,600 French troops under the command of Colonel Nieger were able to control southern Lebanon, not without recourse to executions, collective punishment and 'scorched earth'. In Beirut, an assassination attempt against As`ad Khurshid Pasha, the Sunni director-general of the interior, led to the arrest and banishment of Salim `Ali Salam and three other of the city's notables.

The opposition of the annexed territories

While Christian opponents of the mandate invoked the rights of nations to self-determination, Muslim annexationists expressed their opposition to the mandate and the partition of Syria as a necessarily unjust economic, political, fiscal and administrative system. Indeed, in their *Mémorandum de protestation des populations des territoires annexés* (1921), the notables of Beirut, Tripoli, Sidon, Tyre and Ba`albak refuted the historical justifications for 'natural Lebanon', which, they maintained, had never existed historically. The same thesis would be reiterated by the Congress of the Coast and the Four *Cazas* in its meetings of 1928, 1933 and 1936. But the population of the annexed territories mainly expressed their opposition to economic, administrative and fiscal injustices. The annexed territories had a greater population than Mount Lebanon (380,000 as opposed to 330,000 inhabitants) and their financial resources were richer, as 83 per cent of the fiscal revenues of the new state came from the annexed territories; 80 per cent of those revenues were spent in Mount Lebanon. Regarding administrative posts, the majority of the functionaries of the administration of Greater Lebanon came from the ancient *Mutasarrifiya* and replaced the functionaries of the *wilaya* of Beirut. Last but not least, the coastal cities (Tripoli, Sidon, Beirut and Tyre) incurred heavy economic losses because their ports had been severed from the Syrian hinterland. The signatories of the memorandum concluded that 'the commercial interests of the *Wilaya* [of Beirut] and of all Syria require an immediate reestablishment of Syrian unity'. This last argument identifies economic interests with political unity. The first rupture in the Muslim unionists' discourse would be exactly on this issue and lead to the dissociation between economic and political unity.

A substantial number of non-Maronite Christians (Orthodox and Greek Catholics) had expressed similar wishes to those of the Muslims. The majority of the inhabitants of Zahleh, with its Greek Catholic majority, voted in favour of annexation to Syria and against the mandate. Five hundred of its notables signed a petition to that effect, addressed to the King–Crane commission.

The position of the Maronites does not lend itself to over-simplification. There was much truth in what the Muslim representatives of the Coast and Four *Cazas* said in their memorandum to the peace conference: Patriarch Ilias Huwayik – imposed by the French as the spokesman for the 'Lebanese nation' – with the exception of the Sunnis – did not even represent the majority of the Maronites. To begin with, the majority of the members of the Administrative Council, the only elected body capable of expressing public opinion of the time, including its Maronite members, had opposed the French mandate and opted for an independent Lebanon on close terms with Syria. Though an exact typology of the positions of the Maronites is difficult to determine, given the diversity of their political projects and the constant shifting of positions that partly followed the meanderings of European diplomacy, four main currents can nevertheless be detected:

The Arab federalists were a small elite that supported the Arab kingdom in Damascus and an independent and united Arab state. They counted among their ranks Iskandar `Ammun, president of the Lebanese Union (who resigned his post and accepted a position as Faysal's ambassador in Washington), and members of Beirut's merchant aristocratic families and of mainly notable Maronite families from Mount Lebanon (`Aziz al-Hashim, Edward Dahdah, Farid al-Khazin, Emile Khuri, Emile Yazbak and others). The only known Greek Catholic was Amin Ma`luf.

The Syrian federalists, partisans of the federal unity of 'natural Syria', were mainly represented by the French-based Comité d'Orient and the Comité Central Syrien. The latter, led by Georges Samné and Chucri Ghanem (Francophone poet and playwright), included a large number of Greek Catholics and Greek Orthodox Christians. They were based in Paris with branches in Cairo, London and a support committee in New York, which counted Gibran Khalil Gibran as a member. Some of them called for a 'Christian homeland' inside the federation. But the Syrian federalists split on their position toward the mandate. Samné and Ghanem were supporters of the French mandate (they were even believed to be on the French government's payroll) while others maintained the call for a united independent Syria.

The protectionists, in their extreme form, demanded the annexation of Christian Lebanon by France. Ferdinand Tyan, who describes the Maronites as 'French since times immemorial' and historic allies of France in its 'struggle against Islam', called for a return to a Christian emirate attached to France on the Algerian colonial model. Its official language would be French and the Druze would have the choice between accepting their minority status (and learning French) or simply leaving the country.[3] This tendency conceived of Lebanon as a 'Christian refuge' whose 'Frenchness' differentiated it from Arab identity and Islam, both part of 'barbaric Asia'. Another, more moderate version conceived of French protection as a guarantee against the submersion of the Christians in the surrounding Arab/ Islamic world. Patriarch Huwayik viewed Lebanon's 'autonomy' as its independence from the rest of Syria, on the one hand, and its attachment to France, on the other. In a memorandum to the Quai d'Orsay, the patriarch spoke of Lebanon as a 'faraway extension of France'.[4] Emile Iddi was the politician most representative of the protectionists and Charles Corm its intellectual spokesman.

The Lebanese independentists drew heavily on the traditions of the nationalists and reformers of the Administrative Council (AC). Their chief organ was *Al-Ittihad al-Lubnani* (the Lebanese Union), founded in Cairo by Yusuf al-Sawda. *Al-Ittihad* had been opposed, since the beginning of World War I, to the reintegration of Mount Lebanon into the Ottoman Empire and demanded its neutrality and independence 'without protection or annexation'.[5] This group imagined Greater Lebanon as an independent, democratic and multi-sectarian republic where Christians would coexist with Muslims inside and outside Lebanon. The argument of the Lebanonists for Greater Lebanon was mainly economic: the need to provide Mount Lebanon with the required self-sufficiency in food and an outlet on the Mediterranean. Auguste Pasha Adib, president of the Lebanese Union, envisaged the annexation of the Biqaʿ as a colonial enterprise. Underpopulated, 'its land abandoned and its inhabitants incapable of exploiting it in a fructuous manner', the valley would best prosper if put in the hands of the 'Lebanese'.[6] Whatever the case, Lebanonists such as Adib, al-Sawda, K.T. Khairallah and Bulus Nujaym emphasised the 'integral independence of Lebanon in its natural and historic frontiers' with or without the guarantee of the Great Powers. Al-Sawda departed from his colleagues with his clear anti-colonial position. While paying due respect to France's 'moral position' among the Lebanese, he maintained that 'French colonisation in Lebanon' would only benefit a few 'monopolist capitalists' among the French and 'a minority of job-seekers' among the Lebanese.[7] Further, al-Sawda called for close Syrian–Lebanese relations based on 'mutual respect of the independence of both countries' (al-Sawda). Bulus Nujaym, a pioneer of Lebanonism and a protectionist before the defeat of the Ottoman Empire, would later oppose the mandate and call for a 'democratic Lebanon, economically viable and multi-sectarian'. He attributed to the Lebanese the role of the 'Piedmontese of Syria', which presupposed a leading Lebanese part in a Syrian unity to which they would belong.[8] K.T. Khairallah, also an early protectionist, soon opted for a Greater Lebanon in collaboration with the Muslims and called for solidarity with the independence of Syria and the other Arab countries, 'brothers in ethnicity and language'. Sulayman Kan`an, councillor for Jizzin, proposed two arguments against the mandate. First, the Lebanese had proved their capacity to rule themselves by themselves and had thus earned their right to self-determination, according to President Wilson's principles. Second, the protection of a foreign power would be detrimental to the interests of the Christians themselves. Khairallah wrote in a memorandum addressed to an American conference:

We want to live at peace with our neighbors; but we cannot ever hope to do so while there is a foreign power in Syria, for which the majority of Mohammedans hold the minority Christians responsible. Thus those who come to protect us only arouse against us the enmity of our neighbors. We are indeed safer with them, as the past has proven, without this European protection... The ambition of France to have a naval base in Syria, and to extend her commerce, should not be realised at the expense of a people who have always admired her own political and social ideals at home and who are now being used as a pretext for occupation.[9]

Partisans of a mandated Greater Lebanon

Hardly any sizeable Christian current called simultaneously for Greater Lebanon and the French mandate. Partisans of the mandate were mainly defectors from different currents who adapted to the new mandate *status quo*. From the federalists came Samné, Ghanem, Petro Trad, Ayub Thabit (the latter two would serve as prime minister and president of the republic, respectively) and Habib Pasha al-Sa`d, governor of Mount Lebanon under the Faysal regime, who rallied to the mandate and was appointed president of the republic in 1934. From the independentist camp came Auguste Adib, a future prime minister. Even Bishara al-Khuri and his brother-in-law Michel Chiha had started as partisans of Sawda's Lebanese Union. In December 1921, the partisans of the mandate launched the Party of Progress (*Hizb al-Taraqqi*) under the slogan 'for the preservation of the independence of Greater Lebanon under French mandate'. They conceived of Lebanon's independence as primarily vis-à-vis Syria and guaranteed by France. The party's platform called for the defence of national traditions, freedom of religious belief and the nomination of government functionaries on the basis of competence and merit. Exclusively Maronite and Catholic, the party was the first political manifestation of the alliance of the Mount Lebanon notables with Beirut's commercial/financial bourgeoisie. The former were represented by Emile Iddi and Bishara al-Khuri, whose rivalry would dominate the political life of Lebanon throughout the mandate.[10]

GREATER, SMALLER OR 'MIDDLE' LEBANON: ECONOMY OR AUTONOMY?

Christian partisans of an 'independent' Lebanon obtained a 'bigger' Lebanon than they had asked for. The creation of Greater Lebanon under the French mandate launched a series of debates and revisionist projects that was to last for over fifteen years. In these debates, the question of attachment/detachment had two dimensions. It involved the attachment/detachment of Greater Lebanon vis-à-vis Syria as well as the attachment/detachment of the Christians, especially the Maronites, vis-à-vis the inhabitants of the newly annexed territories, with their Muslim majority. The Maronite discourse was torn between the desire for a Christian state and the need to guarantee a minimum of economic viability and financial resources for the new political entity. It was indeed a tragic choice between the 'Christian refuge' and the spectre of the World War I famine.[11]

George Samné eloquently expressed this contradiction in what he saw as Greater Lebanon's detachment from Syria being self-defeating for the Christians. For him, the choice was clear: either a Syrian federation inside which Lebanese territory would be reduced to Mount Lebanon, or a Greater Lebanon that would renounce its claim to be a 'Christian refuge' in order to cooperate with the rest of Syria. The fact that Greater Lebanon corresponded to neither option led Samné to exclaim: what kind of a 'Christian homeland' was this, where half of the population was Muslim?[12]

French officials were also divided on the question of the size of Greater Lebanon. Of course, they approached the question from a different angle: which was the better method to dominate the whole of Syria, especially its rebellious Sunni majority? Gouraud favoured partition into big entities: 'It will be easy to maintain a balance among three or four [Syrian] states that will be large enough to achieve self-sufficiency and, if need be, pit one against the other,' he wrote in a memorandum to his superiors.[13] In September 1920, he had it his way. However, he included Tripoli in Greater Lebanon against the will of the French government and was reprimanded for that move by Prime Minister Millerand who ordered him to consider the arrangement a trial period.[14] For his part, de Caix envisaged a proliferation of mini-states – up to ten in number – in order to guarantee the weakening of the largely Sunni independentist and pan-Arab movement. He was critical of what he termed 'Lebanese [Christian] megalomania' demanding Greater Lebanon and warned against the annexation of Muslim regions of Tripoli, the Biqa` and `Akkar as a threat to the stability of the future Christian state.

As early as 1921, Aristide Bryant had suggested that the separation of Tripoli would assure Lebanon's Christians a numerical majority. In 1926, de Caix (supported by Henri de Jouvenel) admitted that a mistake had been made in administrating a 'much Greater Lebanon', suggesting that Tripoli and the Muslim parts of `Akkar and the Biqa` be reintegrated into Syria. The resulting 'Middle Lebanon' was supposed to reduce the number of Sunnis who, according to de Caix, had proved after six years of mandate that they did not consider themselves Lebanese but Muslims. Whatever the case, both the economic interests of the mandate and those of Beirut's bourgeoisie were opposed to the return of the port of Tripoli to Syria. Retained inside Mount Lebanon, Tripoli was less likely to endanger Beirut's preponderant economic position. As part of Syria, the risk involved seeing it become Syria's principal port at the expense of the port of Beirut.[15]

DRAWING THE SOUTHERN BORDERS

The declaration of Greater Lebanon left the question of its southern borders pending, awaiting the delimitation of the Palestinian–Syrian borders. In fact, there were few partisans of Greater Lebanon who had demanded the annexation of Jabal `Amil to the new entity. There were even Christian voices that explicitly opposed the inclusion of the south, notably the Maronite Church and a number of Khazin sheikhs.[16]

A joint military Franco-British commission headed by Colonels Paulet and Newcombe negotiated the demarcation of Lebanon's southern borders from June 1921 to February 1922. The British asked that Palestine's northern borders be set at the Litani river, to meet their commitment to provide a 'national homeland for the Jews' in Palestine. In its memorandum of 3 February 1919 to the peace conference, the Zionist Organisation had set the northern borders of the 'national homeland for the Jews' at Sidon and the 'elbow of the Litani' – the river's westward diversion to join the Mediterranean where it is known as al-Qasmiya. In this case, Palestine was to include not only the (Lebanese) regions of Tyre and Jabal `Amil but also the (Syrian) Golan Heights, Jabal al-Shaykh and Hawran. At stake were the tributaries of the Jordan river. The British wanted the Jordan and its tributaries in their mandatory zone. The French, determined not to make any new concession on the borders or on the waters of the Litani and the Yarmuk rivers, ultimately prevailed, despite Zionist objections, and the Galilee was divided between the two mandatory powers.[17] The final accord between the two governments was ratified on 7 March 1923. It fixed the borders within a safe distance south of the Litani basin, retained the tributaries of the Jordan inside the French zone, ceded Hula Lake to Palestine and fixed the western borders at Ras al-Naqura on the Mediterranean.

But the question of Lebanon's size and borders was far from being settled.

6
From Mandate to Independence (1920–1943)

By splitting off Greater Lebanon from its natural hinterland the French not only confirmed the financial and commercial hegemony of Beirut over the Mountain, but also strengthened a pattern of economic activity in which agriculture and industry had become subordinated to banking and trade.

Roger Owen, 'The Political Economy of Grand Liban',
Essays on the Crisis in Lebanon

Partisans of the mandate imagined their country ruled by a Lebanese governor and Lebanese administrators under French protection. All they got was a French-imposed 'regime of direct rule' (Edmond Rabbath). In 1921, de Caix explained that the mandate implied 'a gradual work of civic education and political emancipation'. High Commissioner Gouraud appointed Major Trabaud governor of Lebanon, supported by an executive of seven directors-general (of whom only two were Muslims), but real power in the administration lay in the hands of the French 'advisers'. Gouraud also appointed an Administrative Commission (AC) of 15 members, of whom only five were Muslims. Faced with massive Muslim boycott, the high commissioner enlarged the commission to 17 members (6 Maronites, 3 Greek Orthodox, 1 Greek Catholic, 1 Druze, 4 Sunnis and 2 Shiites) the majority of whom were landowners and merchant notables. Already, the sectarian quotas were established. Substantially, the commission held mainly consultative powers, just like its *Mutasarrifiya* predecessor. On 9 March 1922 the AC was replaced by a partly elected Representative Council, the elections to which were also boycotted by large sections of the Muslim population. Nevertheless, the AC, headed alternatively by Habib Pasha al-Sa`d, Na`um Labaki and Emile Iddi, began to slowly attract Muslim participation.

High Commissioner Maurice Sarrail's period of office (1924–26) deserves mention as the Freemason and secular general represented the republican exception in French policy toward Lebanon. He wanted to appoint a Lebanese governor, but opposed the choice of Emile Iddi, the patriarch's candidate, and finally appointed a

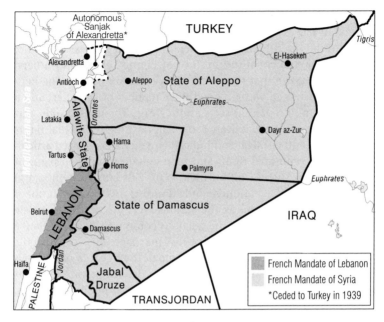

Map 4   Greater Lebanon in the partition of Syria, 1920

Frenchman, de Cayla, as provisional governor. Sarrail initiated a series of courageous reforms. He unified the fiscal system, reducing inequalities in imposition between the inhabitants of the annexed territories and those of Mount Lebanon, opened administrative posts to Muslims and proposed a secular and public education system. Sarrail also divided Lebanon into 11 mixed *muhafazas* and did not apply sectarian representation in the electoral system. A new Representative Council presided over by Mussa Nammour, a Maronite from Zahleh who had turned to Freemasonry, elected de Cayla governor of Lebanon. But most of Sarrail's reforms were rejected by the Quai d'Orsay under pressure from the Maronite Church and his policy of appeasement toward the Muslims was soon drowned in the blood of his repression against the Syrian revolt of 1925–27.

The shock of the Syrian revolt and the imminence of the League of Nations Mandate Commission drove France to grant Lebanon and Syria a constitution. High Commissionner de Jouvenel (1926–29) appointed a parliamentary drafting commission, including Petro Trad, `Umar Da`uq, Shibl Dammus and Michel Chiha, which was immediately boycotted by the majority of Sunni and Shi`i leaders. Nevertheless, the final version of the constitutional text, adopted on 23 May 1926, renamed Greater Lebanon the 'Lebanese Republic', defined its flag as the tricolour French flag with a cedar in the white strip and adopted French an official language alongside Arabic. Significantly, the constitution did not define Lebanon's borders, as if to emphasise that they were open to modification. The Representative Council was renamed the Chamber of Deputies, and a Senate set up to represent sects and regions. The constitution was a hybrid one: on a republican body, emphasising individual rights and liberties and political and judicial equality were grafted articles concerning communal rights and representation most probably at the initiative of Michel Chiha. Article 95 provided for the (temporary) fair distribution of government and administrative posts (but not of parliamentary seats) among the various sects. According to article 9, the state relinquished to the religious communities its legislative rights and rulings on personal status (marriage, divorce, custody, adoption, inheritance, etc.) in the name of the freedom of religious belief. Article 10 summoned the state to defend private religious education on condition it did not conflict with public education. But above all, the constitution legalised the mandate, with French control over the country's foreign and military affairs and public security. The president of the republic was given extensive executive powers, helped by the cabinet whose ministers he had the right to dismiss; yet he was responsible to no one and no institution except the French high commissioner.

On 26 May 1926 Charles Dabbas, a Greek Orthodox notable, was elected head of state for three years in a joint meeting of the Chamber of Deputies and the Senate whose 16 members were appointed by de Jouvenel. Nevertheless, the Senate was abolished a year later, and in 1929 the presidential mandate was prolonged from four to six years. From that time onwards, the Chamber of Deputies was elected on a sectarian basis.

At another level, the debate over attachment and detachment continued unabated. On the French side, some mandate functionaries found they had created a 'too great a Lebanon' that needed reduction. Among the Lebanese, Riad al-Sulh declared, in July 1928, that French Prime Minister Aristide Bryant had promised him to reannex the whole of Lebanon to Syria.[1] At the other extreme, Emile Iddi presented a memorandum to the Quai d'Orsay in which he argued that a Greater Lebanon with a population of 405,000 Muslims to 425,000 Christians did not contain a majority strong enough to 'defend the country'. He proposed that Tripoli become a 'free city' under French administration – its Christian inhabitants would be given Lebanese nationality and the Muslims, Syrian nationality – and south Lebanon would acquire an autonomous status similar to that of the Alawite country. As for the rest of the country – rid of some 55,000 Muslims from Tripoli and an additional 140,000 Sunnis and Shi`i from the south – it would constitute a reduced Lebanon but with a 'secure' Christian numerical majority of 80 per cent and sufficient agricultural area of the Biqa` to avert the danger of famine.[2]

The French opted for a different solution based not on the Christian/Muslim divide but on the notion that Lebanon was a land of religious minorities. The political supremacy of the Maronites was ensured in their capacity as the biggest numerical minority according to the 1932 census, the last to be organised in Lebanon.[3] However that year closed with an interruption of constitutional life on the occasion of the presidential elections planned for May. Tripoli leader, Sheikh Muhammad al-Jisr, submitted his candidature to make the point that a Muslim has the right to the post of head of state. Emile Iddi, fearing he might lose the contest to his rival Bishara al-Khuri, withdrew in favour of Jisr, upon which High Commisioner Henri Ponsot (1929–32), refusing to create such a precedent, decreed the suspension of the constitution and disbanded the Chamber of Deputies.

THE ECONOMIC MANDATE: PHOENICIA AND SWITZERLAND

France treated Syria and Lebanon as one economic unit controlled by two sets of French companies – the Common Interests (*Intérêts communs*) and the Franchise-Holding Companies (*Sociétés conces-sionaires*) – that held between them a monopoly of public services and the main sectors of the economy.[4]

From the beginning, the definition of the borders of Greater Lebanon followed a precise vision of its economic role. As Roger Owen has noted, Lebanon's political detachment from Syria was the condition for its role as economic intermediary vis-à-vis the Syrian hinterland.[5] The mandate authorities encouraged that outward-looking role. Beirut port, confirmed as the principal port of the Syrian interior, was enlarged and modernised, a second dock was constructed and the city, provided with an airport, progressed to become a centre for international communication. According to a new urban plan, the city was recentred on Place de l'Étoile, designed on the model of that of the French capital, and the Parliament and a new business quarter were inaugurated there on the occasion of the

French Colonial Exposition of 1921. These projects contributed to the development of a tertiary sector dominated by a merchant/financial bourgeoisie, which was becoming more and more embedded into the mandate system. On the other hand, the development of education, another mandate policy, helped create a middle class from which to recruit for liberal professions and the bureaucracy.

In agriculture, the mandatory authorities initially envisaged encouraging the emergence of a class of middle farmers to serve as a social base for the mandate. But political considerations ultimately prevailed in favour of attracting the loyalty of the inhabitants of the annexed territories by patronising their traditional landed notables. In `Akkar, the Biqa` and the south, French governors backed leading landowners, who became the main beneficiaries from government aid and projects of agricultural development. Paradoxically, sericulture, one of the original causes of French interest in Lebanon, hardly survived the crisis of the 1920s and finally collapsed in the 1930s, contributing to a new wave of emigration. The Lebanese writer Amin al-Rihani, an émigré to the USA, described when revisiting his homeland the combined effect of emigration and the collapse of sericulture:

Here are the ghost villages, inhabited by unemployment, laziness and desolation. Nothing remains except factories and churches to console you for their disappearance... Here is the lost wealth, lamented by the newspapers... and the gentlemen dressed in European attire. National pride, dressed in artificial silk, eats its bread drenched in the sweat of Africa.[6]

A new role was conjured up for Mount Lebanon: estivation and tourism. The idea was proposed by the New Phoenicians, who were Christian and mainly Maronite intellectuals of the francophile Beirut bourgeoisie. Grouped around Charles Corm's *La Revue Phénicienne*, Michel Chiha, Albert and Alfred Naccache, Fu'ad al-Khuri, Jacques Tabet and others had revived Phoenicia as a cultural and national identity differentiated from the Arabs and as a model for an outward-looking service economy. The Phoenician model was complemented by the notion of 'Lebanon, Switzerland of the East'. The term, first used by the French travellers Lamartine and Gérard de Nerval to compare the landscape of Mount Lebanon to that of the Alpine country, soon became a multifunctional model: Lebanon, banker of the region, federation of sectarian cantons and a country that exploits its natural beauty in tourism and estivation. While Rihani and his like were bemoaning the wounds and ruptures of emigration, the New Phoenicians glorified the peasants' 'dignified misery' in Mount Lebanon, now presented as an abode of the Spirit and of Faith (Charles Corm). They hailed migration as an age-old vocation of an entire people, expressing its spirit of freedom and adventure.

Interests of the city, notables of the Mountain

Under the mandate, Beirut enjoyed economic domination over Mount Lebanon and the rest of Greater Lebanon, but it was the Mountain that controlled the city politically and administratively. Soon, Sunni and Greek Orthodox politicians and functionaries of the city were replaced by those of the Mount Lebanon middle classes, who quickly linked up with the city's commercial/financial interests.

But these political newcomers were far from being united. A great part of the political history of the mandate was dominated by the rivalry between Emile Iddi and Bishara al-Khuri, exploited to the full by successive high commissioners. Both men had studied law at the Jesuit College in Beirut. Iddi, a Francophile and the son of a drogoman at the French consulate in Damascus, was from Jubayl, in the heart of the Christian north, and the favourite Maronite politician of Patriarch Huwayik. Khuri, a notable of Richmaya, in the mixed districts of the southern part of the Mountain, was the son of an administrator of the *Mutasarrifiya*. He was a journalist and talented speaker, at ease in Arabic literature and Arab history, with a perfect and eloquent command of Arabic.

In Cairo, where the two men were exiled during the war, Khuri was close to the *Union libanaise* of Yusuf al-Sawda, while Iddi, already considered France's man, recruited Lebanese and Syrian volunteers to fight alongside the Franco-British troops of the *Légion d'Orient*. At the end of the war, Iddi was brought home by the French navy and named first counsellor to the high comissioner. Khuri was named secretary-general of the administration of Mount Lebanon and counsellor to the French military governor, but he resigned his post two years later in opposition to the nomination of a French governor instead of a Lebanese; Iddi, for his part, continued to serve the mandate. Both men had been members of the legislature since 1922, and Iddi was appointed prime minister for a short while in 1929–30, whereas Khuri occupied the post three times and the two men remained rivals for the presidency of the republic.

As a reaction to the suspension of the constitution in 1932, Khuri created the Constitutionalist Bloc, calling for the immediate activation of the constitution and the signing of a new agreement with France. Khuri's men were grouped around the daily *Le Jour*, founded by Michel Chiha in 1934, while *L'Orient*, edited by Gabriel Khabbaz and Georges Naccache, was the mouthpiece of Iddi's partisans of the National Bloc.

The positions of the two groups soon began to diverge. Iddi envisaged Lebanon primarily as a Christian homeland, insisting on its Mediterranean identity, which differentiated it 'ethnically' from the rest of Syria and the Arabs, and looked upon the Muslims as a threat that necessitated his proposed territorial and demographic reduction. In a famous remark, he admonished Muslims who did not want to live in a Christian Lebanon to emigrate to Mecca. In addition, Iddi was a strong partisan of private religious education, with a strong bias toward the Christian missionaries. During his term as prime minister in 1930, he created a scandal by abolishing 111 public schools, most of which were in Muslim-dominated regions. Khuri, by contrast, envisaged Lebanon as an independent country built in collaboration with its Muslim population and enjoying close relations with Syria and the rest of the Arab countries. Christian rights, instead of being protected by foreign troops, were to be inscribed in the constitution, which guaranteed Maronite political supremacy.

Furthermore, the two men were considerably different when it came to their social status and interests. Iddi was linked to the families of the declining merchant aristocracy of the Sursuq quarter and himself was married to a Sursuq, his law firm representing those families in addition to the French consulate and the big French corporations of the time. Khuri, by his marriage to Laure Chiha and that of his brother Fuad to Renée Haddad, the rich inheritor of a large firm that imported iron and construction material, were embedded in the rising financial and commerical bourgeoisie that rapidly developed under the mandate. Among Khuri's legal clients were the Établissements Darwich I. Haddad and its cement factory in Shikka (built in 1929), both run by his brother Fuad, and the Banque Misr, Syrie et Liban of Midhat Pasha and Tal`at Harb, the first bank established with British and Arab capital in Lebanon in 1929. More importantly, Khuri and his Constitutionalist Bloc had at their disposal the resources of Banque Pharaon-Chiha, owned by the maternal cousins Michel Chiha and Henri Pharaon. Pharaon participated with French interests in the administration of the French conglomerate, Société du port de Beyrouth, and was active in property development. Politically, Pharaon was deputy for the Biqa` region and patron of the Workers' Front, an anti-communist trade union. Michel Chiha (1891–1954) was the director of the family bank and one of the rare Lebanese to sit on the board of administration of French franchise-holding companies, among which was the Banque de Syrie et du Liban, in addition to being the president of the Beirut Stock Market and the vice-president of the Beirut Chamber of Commerce. Chiha was appointed deputy for the minority seat in Beirut and played a major role in drafting the Lebanese constitution of 1926.

The rivalry between Khuri and Iddi was also expressed in the dominant intellectual figures of the times: Michel Chiha and Charles Corm. Corm, the apostle of a Christian Lebanon, considered Muslims as religious and historic adversaries who lacked loyalty to the polity. He emphasised French as the language of the Lebanese Christians and despised Arabic as 'an Asian language' that had been imposed by 'massacres and fright'. In his long poem *La Montagne inspirée* (1934) Corm writes:

> Jesus made me love Mohamet and Moses/
> ... to love our enemy, especially that he hurts us
> Is to triumph against evil...

His identification between Lebanon and the Christians was complete:

> Muslim brother, understand my candour/
> I am the real Lebanon, authentic and devoted...

According to Corm, Christianity, the historical inheritor of Phoenicia, accomplished the elaboration of a Lebanese cultural identity distinct from that of the rest of the Arab world. Chiha, on his part, was no less a Phoenicianist, but he restricted Phoenicianism to the economic sphere, refusing to consider it the hallmark of Lebanese identity. The Lebanese were a 'Mediterranean variety', a confounded mix of many origins; Lebanon had existed even before Phoenicia and its inhabitants were simply Lebanese. Chiha's Lebanon was defined as both a 'people of merchants' and a 'country of associated sectarian minorities'. He would be mainly known as the intellectual of the commercial/financial bourgeoisie.

ECONOMIC DIFFICULTIES AND SOCIAL AGITATION

The 1930s were a decade of great transformations and troubles in the economic, social and political spheres for Mandate Lebanon.

To begin with, the port of Beirut was losing ground to the Palestinian port of Hayfa, which was developed at a rapid pace by the British mandatory authorities and also benefited from the growth of the Jewish sector in the Palestinian economy. Enlarged and modernised, the main dock of the Palestinian port had a surface of 35 hectares compared to 23 for its Beirut counterpart. For years, business circles in Beirut had been pressing the French to enlarge the city's port facilities, create a free zone and modernise the Beirut–Damascus railway line. They also complained about the high customs duties on imports (10 to 30 per cent higher than Palestinian rates), which allowed Palestinian merchants and industrialists to compete with Lebanese products in Arab markets and inside Lebanon itself. In addition, Palestine had become the centre for air traffic between Europe and the Far East. Finally, by 1934, the port of Hayfa had surpassed Beirut port despite the eventual enlargement and opening of a free zone in the latter facility.

On the other hand, the economic privileges of the Mandate were alienating larger sectors of society. Bourgeois interests were coalescing against the monopoly exercised by the French concessionary companies, their fiscal exemptions and the export of their profits to France. They were calling for Syro-Lebanese control over the Common Interests. In 1931, a general strike by taxi drivers against competition from tramways merged with a protest by the inhabitants of Beirut and Tripoli against the high electricity prices to unleash a mass boycott of the services of the Tramways et éclairage de Beyrouth (TEB), the French concessionary company that ran both the city's tramway lines and its electricity supply. After some months, the movement succeeded, and imposed a reduction of the company's fares by 49 per cent.

Socially, the repercussions of the Great Depression of 1929 further aggravated the collapse of the general standard of living. The ensuing years witnessed a number of workers' strikes against unemployment and the rise in the cost of living, all calling for wage increases and the amelioration of working conditions.

The situation in the rest of the country was no better. In November 1934, the French granted a monopoly for the cultivation of and commerce in tobacco (the second largest source of revenue for the Lebanese) and the manufacture of cigarettes to a French franchise-holding company, the Régie co-intéressée libano-syrienne des tabacs et des tombacs, controlled by the French colonial bank, the Crédit foncier d'Algérie et de Tunisie. A general protest strike was called in the two major areas of tobacco cultivation, the predominantly Maronite regions of Jubayl and Batrun in the north and the predominantly Shi`i region of Jabal `Amil in the south. Significantly, Maronite Patriarch `Arida led the movement, backed by a number of Maronite politicians. His conflict with the mandatory powers on this issue led him to a major breakthrough in Syrian–Lebanese relations when negotiations between Bkirki and the Syrian independentist National Bloc started at the end of 1935. In February 1936, `Arida came out with a clear declaration in favour of Lebanon's independence and sovereignty while calling for a strengthening of Lebanon's relations with 'sister Syria' in the economic and social fields. Later, the patriarch called upon the Lebanese to help the victims of the independence demonstrations in Syrian cities, which had been brutally suppressed by the French authorities. During that period, `Arida addressed numerous letters and memos to the French authorities in which he reminded them that the promise of independence made by Clemenceau to his predecessor, Patriarch Huwayik, had ended in colonial occupation. He went on to enumerate the abuses of the mandatory powers: the submission of the Lebanese security forces to the French high commissioner, the domination of French so-called advisers over the administration, the constant intervention of the mandatory authorities in the workings of mixed tribunals (which examined the juridicial conflict between Lebanese and Frenchmen), the constant violations of public liberties (suspension of the publication of newspapers, subjecting political parties to an official licensing, etc.), tax increases (from 330,000 piasters before 1914 to 10 million under the Mandate when the demographic increase did not exceed 50 per cent) and, last but not least, monopoly control over the economy by the concessionary societies. In conclusion, the patriarch criticised the 'short-sighted' politics that saw friendship between the Lebanese and the Syrians as a 'hostile act against France'.[7]

In February 1935, a new wave of strikes had broken out against the TEB and the Société des chemins de fer Damas-Hamah et Prolongements (DHP), which were accused of imposing the cost of their financial deficits on the Lebanese and Syrians while distributing profit dividends to their stockholders with 5–6 per cent interest. In Lebanon, but mainly in the Syrian cities, the strike turned into a political protest and had a decisive effect on defining negotiations for the independence of the two countries.

1936: the year of crises

1936 was a turning point in Lebanon's history in more than one sense. Various events and crises reactivated the polemics on attachment/

detachment. But though sectarian and political tensions increased, social and regional developments gave rise to a new alignment of forces and the crystallisation of a multi-sectarian current aspiring to independence from France.

Events in Lebanon and Syria that year formed part of a renewed cycle of nationalist and independentist contestation at the regional level. In Egypt, the nationalist movement fought for an Anglo-Egyptian treaty, signed on 26 August 1936, which declared Egypt's independence but ceded the administration of its foreign policy to Great Britain and a continued military presence of British troops in the Suez Canal zone for another twenty years. Palestine was the scene of a large-scale popular uprising against the British mandate and Jewish immigration; it paralysed the country and would last until the outbreak of World War II. A general strike from April to October, suspended upon the request of Arab rulers, was followed by prolonged guerrilla warfare, which mobilised some 30,000 British troops, the biggest challenge to British colonialism in its history.[8] In Syria, the anti-mandate demonstrations led the French high commissioner, Comte de Martel, to promise, on 24 February 1936, the reestablishment of parliamentary life and the conclusion of a treaty recognising Syria's independence and backing its admission to the League of Nations.

In Lebanon, 1936 began with the election of Emile Iddi as president of the republic by only one vote, against Bishara al-Khuri. Following the Syrian precedent, seven deputies from the Constitutionalist Bloc addressed a memorandum to de Martel on 2 March demanding that Lebanon be treated on an equal footing with Syria by the application of the constitution and backing Lebanon's admission to the League of Nations. A few weeks later, Viénot, director-general of the Quai d'Orsay, confirmed de Martel's commitments. But whereas Syria was promised independence, Lebanon had to be content with a mere 'alliance of friendship' and an 'internal independence': the country's defence and foreign relations were to be remain in French hands.

The imminence of a Franco-Syrian treaty created two kinds of apprehensions in Lebanon: Christian 'protectionists' feared that Lebanon, 'independent' from France, might soon be annexed by Syria, while Muslim 'unionists' feared that the country's independence would legitimise the Lebanese borders of 1 September 1920 and destroy their hope of annexation.

In the first week of March, the Congress of the Coast and the Four *Cazas* which had reconvened to reiterate the 'annexionist' demands, suffered the defection of a moderate current represented by Riad al-Sulh and his cousins Kazim and Taqi al-Din. Although Sulh was a strong opponent of the mandate in Syria and Lebanon, he had maintained a distance from the Muslim unionists since the Congress of the Coast of 1928 and opened up dialogue with the Christian forces, advocating an inter-sectarian alliance against the Mandate. In 1931–33, he was active with Monseigneur Mubarak, the Maronite bishop of Beirut, in the transport and electricity strike. Settled in Beirut, Sulh, who shared the leadership of the south with the As`ads, also aspired to the leadership of the Muslims of the capital against their traditional leader, Salim `Ali Salam. He was also opposed to the mufti and leader of Tripoli, `Abd al-Hamid Karami, and publicly supported (in 1934) the maintenance of Tripoli within Lebanon's borders. In 1935, Sulh served as intermediary between Patriarch `Arida and the Syrian national movement. With his two cousins, Kazim and Taki al-Din, he founded the Republican Party for Independence (*Hizb al-Istiqlal al-Jumhuri*), headed by `Aziz al-Hashim, a Maronite notable from `Aqura in the Jubayl highlands. The party, representing a section of the professional middle classes, agitated for the political independence of Syria and Lebanon and their economic unity. For the first time, the economic interests of the inhabitants of the coast and the four *cazas* were not linked to political unity with Syria.

Riad al-Sulh had not attended the Congress of the Coast in 1936 as he was banished to the Syrian Jazira for his role in the pro-independence strikes of the preceding year. Upon his release, he travelled to Paris to join the Syrian delegation negotiating the independence treaty. Riad's cousin Kazim, writing in a brochure that appeared a few days after the end of the congress, accused the majority of the congressmen of ignoring the new realities in the country. At the beginning of the Mandate, he argued, 'Lebanonism' was synonymous with Christianity and 'unionism' synonymous with Islamism. At that moment, the Christians were increasingly disappointed by France and 'becoming aware that a great number of economic factors render their daily life as well as their destinies intimately linked to those of the destinies of the sons of Syria'.[9] Prime among those factors was the Syrian–Lebanese desire to control the Common Interests as a shared terrain between the two 'nationalisms'. Facing this new fact, the question of attachment had become secondary, for, 'how would the Syrian unionists benefit if the [annexed Lebanese] "territories" were "returned" to Syria while [Lesser] Lebanon becomes a colonial base that will menace Syria itself?'[10] In return, Sulh proposed supporting the emergence of a new Lebanese patriotism that would surpass the attachment/detachment dilemma in favour of a wider vision of Lebanon's Arab national roots, but which would not necessarily mean a merger between Arab countries.

ABORTED INDEPENDENCE

In this atmosphere of flux opened the independence negotiations in Paris. The Lebanese delegation was led by President Iddi and included Prime Minister Khayr al-Din al-Ahdab – a notable from Tripoli and one of the first Sunnis to collaborate with the mandate – in addition to opposition leader Bishara al-Khuri. In order to appease Christian fears, Viénot reiterated, in a letter to President Iddi on 23 April 1936, France's guarantee of Lebanon's independence in its 1 September 1920 borders. But this only fanned Muslim dissent. A congress in Sidon reiterated the demand for annexation and organised street demonstrations, which the gendarmes fired upon, killing one demonstrator.[11]

In this context, the question of sectarian representation took a different turn. The Muslim negotiators in the Paris delegation, Najib `Usayran for the Shi`as and Khayr al-Din al-Ahdab for the Sunnis, insisted that France commit itself to defend the interests of the sectarian 'minorities' in an independent Lebanon. Those Muslims who believed in an independent Lebanon not annexed to Syria were certain that that entity would be evidently under Christian, and particularly Maronite, domination. A few months before, Patriarch `Arida had asked that the office of president of the republic be officially reserved for a Maronite Christian. Thus, while the Christian negotiators were looking for French guarantees vis-à-vis Syria and the Lebanese Muslims, the Muslim negotiators were looking for French guarantees vis-à-vis the Christians.

The treaty of Friendship and Alliance Between France and Lebanon, signed on 13 November 1936 by President Iddi, State Secretary Ayub Thabit and High Commissioner de Martel, was approved unanimously four days later by the Lebanese Chamber of Deputies. France recognised Lebanon as an independent state and undertook to help its admission to the League of Nations. In return, Lebanon guaranteed French capital and interests, and the continuation of the monetary parity between the two countries, and vowed to remain an ally of France in the event of war. France undertook to provide military aid to Lebanon if attacked by a third party. Lebanon would have its own army but France would maintain a military presence for its Levantine troops (air force and navy) and would enjoy transport and communication facilities. For its part, France would provide military technical aid and advice to the Lebanese armed forces. Emile Iddi threw his weight behind an unlimited French military presence in Lebanon; he received a 25-year period renewable by tacit automatic renewal for the same duration.

Thus, the Franco-Syrian treaty, signed on 9 September 1936, contributed in three fundamental ways to solving important aspects of the above-mentioned problems.

To begin with, the Syrian official delegation dropped its annexionist demands concerning Lebanon in return for France's integration of the Druze and ´Alawite autonomous zones into the Syrian Republic (whereas Alexandretta was definitely ceded to Turkey). Nonetheless, in their declarations to the press after the signature of the treaty, Hashim al-Atassi and Jamil Mardam insisted on a federal union between the two countries.

Second, in terms of independence and sovereignty, the Lebanese obtained more than the initially promised 'internal independence'.

Finally, the question of 'minorities' rights', which was not included in the text of the treaty, was relegated to an exchange of letters between de Martell and Iddi, attached as annexes to the treaty. In letter no. 6, the President of the Lebanese Republic vowed to guarantee equal civic and political rights and to ensure the equitable representation of the country's different 'components' (read 'sects') in government posts. Also, in letter no. 6B, the President informed the High Commissionner (HC) that he would implement administrative reform aiming at a larger measure of administrative decentralisation and grant municipal and governing (*muhafaza*) councils a consultative vote concerning their respective shares of state expenditure. A few weeks later, the HC designated that Tripoli and its port become an independent qaimaqamate. But nothing else was achieved in terms of decentralisation, an increase in the rights of municipal councils, or the setting up of regional councils in the *muhafazas*.[12]

Nevertheless, the independence treaties did not satisfy many, especially in regard to the clause concerning the stationing of French troops. Tripoli, Sidon, Tyre, Nabatiyeh and Bint Jubayl were rocked by waves of demonstrations and strikes from September to November 1936. During his visit to the northern port, President Iddi was met by demonstrators raising the Syrian flag and shouting slogans in support of unity with Syria. Some 20 persons were wounded as the gendarmes fired on the demonstrators, and `Abd al-Hamid Karami was arrested. The resulting general strike did not end until a delegation from the Syrian National Bloc intervened with the city's leaders and obtained the release of Karami. In Beirut, bloody clashes between the popular quarters of Basta (Sunni) and Jummayzeh (Maronite) announced the rise of paramilitary youth organisations expressing the mounting sectarian tensions and the influence of the fascist parties of Europe.

The first of these was the Syrian Nationalist Social Party (SNSP), founded in 1932 by Antoun Sa`adeh and advocating integral Syrian unity including Lebanon, Syria, Transjordan, Palestine, Cyprus and the northern parts of Iraq. The SNSP was anti-communist, anti-Jewish, corporatist and secularist. It was followed by the Party of Lebanese Unity, the 'white shirts' of Tawfic `Awwad, sponsored by Patriarch `Arida and founded as a reaction to the resolutions of the Congress of the Coast, whose members were branded 'secessionists'. In November 1936, the Kata'ib party (Phalange) was founded by Pierre Jumayil, a pharmacist and football referee who was inspired by the discipline of the Hitler Youth during the 1936 Olympic Games in Munich. The party said Lebanon was the definitive homeland for its inhabitants within its 1920 borders, and professed a Lebanese nationalism distinct from that of the Arabs, all the while campaigning for Lebanon's independence. The same month saw the founding of the *Najjada* (Rescuers) of `Adnan al-Hakim. These were Muslim independentists who called for integral Arab unity (which was clearly demarcated from Islamic unity), but did not insist on Syrian–Lebanese unity. In 1937, Rashid Baydun, a businessman and school owner in Beirut, founded *al-Tala'i`* (The Vanguards), a Shi`i paramilitary organisation.

Clearly, the identity debate had taken new forms and had been extended to new social forces, primarily urban and popular. It had became more ideological compared to the simple debate between Christian protectionism and Muslim unionism. Two versions of the identity of the country now clashed: Lebanonism versus Arabism. Between the two stood a third variant, the Syrian nationalism of Sa`adeh's SNSP, representing non-Maronite Christians and the Muslims on the peripheries. More importantly, the stakes had changed: the identity debate was no longer defined in relation to the outside world (attachment/detachment) but articulated the relations of power within the country itself.

Curiously, while the rank and file was being radicalised and polarised, the notables drew closer together. The opposition, led by Bishara al-Khuri, understood the Franco-Lebanese treaty as an undertaking on the part of France to end the Mandate in favour of Lebanese self-rule and independence. The guarantees for the Christians were written into the constitution and the electoral system, and would be embodied in inter-sectarian alliances and in the relations between the leaders of Syria and the other Arab countries – 'brothers and partners in the struggle against colonialism and for freedom and independence', as Khuri called them.[13] The legislative elections of 1937 brought a large number of Constitutionalists to the Chamber, the Pharaon-Chiha bank having contributed financially to that result. Khuri was nominated prime minister and the bank, representing the power of money in the capital, exerted a considerable influence on the economic and financial policies of the government in addition to benefiting greatly from the beneficence of the prime minister.

In addition to his strong support in business circles, Khuri was privileged vis-à-vis Iddi by his inter-sectarian alliances. In contrast to the latter's difficult relations with the Muslims, Khuri's Constitutionalist Bloc included a number of Muslim notables, especially from the peripheries: Muhammad `Abd al-Razzaq in `Akkar, Majid Arsalan in `Alay and the Shuf, Sabri Hamadeh in the Biqa` and `Adil `Usayran in the south.

This period also witnessed the emergence of a third force, which was democratic, reformist and multi-sectarian and reflected the social and anti-monopolist struggles of the 1930s. This group crystallised around the National and Democratic Congress (NDC), which convened in Beirut in November 1938 at the initiative of the Lebanese Communist Party (LCP). The congress included members of the professional middle class, economists and trade unionists, in addition to merchants and notables opposed to the traditional *za'im*s. The congress's resolutions condemned the intervention of the mandate functionaries in the work of the ministries, administrative corruption and of mandatory authorities' support for the franchise-holding companies. They advocated a united budget for the state and the Common Interests. Politically, the resolutions stigmatised the Chamber of Deputies as a 'chamber of notables and big landowners', in which a dozen MPs were ready to be bought and sold, and called for its dissolution and the election of a parliament of 44 deputies through popular suffrage. Other reforms proposed were the election of the president of the republic by direct popular vote and the ban on combining the posts of MP and cabinet minister. Noting that the 80 per cent of fiscal revenues came from indirect taxes, a system detrimental to the poor and the middle classes, the congress called for the adoption of a direct and progressive income and inheritance tax.[14]

The outbreak of war in 1939 suspended the crises of that fateful year. The French National Assembly did not ratify the independence treaties with Syria and Lebanon. In Lebanon, the high commissioner suspended the constitution and dissolved the Chamber of Deputies in early 1939, and though Iddi was still nominally president of the republic, real power returned into the hands of the French high commissioners. In 1941, Iddi was dismissed when the Vichy administration of General Dentz appointed Alfred Naccache to replace him as head of state.

TOWARD INDEPENDENCE

As World War I created the conditions for the emergence of Greater Lebanon under French mandate, it was during World War II that the conditions for Lebanon's independence from France matured, in the context of Franco-British competition over the destinies of the peoples of the Near East. In 1940, France collapsed under Nazi occupation. In 1941 the Free French and British troops attacked from three directions and overthrew the pro-Vichy administration in Syria and Lebanon. General de Gaulle was increasingly apprehensive that Britain's intentions were motivated by the 'preconceived idea of evicting' France from the entire region. On 26 November 1941, in order to thwart the British outbidding the French, Catroux, who was nominated general delegate of Free France in Syria and Lebanon, declared France's recognition of the two countries' independence and invited their respective governments to sign a new treaty with France to terminate the mandate. The declaration came to nothing. The Syrian and Lebanese independentists rejected the idea of a new treaty as there already was one, and the French retorted by claiming that independence could not be accomplished before the League of Nations relieved French of its mandate. Nevertheless, Catroux confirmed Alfred Naccache as president and continued to behave as an all-powerful high commissioner. Britain, the USA, Turkey, Egypt, Saudi Arabia and Iraq immediately recognised the independence of the two countries. Lebanese independentists of all colours – the Constitutionalist Bloc, Riad al-Sulh and his friends, and Bkirki, who called for a national congress under the patronage of Patriarch `Arida – stood up against that illusory and incomplete independence, calling for new elections and the complete handing over of power to the Lebanese, including their right to elect their own president. The refusal of the French authorities was confirmed during General de Gaulle's visit to Damascus and Beirut in August 1942, when he declared that war conditions did not allow the exercise of full independence.

General Edward Spears was appointed mission chief for Great Britain in both countries, based in Beirut. Moreover, the Near East, as the region was then called, was a unified theatre of military operations and an economic union organised to support the war effort, with a HQ in Cairo, home of the Middle East Supply Centre, a body that administered the Allies' communication lines and logistics, while controlling agricultural and industrial production. In short, Britain dominated the whole region.

Two economic factors motivated the financial/commercial oligarchy to opt for independence. The first was its desire, all sectarian factions included, to privatise and control the French 'Common Interests' as well as the franchise-holding companies.[15] The second was the oligarchy's desire to liberate itself from the constraints and restrictions of a weak and closed French monetary zone.[16] In addition, the oligarchy had accumulated huge profits during the war and established many links with Anglo-Saxon markets and the Arab oil-producing states. Already, Beirut was the centre of communication between Europe and the Gulf States and Saudi Arabia. The greater part of the gold purchased by the emirs and sheikhs of that oil-producing region transited through its port, and its banks had begun receiving the first deposits and investing Gulf money in property.

It was in Cairo that the accords concerning Lebanon's independence were negotiated. Meeting under the patronage of Egypt's prime minister, Mustafa Nahhas Pasha, in June 1942, Bishara al-Khuri and the nationalist Syrian leader Jamil Mardam agreed on the return to constitutional life and the integral independence of both countries, while refusing any privileges for France after independence. The two leaders also decided to take charge of the Common Interests. Khuri was thereby recognised by the Syrian nationalists as the representative of the majority of the Lebanese Christians and Muslims. Also during that visit, the alliance between Bishara al-Khuri and Riad al-Sulh was sealed and elaborated in the famous National Pact, in which the former traded French protection for Christian political primacy guaranteed by the constitution and the latter dropped the idea of Muslim annexation to Syria in return for Muslim partnership in running the affairs of the country. Sulh, like many Arab nationalists of the time, had become closer to Britain as the Allies appeared to be heading for victory. During another visit to Cairo in May 1943, Khuri, already treated as the forthcoming president of Lebanon, signed an economic treaty with Egypt, Iraq, Syria and Jordan. In a declaration to the press – immediately denied by the Constitutionalist Bloc in Beirut – he even declared his willingness to sign a federal union between Lebanon and Syria. Khuri was not an obvious British choice from the beginning, though Nahhas Pasha had already adopted him. Spears, though a sworn enemy of Iddi, whom he called a 'French stooge', was not very enthusiastic for Khuri and hoped to advance Kamil Sham`un. As late as July 1943, Britain's men in the region were still testing the two candidates. Iraq's prime minister, Nuri al-Sa`id, met Sham`un and Khuri in July 1943 and was more convinced by the latter. No doubt Khuri's support for a Syrian–Lebanese federal union struck a favourable note with the champion of the Greater Syria project.

Nevertheless, Lebanon's transition to independence did not occur without clashes and violence. The return to constitutional life was not implemented until late 1942, under pressure from Spears, who insisted on the need to organise national elections and did not hide his sympathies for the independence of the two countries.[17] When the French finally agreed to manage the elections, Ayub Thabit, a Protestant politician close to Iddi, was appointed to head an interim government. He decreed a ratio of 32 Christian to 22 Muslim seats and granted immigrants (estimated at 160,000, mostly Christians) the right to vote. Both provisions were rejected by the Muslim politicians and Thabit resigned; he was replaced by a Greek Orthodox lawyer, Petro Trad. Upon the mediation of Nahhas Pasha, an electoral law was decreed in the summer of 1943. It dropped the voting by immigrants and set up a parliament of 55 seats, 30 for Christians and 25 for Muslims. This ratio of 6/5 remained the guideline for Christian–Muslim sectarian quotas until 1990, when it was replaced by parity according to the Ta'if accords.

On 21 September 1943, the result of the summer's elections was a net victory for the Constitutionalists. Bishara al-Khuri, who was elected president of the republic on 21 September, immediately invited Riad al-Sulh to form the government. In October, a high-level Syrian delegation arrived in Beirut, headed by Prime Minister Jamil Mardam Bey, who agreed on three vital points with his Lebanese counterpart: first, Syria recognised and defended the independence and sovereignty of both countries; second, Lebanon made the commitment that its territory would not be used as a base or passageway for any foreign force that endangered Syria's independence or security; and third, close collaboration between the two countries would take place in the economic and social domains. Following that, Lebanon asked the National Committee of Free France (CNFL) for a transfer of powers and of the Common Interests to the Lebanese authorities. The response was negative, with France declaring that as long as the country was still under mandate, there would be no question of terminating the mandate without a new treaty. In fact, General de Gaulle wanted a new treaty that would guarantee for France a privileged position in Lebanon and Syria in the cultural, economic and military domains. Lebanon replied that the CNFL had no legal status or legitimacy to sign such treaties and that Lebanon would not grant privileged status to any foreign power.

On 8 November 1943, the Chamber of Deputies passed a series of constitutional revisions that abolished the clause stating that the French mandatory authority was the sole source of political power and jurisdiction, reinstated Arabic as the country's only official language and adopted a new design for the Lebanese flag. Thus Lebanon's independence was imposed as a *fait accompli*. On the following day, President Khuri promptly ratified the revisions. French Delegate-General Jean Helleu declared the constitutional revisions null and void, as they had been unilaterally carried out without prior consultation with the French authorities. On 11 November, at dawn, Khuri, Sulh, `Abd al-Hamid Karami and ministers Salim Taqla and Kamil Sham`un were arrested and incarcerated in the fort of Rashaya in the southern Biqa`. Emile Iddi, who had abstained from voting the constitutional amendments, was appointed head of state and prime minister. Boycotted by the entire political class, Iddi was incapable of forming a government as news of the arrests led to violent popular reaction. A country-wide general strike was decreed, the officials who were still at large formed a provisional government under Habib Abi Shahla, the speaker of parliament, and Majid Arsalan, the defence minister, and launched an appeal for national resistance. In Beirut, the Phalange and the Najjada formed a united command to wage this common battle, and demonstrators took over the Parliament building, claiming the liberation of the incarcerated leaders. Helleu imposed a curfew and sent French and Senegalese troops to repress the demonstrations, leaving 18 killed and 66 wounded.

Pressed by the monarchs of Egypt, Saudi Arabia and Iraq, British Prime Minister Winston Churchill intervened with General de Gaulle who dispatched General Catroux to Beirut to resolve the crisis. On 19 November, Spears submitted an ultimatum from his government to the Free French, demanding the liberation of Khuri and his friends, or else they would be freed by British troops. On the morning of 22 November, a few hours before the expiration of the ultimatum, Catroux ordered the release of Khuri, Sulh and their companions, dismissed Helleu and declared the end of the French mandate in Lebanon.[18]

Lebanon's independence was largely a product of an entente between Great Britian and Egypt. The former's role was decisive in the termination of the French mandate and the choice of the ruling tandem. Explaining why the Francophile oligarchy had accepted independence from the French, Michel Chiha cynically told his friend Charles Hilu that Lebanon could not remain a French trading post in a dominantly British region. Egypt – the first Arab country to recognise Lebanon's independence – was the Arab guarantor of Lebanon's 'independence', notably vis-à-vis Syria. Significantly, two months after the Lebanese crisis, the Syrian parliament passed a law amending the Syrian constitution to abolish all references to the French mandate.

A new tradition had been inaugurated by virtue of which the Lebanese entity was to be periodically reproduced by means of a compromise between the dominant regional and international powers.

7
The Merchant Republic (1943–1952)

Enrichissez-vous.
Michel Chiha

Prosperity, currency, money, prices, buildings and cars, the airport, the oil terminals, the banks, industry, commerce, hotels, cabarets...

Matter, matter, all is matter, matter that dazzles the eye, fills the pocket, satisfies the body...

Independence, sir, is an empty dark word if its letters are not illuminated by rays of the Spirit.

Yusuf al-Sawda

TWO FOUNDING TEXTS

Lebanon's independent republic took off with two 'founding documents': a formal constitution and an informal verbal understanding between Bishara al-Khuri and Riad al-Sulh known as the 'National Pact', the only written trace of which is found in the latter's ministerial declaration of 7 October 1943.

The constitution itself contains a fundamental dichotomy. It establishes the judicial, civic and political equality of all Lebanese as citizens (*muwatinin*), inasmuch as it institutionalises their judicial and political inequality as subjects (*ahlin*) belonging to hierarchised religious communities with unequal access to political power and public office. In this sense, the 1943 constitution left untouched the three main articles concerning sectarianism in the initial 1926 constitution (numbers 9, 10 and 95).[1]

Nevertheless, sectarian pluralism barely concealed Maronite political primacy, represented by the exceptional powers that the constitution bestowed on the president of the republic, now firmly established by tradition as a Maronite. These are the powers of an 'autocrat', or a 'republican monarch', says jurist Antoine Khayr,[2] whereas constitutional jurist Edmond Rabbath notes that the head of state 'corporally incarnates ... all the life of the State'.[3] As uncontested head of the executive, the president names ministers and chooses a prime minister from among them, and holds the right to dismiss his cabinet, individually or collectively. Not only does he initiate legislation, but holds the right to veto legislation passed in parliament. Although himself elected by parliament, the president could dissolve the legislature and call for new elections. More importantly, a head of state enjoying such wide powers was unaccountable for his 'actions during office' except in the case of the violation of the constitution and high treason (article 60).

On the other hand, the National Pact acted to supplement and correct the constitution on essential questions of the country's identity, its Arab and international relations and the incorporation of Muslim communities in the power structure. There were four major principles involved.

First, the pact confirmed the power-sharing formula among the sects already established in article 95 of the constitution: the 6/5 ratio in political and administrative representation as well as the distribution of the three major posts of government, namely a Maronite president, a Shi`i speaker and a Sunni prime minister.

Second, the pact defined the country's identity, relations and obligations vis-à-vis the outside world. Whereas the constitution (article 1) defined Lebanon as an 'independent State enjoying indivisible unity and integral sovereignty', the pact defines it as a 'country with an Arab profile that assimilates all that is beneficial and useful in Western civilisation'. Thus Lebanon's 'Arab profile' was supposed to replace the (Muslim) demand for unity with Syria, and the cultural links with the West replaced the (Christian) demand for French military presence or Western protection in general.

Third, a major principle of foreign policy pledged that 'Lebanon shall not be a base or a passageway for colonialism'. This was designed to reassure traditional Syrian phobias, with General Gouraud's campaign in 1920 to topple the Arab government in Damascus, from Lebanese territory, still fresh in people's minds.

Fourth, striking a different note from the constitution, the pact implied a virtual partnership in the running of the affairs of the state between President Khuri and Prime Minister Sulh, and thus a better participation of the Muslims in power, decision-making and state functions. Sectarian quotas in the administration were supposed to favour Muslim access to it at the expense of traditional Maronite, and generally Christian, primacy in the public service, a legacy of the mandate period and of the Maronites' historically accumulated educational and cultural privileges.

Thus, the National Pact can be seen as a confirmation of political guarantees for the Christians in exchange for political and socio-cultural promises for the Muslims. These provisions were not incorporated in the body of the revised constitution of 1943, no doubt so as not to endow them with constitutional power, a further sign of the unevenness in the relationship between the representatives of the two communities.

The negative impacts of a country 'taking off' with two founding texts, instead of one, cannot be underestimated. A great part of the later history of Lebanon and of its conflicts would be articulated around the way those two texts were read, interpreted and assigned priority. To a great extent, the history of the application of the 1943 compromise is the history of conflict between constitution and custom.

NAVIGATING IN TROUBLED ARAB WATERS

Lebanon's first years of independence were rife with problems and challenges. Looming over Lebanon's new-found independent identity were the two Hashemite unity projects: the Greater Syria project of Emir `Abd Allah of Jordan and the Fertile Crescent project of Iraq Prime Minister Nuri al-Sa`id. In order to attract the Lebanese Christians, King `Abd Allah proposed autonomy for Mount Lebanon inside a united Greater Syria. Khuri's main contribution to Lebanese foreign policy was his capacity to navigate between the conflicting Arab camps of the time. Hashemite designs directed at annexing Syria helped attenuate Syrian politicians' appetites for Lebanon. Official Lebanon, for its part, opted for the Arab League project as an excuse for refusing to join either Hashemite pact and relied on the protection of the anti-Hashemite camp led by Egypt and Saudi Arabia. Nevertheless, these two countries had their unity project embodied in the Arab League. Lebanon's fidelity to its 'Arab engagements' within the context of the Arab League soon became a basic principle of its Arab policy.

But what policy to follow in the Arab League? A skilful manoeuvre by the tandem of advisers, Pharaon and Chiha, provided the answer. `Abd al-Hamid Karami was invited to head a new government in January 1945. One reason given for his appointment was its contribution to the integration of Tripoli into national political life. But there was more. Under Sulh, Lebanon had become a founding member of the Arab League on 25 September 1944 and participated in the drafting of the league's charter known as the Alexandria Protocol. During that session, and at the initiative of the Syrian delegation, a special clause was introduced into the protocol calling upon all the Arab states to respect Lebanon's independence and sovereignty in its current borders. In 1945, the Alexandria Protocol was to be signed and a decision taken on the federal union project presented by Egypt. Khuri and his advisers were afraid that Sulh might commit Lebanon to it. Karami, a local Syrian unionist who lacked the vision and Arab contacts of Sulh, ceded foreign policy to Henri Pharaon, named minister of foreign affairs, who threw all his weight into transforming the Arab League from a federal structure into a guardian of the existing Arab entities.[4] Pharaon objected to compulsory arbitration in disputes between the member states and rejected majority rule: any executive decision of the league's council should be taken unanimously.

The battle for evacuation

Though formally independent, Syria and Lebanon's problems with France were not over. As soon as the latter was liberated, the French government went back to the idea of a bilateral treaty that would give France the privileged status that General – now President – de Gaulle had been asking for. Britain, at that time, backed the French request and advised the Syrian and Lebanese to sign.[5] But Lebanon received an unexpected support as the USA recognised it as a fully independent state on 19 September 1945, rejecting a French request to delay recognition until after the treaty was signed. The USSR followed suit the next day.

The blessing of the two superpowers gave added strength to the Syrian and Lebanese in the crisis that erupted in May 1945. On this occasion, Syria led the confrontation and Lebanon played second fiddle. After the end of military hostilities in Europe, France dispatched military reinforcements, mainly Senegalese troops, to Syria and Lebanon. Immediately, demonstrations were organised in Damascus and Beirut in opposition to the move. A general strike in Syrian cities and towns degenerated into violent clashes with French troops. The French retaliated with an aerial bombardment of Damascus on 29 and 30 May. This was too much for the British. On the next day, British troops in Syria ordered French troops back to their bases and took charge of law and order. In the United Nations, a US-brokered compromise was reached on 13 December 1945 to evacuate French (and British) troops from Syria and Lebanon. By 31 December 1946, all foreign troops had departed.

Palestine 1948: the calamities of some...

Lebanon participated symbolically in the Arab–Israeli war of 1948. Its army's assigned mission was to move from Ras al-Naqura on the coastal road in the direction of Acre and Hayfa. The Syrian army, invited to reinforce the Lebanese front, was assigned the task of advancing from Bint Jubayl in the direction of Safad. The aim of the joint thrust was to reach the village of Malikiya in central Galilee, on the way to Hayfa. The Arab volunteers of *Jaysh al-Inqadh*, the Army of Salvation, led by Fawzi al-Qawuqji, participated actively in the campaign and the forces reached Malikya. But a counter-offensive of the Zionist forces in October 1948 regained Malikiya and occupied a strip of 14 villages inside Lebanese territory.

Careful not to to be the first Arab country to sign the armistice agreement, Lebanon waited for the Israeli–Egyptian armistice to be signed in Rhodes before engaging in Lebanese–Israeli negotiations in Naqura on 1 March 1949. On 23 March, the armistice agreement was signed, as Israel committed itself to withdraw from the territory it occupied in south Lebanon.

The Palestinian *Nakba* and the creation of the state of Israel had grave, yet contradictory consequences for Lebanon. Economically, Lebanon's service economy was the main beneficiary of the Arab economic boycott of Israel. Beirut took over Hayfa's role as the main port of the Arab hinterland and as an international communication centre between Europe, Asia and some parts of Africa.[6] Palestinian capital, estimated at 150 million Palestinian pounds, flowed massively into Lebanon, followed by a large number of rich and middle-class Palestinians. Nevertheless, industry was dealt a severe blow, as the value of its exports to Palestine was greater than its exports to France, Great Britain and the US combined. However, the economies of the regions neighbouring Palestine, whose products were destined for the Palestinian market (tanneries in Mashghara, pottery in Rashaya and shoemaking in Bint Jubayl) practically collapsed, and constituted a major factor in the migration of many southerners and Biqa`is to Beirut and overseas (especially Africa and the US).

Some 120,000 Palestinians from the Galilee had sought refuge in Lebanon. Declaring that they constituted an economic burden the country could not cope with, the Lebanese government made many attempts to dump them over the borders in Syria, in `Abdeh in the north and Masna` in the east. Rebuffed by the Syrian authorities, the Palestinian refugees were ultimately settled, at the urgent request of business interests, in camps close to the citrus plantations of the coastal plain and Beirut's industrial zones.

Politically, the creation of the state of Israel and its expansionist designs added radically new dimensions to the issue of Lebanon's security and protection: it was a challenge with many repercussions to come.

Sa`adeh's coup

Among the interrelated fallouts of the Palestine *Nakba* of 1948 was the Syrian *coup d'etat* of Husni al-Za`im and the failed armed revolt of Antoun Sa`adeh's SNSP in Lebanon. On 31 March 1949, the commander-in-chief of the Syrian army, Husni al-Za`im, blaming the civilian leadership for the military defeat in Palestine, seized power in Damascus in a military coup in which the CIA was heavily implicated.[7] The Lebanese leaders had every reason to be suspicious of Za`im. He had overthrown their Syrian allies of the National Bloc and expressed sympathy for the Fertile Crescent and Greater Syria projects. In addition, Za`im's coup came after the dissolution of the monetary union between the two countries and at a time of extreme anxiety over the future of their economic relations. It took more than a month for the Lebanese authorities to recognise the new regime in Damascus, which infuriated Za`im. Riad al-Sulh was especially targeted, being accused of conspiring with the exiled Syrian leaders to overthrow the new regime.

Za`im's coup fired up the opposition parties in Lebanon, especially the SNSP. After independence, Sa`adeh, hoping for his party's legalisation, had watered down his rejection of the Lebanese entity, declaring that he would accept it on political and religious grounds, not on 'national' grounds. But the *Nakba* in Palestine once again put the party on the path of radical opposition. Sa`adeh wrote that the Arab defeat in 1948 was proof of the bankruptcy of Arab nationalism and held the Lebanese government, especially Sulh, responsible for the debacle. News of contacts between Sa`adeh and Za`im provided additional reasons for the government to be suspicious of him and his party. A clash on 9 June 1949 between the SNSP and the Phalange in the popular quarter of Jummayzeh – in which the building occupied by the SNSP organ *al-Jil al-Jadid* (The New Generation) was burnt to the ground – served as a pretext for a police campaign against the SNSP. Large-scale arrests were made and the discovery of arms fuelled the accusation that the party was plotting to bring down the government. Sa`adeh promptly fled to Damascus, where he was immediately granted political asylum and declared a popular uprising on 1 July 1949. Bands of armed SNSP militants tried to take over government positions in the Biqa` and move from the Shuf and the suburbs to the capital; but they were quickly foiled by the army, and the revolt collapsed within 72 hours, leaving a number of dead and wounded and a witch-hunt against SNSP members.

Meanwhile, Saudi and Egyptian mediation had helped mend fences between Damascus and Beirut as the erratic Syrian dictator switched camps and dropped his Hashemite alliance. Sulh had visited Za`im in Damascus and, on 24 June 1949, Khuri and Sulh received the Syrian leader in Shtura. Saudi and Egyptian pressure, in addition to a Lebanese agreement to sign a treaty for full economic union with Syria, led Za`im to drop his protégé. On 6 July, Sa`adeh was promptly delivered in Damascus to two Lebanese officers, and the SNSP leader summarily judged before a military court in Beirut and sentenced to death on charges of conspiring to overthrow the government and 'collaboration with Israel'. He was executed by firing squad at dawn on 8 July.

THE 'CONSORTIUM'

The Lebanese president's exceptional executive and legislative powers made him the main pole of attraction for the country's dominant economic interests. This tradition, which began under the independence regime, constitutes a major aspect of Lebanon's political economy.

The commercial/financial oligarchy that came to power with independence was thought to comprise some thirty families articulated around a hard nucleus composed of 'the consortium': the president's two brothers, his sons, and a dozen related families.[8] The extent to which those families held monopolistic control over the main axes of the country's economy is impressive, especially when compared to the free trade pretensions of the 'merchant republic'. In sectarian composition, the families of the oligarchy were mainly Christian: there were 24 Christian families (nine Maronites, seven Greek Catholic, one Latin, one Protestant, four Greek Orthodox and one Armenian), to six Muslim (four Sunni, one Shiite and one Druze). Christian families practised extended endogamy in order to preserve or increase family wealth and property and advance business partnerships. In one generation at least ten of the oligarchy's families (Pharaon, Chiha, Khuri, Haddad, Freige, Kettaneh, `Arida, Bustrus, `Asayli, Doumit) were associated by matrimonial bonds. Their capital came from three main sources: the silk economy and the import trade during the *Mutasarrifiya* period; war profits (between 1940 and 1944 allied troops spent £76 million in Syria and Lebanon);[9] and emigrant money repatriated from Africa, the Americas and the oil-producing Arab countries (Iraq and Saudi Arabia especially).

Members of the consortium held controlling positions in all of the country's economic sectors. In finance, they owned a dozen local or mixed banks, headed by the BSL, the bank that issued the currency, administered the state's finances and controlled credit and commercial exchanges with France.[10] The biggest insurance company, the Union Nationale, was a partnership between members of the consortium and French capital. The above-mentioned interests were mainly importers of Western manufactured products and controlled the biggest share of the market for food products, arms and ammunition, agricultural and industrial equipment, beverages, medical and pharmaceutical products, construction materials, electric equipment and telecommunication, stationery, wood, hardware, coffee, cars, spare parts, and many others. Of the 50 agencies representing US firms, half were in the hands of one family, the Kettaneh, and the rest distributed betwen the Fattal, Sahnawi and Pharaon. Families of the consortium were also pionneers in tourism: they owned the country's biggest and most luxurious hotels in Beirut (the St Georges and Bristol hotels), the summer centres of Bhamdun and Sawfar and the ski centres of Faraya and the Cedars. In the services sector, the consortium, in association with French interests, controlled almost all the franchise-holding societies and public services companies: the port of Beirut, the water and electricity companies (Beirut, Qadisha, Nahr al-Barid), the Régie des tabacs et tombacs, and so on. The consortium also controlled the biggest construction companies in the country (la Régie des travaux) and one of the biggest in the Middle East (the CAT of Emile Bustani). The two principal air transport companies, Air Liban and Middle East Airlines, and the biggest land transport company were owned by members of the oligarchy. In industry, the oligarchy directed the main industrial firms in electricity, cement, textile, beer, matches, agricultural products, vegetable oil, paint, glass, etc. They also combined the import and production of the same products in cement and contruction materials. Finally, all the families mentioned had large property holdings in both city and countryside.[11]

An estimated value of the fortunes of fifteen of those families amounted to LL 245 million, the equivalent of nine times the state budget for 1944 and to more than 40 per cent of the national revenue for 1948. A significant portion of those fortunes was invested overseas.

During that period, thirteen of the oligarchy's members were elected deputies, five held cabinet posts and one was nominated prime minister. Most of the MPs of the oligarchy were 'parachuted' into the peripheries, particulary the Biqa` and the south, where they acted to fund the large lists of 'political feudalists'. Iliyas Trabulsi, a rich trader in Dayr al-Qamar, financed Ahmad al-As`ad's list in the south and ran on it. Pierre Pharaon, the cousin of Henri, and Nicolas Salim, were elected MPs for Jizzin. For a time, Henri Pharaon was the political patron of the region of Zahleh and part of the Biqa`, where his relative Musa de Freige had a mechanised farm and a parliamentary seat. A member of the Sursock family, big landowners in the `Ammiq region, was also MP for the Biqa`. Industrialist Butrus al-Khuri financed the lists of the northern leaders before himself running for parliament. Under the Khuri regime 36 deputies (of whom 26 were Christians) were owners or shareholders in the country's biggest 230 firms.[12]

Be that as it may, Michel Chiha had set up an interesting bifurcated model for the relationship between economic power and political power. Economic power was to be exercised mainly through the executive. The president of the republic, rallying point and business partner of the commercial/financial oligarchy, represented, served and defended its economic interests. Similarly, the administration's main task was to speed up business deals and transactions. Hence, in the interest of efficiency, Chiha was opposed to sectarian quotas in the administration.

On the other hand, parliament, defined as an 'assembly of notables', was to be the reserve of the landed Za`ims representing the country's various sects. Its principal, if not exclusive, role was the establishment of 'sectarian peace'. Nevertheless, that conflict-resolution function attributed to the legislative indirectly served the best interests of free trade, as it simply meant minimum legislation and very 'soft' budgets (implying also a minimum of taxes and customs duties).

Chiha's model was not followed to the letter. The oligarchy ceded the administration to the political bosses who soon filled it with their clients, and public function became a means to absorb some of the surplus labour power that the service economy could not absorb.

The intermediary role

The formation of Lebanon's economic system under the independence regime involved a mixture of imposing the interests of the commercial/financial oligarchy and adapting to Arab and international developments, especially the burgeoning oil economies in Iraq, the Gulf and Saudi Arabia, which were encouraged by the Arab economic boycott of Israel and the breakup of the Syrian–Lebanese economic union.

Liberated from the confines of the franc zone and economic union with Syria, the Lebanese commercial/financial oligarchy established itself as an intermediary between Western markets and the entire Arab hinterland. Exchanges with the franc bloc declined in favour of the Anglo-Saxon zone and the Arab countries (Iraq, Jordan, Saudi Arabia and the Gulf Emirates).[13] More important was the growing integration of Lebanon into the Arab oil economy. As early as 1948, 30 per cent of the world's gold transited through Beirut toward the Gulf as the monarchs, sheikhs and emirs exchanged their petrodollars for the precious metal. On the other hand, since 1934 Tripoli had become the terminal for the Iraqi Oil Company (IPC), and in 1946, an agreement was signed with TAPLINE, subsidiairy of the American ARAMCO group, to build a refinery for Saudi oil in Sidon; another contract gave Standard Oil a concession to build a second refinery in Tripoli.

Beirut was rapidly becoming a centre for international communications. Its modern airport, the privileged relay point for Saudi Arabia and the Gulf, was controlled by two local air transport companies. Air Liban, in which French interests controlled 30 per cent of the shares, was associated with the Busson group (Husayn al-`Uwayni, Antoine Sahnawi, Michel Khattar and Georges Karam) and benefited from `Uwayni's privileged relations with Saudi King `Abd al-`Aziz ibn Sa`ud. Middle East Airlines (MEA) of Sa'ib Salam, associated with Pan American Airlines (PAA), monopolised the Beirut–Kuwayt line for a time, thanks to Salam's excellent ties with the ruling sheikh of the oil emirate. From 60 employees in 1946, MEA jumped to 900 a decade later, and as early as 1951, made a net profit of LL 1.9 million.

The integration into the Arab oil economy introduced Anglo-Saxon interests into the heart of the Lebanese economy and soon led to frantic competition with French interests. In fact, the country's political independence from France had not hindered the recon-struction of neo-colonial ties beween the ancient metropolis and the newly independent country. The control exercised over the whole economy by the Banque de Syrie et du Lebanon (BSL), under its director René Busson, drained a good part of the war profits into France. Issuing bank and depositary of the state budget, the BSL came to control the credit of the banks that financed the big construction projects. In addition, French banks eventually came to dominate and control Lebanese banks: Le Crédit Lyonnais took over Banque G. Trad & Co. and the Banque d'Indochine controlled Banque Sabbagh. Under Busson's supervision, the Banque d'Indochine was responsible for buying gold bullion for the Lebanese lira's gold cover.

The SERIAC group (Société d'études et de réalisation industrielles, agricoles et commerciales) created by Busson provided projects and deals for the French contractors. In addition, it exercised monopoly control over Syria and Lebanon's economic exchanges and financial transactions with France. The group's lawyer was Hamid Franjiyeh and on its adminstrative council sat Fu'ad al-Khuri, the president's brother, side by side with representatives of the BNCI, the Banque française du commerce extérieur (BFCE) and Crédit Lyonnais (CL). On the other hand, *al-Ittihad al-Watani*, the local insurance company owned by the members of the 'consortium' (Yusuf Salim, Jean Fattal, Alfred Kettaneh and Husayn `Uwayni) represented the big French insurance company l'Union Nationale and acquired insurance contracts for the franchise-holding companies (Compagnie du port, TEB, Régie des travaux, Air Liban, etc.)

French neo-colonial interests were better served by the strong presence of their local representatives in the heart of power, ensuring privileges and fiscal exemptions. According to opponents of Khuri's regime, the BSL and other concessionary societies exported to France the tax-exempt sum of LL 50 million in profits annually.

The subordination of industry

Although Lebanese industry witnessed extensive growth during the war, its development was soon to be arrested by the increasing terti-arisation of the economy as the commercial/financial oligarchy used its dominant position in power to subject industrial interests to its own logic and needs. The industrialists, incapable of controlling or even finding a sizeable place in a domestic market dominated by imported goods, were bound to produce for export and distribute their products in the Arab and African markets. The Lebanon of the

1940s was a pioneer in rejecting 'import substitution' in favour of 'export-oriented' industry.

Nevertheless, the intermediary role did not impose itself without resistance. Na`im Amiuni, assistant director-general of the Ministry of National Economy, was among those who presented an alternative view. In a lecture at the American Junior College (the present Lebanese American University) in July 1946, he defined himself as a partisan of the development of the productive sectors, of greater self-sufficiency in staples and a wider differentiation in exports. Reminding his audience that 'commerce is the engine of the economy not the economy itself', he expressed his anxiety at the rapid increase in the number of merchants amd middlemen, the transfer of capital from landed ownership to trade and finance, and the massive importation of consumer and luxury goods. As for tourism, Amiuni remarked that the country's main sources were agricultural and industrial and not touristic. Only two industrial sectors, cotton spinning and tannery, produced two and a half times more revenue than the entire tourism sector (LL 10 million against LL 4 million for 1944–45). Arguing against Chiha's thesis that the Lebanese had refused to be enslaved by industrial labour, he forecast that tourism would transform the Lebanese into a 'class of servants'.

Amiuni discussed at length the lost opportunities for Lebanese agriculture, which used to produce as much citrus fruit as Palestine before World War I, but ten times less at the end of the war, and noted the negative impact of the multiplication of middlemen on the price of agricultural products, which had risen at a rate of 150–200 per cent.

Without underestimating the economic effects of the facilities granted to foreign firms and the country's transit role (for airports, free zones, refineries and pipelines), Amiuni warned against the prevailing optimism. Tripoli, a prosperous port in earlier periods, spent years waiting for Iraqi oil as its population suffered high rates of unemployment. When the oil finally arrived, the dreams collapsed: one cotton-spinning factory in Tripoli employed four times as many workers as the Iraqi Petroleum Company (IPC) terminal and the oil refinery combined.[14]

Breakup of the Lebanese–Syrian economic union

If the creation of Greater Lebanon achieved political detachment from Syria, the country's independence in 1943, under the domination of the importers and middlemen, gradually led to its economic detachment from the 'sister' country. The dream of both Muslim and Christian independentists of a politically independent Lebanon entertaining the best possible economic, social and cultural relations with Syria, not to speak of being united economically with it, suddenly evaporated. Ironically, whereas French colonialism had unified Syria and Lebanon economically, the nationalist leaders of both countries succeeded in breaking up that unity.

By 1950 the rupture of the monetary and customs union between the two countries and the separation of the Common Interests had become final. There were linked political and economic reasons for this. On the Lebanese side, Maronite phobias read economic union as an inevitable step to political unity. Georges Naccache likened the economic union to the Nazi invasion of Austria '... as economic Lebanon became a Syrian province, it would be integrated as such into the Syrian State'.[15] Those phobias merged easily with the *laissez-faire* attitudes of the importers and agents of foreign companies. The elements of conflict were aggravated by the uneven competition between two economic systems and the interests of two competing bourgeoisies. In fact, the Lebanese bourgeoisie was attached to the *status quo ante*: Beirut as an outlet for a Syrian hinterland specialised in agricultural monoproduction (cotton, wheat, cereals), leaving the importation and distribution of manufactured products to the Lebanese. Despite the fact that an active industrial sector had developed during World War II in both countries and sought to defend itself against foreign competition, Lebanese industry was subordinated to the dictates of import trade and progressively expelled from the local market to seek external markets. On the other hand, the industrial and commercial factions of the Syrian bourgeoisie joined forces to conduct a protectionist policy in defence of their internal market against the uneven competition of the outward-looking Lebanese bourgeoisie, so much richer in capital and in relations with world markets.

Post-independence negotiations between the two countries revolved around the three major divisive questions: Lebanon's purchase of Syrian wheat, the monetary and customs union, and the commercial exchanges of the two countries.

First, Greater Lebanon, whose *raison d'être* was to provide its inhabitants with some measure of self-sufficiency, did not produce more than one-third of its basic requirements in cereals, despite the annexation of the Biqa` plain – it was no more in proportion than under the *Mutasarrifiya* and added to the demand for the annexation of the Biqa` and `Akkar plains. The remaining two-thirds were imported from Syria, which demanded to be paid for its wheat in foreign currency, in order to counterbalance the difference of exchange rates between the Lebanese and Syrian liras. The Lebanese wanted to pay in local currency and insisted on reciprocity in exchanges between them: Lebanon would continue to buy wheat from Syria on condition that Syria open its markets for imported goods transited through Lebanon.

Second, the conflict concerning the customs union revolved around two points: the distribution of revenues and the administration of the joint customs' body. Syria reiterated its claim to a better distribution of the revenues as it received 51 per cent, for five times as many inhabitants, and called for a joint administration of the common body, managed solely by a Lebanese. The Lebanese insisted on a higher share than Syria as they imported more than the Syrians (Lebanese journalists even demanded that Lebanon's share be raised to 70 per cent). Even the import statistics of the two countries were interpreted differently. Although an agreement was signed on 10 July 1947, which modified the distribution of revenues in favour of Syria and confirmed two directors, one Syrian and one Lebanese, at the head of the customs authority, Lebanon refused to put the measures into practice.

In 1948 came the breakup of the Syrian–Lebanese monetary union as Lebanon, in order to prevent the devaluation of its currency, in February of that year renewed the monetary accord with France that linked the Lebanese lira to the French franc. Syria, less fearful of devaluation, as its balance of trade was nearly balanced, prefered to exit the Franc zone and French monetary tutelage altogether. This divergence led Syria to suspend the customs and economic union between the two countries, abolish the interdependence of their currencies and impose a licensing system on all Syrian imports through Lebanon. Neither of the two countries benefited from this rupture. As early as September 1949, the Lebanese lira was devalued following the devaluation of sterling. On the other hand, some 500–700 members of Syria's business families moved their capital and operations to Lebanon.[16]

A compromise agreement was signed in July 1949, according to which Syria would maintain a number of selected imports from Lebanon, in return for which Lebanon would give up importing some luxury articles and admit the principle of protection of agriculture and industry. But this agreement was mainly dictated by political considerations, following the Palestine *Nakba*. The two countries could not agree on the list of the concerned foreign goods. Najib Rayyes, referring to the famous consortium, put all the blame on the 'party of import merchants ... whose families are closely linked to political power'. He raised a pertinent question: were the revenues from transit trade more important than the Syrian market, with its four million consumers? The import interests thought yes, they were. There would be no concession on free trade. It was a question of life and death, for the oligarchy and its government at least. Lebanese economist Gabriel Menassa said it in so many words: '*Importer ou mourir!*' ('Import or die!').

No compromise was in sight. On 5 November 1949, an economic congress in Damascus decided to strive for 'economic independence vis-à-vis Lebanon', and Michel Chiha insisted that Lebanon's political independence could only be guaranteed by its economic independence.[17] He was, of course, talking about Lebanon's independence from Syria.

DOWNFALL

Despite a positive economic balance and unprecedented economic growth, the Khuri regime did not fail to give rise to a fierce opposition, which was triggered after the truncated elections of May 1947, designed to give Khuri the two-thirds majority parliamentary majority needed to modify the constitution and renew his term of office. The 1947 legislature was appropriately described by the journalist Iskandar Riyashi as 'the Parliament of 15 capitalists and 40 of their lackeys'. Several additional factors contributed to the rise of the oppositon: the Arab defeat in Palestine, the profiteering of the 'President's men', the influence-peddling of his brother Salim (nicknamed Sultan Salim) and the absence of his Sunni partner and supporter Riad al-Sulh, who was assassinated in 1951 by a commando of the SNSP while on a visit in Amman, for his role in the summary execution of Antun Sa`adeh.

But a considerable part of the opposition also had to do with the growing conflict over French neo-colonial policies. Two ministers had opposed Busson and his 'empire'. Kamal Junblat stood against the group's attempts to monopolise the export of citrus fruits and Philippe Taqla, minister of finance, had revised the franchise of the BSL and contributed to the dismissal of Busson, accused by the British shareholders of the BSL (in which the Ottoman Bank of London held 25 per cent of the shares) of running the bank as a dictator and using funds for his personal use. Taqla also waged a campaign to tax the franchise-holding companies on a par with Lebanese companies. He revealed that the Tramways et éclairage de Beirut (TEB) bought electricity from the Compagnie libanaise d'électricité de Nahr Ibrahim for 400,000 LL per year, for which it paid LL 125,000 in taxes, before reselling it to Lebanese consumers for double the purchase price at LL 800,000, and the TEB profits were tax-exempt. In fact, the opposition called for nationalising the TEB, and critics detailed its surplus profits, bad service, huge production costs and lack of planning for Lebanon's future needs. An American company offered to generate electricity from the waters of the Litani river and sell it at 3 piastres/kilowatt, that is, three times less than the price at which the kilowatt was sold by the Nahr Ibrahim electricity company. But the TEB stood its ground and sabotaged the project, backed by its lawyer, no other than Sheikh Khalil al-Khuri, the president's son. On 15 January 1952, parliament decreed – upon a motion tabled by Kamal Junblat and Kamil Sham`un – to revise the agreements with the Compagnie du port, the DHP and the TEB, and abolish all the privileges and concessions granted to foreign firms under the Ottoman Empire and the French mandate. When the government decided to submit the TEB to taxation, after a general strike and a boycott of the company's services in autumn 1952, the company promised to pay, starting from 1953. But it was nationalised by the Lebanese government under Sham`un in 1954 before having paid a penny in terms of taxes or customs duties.

The consequences of the Korean war aggravated the social crisis. Whereas the oligarchy made enormous profits on speculation in currency and goods, the population suffered a dramatic rise in its cost of living and unemployment. In 1951, Lebanon counted 57,000 unemployed out of a population of 1,250,000.[18] The Sami al-Sulh cabinet, formed in February 1952, faced a widespead strike movement calling for reductions in the price of meat and bread and the abolition of the monopoly held by the franchise-holding companies. There were strikes in a variety of sectors, such as industrial workers, postal workers, contractors, teachers, taxi drivers, journalists and lawyers. The latter were protesting against the two-headed system of civil and religious legislation and courts, calling for a unified civil code for matters of personal status.

An alliance of the opposition forces and figures, led by Kamal Junblat, Kamil Sham`un, Raymond and Pierre Iddi, in addition to the Phalange, the Najjadeh, the PSNS and the LCP, formed the Patriotic Socialist Front (PSF) in early 1950. On 16 May 1952, the PSF adopted an ambitious programme of democratic and anti-monopolist policies mainly inspired by Junblat's Progressive Socialist Party: the independence of the judiciary, freedom of the press and of political parties, and the abolition of noble titles. Socially, the programme called for social security, an unemployment insurance scheme for workers, peasants and intellectuals, and the transformation of 'exploitative companies' into cooperatives in which the salaried would be shareholders. Signed by Junblat, Sham`un, Anwar al-Khatib, Ghassan Tuwayni, `Abd Allah al-Hajj and Emile Bustani, the programme was made public during a mass rally by the PSF in Dayr al-Qamar in August of that year. In his speech, Junblat insisted on the abolition of the sectarian quotas in the elections to the chamber of deputies and called upon the president to apply those reforms or resign.

At the new parliamentary session on 9 September, Prime Minister Sami al-Sulh exploded his political 'bomb'. He declared that a 'covert power' led the republic and blocked all reforms: 'Men with authority hold power without being accountable and they interfere in all the affairs of the State,' he said in direct reference to the President's advisers, whom he accused of influence-peddling, intervention in the course of justice and financial scandals.[19] Those whose fortunes were 'safely outside the country', Sulh continued, 'have impoverished the people and oppressed them', and concluded by accusing that same clique of the assassination of his cousin Riad and presenting his government's resignation and his own.[20] The next day, Michel Chiha replied in his *Le Jour* editorial, with a hefty dose of cynicism: 'It may well be that authority and responsibility are disassociated whereas they should be joined. That may well be a mistake, but that is the way things are.'[21]

Whatever the case, the death-knell of the Khuri regime had sounded, despite the fact that it could still count on a sizeable parliamentary majority. Khuri appointed Sa'ib Salam as prime minister, heading a three-man government. On 17 September, the opposition declared an open general political strike until Khuri resigned. The president stood his ground and rejected a parliamentary note signed by a number of deputies asking for his resignation. Salam then resigned and Khuri's last card was to call upon General Fu'ad Shihab, commander-in-chief of the army, to break the strike by force. Shihab declared his readiness to engage the army in keeping law and order but not to use it against the people. Khuri's resignation was announced on midday of 18 September 1952.

An external factor in Khuri's downfall was related to the question of Lebanon's membership in Western military pacts. On this issue, the two guarantors of Lebanon's independence – Great Britain and Egypt – were at odds. In early 1950 the USA and Britain (in addition to France and Turkey) launched the Pact for the Collective Defense of the Mediterranean against communism. Egypt, invited to join the Western military pact with Syria and Lebanon, rejected the offer, setting as precondition the closing of British military bases on Egyptian territory. At the initiative of Egypt, the countries of the Arab League signed a Treaty of Arab Collective Security (TACS) on 13 April of that year and asked European countries for arms to strengthen their defences against Israel. The Tripartite Declaration of May 1951, issued by the US, Britain and France, was a reply to that treaty. In it the signatories gave priority to defending the region against communism, criticised the Arab–Israeli arms race and declared the inviolability of the Middle East's borders and the 1949 armistice lines. In their collective response of June 1951, the Arab League states retained from the Tripartite Declaration its opposition to resorting to violence to solve the problems of the region or modify armistice lines. It insisted on the defensive character of Arab armaments, rejected all pressures to impose the *status quo* or negotiations with Israel, and reiterated its demand for the implementation of UN resolutions concerning the right of return for Palestinian refugees and compensation for their properties. The Arab states' response concluded with the affirmation of the sovereignty and independence of their countries.[22]

Official Lebanon sided with Egypt, adhered to the TACS and signed the collective declaration. As early as 1950, Khuri and Sulh had rejected British offers to join the Mediterranean Collective Defense Pact; they had decided that Lebanon would be the last Arab state to join any foreign military pact. At best, both were ready for a bilateral defence agreement with any Western power, but not a collective military pact. Facing increased British pressures, Khuri convened an assembly of some 40 notables of the Constitutionalist Bloc, who reiterated his positon. The only dissenting voice was that of Henri Pharaon, who also expressed the opinion of his cousin Michel Chiha, the most vocal advocate of an immediate membership in the pact. Chiha had strongly disagreed with Khuri on that issue to the point that relations between the president and his brother-in-law reached the point of rupture.

Be that as it may, the divisions inside the Constitutionalist Party between 'protectionists' and 'neutralists' broke out in the open when their respective leaders ran to succeed Khuri: Kamil Sham`un, the protectionist, and Hamid Franjiyeh, known for his neutralist positions. Franjiyeh withdrew from the race when Ahmad al-As`ad's southern bloc of 14 deputies declared their intention to vote for Sham`un.[23] On 23 September 1952, Sham`un was elected president. He had agreed to engage Lebanon in the Western pacts, and he kept his promise.

8

The Pro-Western Authoritarianism of Kamil Sham'un (1952–1958)

Lebanon is important to the United States because of its lines of communication and bases which could be provided in the development of a forward defense in the Middle East. Lebanon posseses one of the best harbors and communications centers on the Eastern Mediterranean shore and potentially good air bases. Most of the pipelines which transport oil from the Persian Gulf area and Iraq terminate in Lebanon ports on the Mediterranean.

(US Joint Chiefs of Staff, *A Report by the Joint Committee on Programs for Military Aid for the Middle East*, 3 February 1957)

During the presidency of Kamil Sham'un, Lebanon witnessed a period of economic prosperity that drew on favourable regional conditions: the boom in the oil economies of the Gulf and Saudi Arabia; the economic effects of the creation of the state of Israel; and the flow of Arab capital to Lebanese banks fleeing the first wave of nationalisations in Syria, Iraq and Egypt. The rise in GDP exceeded the demographic increase, and record rates were registered in the construction, banking and tourism sectors, and in the number of agencies of foreign firms established in Lebanon. Revenues accruing from transit trade with Jordan, Iraq and Saudi Arabia more than compensated for the losses incurred following the breakup of the customs and monetary union with Syria. Sham'un's uncontested merit was to provide the appropriate judicial framework, such as the 1954 law on the creation of joint stock companies (which were exempted from taxes for six years) and the banking secrecy law of 1956.

Yet Lebanon's prosperity aggravated social and regional disparities and tensions as most of the profits were absorbed by the commercial and financial sectors of the economy and concentrated in parts of the capital and Mount Lebanon. Sham'un was immediately surrounded by the same consortium of the Khuri days, enlarged to accommodate the new president's men and the *nouveaux riches* of emigration. The first thing the newly elected president did was to break with his former partner in the Patriotic Socialist Front (PSF) after representatives of US oil interests officially asked Sham`un not to give Junblat any ministerial post, as they suspected him to be a supporter of nationalising the oil interests.[1] Nevertheless, in his nomination speech on 23 September 1952, the new president promised to fight corruption, talked about the 'modesty and asceticism' of the president's post and promised to abolish the privileges and formalities attached to it, including the secret funds at the discretion of the president. In the PSF charter, he had committed himself to achieve Lebanese neutrality in international affairs, reform the administration, create a state council to examine the constitutionality of legislation and abuses of power. The extent to which the new president did exactly the opposite of what he had committed himself to do is quite amazing.

PRESIDENTIAL AUTHORITARIANISM

Sham`un pushed his exercise of power to the limits of autocracy, relying on the textual interpretation of the constitution at the expense of the spirit of the National Pact.

Not only was an unprecedented pomp and ceremony attached to the presidency, but Sham`un established two traditions that contributed greatly to the concentration of power in his hands. First, he chose weak prime ministers who, rather than represent their community's interests and aspirations, were dependent on the favours and privileges of the president. Second, the president ruled by direct liasion with the directors-general of the major ministries (Foreign Affairs, Defence, Finance, Justice and Internal security – almost all those functionaries were Maronites), which meant beyond the control of the respective ministers.

Presidential control over the executive branch was further complemented by the subordination of the legislature. Sham`un opted for the small electoral district but reduced the number of deputies. According to the new electoral law of November 1952, the country was divided into 33 electoral districts (instead of the previous nine) and the number of deputies reduced from 77 to 44. This last measure was justified by the president's alleged desire to 'replace quantity by quality'.[2] Theoretically, the adoption of smaller electoral districts would break the monopoly of the traditional leaders over the chamber but in practical terms, it guaranteed the president a safe majority in the legislature and amplified the sectarian character of the electoral district. According to the new legislation, women were granted the right to vote for the first time, a measure that crowned the women's movement's long struggle for legal and political rights.

The results of the 1952 elections partially fulfilled Sham`un's goal. Twenty-two new individuals entered parliament for the first time and the major heads of lists were weakened. Sham`un's authoritarianism reached such proportions that the leader writer of *l'Orient*, the Francophone Christian daily, was prompted to write in 1956: 'The Head of State has become the entire Legislature and Executive. This is so true that we notice each time he is absent, all the [state's] prerogatives are absent with him'.[3] Strengthened by foreign backing, the complicity of the bourgeoisie and by Maronite mobilisation, Sham`un exacerbated sectarian tensions as no other political leader had done before him. With the majority of the Muslim leaders outside parliament, the Muslim 'street' was massively attracted to the Nasserist nationalist and anti-colonialist discourse.

THE ANGLO-SAXON ALIGNMENT

Undoubtedly, the rise of Jamal `Abd al-Nasir in Egypt increased the US administration's interest in Lebanon. Arab nationalism was seen as the enemy and its policy of non-alignment as a tacit alliance with the Soviet camp. In response, Washington's strategy was based on three axes: to wean Saudi Arabia from `Abd al-Nasir, to transform Iraq into a competitor of Egypt, and to reinforce the Lebanese authorities. Secretary John Foster Dulles designated Israel, the oil of the Gulf and Saudi Arabia and Lebanon as the 'American positions' to be defended against the rise of Arab nationalism.[4] In economic terms, the US was interested in Lebanon as an oil terminal and a rapidly developing centre for agencies representing US firms in the entire region. Strategically, Lebanon attracted US interest for its infrastructure: military bases, ports, communication networks and other facilities that could serve as a bridgehead in the event of military intervention in the region. In 1953, the Lebanese government received $6 million in US arms and economic aid, and by 1954, Sham`un had allowed the US air force to use Lebanese air space for reconnaissance missions. A year later, a preferential commercial treaty long desired by Lebanese officials was finally signed.

The Baghdad Pact, declared in 1955 between the Iraq of Faysal and Nuri al-Sa`id, Pakistan, Turkey and Iran, was the best that Western powers could impose on the region. Although Sham`un did not adhere officially to the anti-communist pact, he made it clear that he supported it without reservation. King Sa`ud even accused Sham`un of exerting pressure on his friend King Husayn of Jordan to join the Baghdad Pact. The latter's hands were tied with nationalist agitation that had swept across Jordan, including the army, and imposed the nationalist Sulayman Nabulsi to head a pro-Nasir government. But, on the other hand, Sham`un refused to join the Arab Defence Pact signed by Egypt, Saudi Arabia and Syria in March 1955 as a response to the Baghdad Pact.

The declaration of the Baghdad Pact was met with violent student and popular demonstrations across Lebanon, from Tripoli to Bint Jubayl. In the capital, the police opened fire on demonstrators at the gate of the AUB, killing the student Hassan Abu Isma`il, a militant of Junblat's PSP, and wounding many others. Incapable of adapting to the president's foreign policy, Hamid Franjiyeh resigned as minister of foreign affairs, in September 1955: he had assured `Abd al-Nasir, in the name of his government, that Lebanon would oppose Western military pacts.

Thus Sham`un undermined the bases of his predecessor's neutralist Arab policy. His position on the Baghdad Pact put him at odds with `Abd al-Nasir's Egypt, all the while poisoning his relations with neighbouring Syria. During the Suez crisis of 1956, official Lebanon offered qualified support to Egypt, while criticising the 'abruptness' of the nationalisation of the Suez Canal Company. As a reaction to the tripartite aggression against Egypt, Sham`un called for a summit of Arab rulers in Beirut, a manoeuvre to outbid his domestic opposition. In the meantime, he left on an official visit to the Shah of Iran. When the Arab summit finally convened, the fighting on the Suez Canal zone had ended and Sham`un tried to divert discussions away from sanctions against France and Britain to demands for an Israeli withdrawal from Egyptian territory. Nevertheless, when the summit resolved to sever all diplomatic relations with France and Britain, official Lebanon refused to comply. This step marked the final break with Prime Minister `Abd Allah al-Yafi and Minister of State Sa'ib Salam. Both men resigned and joined the opposition. Sham`un reacted by forming a five-man government headed by Sami al-Sulh. The portfolio of defence was entrusted to General Shihab, who was asked to declare a state of emergency. More challenging was the appointment of Charles Malik to the post of minister of foreign affairs, given his extremely pro-American stances. In April of that year, Sham`un, accompanied by his prime minister, went on an official visit to Ankara. The joint declaration insisted on the identity of views and policies of the two countries at a time when Turkey was menacing Syria and massing troops on its borders.

On 16 March 1957, Sham`un formally linked Lebanon to the Eisenhower doctrine via a joint communiqué by the two governments approved by a vote in parliament on 4 April. In May that year Sham`un organised national elections 'bought for' him by the CIA, to use the term of Wilbur Crane Eveland who wrote:

Throughout the elections I travelled regularly to the presidential palace with a briefcase of Lebanese pounds, then returned late at night to the embassy with an empty twin case I'd carried away for Harvey Armada's CIA finance-office to replenish. Soon my gold DeSoto with its stark white top was a common sight outside the palace, and I proposed to Chamoun that he use an intermediary and a more remote spot. When the president insisted that he can handle each transaction by himself, I reconciled myself to the probability that anybody in Lebanon who really cared would have no trouble guessing precisely what I was doing.[5]

The number of seats was increased from 44 to 66 but leading Muslim figures Salam, Junblat, Yafi, As`ad and others, lost their seats and were replaced by candidates loyal to the president. On 30 May police fired upon a demonstration objecting to the election results, with several deaths resulting.

Sham`un's policies not only alienated Muslim elites and the Muslim 'street' but divided Christian ranks. In addition to the growing Muslim opposition against him, there developed a predominantly Christian 'third force' that included Pharaon, Yusuf Salim, Charles Hilu and Georges Naccache, who called for Lebanese neutrality in Arab conflicts. Raymond Iddi, who succeeded his father as the head of the National Bloc, openly opposed the renewal of the president's mandate. More important was the opposition of Patriarch Ma`ushi, who was eager to react to the new developments in the country and the region. He had urged the Lebanese government to reject the Baghdad Pact and expressed courageous and lucid opinions on Christian–Muslim relations. The time had come, he confided to US Ambassador McClintock, for the Christians to face the realities of life: they were a minority in Lebanon and a small minority in the Arab world, although they still controlled the best posts and entertained the fiction that they were a majority. The only way to preserve the existence of my people, he went on, would be to get used to the fact that the Christians constituted a minority, and the first step in that direction would be to put the greatest possible number of administrative posts in Lebanon at the disposal of the Muslims without delay.[6]

Corruption under Sham`un had reached dramatic proportions: the president's brokers imposed the granting of shares in the form of 'gifts' to the president and his coterie in return for each licence granted to form a joint stock company.[7] The president was also accused of diverting to his own accounts funds sent by Lebanese émigrés to the victims for the earthquake of 1956. The resignation of businessman Emile Bustani, minister in charge of reconstruction, lent weight to the accusations.

On 1 February 1958, the union of Syria and Egypt as the United Arab Republic (UAR) was celebrated by demonstrations of joy in Beirut and the coastal cities. When `Abd al-Nasir visited Damascus, tens of thousands of Lebanese headed to the Syrian capital, led by Salam, Junblat, Yafi, Ahmad al-As`ad, Sabri Hamadeh, Fu'ad `Ammun, Rashid Karami, Ma`ruf Sa`d and others.

THE 1958 INSURRECTION

The crisis, which would develop into an armed insurrection, started in March 1958, when Sham`un refused to deny rumours about his intention to renew his mandate.

The American administration was not opposed in principle to a new mandate, but the embassy in Beirut feared that the division of Christian ranks on this issue would endanger Christian political dominance over the country. It sent highly sophisticated analyses to Washington on political discontent, economic and social difficulties, Christian privileges and the status of the country's Muslim population as second-class citizens. Many leaders of the opposition did not hide their pro-American sympathies. Despite its knowledge of the general corruption of his regime, his many violations of the National Pact, and the need for economic and social reforms, the American administration decided to defend Sham`un in case he sought a second mandate.

On 27 March 1958, 85 figures from the opposition and the 'third force', of whom half were Christians, met and elected a steering committee of three: Henri Pharaon (president) `Abd Allah al-Yafi (vice-president) and Kamal Junblat (secretary). The meeting declared its opposition to a second mandate and accused Sham`un of promoting fears about the country's security to serve his personal ends. Sham`un was seen as attempting to impose on the Lebanese the identification of patriotism with allegiance to his own person. 'A new political creed has been proposed to the Lebanese for the past eight months', wrote Georges Naccache. "If you are not a Sham`unist, that means that you are a traitor or a Syrian-Bolshevik"'.[8]

By the end of April, observers described Lebanon as a powder keg. The spark came with the assassination on 7 May of the leftist journalist Nasib al-Matni, the Maronite editor-in-chief and owner of a popular opposition daily, *Al-Tallaghraf* (The Telegraph), known for his violent criticism of Sham`un's foreign policy and his regime's corruption. On the next day, the opposition called for a general strike, and the occasion of the assassinated journalist's funeral turned into massive demonstrations in `Akkar, Minyeh, Shuf, the Biqa` and Sidon. There were angry scenes, with hostile denunciations of foreign military pacts and demands for the resignation of the president. In Tripoli the partisans of Rashid Karami clashed with the army and barricades appeared in the streets of West Beirut.

After two months of fighting, the opposition came to control three-quarters of Lebanese territory. The army, under Fu'ad Shihab, observed a policy of 'active neutrality', trying to contain the insurrection rather than crush it, an impossible mission in any event given the rebellion's geographical scope compared with the means at his disposal and the sectarian composition of his army.[9] Be that as it may, Shihab resisted Sham`un's orders to occupy the bastions of the insurrection in Basta, Musaytibeh and Tariq al-Jadideh, but he nevertheless managed to stabilise the fronts in Tripoli and stop the offensive of the partisans of Kamal Junblat on two major axes: their attempt to control the Beirut–Damascus road (on the `Alay-Sawfar front) and occupy Beirut international airport. Fierce combats raged on this second axis in Shimlan, where the army was backed by armed partisans of the SNSP, Sham`un and his Druze ally, Majid Arsalan.

Upon the outbreak of fighting, Charles Malik officially requested the US to intervene militarily in Lebanon. A month later, the White House was still opposed to engaging its troops. In a telegram to the embassy in Beirut, Secretary of State Dulles explained that military intervention ran the danger of provoking 'sectarian conflicts' or even leading to 'partition or the territorial amputation of the country'.[10] On the other hand, the Americans considered the Lebanese army sufficiently strong to fulfil the demands of internal security, especially since it had recently received large shipments of new US arms and ammunitions. Nevertheless, from the autumn of 1957, plans for possible military intervention in Lebanon had been ready in the Pentagon, under the codename 'Operation Blue Bat'. However, this plan was drafted in relation to a much wider regional context, as we shall soon see.

Meanwhile, an American emissary was dispatched to Jamal `Abd al-Nasir, whose relations with the Soviet Union had suddenly turned sour that year. The Egyptian leader – all the while criticising the American lack of understanding for the aspirations of the Arab peoples to liberate themselves from the established powers – proposed a compromise solution. He suggested a general amnesty; the nomination of Shihab as prime minister; a declaration by Sham`un that he would not seek a renewal of his mandate in return for serving the remainder of his term; and the organisation of immediate elections. `Abd al-Nasir's proposal was even more moderate than that of Patriarch Ma`ushi, who had suggested that Sham`un leave the country, on the pretext of taking a vacation, and that new elections be organised in his absence. However, Sham`un rejected the amnesty, and to head off any accord between the US and the UAR, issued arrest warrants against 15 of the opposition leaders.

In June 1958, the military situation had become untenable for Sham`un: the Popular Resistance of Sa'ib Salam was threatening the Presidential Palace in the Qantari district of West Beirut and, Junblat's rebels were preparing for a final assault on the airport. The authorities' biggest worry was seeing the two groups join forces in an operation to take over the airport. On the other hand, the UN group of observers (UNOGIL) dispatched to investigate the military intervention of the UAR in Lebanese internal affairs confirmed the flow of arms from Syria but not the Lebanese government's allegations about the participation of Syrian or Egyptian troops in the fighting.[11]

'OPERATION BLUE BAT'

On 14 July 1958, the Iraqi monarchy fell to rebel army units led by a group of Free Officers, as the mob took to the streets of Baghdad and reacted with unprecedented violence against the symbols and figures of the regime. The diplomatic exchanges between Washington and London make for interesting reading. When Eisenhower telephoned the British prime minister to tell him that the Americans would put the plan into action, an unusual *quid pro quo* arose. While the US president was thinking of intervention in Lebanon, Harold

Macmillan, believing that 'oil was in jeopardy', saw the Iraqi coup as a 'showdown' and viewed Lebanon as only one part in a wider military operation that would reach the Gulf, running all the way through Syria and Iraq. There was nothing surprising in this aggressive attitude toward the Syrian regime, as it was already known that Britain and the US were trying to topple it in 1957. But declassified British documents reveal that Prime Minister Macmillan and President Eisenhower approved in that year a CIA/MI6 plan to stage border incidents and even acts of sabotage in the neighbouring countries, which would be used as a pretext for Syria's neighours (Lebanon, Jordan, Iraq and Turkey) to invade Syria and topple its Ba`thi Leftist regime. To facilitate the execution of this plan, fomenting internal uprisings in Syria itself was envisaged and it was decided to physically eliminate key figures of that regime, namely `Abd al-Hamid al-Sarraj, head of military intelligence, `Afif al-Bizri, the chief of staff, and Khalid Bakdash, secretary-general of the Syrian Communist Party.[12]

Apart from Turkey, no neighbouring country agreed to participate in the Anglo-American plan. The following year, the Ba`thists and Nasserites moved against their Communist allies and pressurised `Abd al-Nasir to make a complete merger between Syria and Egypt or else the former would fall in the hands of the Communists. The US President referred to Congressional restraints concerning a large military operation and settled with Macmillan on American intervention in Lebanon and British intervention in Jordan to save the two remaining pro-Western regimes. On that same 14 July, Sham`un reiterated his request for a US military intervention within 48 hours, 'or else a second pro-western Arab regime will fall in its turn'. The US administration obliged in less than 24 hours.[13] On the afternoon of 15 July, while British troopers were landing in Amman airport, the first marines disembarked on the coast of Khaldeh, south of Beirut, and their tanks encircled the city, cannons pointing toward West Beirut. In the four days that followed, 15,000 American soldiers landed, backed by another 40,000 on the 70 warships of the US Navy's Sixth Fleet, in the first operation of its kind since the War.

Sham`un, who had believed the landing represented strategic support for him to achieve victory over his enemies, increased pressure on his commander-in-chief to occupy rebel neighbourhoods and 'clean up Beirut'. Shihab seemed more concerned with expressing his apprehension at the entry of a foreign army, albeit a friendly one, into his country's capital. On the following day, Robert Murphy, under-secretary of state and special presidential envoy, arrived in Beirut, tasked with finding a peaceful settlement to the crisis 'at any cost'. In the best tradition of gunboat diplomacy, Murphy sent a message to Sa'ib Salam that the firepower at his disposal could annihilate Basta in a few seconds. On the other hand, he amicably informed General Shihab in their first meeting that the aircraft carrier *Saratoga* anchored opposite the coast of Beirut was armed with nuclear warheads. It did not take much more talking to reach a compromise: American troops entered the Lebanese capital escorted by elements of the Lebanese army. The airport, occupied by the marines, was now safe from Junblat's partisans; the rebellion was practically contained and the American emissary could now look at a political solution.

It soon turned out that the Sixth Fleet came to Beirut to impose a successor to Sham`un rather than defend him against the rebellion. The choice of Fu'ad Shihab was not surprising, as many factors favoured him. His name had already been mentioned during the negotiations with `Abd al-Nasir, and he fulfilled the condition of Eisenhower, who wanted a military man. On 31 July 1958, parliament convened and elected Fu'ad Shihab with 48 votes, with ten Sham`un loyalists staying away. Raymond Iddi, who had presented his candidacy to protest at the election of a military man to the presidency, received seven votes.

On 23 September Sham`un left office at the end of his term, and Shihab was finally sworn in. The new president asked Rashid Karami, the leader of the rebellion in Tripoli, to form the new government. Karami duly unveiled an eight-man cabinet that was immediately judged to be too biased in favour of the opposition, especially since the prime minister had declared his government's intention to 'reap the fruits of the rebellion'. That same day saw the abduction of Fu'ad Haddad, editor-in-chief of the Phalangist daily *Al-`Amal*, known for his bitter diatribes against President `Abd al-Nasir. On the following day, a general strike observed in the Christian regions following a call by the Phalange Party, opened three weeks of armed conflict known as the 'counter-rebellion', which were characterised by sectarian clashes, kidnapping and violence in Beirut and the Mountain. The guns were silenced only after a four-man cabinet was formed, split between representatives of the loyalists and the rebels: Karami and `Uwayni for the Muslims and Pierre Jumayil and Raymond Iddi for the Christians, with reconciliation signalled by the slogan 'no victor and vanquished.'

By the end of October, the American troops had left the country.

9
Shihabism and the Difficult
Autonomy of the State (1958–1970)

The Lebanese State is but a pretext. It exists just enough to make the country into a fiscal paradise.

Philippe Simmonot, *Le Monde*, 29 October 1968

THE SHIHAB REFORMS

Fu'ad Shihab's personality and his political and social project dominated an entire decade of Lebanon's life, spanning two presidential mandates. The man had drawn many lessons from his job as commander of the army and from the experience of the 1958 rebellion. In direct contact with his NCOs and soldiers, who came mainly from the peripheries, he was conscious of the social and political effects of regional disparities, a factor that explained the ease with which people in those parts of Lebanon – Muslim in their majority – rose up in arms against the state and its legitimate authorities.

It was no surprise that Shihab would inaugurate his term with a meeting with President ʿAbd al-Nasir on the Lebanese–Syrian border. He followed a policy of neutrality in Arab politics, in contrast to Shamʿun's blatant anti-Nasir policies and pro-Western pacts, combined with close collaboration with the UAR, which included security. The UAR's ambassador in Beirut, ʿAbd al-Hamid Ghalib, soon enjoyed major influence in Lebanese politics.

Benefiting from a relative lull in inter-Arab tensions, Shihab directed his attention to the principal task of building 'the State of independence', assuming that the independence of the state had been achieved in 1943. The first two years of his mandate were devoted to defusing tensions, appeals for a return to national unity and the insistence on equality between the Lebanese, while the second phase was initiated by Shihab's speech on the eve of Independence Day on 21 November 1960. He called for 'comprehensive social reform' and the 'building of a new society'. The message was clear: 'those who benefited from prosperity should take care of the deprived Lebanese…

some should sacrifice and the others should be patient'. His version of Lebanese nationalism was unifying and egalitarian, for, said he, 'in being Lebanese there is no discrimination nor privilege'.

The major domestic political event of this period contributed to strengthening the regime, but involved seriously negative repercussions. On New Year's eve – the night of 31 December 1961/1 January 1962 – Lebanon experienced its first military *coup d'etat* when army units led by officers from the Syrian National Social Party (SNSP), backed by armed militias of the party, took over the Ministry of Defence, occupied officers' quarters and kidnapped a number of senior officers. The coup was foiled by loyal troops, however, and the rebel officers arrested. Internally, the coup was largely a reaction to the way the 1958 crisis was resolved: the SNSP, excluded from the solution that put an end to the fighting, felt that the crisis ended in an undeserved victory for the anti-Sham`un forces and an overstated influence of Nasserism in Lebanon. Regionally, there were serious suspicions that the SNSP's anti-Nasserite and anti-Communist coup was encouraged and even financed by the British and Jordanians desiring to form an anti-Nasser federation comprising Syria, Jordan, Lebanon and Iraq.[1]

The aborted *coup d'etat* rallied wide sectors of the public around Shihab, fed by Christian phobias about Greater Syria and by Muslim hostility against Sham`un (the SNSP's ally), a convergence that the regime did not fail to exploit. The authorities arrested some 12,000 suspects and put 300 of them on trial, while torture became a standard practice in detention centres and prisons. The SNSP coup gave the security agencies a golden opportunity to entrench themselves even more in Lebanese politics. Transforming itself into a new patronage network, the men of the famous *Deuxième bureau* – army intelligence – intervened in trade unions, rallied the *qabadays* (power brokers) in local neighbourhoods, controlled the carrying of arms and exploited the state of emergency in the border regions (in the south and the Biqa`) to impose firm control over Lebanese life.

In fact, the Shihab project sought to provide the country with an alternative political body by co-opting the armed protagonists of the events of 1958, using the army, the intelligence agencies and the technocrats. This meant displacing the centre of power again, from the legislature to the executive. A new electoral law, which readopted small electoral districts but increased the number of deputies, had two functions: to aid the return of the notables excluded during the 1957 elections, and to encourage the rise of new figures backed by the security agencies. A firm parliamentary majority gave extraordinary powers to the long cabinets of Rashid Karami to rule by decree-laws, without the need to refer to the legislature.

The creation of a parallel administration by resorting to independent services and agencies was one way of building a state sector without acknowledging it and isolating the bureaucracy from the encroachment of the 'political feudalists'. Thus the state administration doubled in size through the employment of some 10,000 new functionaries, vetted by a Civil Service Council and a Central Inspection Council, which limited the role of MPs in job patronage, reduced administrative corruption and favoured recruitment on the basis of merit and specialisation. In addition, the sectarian composition inside the administration was clearly modified in favour of the Muslim communities, and the Shiites in particular. Under Sham`un, the Maronites constituted 29 per cent of the population but held at least half of the administrative posts; by the end of Shihab's mandate they held no more than a third.[2]

Shihab contented himself with those measures without questioning political sectarianism as such. His constitutionalist approach was limited to establishing sectarian equilibrium rather than abolishing sectarianism. In effect, Shihab wanted to correct the failures of the sectarian system by injecting it with large doses of economic and social justice.

Economically, a rationalisation and regaining of control over the development of Lebanese capitalism was needed for two major reasons. One was the anarchic development of the economy during the 'boom' years under Sham`un, especially in the banking sector. The other was the change in the basis of the economy itself, from domination by the productive sector to that by the tertiary sector. In 1939 the productive sector yielded 50 per cent of national revenue; by the 1960s, that contribution had been slashed by half.

The principal task involved organising the banking sector, the bellwether sector of the economy. When the Banque de Syrie et du Liban's concession ended in 1964 the Banque du Liban (BDL) was established as the central bank. The Law on Credit and Currency, passed the year before, gave the BDL the right to issue currency, stabilise exchange rates of the Lebanese pound and, in general, direct economic performance. To achieve this, the BDL imposed on the banks a compulsory deposit in its safes in order to regulate the interest rate and act as a safety valve for helping banks in difficulty. The Law on Credit and Currency was violently contested by the liberal bourgeoisie although Shihab named Philippe Taqla, a banker and liberal politician from the Constitutionlists' ranks, to head the BDL.

On the other hand, labour relations were subject to strict regulation in the Law on Collective Labour Agreements, which organised the relations between the state, employers and employees and codified regulations on strikes. But Shihab's major social reform was the establishment of the National Social Security Fund (NSSF), largely inspired by the French model. Nevertheless, social conflicts were contained and the trade unions controlled by the intelligence agencies: there were practically no labour strikes during Shihab's mandate.[3]

The state played an active role in regional development and in the modification of the social distribution of economic growth. Sizeable funds were spent on building an economic infrastructure and unifying the domestic market via road construction and bringing water and electricity to remote villages – thus fuelling accusations that Shihab had depleted the treasury. Hospitals were built in rural areas and medical dispensaries in villages. Two major projects were carried out for agricultural development. The first was the building of a dam on the Litani river that irrigated large surfaces in the western Biqa` and allowed for the irrigation of southern Lebanon (this was never implemented because of the objection of the As`ads). The second was the ambitious Green Plan for clearing land for cultivation.

A favoured Shihabist reform was development of public education. In 1959, a law school was added to the Lebanese University, finally breaking the Jesuit University's monopoly on teaching that profession. Thus began the rapid development of the free, public Lebanese University (LU), where instruction was in Arabic. In addition, members of the middle and lower middle classes, attracted by the chance of social promotion, began sending their sons to European universities, benefiting from the strong position of the Lebanese pound. Others obtained grants to study in the universities of the Soviet Union and the countries of Eastern Europe.

Despite these reforms, three major interests were to coalesce against Shihab's programmes. First, a large section of the oligarchy, in both its Muslim and Christian factions, rejected any infringement on its rents and profits, in order to safeguard its mid- and long-range interests. Second, the 'political feudalists' reacted negatively against the new forms of patronage exercised by the Shihabist 'services' and to their own reduced influence in the administration. Third, Maronite autonomism was challenged by what appeared as the state's bias toward Muslims and by increased state intervention in society. In fact, these forces were bound by a common aversion to what constituted the salient character of the Shihab project, described by Waddah Sharara as 'the extension of the roots of the State into the heart of society and the founding of political domination on the ramparts and trenches of civil society'.[4]

At the vanguard of the ideological campaign against Shihabism was Ghassan Tuwayni's daily *Al-Nahar*, an influential forum of liberal, pro-Western opposition to Nasserism and socialism. It was practically the only newspaper that dared publish Raymond Iddi's fiery denunciations of Shihab and his regime. *Al-Nahar* had come by default to play the role of 'collective intellectual' of the bourgeoisie, speaking for a wide section of the professional middle classes and some of the intelligentsia.

Political opposition was mainly represented by Raymond Iddi, Kamil Sham`un and Sa'ib Salam. The latter, deprived of the premiership in favour of his northern rival, Rashid Karami, and frightened, like many among the Sunni bourgeoisie, by `Abd al-Nasir's nationalisations in Egypt in 1961, was tilting more toward Saudi Arabia. The opposition succeeded in linking political liberalism to economic liberalism, while still addressing Christian fears of Nasserism. Its chief target was the army's Deuxième bureau. In a stormy and memorable session of parliament on 23 June 1963, Raymond Iddi stood up against the marginalisation of the chamber and sniped against deputies for ceding their legislative rights to the executive. The MP for Jubayl accused the Deuxième bureau of exploiting the SNSP coup to extend police control over the country. Though only responsible for external security, that service interfered in domestic political life, the administration, legislative and municipal elections, distributed licences for carrying firearms and engaged in arbitrary arrests. Iddi denounced the 'self-censorship' of the Press Syndicate, imposed by an officer from the Deuxième bureau. Finally, the leader of the National Bloc accused the Phalange of backing all of the country's regimes at the beginning only to turn against them later. Commenting on the Phalangist call for abolishing the income tax, he said: 'At a time when socialism is at our doorstep, the Phalangists think of abolishing the only tax adopted by all the developed countries of the world in order to attain some measure of equality between rich and poor!'

On the other hand, the Shihab regime attracted those forces in society that shared an immediate interest in the building of a state:

a bourgeois faction that was either fighting against the monopoly powers of the 'consortium' or seeking political recognition and a place in the system; middle classes that had acceded to social mobility through Arab capital invested in Lebanon; large sectors of the petite bourgeoisie, including some intellectuals and many civil servants; and generally, the Muslim public.

The two main protagonists of 1958 – Jumayil's Phalange party and Junblat's PSP – constituted the social and political base of Shihab's regime. Junblat aimed at linking his marginalised and frustrated community with the pro-`Abd al-Nasir Sunni 'street', deprived of leadership after the defection of Sa'ib Salam. A recent convert to Nasserism – after having announced many reservations about the lack of democracy in the new Egyptian regime – Junblat saw in it a confirmation of his own socialistic ideas and in `Abd al-Nasir a strong and prestigious external ally. The Phalange's relationship to Shihabism was more problematic. Their presence in the executive for the first time confirmed them as a serious Christian political force and allowed them to provide services to an increasing number of clients; the big boost they received from the oppression that struck their main rival, the SNSP, and their traditional role as the surrogate force for the state and the army were among the many factors that attracted them to Shihabism. However, they were repulsed by Shihab's statism and the growing influence of `Abd al-Nasir in Lebanon, which went against their Maronite autonomism, their extreme Lebanese nationalism and their *laissez-faire*, anti-Nasserite and anti-Communist ideology. Whatever the case, both populist political forces were very keen to preserve their political positions, which allowed them to modify the balance of power inside their respective communities in their own favour.

Elections in the spring of 1964 gave a sweeping majority to the Shihabists. Money had played its role, largely dispensed by the sponsors of Shihabism (*parvenus* from emigration, arms dealers and contractors) and so did the strong-arm tactics of the Deuxième bureau. A few weeks later, a petition by 79 loyalist MPs called for the renewal of Shihab's mandate. A severe crisis broke out as the largely Christian opposition, led by Sham`un and Iddi, threatened to resort to a '1958 in reverse': just as the Muslims rebelled when the Christians sought to renew Sham`un's mandate in 1958, the Christians would rebel if the Muslims tried to renew Shihab's mandate. The crisis was defused on 17 August when Shihab announced that he had no intention of renewing his term of office. A compromise candidate was chosen in the person of Charles Hilu, who was elected with 92 votes against the votes of the Phalange bloc: Pierre Jumayil had presented his candidacy to distinguish himself and his party from both factions of the political elite.

DUALITIES AND DIVISIONS OF THE HILU REGIME

Charles Hilu was the first Lebanese president without a sizeable regional and popular base. A journalist and lawyer, and fervent disciple of Michel Chiha, he edited *Le Jour* before becoming Lebanon's first ambassador to the Vatican. Politically, he participated in the foundation of the Phalange and belonged to the Constitutionalist Bloc at the same time. Though those credentials were instrumental in bringing him to power as a compromise president, Hilu soon fell victim to the polarisation between the Shihabists (the *Nahj*) and their opponents (the *Hilf*) as well as the polarisation between the two populist parties that constituted the basis of the preceding regime, Pierre Jumayil's Phalange and Junblat's PSP. These 'dualities' and the reigning social and political divisions dominated his mandate.

Although Hilu dropped Rashid Karami as prime minister of his first cabinet, the Shihabists were still a majority in the chamber and firmly entrenched in the 'agencies' and the administration. In addition, Iliyas Sarkis, first lieutenant of the ex-president, was secretary of the presidency and Gaby Lahud, in his capacity as head of the army's Deuxième bureau and commander of the Unified Security Agency (which subjected all the security organisation to the army), attended all serious decision-making meetings, including those in which ministers were appointed.

Regionally, the Hilu regime corresponded to a period of intensification of the 'Arab cold war' between `Abd al-Nasir and his Saudi and conservative rivals.[5] While the former successfully managed Lebanon's fragile neutrality, the latter used their economic and financial means to press for Lebanon's decisive engagement with the Arab conservative camp, going as far as to threaten to abrogate the preferential commercial treaty between the two countries. The stakes were great, as no less than 40 per cent of the country's exports were destined for the oil kingdom.

Another burning issue was Israel's diversion of the waters of the Jordan river and Arab efforts to counter this. `Ali `Ali `Amir, the Egyptian commander-in-chief of the Unified Arab Command, considered introducing Arab troops (mainly Egyptian) under his command into Lebanon, to reinforce that part of the Northern Front. Philippe Taqla, the minister of foreign affairs, objected in Lebanon's name, arguing that the presence of these troops would become a pretext for Israeli aggression against his country. A compromise elaborated by ʿAbd al-Nasir and Hilu deferred the military deployment and admitted Lebanon's right to submit any decision of the Council of Arab Defence for prior approval in its parliament. Nevertheless, for the first time since signing the armistice, Lebanon was being confronted by its obligations toward the Arab–Israeli conflict. Its traditional policy, based on the motto that 'Lebanon's strength lies in its weakness', would be severely tested in coming years.

SOCIAL MOVEMENTS IN THE POLITICAL QUAGMIRE

In economic policy, Hilu was keen to reassure the anti-statist oligarchy. Conceding that free enterprise was a necessary but not sufficient condition for a sound economic policy, he maintained that the role of the state should be limited to building the infrastructure for the development of the services sector. He nevertheless concluded that 'the Lebanese businessman is more enterprising and a better administrator than his government'.[6] To back this role of the state, Hilu got parliament to approve on 22 November 1965 an ambitious development plan for LL 272 million, which included the building of popular housing units, clinics, laboratories, technical schools and a university campus for the LU, among others – a diluted form of Shihabist developmentalism and planification.[7] Ebbs and flows in economic and social choices would last throughout his mandate. But in the short term, at stake were the problems left unsettled by the Shihab reforms and the impressive rebirth of the social movement frozen under the former president.

A nearly uninterrupted series of strikes and protest movements unfolded in the period leading up to the June 1967 war. In the autumn of 1964, employees of the oil sector, public transport, the electricity company and of the central bank forced the General Workers Union in Lebanon (GWUL) to threaten a general strike if their demands were not met: a wage increase and a rise in the minimum wage. Parliament reacted in a manner that would become chronic: it decreed an 8 per cent wage increase for workers and a 20 per cent salary increase for the deputies!

This took place during Husayn ʿUwayni Cabinet, nicknamed the 'millionaires' government,[8] which had, upon the suggestion of the

US administration, tabled a draft law guaranteeing foreign capital investments in Lebanon. Had the law been adopted, it would have allowed the governments of Europe and the US to represent their nationals in the collection of debts and settlement of disputes. But a campaign launched by leftist and nationalist parties against the legislation, led by the PSP, the LCP and the Arab Nationalist Movement (ANM), managed to foil the plans.

The social movement continued unabated despite the wage increase. First, the trade union movement opposed the 1964 law on Collective Labour Agreements, which imposed obligatory arbitration of 15 days in labour disputes and curtailed the right to strike. The second and more important conflict revolved around the National Social Security Law, passed at the end of Shihab's mandate in September 1963. Employers were sabotaging the law that came into effect in April 1965 by launching a massive wave of worker dismissals to evade paying the social security fees. The working class thus found itself in a vicious circle: what they won in terms of social services was lost in terms of job security, as article 50 of the Labour Code, which allowed 'arbitrary dismissal', hung over them like the sword of Damocles. In the summer of 1966, public sector workers went on strike and imposed a 6.8 per cent wage increase and a rise in the monthly minimum wage from LL 145 to 175.

In education, primary school teachers went on strike, demanding a salary increase and a rise in the cost of living premium, but were forced back to school under a government threat to consider them all as having resigned. Law students at the Arab University and the LU also resorted to a strike to force the recognition of their law degrees and their right to practise the profession.

The extent and gravity of the social struggles were such that they required a new definition of national unity, which became 'the unity of all the social classes that compose the Lebanese people', according to Prime Minister ʿAbd Allah al-Yafi.

But these years were dominated mostly by the crisis in agribusiness. Peasants and farmers launched a countrywide movement in opposition to the monopolies in agro-industries and to the exploitation of small and middle-level producers by the commercial/financial network. In the south, the tobacco planters refused to deliver their product to the *Régie* unless better terms of sale were agreed upon.[9] In the Biqaʿ, thousands of beetroot planters were in conflict with the sugar factory, the industrial monopoly and sole buyer of their product, and vegetable producers rose up against brokers and middlemen who tripled the price of their produce when selling to consumers. Some 60 per cent of Mount Lebanon's farmers were apple cultivators, who were objecting to the high costs of production (including cold storage and distribution) and the control by middlemen over the price of the products. In February 1965, the farmers' unions of the Matn, Shuf, `Alay and North Lebanon jointly called for a set of actions that were intended to end with a general strike.

In August of that year, in solidarity with the agrarian movement, which had failed to attract the attention of the authorities, a big popular rally of the planters of fruit trees was organised by the Left (the PSP, LCP, ANM) in addition to trade unionists and independent figures. In Btikhnay, in the *Caza* of `Alay, Kamal Junblat read the list of farmers' demands, which went to the heart of the malaise: commercial monopoly.[10] The Phalange's reaction was not long in coming. In a press communiqué on 8 August 1965, Pierre Jumayil accused the organisers of the Btikhnay rally of being foreign-inspired and seeking to destabilise the economy, whose prosperity was unfavourable to the propagation of Junblat's socialist ideas. Jumayil joined Majid Arsalan, Junblat's traditional Druze rival, to organise a counter-rally in which the speakers, putting aside agricultural problems, outbid each other in their profession of faith in the merits of free enterprise and their attacks on 'destructive socialism', a term they replaced by … 'socialism *à la libanaise*'.

SCAPEGOATS AND THE 'SPECTRE OF MARX'

In the autumn of 1965 the Maronite religious brotherhoods raised the question of the Karantina (Quarantine) shantytown, built on the 'property of others' in the eastern suburb of Beirut. Soon the Maronite League took up the issue and convened a 'national congress' in which voices were raised accusing the state of 'selling out Lebanon', and resolutions were passed demanding a ban on the sale of landed property to 'foreigners'. The link was being made between two elements not so easily assimilable: those who bought landed property were the rich Arabs of the Gulf and Saudi Arabia, while the Karantina dwellers were poor Lebanese with a minority of Syrians and non-naturalised Kurds. In any event, the campaign opened the wider issue of the presence of 'foreigners' in Lebanon (Palestinians and Syrians in particular), and voices were raised against the widespread granting of Lebanese nationality to 'outsiders'.[11] In successive and rapid slippages, the connection was made between 'poor' and 'strangers'. The scapegoat had been found. Father Sim`an Duwayhi, MP for Zughurta, in a speech in parliament, called for a census of those 'miserable' individuals who constituted a 'source of corruption, petrifaction and illness that saps the moral, human and spiritual values of Lebanon'. Duwayhi went on to denounce the decrease in the number of Lebanese owing to emigration and the increase in the number of illegal immigrants. For those 'miserable' were the strangers who 'spread among us, Lebanese, epidemics from those hotbeds of contagion and slums deposited, in all their noisiness, on the heart of our capital'. All strangers confounded were lumped together and accused of 'snatching the piece of bread from the mouth of the Lebanese'; whether they were 'miserable' shantytown dwellers or 'those who take our banking secrets and sell them to the first customer for profit's sake'.[12] The last insinuation was barely veiled: it concerned the biggest bank in Lebanon, Intra Bank, directed by Yusuf Baydas, a Palestinian Christian of whom we shall hear more later. Pierre Jumayil, in his capacity as minister of interior, obtained the cabinet's approval for a law, hurriedly passed in parliament, that banned the sale of landed property to non-Lebanese. Commenting on the parliamentary discussion of a new rent law, *Al-`Amal* opened fire on the 'intruders' and diverted attention from high rents, and the existence of 10,000 unrented luxury flats in Beirut alone, to a denunciation of the existence of tents, huts, tin-roofed shanties and refugee camps!

Thus, the country's problems were exteriorised: poverty was attributed to strangers and social problems seen as manifestations of a 'foreign' conspiracy aiming at destabilising the economy! Under the title 'Marx is on our doorsteps', *Al-`Amal*'s leader writer warned his readers that Syria was becoming the 'Middle Eastern Cuba' and that 'international communism' was the party pulling the strings in Cairo, as well as Damascus or Baghdad. In order to confront this danger, the Phalangist daily called for no less than 'national resistance':

... when Communism is knocking at Lebanon's doors from the borders of Maysalun and Wadi al-Harir, it becomes our duty to mobilise all the vital forces of the Nation to stop this dangerous invasion and save Lebanon as it is, and it should remain for ever: a citadel of freedom and a haven of security, stability and prosperity.[13]

'Marx is inside the borders', reminded Jibran Hayik in the editorial of his afternoon daily *Lisan al-Hal*, embodied by poverty in 'some Lebanese regions', huge inequalities between rich and poor and unemployment and vagrancy, all aggravated by the failure of government, its carelessness and lack of foresight. Hayik concluded with a solemn appeal to officials to deal with these problems with the greatest lucidity or else 'the Marx of the interior will rise up to assassinate democracy in collaboration with the Syrian Marx and other Marxs'.[14]

THE INTRA BANK CRASH

While the bourgeois press was exorcising the spectre of Marx, a real malaise was striking the heart of the Lebanese economy. On 14 October 1966 Intra Bank was declared insolvent, plunging the economy into one of its most serious crises since independence and signalling the drying up of the prosperity the country had enjoyed during the two previous decades.

Yusuf Baydas had built an impressive financial empire. His bank, the biggest and strongest of the banks with Lebanese and Arab capital, had acquired international stature for attracting a big share of the influx of Arab capital into Lebanon and for investing in the Arab world and Africa in association with émigré capital. The Intra group controlled a number of the country's major companies: the Compagnie du port de Beyrouth, Middle East Airlines, Radio Orient (the ex-franchise-holding French company) and eight others in property development (including the Société immobilière libanaise, the owner of the luxury Phœnicia Hotel), services, tourism and industry. Intra also financed the government's infrastructure and transactions such as the import of wheat. Overseas, the group had substantial investments in property in France (including the Champs Elysées), controlling shares in the naval docks of La Ciotat, and a number of small banks in Switzerland. Yusuf Baydas's bank was particularly proud of the high number of its small depositors, some 19,000 accounts. These individuals would be the biggest victims of the crash.

The Intra Bank crash expressed a tendency for the reduction of the intermediary role of the Lebanese financial sector in favour of more direct relations between the two poles of that mediation: the oil-producing countries of the Gulf, on the one hand, and the Western financial centres, on the other. It was no secret that the financial powers in the West had raised interest rates and even employed direct political pressure in order to encourage direct investment and deposits in their capitals. But the bank's solvency crisis resulted from a deeper cause: the contradiction between its mainly short-term deposits and its long-term investments, especially in property. Indeed the crisis revealed the adventurism and speculative character of the new bourgeois faction linked to Shihabism, represented by Baydas and his associates. A great portion of the favours that Intra benefited from were provided by the Deuxième bureau, in return for which the bank financed elections, distributed cash gifts in the guise of loans, employed clients of Shihabist notables and paid bribes of all types.

Nevertheless, when the bank stopped payment, its assets greatly surpassed its liabilities. Recent research and revelations tend to point out that the bank was most probably 'sunk' by a governmental decision to not 'float' it, under pressure from the traditional oligarchy linked to Western financial capital. Yusuf Baydas, who was in Europe when the crisis broke out, spoke of his 'national bourgeois' project, which was sabotaged by the agents of Western interests.

In the immediate fallout of the Intra crash were the bankruptcy of a number of local banks and capital flight. Between 30 September and 14 October 1966, LL 18.6 million was withdrawn from 20 Lebanese banks and reinvested abroad.

The Lebanese ruling class was seized with panic while its various factions traded accusations over responsibility for the crash. Kamil Sham`un, who declared the end of Lebanon as 'the Switzerland of the Orient', condemned the 'adventurist policy of Intra Bank', inaugurating a campaign to put the blame for the crash on the Shihabists. A more upbeat approach tried to raise morale on the state of the economy, all the while settling accounts with the statism of the Shihabists.

This was the case of *al-Nahar* and its talented editor Michel Abu-Jawda, whose first reaction to the crash was to call for endowing Lebanon with a 'capitalist state' on the model of those of Europe and the United States.[15] When the Shihabist Rashid Karami was recalled to form a new government of technocrats, Abu-Jawda saluted him as a representative of the 'intelligent Right' and charged him with the task of building the 'intelligent free economy'.[16] But the financial scandals revealed by the Intra crash – and the arrest of a number of the banks' major shareholders and Shihabist politicians – split the ruling class to the point that Abu-Jawda forgot all reform projects and launched a vibrant appeal to the 'hundred families that govern the country to stop betraying each other and safeguard their unity'.[17]

'The Miracle, shall we make it ourselves?'[18] was the theme of an ardent editorial by Ghassan Tuwayni for *al-Nahar*'s 1967 yearly supplement, in which he attacked statism and insisted that the

Miracle was and always would be the achievement of the Lebanese individual, 'who is stronger than his government, more lucid, more patient, and more resourceful and farsighted... the Lebanese barely needs government, as government can only bridle him and paralyse his efficiency'.

Tuwayni went on to establish a number of basic principles highly representative of the ideology of the Lebanese ruling class in socio-economic matters. Denying the existence of big fortunes in Lebanon, since the Lebanese 'fructify money that is not theirs, and the exception confirms the rule', he admited that a 'temporary class war' had recently erupted in Lebanon. However, its danger lay not in the social inequalities it revealed – as those hardly existed – but in the effects of the 'scrambling up on the ladder of wealth' practised in the same manner by all classes: by 'over-indebtedness and spending (beyond their means)'. The danger in that 'scrambling up on the ladder of wealth' was that it 'abolishes the real differences between rich and poor' and creates 'physical and mental gaps' that separate the Lebanese. That is why, Tuwayni continued, all classes of Lebanese society were to be held responsible for the 'suicidal turn' that economic and social relations had recently taken. The labouring classes, 'be they rich or poor [sic] ... try hard to hate the only regime that allows them to aspire to more wealth', whereas the rich classes – 'whether their wealth is mere appearance or real' – 'are governed by fear, which prompts them to export their money or shy away from investment'.

For all of these reasons, there was no historical basis for Right or Left in Lebanon. The country's future would be made by the 'partnership in wealth rather than in the generalisation of poverty and depravation'. As for the role of the state, it was to 'create the adequate legal context for prosperity and transform the budget and fiscal policy into means of development and justice'. This was the condition for developing trust between the individuals and the state. Tuwayni concluded by suggesting that 1967 be declared the year for achieving the 'partnership in prosperity between Money and Labour', a partnership that amounted to the Miracle that people would perform themselves.

On a different level, the Intra crisis was the occasion for the Muslim faction of the oligarchy and the political class to reiterate its demand for a greater share in political power and decision-making. `Aliya' al-Sulh, daughter of Riyad, wrote in *Al-Nahar* that the socio-economic privileges of the Christians had always been the source of all the country's crises, while Sa'ib Salam revisited the question of parity in sectarian representation between Christians and Muslims (to replace the 6/5 ratio) and called for a 'constituent assembly' to revise the National Pact of 1943.

The politicisation of the crisis involved the settling of accounts between the different factions of the bourgeoisie and the ruling class. Rare were the voices that asked about the responsibility by the regime and its men for the crisis. Reform projects were plentiful but the only one that attracted attention was a project for administrative reform initiated before the Intra crisis. It was nevertheless sunk in the infighting between the factions of the ruling class, and ended in October 1966 in a partial laying off of a small number of high functionaries.

Instead of being the year of the 'partnership in prosperity' between rich and poor, 1967 became the year of the crisis of the partnership of the ruling class altogether, as official Lebanon faced the watershed Six Day war.

PLO, SECURITY AND POLARISATION

The June 1967 war plunged Lebanon into the Arab–Israeli conflict, which it had sought to evade for so long. The physical incarnation of that involvement was the entry of Palestinian *fida'iyin* to its territory and their accelerated implantation in the south, where they launched their raids against the Jewish state, triggering a policy of Israeli military retaliations that escalated to 'preventive strikes', which transformed the southern part of the country into a battlefront for years to come.

At first, the Palestinian commandos established their bases in the `Arqub region along the Syrian–Lebanese borders, baptised 'Fatahland' by the Western press and the Israeli military. It should be said that the *fida'iyin* were favourably welcomed by a population shocked by the Arab defeat of 1967, during which the Lebanese army contented itself with defending foreign embassies and the headquarters of British and American oil companies in Beirut from an angry population. Young Lebanese joined their ranks and the death of Khalil Jamal, the first Lebanese martyr (*shahid*), was the occasion for a massive and moving demonstration in Beirut in support of the PLO. In the south, the armed Palestinian presence acquired a domestic function as a large part of the population found in it a recourse against two alien forces:

the traditional leadership of the As`ads, on the one hand, and the iron hand of the Shihabist 'agencies', on the other.

The government was initially complicit with the establishment of *fida'iyin* bases in the south, but soon found itself facing the hammer of the Israeli military and the anvil of Syrian pressure. The latter took the form of closures of the Syrian–Lebanese borders and economic sanctions. On 1 March 1968, the first of a series of armed clashes between the army and the *fida'iyin* took place.

On the other hand, with `Abd al-Nasir's astounding defeat in the June 1967 war, the inter-Arab balance of power started tipping, slowly but surely, in favour of the Saudi-led conservative camp. The repercussion for Lebanon was the formation of the Tripartite Alliance (*al-Hilf al-Thulathi*) by Sham`un, Iddi and Jumayil against 'Nasserism, Communism and Zionism'. In April 1969, the *Hilf* registered a substantial victory in the parliamentary elections resulting in a parliament divided between the *Hilf* and the *Nahj*. In internal politics, the campaign against 'strangers', the first reactions to the armed Palestinian presence and the increasing hostility of large sections of Christian public opinion to the Shihab 'security agencies', contributed to that electoral victory. In October 1968, Hilu, hoping to profit from all these changes, submitted his resignation as a means of pressure on the *Nahj* and 'services'. He withdrew it after having received the support of the *Hilf* and imposed `Abd Allah al-Yafi as prime minister with a four-man government from which the *Nahj*-ists were excluded. Non-Shihabist moderate Muslims (Yafi himself and Husayn `Uwayni) sat with two leaders of the *Hilf*, Raymond Iddi and Pierre Jumayil.

Hilu's bias toward the *Hilf* was cut short by the first crisis on the presence of the Palestinian resistance. On 28 December 1968, 13 Middle East Airlines planes were destroyed on the ground by an Israeli commando unit as retaliation for the hijacking of an El-Al plane to Athens claimed by George Habash's Popular Front for the Liberation of Palestine (PFLP). Caught between popular anger at the state's inability to defend its own airport, on the one hand, and the accusations of the *Hilf* that he was encouraging Palestinian armed presence, on the other, Yafi resigned. Hilu placed the army command in charge of internal security and designated Rashid Karami, leader of the Shihabist bloc, to head a new government. All that Karami could do was ask parliament to recognise the right of the Palestinians to armed struggle. But not everybody was ready to accept this solution. On 23 April 1969, the army opened fire at a massive demonstration in solidarity with the Palestinian resistance in Sidon and Beirut, leaving a number of dead and wounded. The violent reactions to the army's behaviour – especially in his home town, Tripoli – prompted Karami to resign. He was charged to form a new government and declare a state of emergency; but the country plunged into a ministerial and political crisis that would last for 215 days.

At the end of September, after a series of confrontations with the resistance, the army launched a last attempt to control the situation. Syria reacted by closing its borders with Lebanon and imposing a number of severe economic sanctions. The crisis was temporarily resolved with the signature, on 8 November 1969, of the Cairo Accords by Yasir `Arafat, soon to be elected PLO chairman, and General Emile Bustani, commander-in-chief of the Lebanese army, under the patronage of President `Abd al-Nasir. The accords, whose terms were kept secret at the time, were quickly ratified in parliament behind closed doors. Only Raymond Iddi and his parliamentary group voted against the accord, which they viewed as an infringement on Lebanese sovereignty. The accord recognised the armed *fida'iyin*'s right to be present on and move around Lebanese territory, especially to and from the `Arqub region, and provided a form of extra-territoriality for the Palestinian camps, long under the heavy hand of the Lebanese security services, and recognised a Higher Palestinian Commission, headed by a Palestinian veteran Shafiq al-Hut, as a *de facto* Palestine embassy in Lebanon.

With the Syrian borders finally opened, Karami formed a government of national unity on 26 November 1969 with Kamal Junblat as minister of the interior, responsible for applying the Cairo Accords. But the crisis had already consummated the break between the Muslim 'street' and the 'services', and constituted the founding act for the alliance between the nationalist and leftist parties and the PLO.

Junblat and Jumayil, who had alternated in occupying the post of minister of interior, each presented his security policy to a divided ruling class and a hesitant bourgeoisie, while waging his own struggle to put an end to the power of the Shihabist 'services'. Junblat proposed separating the security services from the army (a measure mainly directed at Gaby Lahud's Common Security Agency), the abolition of military zones, in the south and the Hirmil region – which were pretexts for the Shihabist services to reinforce their political control over those regions – and the reorganisation of the Palestinian presence on the basis of the Cairo Accords. In so doing,

Junblat – who accused the Deuxième bureau of seeking to liquidate the Palestinian presence in Lebanon – presented himself as a mediator between the Lebanese state and the PLO in return for reforms and an enhanced share of political power for the Muslims. Pierre Jumayil responded by demanding that all of Lebanon be declared a military zone and reiterated his desire to see a 'benevolent despot' rule the country.[19]

In September 1970, Sulayman Franjiyeh, a member of the Centrist group with Sa'ib Salam and Kamil al-As`ad, backed by the *Hilf*, was elected president against the Shihabist candidate Elias Sarkis. He owed his one-vote edge to Junblat, who had rallied the opponents of the Deuxième bureau. His last act as minister of interior was to legalise the nationalist and leftist parties: the LCP, the Arab Nationalist Movement (ANM), the SNSP and the pro-Iraqi Ba`th.

At the end of the Hilu regime, the bourgeoisie, shocked and its unity threatened by the fallout of the Intra Bank crash and the political divisions between *Hilf* and *Nahj*, managed to rebuild some measure of understanding concerning economic policies and the role of the state in the economy. The opposition dropped its call for the abolition of the Central Bank and the Civil Service Council, but tried to curtail the state's role in the economy. As for social security, the conflicts shifted to confrontations between employers and employees. Nevertheless, new divisions threatened the reconstituted unity in the socio-economic field. As seen above, the contradictory reactions to the social crisis and to the Palestinian armed presence destabilised the very foundations of Shihabism by dividing its social base represented by the two 'populist' components: the Phalange party, on the one hand, and Junblat and the nationalist and leftist parties, on the other. But these were also the parties that were the more representative of the petty bourgeoisie and the middle classes, classes that also constituted the social base of the Lebanese system.

They would become the protagonists of the 1975 civil wars.

10
From Social Crisis to Civil War
(1968–1975)

If it were again a question of the liberal economy in which the strong oppresses and exploits the weak, if it were the case of the prosperity of the tiny capitalist minority and of bourgeois society, if the Lebanese Miracle should continue to express itself in terms of improvisation, approximation, lack of foresight, invisible revenues and non taxable returns, if it were finally the case of the Lebanon of the privileged few, we shall quickly see the positive security of the majority threatened by the gravest of dangers and face a catastrophe from which Lebanon will not stand up again.

Grégoire Haddad, Greek Catholic archbishop of Beirut, 1975

The Intra Bank crash inaugurated a tendency that would manifest itself fully in the 1970s: the rise in interest rates in Europe and the USA and the strong pressures on the rulers and the rich of the Gulf and Saudi Arabia had succeeded in attracting petrodollars to be deposited and invested in Western capitals. This development would henceforth make Lebanon into a 'place' for recycling petrodollars toward Western networks. The result further subjected the economy to foreign capital, while exaggerating its monopolistic structure and strengthening the domination of the commercial/financial complex.

MONOPOLISTIC 'LAISSEZ-FAIRE'

By 1969, non-Arab foreign banks already controlled 40 per cent of bank deposits in Lebanon. Five years later, this percentage had doubled. By 1970, a third of the Lebanon's joint stock companies (SARLs) and 20 per cent of limited liability companies (SALs) with mixed capital had become branches of foreign companies.[1]

It should be noted that this outward-looking function of banks had an adverse impact on the country's economic development. Although banks operating in Lebanon possessed an impressive monetary mass, which exceeded LL 6 billion, they contributed very meagrely to the development of the country's productive sectors. Their major operations involved speculation in foreign currency and bonds in Europe and the US (LL 2 billion in 1970), commercial short-term loans (60 per cent of total bank loans in 1971) and international long-term loans to the Régie Renault in France, the Indian government and even the World Bank.

The commercial/financial oligarchy continued to dominate the economy. According to a survey carried out in 1973, 41 of a total of 800 families controlled the majority of shares in 103 joint stock companies in trade and services (a third of the total), accounting for 70 per cent of their turnover.[2] Five families among those controlled half of the country's import/export trade.[3] Five agents of European and American companies controlled 22 per cent of the market for the exports of these countries, and 20 merchants controlled 85 per cent of the import of food products. Four of those families belonged to the 'consortium'. Furthermore, commercial monopoly was legally enshrined in law decree no. 134 of August 1967, which limited commercial representation of foreign companies to an exclusive agent.

However, the salient characteristic of this period was the rising encroachment by the commercial/financial complex on industry and agriculture. In the banking sector, 57 family 'holdings' – representing 32 per cent of the total – controlled 72 per cent of the capital of the industrial SARLs, 75 per cent of the deposits in Lebanese banks, 52 per cent of the capital of the SARLs in trade, agriculture and services, 64 per cent of the capital of the insurance companies, 71 per cent of the capital of transport companies, 92 per cent of the capital of financial joint stock companies and 37 per cent of the capital of property companies.[4]

A dependent industrial mediation

During the post-Intra years Lebanon witnessed rapid industrial growth. The industrial share of GDP rose from 14 to 18 per cent and investments in that sector grew from LL 987 million in 1966 to LL 1,234 million in 1970. Closely related to foreign capital investments, this expansion followed the logic of the recuperation of petrodollars by Western capital. Thus, multinationals came to directly control existing industries or established processing industries for their own products in Lebanon, producing mainly for Arab markets. Interestingly, the majority of these new industrial firms were financed by loans from Lebanese banks.

It should be noted that industrial growth depended heavily on the intensive employment of labour. Numbers of industrial workers nearly doubled in ten years, from 65,000 workers in 1965 to 120,000 when the war broke out.

Four major effects of this boom should be noted. First, as half of the domestic market had already been ceded to imported goods, foreign capital competed with local industry for the other half and for Arab markets (exports to Arab markets accounted for 80 per cent of total Lebanese exports, 40 per cent of which were destined for Saudi Arabia alone). Second, the external dependence of the industrial sector was aggravated by the rise in imports of raw materials and the payment of various royalties and licences. This led to a third result, namely that exports increased at a much slower rate than the increase in imports, and the deficit in the balance of trade shot up to LL 1.5 billion, four times the volume of exports. Fourth, industrial growth gave rise to a double concentration: in the volume of industrial firms (50 per cent of the enterprises employed more than 187 workers) and in the share of industrial firms in production (20 enterprises produced half of total industrial production in 1973).[5]

The crisis of agriculture

For its part, agriculture was invaded by the financial/commercial complex, which controlled direct producers through credit, prices, the sale of insecticides, fertilisers, agricultural machinery and tools, the packing and refrigeration industries and, finally, distribution. Here, concentration was no different from that in other sectors. Twenty-five brokers who also owned the main refrigerated storehouses controlled two-thirds of the market for apples; 20 brokers controlled 81 per cent of the market for citrus fruits (three of whom controlled a third of the market), and two firms practically controlled the imports of insecticides and fertilisers.[6]

By the 1970s, share-cropping had practically disappeared. Despite the development of relatively large capitalist farms using salaried workers, the better part of agricultural production was still coming from relatively small family-based units that nevertheless increasingly resorted to Syrian agricultural workers. Between those two poles developed two hybrid forms of production. One, prevalent in the Biqa`, was a capitalist form of share-cropping: according to a yearly contract between a number of small land-owning farmers and a capitalist entrepreneur, the latter would provide credit, grain, pesticides and the use of machinery and pumps in return for a share of the harvest. The other form tied thousands of farmers and peasants to agribusiness monopolies. This was the case of hundreds of families of beetroot farmers in the Biqa`, producing for the benefit of one sugar factory at `Anjar and the 45,000 tobacco producers in the predominantly Shi`i south (and also in the Maronite districts of Jubayl and Batrun) producing for the tobacco monopoly, the *Régie*.

However, commercial/financial control over agriculture followed the same logic as that of its control over industry since larger portions of the local market for agricultural products had already been taken over by importers (only 15 per cent of food consumption was being locally produced), and agricultural production was driven to produce for external markets (two-thirds of exports were fruit and poultry products).[7]

Debts and exploitation by merchants, moneylenders, banks and suppliers of machinery, fertilisers and pesticides forced small farmers to leave for the cities and overseas at an accelerated pace. Half of the Lebanese population made their living from agriculture at the end of the 1950s but, by 1975, only 20 per cent remained engaged in that sector. Agriculture had lost some 100,000 active members in barely two decades.[8]

SOCIAL CONSEQUENCES

Demographic and social mobility

Since its attachment to the world market, Lebanon has been characterised by a demographic flux in which rural migration and emigration carry out a permanent reconstruction of the country's social stratification. Emigration is the process by which Lebanese society hides its high rates of unemployment and rids itself of the human surplus. It developed at an average rate of 8,566 per year for the years 1960–70 and rose to 10,000 for the years 1970–74. The share of émigré remittances of GNP showed dramatic growth, rising from 5.38 per cent in 1951 to 30 per cent in 1974. While the local labour force was exported, non-Lebanese labour was brought in to replace those who left, or those who refused to be reduced to wage labour. Before the war, Syrian workers in Lebanon already constituted the majority of agricultural workers and a high percentage of construction workers.

On the other hand, many of the returnee émigrés had been elevated to middle-class status or even joined the ranks of the bourgeoisie, bolstering in both cases the dominant sectors of the economy by investing principally in commerce, finance and property. Social promotion acquired by political rent and work abroad spilled directly into politics, for it was principally through politics that the socially promoted hoped to obtain social distinction. Contemporary Lebanon became a country in which middle- and high-income *nouveaux riches* constituted a large part of the middle and upper classes. The dialectics of wealth/honour were implanted in the heart of social relations and regulated the relationship between the political and the social.

High cost of living

The increasingly outward-looking nature of the economy, the absence of any price controls to check merchants' lust for profits and monopoly control directly impacted on the standards of living of the majority of Lebanese. Between 1967 and 1975 the cost of living had doubled,[9] and during this time Beirut had been classified as more expensive than Washington. In one year, 1972–73, the price of imported goods rose by 10–15 per cent despite the fact that the Lebanese pound had registered a net rise compared to the US dollar and sterling. The only possible explanation for this was the arbitrary decision-making by importers and middlemen, opined Marwan Iskandar, a liberal conservative economist. He went on to add that the market price of imported meat was eight to ten times more than its purchase price c.i.f. Beirut and that the price of agricultural products in Saudi Arabia (imported from Lebanon) was 40 per cent lower than in Lebanon! The same could be said for the high prices of pharmaceutical products, medicine and hospitalisation, determined by monopoly control and by the extroverted orientation of medical services, to satisfy the needs of the rich of the Gulf.

Property speculation – the main form of investment by the commercial/financial oligarchy, the Gulf sheikhs and the émigrés – raised the price of land and imposed the construction of luxury apartment buildings. In the 'forest of stone' that Beirut had become, rent gobbled up no less than 40 per cent of family budgets, while low-cost public housing, promised for so long in ministerial speeches, never materialised. On the eve of the war, there were between 40,000 and 50,000 empty luxury apartments in Beirut alone, while successive waves of migrants from the rural areas crammed into shantytowns and squats and ravaged entire suburbs.

Class, sectarian and regional inequalities

On the eve of the 1967 war Lebanon's social structure was one of small-scale privileges and distinctions produced by patronage and the sectarian system, along with large-scale class privileges and divisions.

The majority of the Lebanese had no more than 12–15 per cent of national income.[10] Bishop Gregoire Haddad wrote that 79 per cent of the Lebanese received less than the minimum income, estimated by him at LL 10,480/month.[11] Meanwhile, 72 per cent of the workers did not earn more than LL 561/month,[12] and the official minimum wage increased only from LL 205 to LL 310 between 1970 and 1975.

Despite the ambitious Shihab reforms, great disparities persisted between centre and periphery. While the annual per capita revenue in Beirut was estimated at $803, it was $151 in south Lebanon. Beirut and the surrounding Mount Lebanon totalled 64 per cent of private primary and complementary educational institutions, 73 per cent of those in secondary education and the entirety of university teaching. In the early 1970s, 65 per cent of all medical doctors lived and worked in Beirut, which accounted for 27 per cent of the population; 5.5 per cent were in the south for 18 per cent of the population, and only 3 per cent in the Biqa', where 13 per cent of the Lebanese lived.[13]

Beirut's 'poverty belt'

Rapid urbanisation surrounded Beirut with a 'poverty belt' stretching from Karantina in the east to Raml al-`Ali and Laylaki neighbourhoods in the west, between which lay a number of villages that had been rapidly transformed into the poor and working-class suburbs of Judaydeh, Sin al-Fil, Mudawar, Burj Hammud, Nab`a, Dikwaneh, in the east bordering Nahr Beyrut, and Ghubayri, `Ayn al Rummaneh, Shiyah, Harit Hurayk, Burj al Barajineh and Murayjeh, stretching to the airport. The 'belt' was punctuated by the Palestinian camps of Tall al-Za`tar in the east, and Mar Iliyas, Sabra, Shatila and Burj al-Barajineh, further to the west. Some 400,000 out of a total population of Beirut that had attained one million lived in these neighbourhoods, which mushroomed within two decades, swelled by rural migrants who were victims of the collapse of share-cropping and the crisis of agriculture. But this rapid urbanisation was considerably accelerated by additional factors: the collapse of the economy of Jabal 'Amil and the Southern Biqa` after the creation of the state of Israel in 1948 and those displaced by Israeli retaliation for *fida'iyin* operations against the villages of the south.

Although it primarily served the industrial locations of Mukallis in the east and Shuwayfat in the west, the 'poverty belt' was also the location for a mass of sub-proletarians, whether members of a growing 'informal' artisan and manufacturing sector or simply masses of unemployed. The inhabitants were mixed. While Harit Hurayk and Murayjeh, in the west, were still nearly exclusively Christian, the eastern suburb had become home to some 250,000 Shi`a in the mainly Armenian neighbourhoods of Burj Hammud, Nab`a, and in Dikwaneh, the latter surrounding Tall al-Za`tar Palestinian camp. But the most impressive process of urbanisation concerned the Shi`a. While most of the community was rural in the post-independence years, more than three-quarters of it had become urbanised by the 1970s.

Those were not the *favelas* of Rio de Janiero, but their high density per square mile, squatting, very poor sanitary and health conditions, scarce water supply and stolen electricity, made these suburbs breeding grounds for the populist parties of the Left and the Right; the proximity of the Palestinian camps provided one with hope for change, the other with the needed scapegoats.

Sectarian distinctions

In the 1970s, business was still basically under Christian control. At the end of the 1950s, Yusuf Sayigh, in his pioneer study of Lebanese entrepreneurs, found that the ratio of Christians to Muslims was 10:2 in industry, 11:2 in finance and 16:2 in services.[14] In a later study in 1973, Boutros Labaki demonstrated that these ratios had been sizeably modified but remained quite uneven: 75.5 per cent Christians to 24.5 per cent Muslims in commercial firms (family firms and SARL); 67.5 per cent/32.4 per cent in industrial firms, and 71 per cent/29 per cent in the banking sector.[15] Conversely, among the industrial working class, 75 per cent of the workers were Muslims, Shi`a in particular, against 25 per cent Christians, though the percentage of Christian wage earners would markedly increase when it came to the services sector. Kinship relations and regionalism played an important role in employment and in maintaining a balance of power inside firms that was favourable to employers.

The middle classes: unity and differences

The inflation of the middle classes was a salient characteristic of Lebanon's social structure in the prewar period owing primarily to emigration, the development of education, the inflated bureaucracy and the sizeable increase in the members of the liberal professions. By 1973, the middle classes accounted for 67 per cent of the population, according to some estimates.[16]

Among the large lower middle and middle classes, small privileges based on sect and region immediately translated into socio-economic advantages. Two major domains of sectarian differentiation were the privileges in the bureaucracy and the education system. As already noted, the Lebanese *laissez-faire* system did not prevent the existence of an inflated administration of some 100,000 functionaries (including the military and security forces). In fact, the development of literacy and the relative equalisation in access to education between the sects combined to exacerbate competition among graduates for a restricted number of posts in the state administration and to an increasing questioning of the validity of the sectarian quotas on both sides of the sectarian divide. Consequently, the education question took on an exaggerated dimension and led directly to political conflicts. Its function in the enlarged reproduction of the class structure operated by transforming the traditional petty bourgeoisie of farmers, tradesmen, artisans, village teachers, and the like into a modern petty bourgeoisie of functionaries in the public sector, employees in the private sector, teachers in public education and the liberal professions. But the chaotic rush toward education widened the gap between the economic system and an education system that prepared 'students for everything and for nothing' and exported a big portion of its graduates to the foreign markets.[17]

Under the impact of the general crisis, the pressures on class and sectarian selection and elimination increased in different ways:

- discrimination in opportunities of access to higher education: only 8 per cent of primary school students reached the end of secondary schooling and 6.1 per cent of those sat for the baccalaureate (secondary school) exams and made it to university;
- the elimination grade (less than 5/20 for French) in intermediate and secondary exams favoured the sons of the rich and Christian families and students of private schools in general who received a relatively good French education or spoke French at home;
- regional selection manifested itself by the concentration of educational institutions in the dominantly Christian 'regional-sectarian zones';
- the flagrant gaps between public and private schooling.

These inequalities were reflected in unequal access to higher posts in the state and the private sector and in differences in salaries. A bank employee who graduated from the American University of Beirut (AUB) would start with a monthly salary of LL 2,000, a graduate of the Jesuit Université St Joseph (USJ) with LL 1,500, and a graduate of the Lebanese University (LU) would only get LL 600.[18]

Thus, while the development of public schooling at the LU integrated young men and women who were meeting for the first time – Christians of modest origins, mainly from the periphery in Jubayl, Batrun, 'Akkar and the north with young Shi`as from the south and the Biqa` – the mass of students were divided on issues of public education versus private education and foreign language versus Arabic. The long struggle for the establishment of the LU, its development and the recognition of its diplomas is a strong example of this.

Nevertheless, the middle classes were unified, 'objectively' at least, by their shared submission to the other and more dangerous effects of the crisis. Whereas the correspondent of *Le Monde* in Beirut spoke of the 'slow death of the petite bourgeoisie', economist Marwan Iskandar expressed the frustrations of the middle classes and their desire for change:

The middle classes, hard-bitten by the high cost of living, are more and more ready to exchange a false liberty – that they supposedly possess – for any system on condition that that system hits at monopoly and demolishes its ramparts. As far as the middle Lebanese were concerned, any system, inasmuch as it contains a part of what its name denotes, is better than the prevailing system of arbitrary privileges and complete blindness.[19]

SOCIAL MOVEMENTS

On the eve of the 1967 war, all segments of the Lebanese population were in motion to contest the established order, resist the crisis and confront the policies of the commercial/financial oligarchy, expressing, in one way or another, a deep desire for political, economic and social change.

From the convents of the north to the plantations of the south

The agrarian crisis set in motion struggles that combined the desire for land with resistance to the introduction of monetary relations into agriculture. In 1970, tenant farmers of the Maronite convents of Tannurin and Mayfuq (the highlands of Batrun and Jabal respectively) organised strikes and demonstrations for a better share of the crops and for the distribution of church lands between them. In Mayfuq, the gendarmes intervened against the peasants. One year later, a violent conflict over land ownership broke out between the peasants of Hanin (southern Lebanon) and Kamil al-As'ad, speaker of the chamber of deputies. Twenty-three villagers were accused of violence and arrested. Qantara, property of the 'Usayran family, experienced a similar dispute in the same year.

But the most important agrarian movement was the revolt of the peasants of the 'Akkar plain, starting in 1968 against a background of difficult conditions for share-cropping and a rush of capitalist entrepreneurs. To finance their new lifestyle in the cities, 'Akkar's absentee landowners imposed a semi-feudal exploitation and exactions on their share-croppers (obligatory gifts, free domestic work by the villagers' womenfolk in the *Beyks'* households, etc.), when they did not sell or rent their lands to capitalist entrepreneurs. These reduced the share-croppers to the status of salaried workers or expelled them from their land and cottages altogether. Caught in the crossfire, share-croppers and peasants resorted to an armed rebellion, assisted by the Sa'iqa, the Palestinian faction of the Syrian Ba'th recently created by the government of Salah Jadid. After the fall of Jadid in 1970, the parties of the Lebanese Left took over the leadership of the movement.

In the south, the *Régie* had become a private reserve of the traditional *za`im*s, who packed it with their clients and controlled cultivation licences, which they distributed to their friends or rented to farmers. A private franchise-holding company since 1935, whose franchise was extended until 1973, the *Régie* also held the exclusive right to export Lebanese-produced tobacco, import cigarettes and produce local cigarettes. Two thousand employees worked in its administration and in the sorting and packaging centres.

The problems of tobacco cultivation had been dragging on for a decade, articulated around the following planters' demands:

- ending speculation in cultivation licences by withdrawing them from those who were not engaged in agriculture;
- limiting the area cultivated to 25 dunums per person (70 per cent of the farmers cultivated 5 dunums, but there were licences that covered 400 dunums);
- increasing the purchase price of tobacco leaves;
- nationalising the *Régie*, a major demand of the tobacco planters, but which ran counter to a project by the Phalange minister Joseph Shadir to lease it to Phillip Morris, the big American cigarette conglomerate.

After many years spent awaiting results, on 22 January 1973 a procession of thousands of tobacco planters occupied the offices of the *Régie* in Nabatiyeh, demanding a 20 per cent increase in the purchase price of their products. The following day, the army shot at the demonstrators and killed two peasants. A few days later, 20,000 people demonstrated in the streets of Beirut in solidarity with the tobacco planters.

Moreover, the agrarian movement was organising itself at a rapid rate. In April 1973, the Unified Syndicate of Tobacco Farmers was born. A month earlier, the first congress of the National Union of Agricultural Workers was convened, representing 163 villages from all parts of the country. In May of the same year, the first congress of the peasants and farmers of the Biqa' launched a campaign against the rise in the price of fertilisers and insecticides (which accounted for 20–30 per cent of production costs), demanded a new tenancy code, attacked the middlemen's network, which contributed to raising the price of agricultural products, and demanded the admission of peasants and farmers to the National Social Security Fund (NSSF).

Militant working-class unity

The struggles for NSSF coverage united workers and employees around a common programme, led by a unified trade union federation, the General Workers' Union of Lebanon (GWUL), inside which the influence of the left-wing federation, the National Union of Workers Trade Unions (NUWTU), and the reformist trade unionists was on the rise. Large segments of the lower-income groups in the cities and countryside were mobilised around a programme that integrated the demands of agricultural workers and mobilised all those who suffered the rise in the cost of living.[20]

The threat of a general strike planned for February 1970 forced the authorities to activate medical coverage by the NSSF that was supposed to benefit some 250,000 employees. But a counter-offensive by employers succeeded in imposing equal representation in the administrative council of the NSSF, which meant practically controlling it. Further, under pressure from business circles, the government agreed to deposit NSSF funds in private banks at an interest rate of 3–4 per cent, much lower than the normal rate of 8–10 per cent. More serious was the extensive campaign of layoffs waged by employers against their old employees (salaried workers would automatically benefit from the NSSF after two years' employment) in order to reduce the number of employees for which they would have to pay social security fees. These layoffs raised the question of job security at work and the right to engage in trade union activity and organisation, which required amending article 50 of the Labour Code.

A new threat of general strike by the GWUL planned for 25 May 1971 demanded the immediate halt of arbitrary layoffs, a salary increase of 11 per cent, a 25 per cent reduction of rents, the importation by the state of medicine and essential foodstuffs, and legislation for agricultural workers within six months. The strike was deferred after a wage increase of 5 per cent was decreed. When the GWUL finally acted on its strike threat on 28 August 1973, it called also for limiting commercial profits and encouraging cooperatives. This was the first time that the trade union movement had touched upon the covert and sacrosanct power and privileges of the commercial/financial oligarchy. The government's answer had become traditional: it decreed a new wage increase of 5 per cent (at a time when the price indexes spoke of a rise in the cost of living of at least 12 per cent) and raised the minimum wage to LL 225 and family allowances to LL 70. A compromise on article 50 of the Labour Code imposed restrictions on the laying off of trade unionists. None of the other demands were met.

On another level, an uninterrupted series of strikes and shopfloor movements had rocked the industrial world since 1968. The rapid industrialisation and the exploitation of young manual workers of rural origin who were being rapidly and aggressively proletarised sharpened their class-consciousness and combativeness. Their demands covered all aspects of working-class life: implementation of labour legislation concerning working hours, the minimum wage, equal pay for men and women, family allowances, maternity and sickness leave, the right to trade union organisation and the recognition of shopfloor committees; opposition to arbitrary layoffs; integration of agricultural workers in the NSSF, including its medical benefits branch; improvements in working conditions, workplace safety, indemnities for work accidents and outlawing of sexual harassment of female workers.

The rank and file workers' struggles culminated in a strike at the Ghandour biscuits and chocolate factory. Its 1,200 workers in Shiyah were the biggest non-unionised element of Lebanese industry. They struck in November 1972, demanding a wage increase, equal pay for men and women workers, the recognition of the shopfloor committee and their right to trade union organisation. During their demonstration of 11 November 1972 at the factory gates, the police fired at the demonstrators, killing Yusuf al-'Attar, a militant of the OCA's Workers' Committees, and Fatima al-Khawaja, a member of the LCP, and wounding 14 others. The GWUL organised a one-day general strike to protest at the official violence and show solidarity with the Ghandour workers; a wave of indignation spread throughout the entire country while the Salam government, unwilling even to investigate police firing on a peaceful demonstration, decided to require organisers of demonstrations to obtain an official permit. At the initiative of progressive and leftist forces, a demonstration of some 20,000, led by Kamal Junblat, ended in a large rally on the steps of parliament where the socialist leader's speech was interrupted by shouts of '99 thieves and 17 ruffians' (for the 99 deputies and the 17 ministers). On 15 December, Ghandour declared a lockout and laid off all his workers. He reopened a week later and reemployed them all, except 100 workers whom he considered the ringleaders. Although the Left organised another demonstration against the arbitrary layoffs, on 26 December, the outcome of the Ghandour battle left only frustration and resentment. The trade union attaché at the US embassy noted that the demonstration and the general strike had been a 'moderate success' for the Left, which had managed to go on the offensive and win the 'propaganda war'. However, he concluded that neither the Left nor the trade unions had secured any concrete gains for workers.[21]

Effectively, the trade union movement had fallen into a vicious circle: wage increases, paid for mainly by the industrialists and the government were sapped by the merchants, who immediately raised prices. The meagre results of years of trade union activity drove popular protest 'to the street'. When, on 5 February 1973, the GWUL announced another postponement of its general strike, a movement of wildcat strikes and violent demonstrations swept the country: in Beirut, Sidon, Tyre, Bint Jubayl, the south, the Biqa' and Tripoli (where, the demonstrators set fire to the offices of the pro-government Federation of Trade Unions of the North). More important were the demonstrations in the Christian localities of Juniyeh, Jubayl and Hammana, not to speak of the mixed regions of the Shuf, 'Alay, Shuwayfat and Jiyeh. On the following day a wildcat strike, organised by the Workers Committees of the Organisation of Communist Action (OCA) closed the factories of the industrial zone of Mukallis-Tall al Za'tar (affecting some 10,000 workers) and a workers' demonstration blocked the Beirut–Bayt Miri road for two days. 'This wild strike cannot be reduced to its mere demands', commented René Aggiouri, editor of the French-language daily *Al-Safa*, 'as it calls into question the political leaders in Lebanese society and, more importantly, its trade union leaders.'[22]

Students against the 'merchant society'

'A revolt against our merchant society': in these words Edward Saab, the astute correspondent of *Le Monde* in Beirut, described the student movement.[23] Much more than a protest movement, it was a radical questioning of Lebanese and Arab societies from a moral and cultural point of view, greatly influenced by the defeat of June 1967, the emergence of the Palestinian resistance and the impact of May 1968 in France.

The movement started with a long strike by secondary students in March 1967, demanding lower fees, getting rid of the elimination grade in exams for foreign languages and the unification of school textbooks. In Tyre, the gendarmes fired on a demonstration, killing a student, Edward Ghanima. June 1967 and the following months were marked by intense student activity concerning the Arab–Israeli war, which ultimately led to the official closure of the schools and universities and the occupation of AUB campus by police and the expulsion of striking students.

A fifty-day strike by both the students and teachers of the Lebanese University (LU) began in April 1968. The latter were demanding a wage increase and tenure, the former sought the building of a unified university campus, an increase in scholarships and the provision of university restaurants. None of those demands was met, but the students managed to impose the formation of the National Union of Lebanese University Students (NULUS). As a sign of the radicalisation of the student movement, the Left alliance (PSP, LCP and OCA) gained control over NULUS, which in March/April 1972 launched a massive strike to press for its demands. Private universities – AUB, USJ, and the Beirut Arab University (BAU) – joined the strike in solidarity.

The LU strike was renewed the following year and was interrupted by police intervention and the laying off of a number of teachers. Three times during that year, 1969, teachers and students from the private and public sectors went on strike to demand wage increases and mutual aid funds, to no avail.

In the cities and the countryside, technical schools saw considerable mobilisation in support of improving teaching conditions and a better diversification of specialisations and job opportunities. Their movement culminated in a general strike at the beginning of 1974, although practically no substantial results were achieved.

In the private university sector, AUB students, mainly belonging to the middle and upper classes, went on strike in 1971, to protest at fee increases. They occupied the premises and organised big demonstrations. The police and the Phalange militia intervened and students were expelled.

In 1972, Lebanon witnessed a major nationwide strike movement by the 16,000 public education school teachers demanding a wage increase, the right of trade union organisation and retirement after 25 years of service. The strike, which lasted for two months, was broken after the ministry suspended the payment of salaries. When the strike was renewed from January to July 1973, 324 teachers were laid off, condemned as 'agitators' by Prime Minister Sa'ib Salam. Protest and solidarity movements with the teachers covered the entire country while their sit-ins and hunger strikes became a rallying point for all social movements. Even the Maronite Church intervened to demand that the expelled teachers be reinstated, also to no avail.

Student demonstrations, at times 25,000-strong, became an everyday scene in Beirut and major Lebanese cities. Police repression only produced new demonstrations, so much so that President Franjiyeh contemplated closing the LU for that academic year, fearing that 'university agitation might unleash a revolutionary situation'.[24] The last student demonstration occurred a few days before the beginning of the fighting.

POLITICAL SCLEROSIS

A flagrant contradiction dominated political life in the 1970s between the gravity of the socio-economic crisis and the return of the traditional notables to power. The 'centrist' ruling troika – Franjiyeh/al-Asad/Salam – had given priority to its fight against the intervention of the army in political and civil life, and Franjiyeh inaugurated his mandate with a purge of the Shihabist intelligence officers. The death, in a helicopter accident, of the Shihabist Jean Nujaym, the commander-in-chief of the army, was the occasion for his replacement by Iskandar Ghanim, a friend of the president. On the other hand, the patronage of the Shihabist security 'agencies' was quickly replaced by the 'northern' clients of the president's son,

Tony, the eternal minister of communications who was accused of having made a fortune from telecommunication contracts.

A dissociated representative system

The structure of parliament and the electoral system were particularly indicative of the flagrant contradiction between the political system and the country's new socio-economic realities. The chamber was dominated by true political dynasties: out of a total 425 deputies elected since 1920, 245 belonged to families of parliamentarians.[25] On the other hand, the influence of 'funders' was increasing. Parliament, that 'arrogant alliance between money and the feudal system', according to Georges Naccache, was being increasingly dominated by moneyed interests, and the landed notables themselves (the 'political feudalists') were rapidly transformed into capitalist businessmen, shareholders in joint stock companies and holders of import quotas distributed by the state.

The rapid monetarisation of political mediation became a way to bridge the widening gap between those notables, increasingly incapable of providing effective services to their clients, and their public. In fact, massive migration toward the cities rendered the rural basis of the electoral system obsolete. A great part of the Lebanese were obliged to vote in villages where their parents had been born, in which they had no longer any interests or links, save perhaps memories of clan or family allegiances and disputes. Meanwhile, they were deprived of the right to vote in cities where they had been living for decades – where they worked, paid their taxes and fees, became individualised and grouped into socio-professional and class forms of representation – in short, where they had interests to be defended and represented. For example, no more than 20 per cent of the inhabitants of the suburbs of Beirut voted in their localities. On election day, they would make the trek to their respective villages, where the effects of socio-economic integration were being erased and family, clan and sectarian allegiances reproduced.

Nevertheless, the traditional rentier hierarchy that underwrote politics refused to admit change. On the eve of the 1972 elections, during one of his many polemics with Junblat, Prime Minister Sa'ib Salam gave a perfect illustration of this logic. 'We welcome Kamal Junblat, in his capacity as the son of a well-bred "house" and as an honourable chief of his [Druze] sect', said Salam, 'but we categorically refuse to deal with him as one who invites destruction and sabotage, poses as the protector of the Left and of Communism and exploits popular problems [for his own interests].' If anything, the 1972 elections revealed the degree of impermeability to change that characterised the Lebanese political system and the many blockages that it imposed on the participation of new forces in society, especially as represented by cross-sectarian political parties. A few 'independent' candidates who ran on traditional lists managed to get elected. For the rest, the title of Le Monde's article says it all: 'A team that hardly represents public opinion'.[26]

Aborted 'revolution from above'

Sa'ib Salam, who formed the first cabinet under Franjiyeh, named it a 'youth government' and committed himself and his team to 'carry out a revolution from above' to undercut the possibility of 'one from below'. But his ministers, technocrats and professionals had to face the covert power of the commercial/financial oligarchy; they ended up resigning, one after the other. Ilias Saba, economic adviser to the president and minister of the economy, issued ministerial decree no. 1943, which contained a set of fiscal reforms and protective measures for national industry, but had to back down after the Merchants' Association threatened to strike. Emile Bitar, minister of public health and member of a new reformist political formation, the Democratic Party, proposed government control over the price of medicine (fixing profit rates equal to those in France) and seeing the NSSF import a number of pharmaceuticals. That last suggestion meant discovering the cost price of medicine and, consequently, the profits of the importers. Vital medicines such as insulin disappeared from the market as the syndicates of drugstore owners and pharmacists threatened to strike, also backed by the Merchants' Association. Eventually, Franjiyeh, who had friends and funders among the agents of big pharmaceutical companies, withdrew support from his minister and Bitar resigned. Architect Henri Iddi, minister of public works, resigned in solidarity. Two other ministers were prompted to resign on the education question: Ghassan Tuwayni, the editor of al-Nahar and minister of education, and his successor Michel Iddi could not enlist the president's support for their projects of educational reforms. In 1973, industrialists finally obtained their long-time demand for a ministry of industry, whose portfolio was entrusted to Pierre Hilu, a rich businessman and industrialist of international stature. A few weeks later, Hilu held a press conference in which he accused the commercial monopolies of controlling the government and sabotaging his attempts to protect national industry and reinstate the workings of free competition.

As early as January 1965, a draft law (no. 189) limiting profit rates had been withdrawn, also under threat of a merchants' strike. No such talk about this type of reform would be heard again. The importers who were hoarding foodstuffs were known; the press had published lists of their names and the nature and quantity of goods they held in the Port's warehouses. But nothing was done about it.

To counter all reform projects, officials made the absurd argument that the state lacked funds, when it was well known that the state systematically refused to increase its budget revenues, the major part of which came from customs duties and taxes; but not any direct taxes. Two-thirds of the country's fiscal revenues came from indirect taxes on consumption and from income tax deducted 'at source' by employers from their employees' salaries. Both were against the interests of the salaried, functionaries and professional categories, while the rich practised tax evasion, not to speak of enjoying their 'invisible returns'. And forget about a progressive income tax, which simply did not exist. Bank profits were taxed according to an inclusive rate of 15–22 per cent. Moreover, one of the rare pieces of fiscal legislation of those years increased by 50 per cent the income tax on the revenues of the middle-income groups (those who paid more than LL 1,000 in annual tax) without any increase for the higher-income categories! Furthermore, the 'fiscal paradise' knew no tax on wealth or any form of inheritance rights, and many economic activities were not even taxed, such as interest on government bonds, property surplus value and the sale of bank licences (a lucrative activity as the government stopped issuing permits to open new banks after the Intra crash).

Thus, the reformist pretensions of the first two years of Franjiyeh's mandate ended in fiasco. 'The Lebanese bourgeoisie and political establishment, in both their Muslim and Christian sectors, were unwilling to surrender any privileges for the cause of reform,' commented Kamal Salibi.[27]

This was at a time when the oil boom had started and any vigilant self-interested businessman could have predicted the benefits accruing to his class and to Lebanon in general, provided some concessions were made to reinforce social peace in the country. Perhaps a few harboured such thoughts, but almost all refused to do anything about it. As revolution was not made 'from above', it was to be made, in the most vicious and destructive manner, 'from below'. In a country where the rights and obligations of people are nearly always defined by the individual's belonging by birth to a sectarian political community, social frustrations and blocked social demands gradually slipped toward sectarian and regional division, aggravated by the political conflict between reform and security, the latter centred on the Palestinian armed presence.

The army: for internal control or national defence?

Salam's second cabinet of 1972, composed of politicians this time, revealed a marked propensity for repression. Unable and unwilling to impose concessions on the bourgeoisie or defend Lebanon's territory against Israeli incursions and air strikes, the state revealed its power through internal repression.

This government was in office during the shootings of the workers at the Ghandour factory and the tobacco planters of Nabatiyeh, the mass layoff of teachers and the repression of student demonstrations. The anti-Shihab notables, who had returned to power, took their revenge by putting the ex-officers of the Deuxième bureau on trial; even though they had advocated the return of the military to their barracks, they were quick to send the army against workers, students, peasants and resort to the worst methods of the defunct 'agencies': telephone tapping and violations of the freedom of opinion and the press, including the arrest of journalists (half a dozen had been incarcerated among whom was editor of al-Nahar, Ghassan Tuwayni). Finally, it was also under Salam that a law on political parties was drafted that greatly curtailed freedom of thought and association. The opposition to this draft law was the occasion for the launching of the Rally of National and Democratic Parties and Personalities (later to be known as the Lebanese National Movement – LNM) during a mass meeting at Byblos Cinema in June 1973.

But many in Lebanon demanded the defence of the south and the building of fortifications in border villages, if not the defence of the borders themselves, and at the least the retaliation by the army for Israeli incursions on Lebanese territory. A Libyan offer to provide the country with an air defence system was rejected. Official Lebanon was seeking US guarantees for its security that never came. The official philosophy was expressed by Pierre Jumayil's famous formula: 'Lebanon's strength lies in its weakness'. Lebanon was desperately trying to extricate itself from any responsibility for belonging to a region dominated by the Arab–Israeli conflict. The army was there to defend the system, not the homeland.

The Christians of Lebanon had never wanted a real national army, for – good merchants descendants of the Phoenicians that they claimed to be – they did not want to pay for it. They did not want to provoke Israel, and they did not want to encourage the growth of an armed force that might then stage a *coup d'etat*, as so often had been the case in other Arab countries. But they were to pay the price.[28]

Be that as it may, some individuals were making good business out of the army and many an official figure was implicated in the scandals of the French Crotales anti-air missiles, the air-defence radar for the Baruk Mountain and the French Mirage jets.[29] In 1969, LL 200 million was disbursed by the state to modernise the army. Since then, every arms purchase was accompanied by a financial scandal, and it was also revealed that arms, bought in the name of national defence, were in fact destined for use in internal repression. General Fuad Lahhud, MP for the Matn and president of parliament's defence committee, exclaimed when he discovered the list of arms required: 'We must define the task of the army. Has it been built to fight against the Left? … Has it been built to fight the *fida'iyin*?' Lahhud revealed flagrant irregularities in the purchase of French AMX 12 tanks, which were light tanks unfit for national defence purposes. Middlemen had pocketed large commissions despite the fact that the transaction was between the French and Lebanese governments. Worse, older models were bought only because the commissions on them were higher (30 per cent compared to 7 per cent for the more recent models).

In April 1973, a special operation Israeli unit called the Serayet Mat'kal, commanded by Lieutenant Ehoud Barak, assassinated two leaders of Fatah, Abu Yusuf al-Najjar, Kamal 'Udwan, and the poet Kamal Nasir, spokesperson for the PLO, in Verdun street in Beirut, a hundred metres from a major police barracks. Prime Minister Sa'ib Salam demanded the resignation of the commander-in-chief of the army. Enjoying political cover by the president, the army and its chief were declared 'untouchable' and it was the prime minister who had to go, as a quarter of a million people took to the streets to bid their last farewell to the assassinated PLO leaders and vent their anger at an army that was always present for internal repression and always absent when it came to national defence.

SLIPPAGES AND DIVISIONS

In the 1970s Lebanese society walked a delicate tightrope, balancing between the drive to rebuild its unity through structural reforms and its conflict-laden division by an obsession with 'security', which failed to guarantee any security. If the unity of the bourgeoisie managed to obstruct any reform, the frustrations and divisions of the middle classes, the petty bourgeoisie and the poorer classes prepared the slippage to armed conflict.

In fact, Junblat and his Leftist and nationalist allies on the one hand, and the Phalange and their allies, on the other, were disputing two contradictory versions of security. A partisan of a strong state based on an army backed by right-wing militias, opposed to any kind of reform, the Phalange party was only repeating, in a situation of crisis, its function as defenders of narrow sectarian privileges in the service of the big class interests. Junblat, now recognised in the Arab world as the leading Muslim figure in Lebanon, emboldened by Syrian and Egyptian support and fully conscious that the presence of the Palestinian commandos had broken the Maronite 'monopoly of violence', proposed a bargain: moderate socio-economic reforms and more equitable participation by Muslims in managing the state, in return for an amicable limitation of PLO military activities by rigourously applying the Cairo Accords. Junblat's rebellion, his calling into question the Lebanese socio-political regime in its entirety, his semi-suicidal adventure of 1975–76 were but the product of his exasperation after having failed to push through that choice.

Meanwhile, two movements deserve mention as they represent the impact of the social movement inside the Christian communities and the level of frustration on the Muslim side.

Renewal and contestation in the religious institutions

On the occasion of Christmas 1968, the Jeunesse Estudiantine Chrétienne (the Christian Student Youth – JEC) issued a manifesto that denounced the 'material wealth and political might of our Church... which participates in the feudal and capitalist exploitation system in Lebanon and justifies it'. They called for a church and Christians who consider themselves 'an integral part of the Arab World and share in its problems, struggles and aspirations for liberation and the building of a developed society that belongs to all its members'. The manifesto concluded with a declaration of solidarity with the struggle of the Palestinian people and called upon fellow believers to commit themselves to a 'radical transformation of Lebanese society'.[30]

A multitude of organisations actively sought a radical renewal of the Maronite Church. Prominent among them were students at the Clerical College of Ghazir, the members of the seminary of Christ-the-King and the parish priests of the poor Christian suburbs of Judaydeh and Dikwaneh. In addition, worker-priests, influenced by the liberation theology of Latin America, had made their appearance in the Matn and the suburbs of Beirut, where they engaged in social work and literacy classes. The Rally of Committed Christians, established in 1974, and close to the Communists and the Lebanese National Movement, called for an open democratic and secular form of Arabism. The Young Orthodox Movement, led by Bishop George Khudr, represented the renaissance of Eastern Christianity, open to dialogue with Islam. In early 1974, a movement for 'ecumenical renewal with an independent perspective' took shape around Grégoire Haddad, Greek Catholic bishop of Beirut. In his magazine *Afaq* (Horizons), Haddad critiqued the 'exploitative social system' in Lebanon, called for a serious commitment to 'the cause of Arab Man' and demanded 'change that will permit our society to become more equitable, more civilized and richer in human values'. Haddad's popularity saved him from excommunication, but he was relieved of his bishopry. He had called for the abolition of religious marriage, which encouraged sectarianism and worked for the adoption of secularism. In the first weeks of the war, Haddad wrote that social gaps constituted the main cause for the crisis that led to the war. The solution lay in social justice, ensuring work, food, housing and health care for all. Rather than evade the security issue, Haddad reversed its terms: it was not change that threatened security; rather the current conditions constituted the gravest threat to it.[31]

Amal: the 'third way'

Musa al-Sadr's short residence in Lebanon was to stamp Lebanon's Shi`as for a whole period of their history. Born in Iran and a member of the Iranian religious institution, he arrived in Lebanon in the early 1960s, with substantial funds to launch social projects for the community. He settled in Tyre, where he attempted to fill in the religious vacuum created by the death of the leading *mujtahid* Sayid `Abd al-Husayn Sharaf al-Din, and the political vacuum created by the death of Muhammad al Zayyat, the popular leader of the Arab Nationalists Movement (ANM) against the al-Khalil clan of local *za`im*s. Sadr, who advocated an enlightened and open religious discourse, tried to build a third force between the traditional leadership of the As`ads and the parties of the Left, especially the LCP, the OCA and the Ba`th, which were highly influential among the southern public, especially the youth. In his first endeavour, he managed to enlist the support of Sabri Hamadeh, Shi`i *Za`im* of Ba`albak-Hirmil. As early as 1966, the reports of the US Embassy in Beirut described al-Sadr as a bulwark against the influence of `Abd al-Nasir on the Shi`i masses.[32] In 1974, Sadr confessed to US Ambassador Godley that his main concern was to counter Communist influence among Shi`i youth.[33]

Snubbed by the Shi`i clergy, traditionally hostile to the central government and the traditional *za`ims* and loyal to the religious authority in Najaf, Sadr attracted the attention of Charles Hilu, the Shihabist 'services' and Michel Asmar's Cénacle libanais, a think-tank of Lebanese nationalism, Maronite-syle. All were in search of a new Muslim ally against the Sunni leadership and the Sunni 'street', considered too committed to 'Abd al-Nasir and the Palestinian *fida'iyin*. Upon Sadr's initiative, the Shi`a completed their transformation into a structured and official sect. Law no. 72/76 of 19 December 1967 recognised the right of the representatives of the Shi`i community to act and express themselves 'in conformity with the fatwas emanating from the supreme authority of the community in the world' (article 1) and granted the Higher Islamic Shi`i Council (HISC) the prerogative of 'defending the rights' of the community and 'improving its social and economic conditions' (article 5). The reference to a religious authority outside Lebanon was not new regarding the rights of Lebanese sects, but granting the HISC the role of defending the political, economic and social rights constituted a precedent. Two years later, in 1969, the HISC was created and Sadr nominated as its president. In May 1970, after an official day of solidarity with the south, the government recognised the new Shi`i body and disbursed $10 million in aid for the south.

During the rise of social movements, Sadr's populist discourse mainly emphasised the sectarian and regionalist aspects. His ambiguous message on the rights of the deprived [*al-mahrumin*] interpellated a multiplicity of social sectors: rich Shi`i émigrés from Africa, looking for a place in the political Lebanese system and a new social status that befitted their newly acquired wealth; a wide sector of Shi`i intellectuals and government functionaries in search of employment or promotion, who were at a disadvantage compared to their Maronite and Sunni counterparts; and those southerners who had traditionally stayed on the fence between the traditional leaders and the Left, many of whom had been organised by the 'agencies' in what was called the Partisans of the Army (*Ansar al-Jaysh*). Fouad Ajami, as American Shi`i intellectual of Lebanese origins, did not fail to notice and laud Sadr's 'concrete sectarian project for Lebanon' that 'crushes class differences'.[34]

Sadr emphasised the need to develop the south as a deprived region 'before a revolution breaks out'. In order to do this, he demanded a share of the national budget, the expansion of the Litani project to irrigate southern land and the construction of hospitals and schools. Nevertheless, he found no contradiction between the armed Palestinian presence and Lebanese sovereignty. In response to demands for the cessation of Palestinian military operations, he said that safeguarding the borders of Israel was not Lebanon's responsibility. Later, he proposed an Arab force for the defence of the south and an Arab fund for its development. Yasir 'Arafat's Fatah movement, looking for allies outside the confines of the Left, played an important role in the creation of the Movement of the Deprived and its development.

A large part of Sadr's struggle on the eve of the war was devoted to imposing himself as principal spokesman for the south and the Shi`i community and confirming his presidency of the HISC. Contested by Kamil al-As'ad – who in July 1972 founded his Democratic Socialist Party, also to 'counter Communist and Ba'thist influence in South Lebanon' – Sadr managed to rally a number of Shi`i deputies, including Husayn al-Husayni, future president of Amal and speaker of parliament. Sadr insisted on the formation of a ministerial committee to discuss Shi`i demands and in a meeting with Franjiyeh, 13 of the 19 Shi`i deputies threatened to resign if their community's full rights were not recognised.

During this period, Sadr distinguished himself by his populist meetings and tours of the south following Israeli bombing raids. In March 1973, during a mass meeting of some 50,000 persons in Ba`albak, he unveiled his famous motto, 'arms are the ornaments of men'. Sidon and Tripoli, cities with a Sunni majority, welcomed him enthusiastically, and 190 personalities from all sects signed a petition in support of his Movement of the Deprived 'that went beyond the Shi`i community'. In 1974, Sadr threatened civil disobedience if his demands were not met. In a mass meeting in Bidnayil (Ba`albak-Hirmil), he exclaimed: 'We are *Matawila* [a pejorative term for the Shi`a] no more, we are rejectionists, avengers, a people in revolt against injustice,' and he threatened to launch his followers in an assault against the palaces of the rich and the mighty if their demands were not met.

'Here is another one lost to the cause of revolution,' exclaimed the correspondent of *The Economist* in March 1974. This was not quite the case. As Sadr's discourse was being radicalised, he became more reconciled with the system and moved closer to Franjiyeh. The president, on bad terms with Salam and isolated in the Sunni 'street', was looking for a Shi'i ally to face the Sunni leaders and the Left. The occasion was quickly seized. In the by-elections of Nabatiyeh in December 1974, Sadr's candidate, a rich and obscure émigré from Africa, defeated Kamil al-As'ad's candidate for the parliamentary seat. On the steps of the Presidential Palace, a few days later, Sadr declared that he had decided to 'open a new page with the State'.

While the Left and Nationalist parties were trying to link the southern question to demands that covered the entire national space, Sadr's exclusivist position appeared problematic, at best. The two currents tested their weight in the elections for the Executive Bureau of the HISC. The result was even: the Left managed to secure half of the body's seats.

Displaced frustrations

Sadr had managed to put his finger on a burning question when he coined his slogan about the alliance between 'those deprived in their homeland and those deprived of their homeland'. Young people humiliated by the defeat of June 1967, which continued to be played out in the daily war that Israel was waging in southern Lebanon, inspired by the example of Che Guevara and contesting the 'merchant society' identified increasingly with the Palestinian resistance. The accumulated failures and frustrations of the social movements pushed some of the public in the same direction. A poem by `Abbas Baydun, the most promising of the new generation of Lebanese poets, is a good illustration of that spirit. His words, put into music by Marcel Khalifa, are addressed to `Ali, symbol of the 'people of the South/the barefooted of the cities':

You have resisted
to liberate your blood
from the garages of grease
and your mouth from the sugar warehouses
and your bones form the seats of the *Beyks* and the charlatans.
But, 'Ali, where will you find a land
For a proud head and two free hands?

Here the liberating influence of the *fida'i* model operates indirectly by a slippage from the national to the social, not devoid of violence:

> Every morning, a gun falls on the mountain
> and we are but silent witnesses.
> But a day will come
> when we will direct our ploughshares
> To their obese
> and debauched hearts.

The evolution of the following events was a succession of attempts at armed liquidation of the *fida'iyin* alternating with concessions that always came too late.

Amin al-Hafiz, an economist and deputy for Tripoli in Karami's parliamentary bloc, known for his good relations with the PLO, was called upon to form a new government in April 1973. Presenting his cabinet as a revised version of the 'youth' cabinet, his short-lived tenure was dominated by an army offensive against the Palestinian camps in Sidon and Beirut. On 3 May, the air force intervened and bombarded Burj al-Barajina refugee camp. Violent battles raged for two weeks between the army, backed by the Phalange, and the PLO, supported by the organisations of the Left. Syria's decision to close its borders with Lebanon, coupled with a threat to close its airspace, imposed a cease-fire and the conclusion of a new accord between the Lebanese government and the PLO, known as the Melkart Accord. A month later, on 14 June, al-Hafiz resigned.

Taqi al-Din al-Sulh, who succeeded him, was chosen primarily because of his Iraqi sympathies, in order to counter Syrian influence and rally the support of Muslim notables. The suggestion that Junblat take the ministry of the interior was met with a veto by Sham'un, Jumayil and Franjiyeh. In August 1973, the government announced 140 appointments to administrative posts and the 'abolition of sectarianism in the public function': Grade One posts of director-general would no longer be reserved to a specific sect and the lower posts would be distributed on a parity basis between Christians and Muslims (compared to the earlier tradition of six Christians to five Muslims). Iddi and Sham'un opposed the new measures in the name of Christian rights while Jumayil accepted them 'grudgingly' as concessions to the 'so-called disfavoured sects at the expense of the Maronites'.[35] In fact the appointments were mainly designed to substitute Shihabist functionaries by partisans of the returning notables, Franjiyeh, Sulh, As`ad, Skaff and Hamadeh, and they left practically no impact on public opinion.

During the Sulh mandate, it had become known that the Phalange and Sham`un's National Liberal Party (NLP) were training and arming their followers, earning Junblat's accusation that they were seeking to 'liquidate' the Palestinian resistance. In July 1973, the first confrontation between armed Palestinians and the army, the Phalange and the partisans of Raymond Iddi broke out in Dikwaneh (the southeast suburb of Beirut, adjacent to the Palestinian camp at Tall al-Za`tar).

But the far more important development was the outbreak of the October 1973 Arab–Israeli war. Lebanon did not participate in the conflict but the Biqa` was transformed into a corridor used by the Israeli air force to raid Damascus and the Syrian cities of the interior, bypassing the strongly fortified southern approaches to the Syrian capital defended by a sophisticated network of Soviet missiles.[36] The war provided the occasion for the beginning of a new friendship between the Lebanese and Syrian presidents. On 7 January 1974, the Franjiyeh–al-Asad summit was a major event: a Syrian president was visiting Lebanon for the first time in 18 years. On the agenda were shared water resources, the problem of Syrian workers in Lebanon, transport, transit and commercial exchange. The visit was crowned by the signature of a joint defence treaty granting Syria early warning facilities on Lebanese territory against air strikes in return for which Damascus commited itself to defend Lebanon against Israeli aggression upon the request of the Lebanese government.

In September 1974, following confrontations in Tarshish (the Matn) between armed Phalange members and the PSP of Junblat – who reacted by suspending the participation of his two ministers in government – Taqi al-Din al-Sulh submitted his resignation, accusing Franjiyeh of covering up a shipment of arms that had arrived at Juniyeh for the Christian militias and was unloaded with the complicity of the army.

When Rashid al-Sulh succeeded his cousin Taqi al-Din, his government was supposed to please or, at least appease Junblat. But the division concerning Palestinian presence and the question of the defence of the south was widening. The year 1975 started with a general strike in the south and demonstrations in Beirut, precisely on that matter. A few weeks later, Jumayil declared that the Lebanese were divided on the Palestinian presence and the military activities of the PLO, evoked the existence of 'two governments and two armies' and called upon the president to organise a referendum on the presence of the *fida'iyin* on Lebanese territory.

On 26 February 1975, a demonstration by fishermen in Sidon protesting against Protein, a fishing company in which Kamil Sham`un was a major shareholder, was fired upon by the army, leaving a number of dead and wounded. Among the casualties was Nasserite deputy Ma`ruf Sa`d, who was at the head of the demonstration, and died a few days later in hospital. The army was still 'untouchable', however, and Franjiyeh blocked an investigation into the shooting. Violent confrontations broke out between the army and the PLO *fida`iyin* and Nasserite and Leftist organisations at the beginning of March in Sidon. In response, the Phalange organised a counter-demonstration of solidarity with the army in East Beirut. It was only on 12 March that the cabinet acceded to some demands by the people of Sidon and the National Movement: two army officers were transferred and the governor of Sidon put on administrative leave for one month. Pierre Jumayil objected to the rotation of the officers; 'they could no longer remain silent in the face of defiance and provocation', he said. A month later, the same cabinet announced the cancellation of the Protein project and its decision to compensate the fishermen. But it was too late, as usual. On the following day, 13 April 1975, a car fired shots at a congregation of Phalange partisans in front of a church in `Ayn al-Rummaneh, wounding a number of people, to which Phalangist militiamen reacted a few hours later by machine-gunning a bus heading for the Tall al-Za`tar refugee camp, killing 21 Palestinians. Fighting broke out throughout the southeastern suburb of Beirut between the Phalange and the Palestinian resistance and their Lebanese allies.

A war that was to last for fifteen years had just begun.

Part III

The Wars of Lebanon

11
Reform by Arms (1975–1976)

The adventure was worth the try…
Kamal Junblat

The 'Two Years War', although commonly referred to as a 'Christian–Palestinian war', was one in which internal factors played a major role. A duel had been engaged between two 'modern' populist forces that sprang from the country's social crisis: the Phalange party and its allies in the Lebanese Front,[1] on the one hand, and the nationalist and progressive movements of the Lebanese National Movement (LNM),[2] on the other. Each attempted to impose itself on the country while simultaneously imposing itself as the unique representative of its own 'camp', at a time when the increased involvement of the PLO in the fighting encouraged the intervention of outside parties, notably Israel and Syria.

SECURITY OR REFORMS?

In the first phase of the war, two dynamics were at work: a game of exclusion between the two protagonists; and an armed 'dialogue' between security (through the deployment of the army) and political reforms.

Throughout this phase of the conflict, the Phalange resisted reforms by arms. When after four days of violent fighting they ageed to hand over two of their militiamen accused of the killing in `Ayn al-Rummaneh, they launched a virulent attack against the Left, qualifying it as 'malicious, vicious and on the payroll of foreigners … to destroy Lebanon and the Palestinian Resistance'; hence the urgency to 'eradicate that infectious source'. The only error that the Phalange acknowledged was that they had 'made too many concessions' and had been exploited by the Left.[3] The LNM's answer was on the same rhetorical level: it called for the 'isolation' of the party, an official ban on its activities and the expulsion of its ministers from the cabinet. Paradoxically, the party of Pierre Jumayil, blamed by the LNM for its 'isolationism' (in`izaliya) vis-à-vis the rest of the Arab world, was

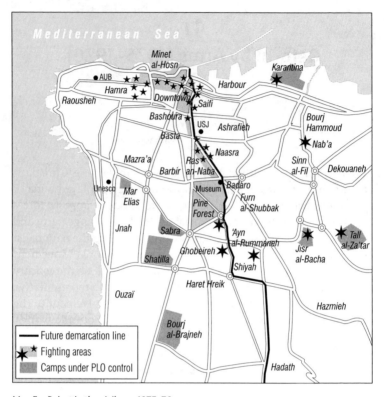

Map 5   Beirut in the civil war 1975–76

being punished by isolation (`azl*)! That slogan only led to increasing the influence of the Phalange among the Christian public.

As the Christian ministers resigned in solidarity with the Phalange, Sulh presented his government's resignation in an accusatory speech against the Phalange during a turbulent session of parliament. Franjiyeh's reaction expressed his inability to manage a crisis on which he had lost all influence. On 23 May, he named a military cabinet headed by a retired army officer, Brigadier-General Nur al-Din al-Rifa`i, charged with 'establishing law and order'. This stillborn military government resigned three days later under pressure from a general strike called by the LNM and backed by the Muslim political community along with Raymond Iddi and a number of Christian figures. Franjiyeh promptly made an about-face and asked Rashid Karami to form a new government. Karami's government, composed of six ministers excluding both the Phalange and Junblat, but providing a triumphant return of Kamil Sham'un to the political scene, negotiated a cease-fire with the help of Syrian mediators – Deputy Prime Minister and Foreign Minister 'Abd al-Halim Khaddam, Hikmat Shihabi, army chief of staff and Naji Jamil, head of Military Intelligence – intervening for the first time in the Lebanese crisis.

The dialogue by fire continued unabated. One party used the fighting to charge the army with the enforcement of 'law and order' while the other used armed pressure to impose reforms. In August 1975, the LNM issued its 'transitional programme for the democratic reform of the Lebanese system'. Its highlights were the abolition of the system of political and administrative sectarian quotas; a voluntary civil code for personal status; a new electoral law based on proportional representation in which Lebanon would become a single electoral district; extensive administrative decentralisation and the convocation of a constituent assembly on a non-sectarian basis. Jumayil's response was to warn that reform meant 'playing with fire', and al-'Amal insisted that the political domination of the Maronites was the only guarantee for a minority condemned to oppression by a majority that was oppressive by its very nature as a majority, 'involuntarily and even unconsciously'.[4] A few days later, on 22 August, Pierre Jumayil, observing the positive reactions to the LNM reform programme, called for the secularisation of the state, reduced to a unified personal status system and the distribution of administrative posts on the basis of competence. But he conceded that secularisation would be a transition toward abolishing political sectarianism in parliamentary representation and administrative posts (sectarian quotas would still apply to the three top state posts). Strangely enough, Jumayil concluded that the constitution and the National Pact of 1943 were untouchable and could only be modified if the unanimous approval of the Lebanese was secured. Jumayil, who had called for a referendum to gauge the opinion of Lebanese about the armed Palestinian presence (requiring a threshold of at least 60 per cent public support), rejected the recourse to a referendum on the abolition of political sectarianism.

'No reforms, no army', was the LNM's response. In September, Karami tasked the army with ensuring internal security after having changed its controversial commander-in-chief. But the veto imposed by the LNM and the PLO against any engagement of the army in keeping order without prior acceptance of the reforms provoked two new rounds of fighting in Zahleh and Zgharta, later known as the fourth and fifth rounds of hostilities. Much of the military tension between Zgharta and Tripoli was attributed to the Liberation Army of Zgharta (later renamed the Marada Forces, after the supposed ancestors of the Maronites), commanded by President Franjiyeh's son Tony. When the army intervened to create a buffer zone between the two northern cities, it was accused of complicity with Zgharta. A call for a general strike by the LNM against the intervention of the army in the north provoked a new round of fighting in Beirut in which the Phalange took the initiative to bombard downtown Beirut while their spokesperson declared that the fighting would not stop until the Lebanese Army was deployed.

SECULARISM AND THE 'ABOLITION OF SECTARIANISM'

A new cease-fire was declared and reinforced by the formation of a 20-member Committee for National Dialogue (CND), presided over jointly by Sham`un and Karami to discuss reforms.[5] The exchanges between the protagonists continued during September and October. Though the fighting did not stop, the dialogue nevertheless sent a message of hope to the embattled country. A PLO delegation submitted to the CND a memorandum in which it reiterated its commitment to respect Lebanese sovereignty and reject any substitute homeland for the Palestinians. Musa al-Sadr exhorted the committee, in the name of the country's religious dignitaries, to return to 'coexistence among the country's spiritual families (sects)', while a joint delegation of the employers' associations and the workers' trade unions led by `Adnan Qassar and Iliyas al-Habr threatened to occupy the CND's headquarters until a programme of reforms was agreed upon.

Inside the CND's subcommittee on political reforms, discussion touched on the vital questions of public life, perhaps for the first time in the country's history. The LNM reform programme dominated the discussions. Pierre Jumayil, who noted that the place for such discussions should be the Chamber of Deputies in circumstances other than those of armed conflict, threatened to leave the committee if it adopted any amendment to the constitution and opposed any modification of the 6/5 Christian/Muslim ratio for sectarian political and administrative representation. When Raymond Iddi called for secularism – reduced to the adoption of a civil code for personal status – as a transitional step toward abolishing political sectarianism, he provoked the expected reaction from the Muslim notables. `Abd Allah al-Yafi opposed civil marriage as a violation of a principal article of the Muslim faith (the ban on the marriage of a Muslim woman with a non-Muslim). Edmond Rabbath, attempting to clarify the matter, started by defining the ongoing civil war as 'sectarian in form, and social in content and demands' and held the system of 'free enterprise' responsible for the 'social inequalities, covered by sectarian packaging' and consequently the prevailing violence. Rabbat went on to distinguish between the abolition of political sectarianism and secularism. Sectarian pluralism, the independence of the sects and the political and administrative representation according to (presumed) numerical percentages of each sect among the population, he noted, were contrary to the fundamental democratic principle of legal and political equality among citizens. He went on to say that the constitution had attempted to reconcile two irreconcilables: equality between citizens before the law and the sectarian system of political representation. From the same angle, Rabbat discussed the question of personal status: the legislation on personal status violated the sovereignty of the state and the constitution as it subjected Lebanese to the legislation and decisions of non-Lebanese authorities such as the Vatican in Rome, al-Azhar in Cairo and the Najaf in Iraq. In conclusion, Rabbat proposed two solutions: either civil court jurisdiction in cases of personal status according to the sect of those concerned, or the adoption of a unified civil code to which citizens would adhere voluntarily, thus consecrating the key principle of democracy, that of personal choice.

   The committee resolved to abolish sectarian quotas in parliamentary representation and in the administration. There was a unanimous vote, which only lacked the approval of Pierre Jumayil. Nevertheless, the Sham`un-Jumayil-Franjiyeh troika sabotaged the CND decisions. Weeks later, Franjiyeh presented the cabinet with a totally different reform programme. Barring the road to any reform by any means – including the use of violence – was the aim of Phalangist politics throughout that phase of the war. Amin Jumayil said it in so many words: 'We have tried to save institutions from any change. Although violence leads nowhere, it has helped us at least to save what could be saved. It was violence to conserve the system.' He concluded: 'We believe in dialogue; this is why we have had recourse to violence.'[6]

MILITARY ESCALATION

After the failure of dialogue on reforms, the dialogue of arms took over. Franjiyeh and his super-minister Sham`un, whose militias were actively participating in the fighting, were directing both the government and commanding the army and the security forces. Marginalised, Karami shut himself up in the government building in West Beirut before suspending his government activity in November 1975 to protest at the army's complicity in unloading an arms shipment for the Christian militias in the port of Jounieh.

Meanwhile, the LNM had gone on the offensive in West Beirut, insisting that it was impossible to establish order as long as Franjiyeh remained in power. They launched the 'Battle of the Hotels', to dislodge the Phalange militia from a mixed quarter of West Beirut that commanded the strategic road to the Central Bank. The offensive was a reaction to 'Black Saturday': on 6 December, as Pierre Jumayil and members of his politburo were on a visit to Damascus, the Phalange militia committed a massacre in East Beirut, triggered by the discovery of the corpses of four slain Phalange members, leading to the killing of some 200 Muslim civilians, mostly port workers.

On 9 December, the intervention of the army to recover the Saint-Georges and Phœnicia hotels led to a more direct intervention of the Palestinian organisations in the fighting. Franjiyeh joined the Phalangist campaign, denouncing the 'Zionist-Leftist conspiracy' and rejecting any dialogue as long as order was not established. The president, more and more isolated, still enjoyed the support of *al-Nahar* and the 'third force' of pro-Syrian parties, especially the Lebanese branch of the Ba`th party and the partisans of Musa al-Sadr. At the beginning of armed hostilities, the Shi`i leader, shocked and sidelined by the war, refused to take sides and declared a hunger strike at the `Amiliya school until the formation of a new government of national unity. A month later, on 6 June 1975, he announced the creation of the Amal movement,[7] and soon an explosion in a Fatah training camp in the Ba`lbak region revealed that the imam already possessed an armed militia.

At the beginning of the new year Sham`un's *Numur* (Tigers) and the Phalange militia launched their first 'cleansing' operation on their territory when al-Dhubayeh Palestinian Christian refugee camp, on the Matn coast, was attacked and its inhabitants expelled from the Christian part of the country. Simultaneously, the first attacks were launched against Karantina (Quarantine) and Maslakh (the public slaughterhouse) shantytowns on Beirut's northern coast. The Joint Forces of the LNM and the PLO responded by laying siege to Damur on the coast of the Shuf, a Maronite-majority town of some 20,000 inhabitants, that controlled the Beirut–Sidon road. Sham`un, entrenched nearby in his villa at Sa`diyat, ordered the army and the air force to defend Damur. Karantina fell to the Phalange militias on 22 January 1976, and two days later, the Joint Forces invaded Damur, Sa`diyat and Jiyeh. Massacres were committed in both cases.

After these rounds of fighting, the Phalange readjusted their aim and directly accused the Palestinians of intervention in the country's internal affairs. Moreover, by February 1976 Pierre Jumayil had started calling for distributing the Palestinians of Lebanon among neighbouring Arab countries. At a time when Franjiyeh's authority had become identified with the right-wing militias, the Phalange politburo found no better solution to the crisis than the 'unity of force and of the will of the State', accusing the Muslims of weakening both.[8] That conception of unicity contributed to the division of the army. Units with a majority of Muslim soldiers in the Biqa`, the north and the south rebelled under the leadership of second-rank Muslim officers. Thus a parallel army was born under the command of Colonel Ahmad al-Khatib, supported by Fatah and financed by Libya. Fighting flared on all fronts, aggravated by the struggle for the control of the army's military barracks.

On 23 January 1976, renewed Syrian mediation negotiated a cease-fire. It was decided to deploy units of the Palestinian Liberation Army (PLA) stationed in Syria along the 'Green Line' separating the two halves of the capital. Karami, who had resigned in opposition to the army's siding with the Lebanese Front, accompanied Franjiyeh to Damascus where a constitutional charter was drafted, establishing parity in political and administrative representation between Muslims and Christians and increasing the prerogatives of the prime minister. Announced in mid-February, the charter was immediately rejected by the LNM, which insisted on abolishing political sectarianism and reforming the electoral system. On the other hand, the formation of a new cabinet was blocked by Sham`un and Jumayil who vetoed Junblat's participation in the government.

As the ministerial crisis unfolded, retired Brigadier-General `Aziz al-Ahdab took control of the state television station on 11 March 1976 and decreed the removal of Sulayman Franjiyeh. Khatib's rebel troops joined the coup. Despite the fact that the 'television general', as he was nicknamed, lacked the means to impose his decision he nevertheless succeeded in putting the president's resignation on the agenda. The only 'legitimacy' remaining in the country, the Chamber of Deputies, soon joined the call for Franjiyeh's departure as its speaker, Kamil al-As`ad, presented the president with a petition

signed by 69 deputies (out of 99), more than the two-thirds consti-
tutionally required for that purpose. Inside the Phalange politburo,
the majority supported Franjiyeh's departure but Jumayil's personal
intervention was required to stop them from publicly announcing
that decision.[9] Al-Asad, Salam and Karami left for Damascus to
request the intervention of Syrian authorities to convince Franjiyeh
to take the ultimate salutary decision. President al-Asad remained
committed to Franjiyeh but found him an honourable discharge: the
election of his successor before the end of his term. But on 25 March,
the Presidential Palace was bombarded and Franjiyeh took refuge in
East Beirut, a sad indication of the breakdown of the state.

Meanwhile, another breakthrough occurred at the end of March,
when Junblat and al-Asad met for the final time. The former, heading
a Palestinian–Lebanese coalition that controlled 80 per cent of
Lebanese territory, was engaging in his last bid to change the political
system. Before him sat a head of state gripped by a strategic vision to
unify under his leadership four peoples and three countries (Syria,
Lebanon, Jordan and the Palestinians) as a counterweight to Sadat,
who was inaugurating his step-by-step march toward a bilateral peace
with Israel. Al-Asad was hardly interested in the question of internal
change in Lebanon, while a democratic and secular Lebanon was
not exactly to his liking. In addition, he had committed himself to
support Franjiyeh and the Phalange. A dialogue of the deaf ensued
and lasted for more than seven hours. Junblat pleaded for Franjiyeh's
departure, the abolition of sectarianism and electoral reform before
the election of the new president. Al-Asad, reminding his visitor that
Syria was a secular state that refused to pose issues in sectarian terms,
continued to back Franjiyeh and to the constitutional document
that confirmed sectarianism! The meeting was doomed to end with
a dangerous rupture between the two men, as each had revealed to
the other his true motives and aims. Junblat avowed that he was
seeking to inflict a military defeat on the Lebanese Front and al-Asad
revealed his intention to carry out a Syrian military incursion into
Lebanon to control the PLO.

THE SYRIAN–ISRAELI 'DETERRENT DIALOGUE'

This sudden and unexpected turnabout in Syrian politics was noticed
by US Secretary of State Henry Kissinger and put to use in his step-by-
step strategy for solving the Arab–Israeli conflict. He could not have
failed to notice also a BBC interview with al-Asad in 1975 in which

the Syrian president declared that he stood for a settlement with Israel formalised by a peace treaty. In his attempt to integrate both Arab protagonists of the October 1973 war, Kissinger had already coined a famous slogan: 'there can be no war in the Middle East without Egypt and no peace without Syria'.

Since January 1976, the US administration had lauded the positive political role of Syria in Lebanon and supported the constitutional document signed in Damascus by Franjiyeh and Karami. But, when on 14 March 1976 Brigadier-General Hikmat Shihabi approached US Ambassador Richard Murphy in Damascus and spoke vaguely of Syria's intention to intervene militarily in Lebanon, Kissinger instructed Murphy to clarify the matter with President al-Asad. On 18 March, al-Asad informed Murphy that President Franjiyeh had requested Syrian military assistance and that he planned to 'extend a helping hand to our brothers'. When Murphy mentioned the sensitive issue of the security of Israel's borders, al-Asad answered that he could not guarantee anything concerning Israel's borders but hoped the US would urge Israel to understand that 'they have nothing to do with this internal Arab affair'.

Israeli Prime Minister Rabin's first reaction was to inform the Americans on 23 March that Israeli forces would occupy strategic positions on Lebanese territory 'as quietly as they can' in the event of Syrian military intervention. Nevertheless, on the following day, an Israeli memorandum specified that the Israeli cabinet would consider a Syrian military presence above brigade size unacceptable and would not tolerate movement of Syrian forces beyond an area of ten kilometres south of the Beirut–Damascus road. The famous 'red lines' between the two regional powers had already been set down.[10]

Upon Kissinger's recommendation, Dean Brown was dispatched to Beirut as a special emissary of US President Ford. Brown, who served as ambassador to Amman during the bloody confrontations between King Husayn's army and the *fida'iyin* in September 1970, arrived in Beirut on 31 March, greeted by a ten-day cease-fire agreement. Brown reported to his superior on 1 April that the Christians 'want the Syrians to save them'. Inside the Lebanese Front, Franjiyeh and the Phalange were already won over to Syrian military intervention. But Sham`un and Charles Malik hoped for an American military intervention under UN auspices. Brown made it clear to them that a new military venture, barely one year after the Vietnam debacle, would not be understood or accepted by American public opinion.[11]

In fact, the Lebanese Front's decision to ask for Syrian military intervention came after failing to directly involve Israel militarily in the Lebanese conflict. The first contacts between the Lebanese Front and Israel began in September 1975 when George `Adwan, a leader of the extreme right-wing organisation Tanzim, known for its close links to the army, arrived at the Israeli embassy in Paris, declared his identity and asked to meet an official. He was received by David Kimche, coordinator of Lebanese activities for Mossad, who happened to be passing through Paris. A few days later, Kimche and Colonel Benyamin bin-Elezier (alias Fuad) arrived in Juniyeh and held separate meetings with Pierre and Bashir Jumayil and with Kamil Sham`un and his son Dany. Another secret meeting was organised in mid-September between Sham`un and Pierre Jumayil and Prime Minister Ytzhak Rabin on board an Israeli navy speedboat off the Lebanese coast. The Israelis decided to give the Phalange arms, ammunitions and training, but there was no question of their direct intervention in the Lebanese conflict.[12] On 12 March 1976, Bashir Jumayil sent a Phalange delegation headed by Joseph Abu Khalil to Tel Aviv where they met Prime Minister Peres and some time later, Elezier visited Lebanon and attended the siege of Tall al-Za`tar.[13] Peres and Elezier reiterated that Israel was neither ready nor willing to engage itself in a direct military intervention in Lebanon. This position was highly instrumental in the Lebanese Front's opting for Syrian military intervention.

Be that as it may, Brown was not worried about the Christian military situation – 'they could probably hold out indefinitely against the Leftist–Moslem alliance alone unless fedayeen gave them all out support', he wrote to Kissinger.[14] On the other hand, the American emissary harboured no illusions that the Lebanese army was capable of putting an end to the armed conflict.[15]

Brown had left the US with instructions from Kissinger that the 'Syrians should be kept out' of Lebanon militarily. During his Lebanese mission, the US-brokered Syrian military intervention had been arranged. Reassured by his superior that Israel would not object to a limited military incursion by Damascus, he did not doubt the Left and the PLO would be its victims:

If Lebanon's neighbor to the East has not overly disturbed Lebanon's neighbor to the South the same cannot be said about the Lebanese Left and the Palestinians, these groups, first informed that there was no significant buildup are now faced with a *fait accompli*, softened only by the alleged assurance (obviously false) that the intervention is designed to strengthen the position of the Left. Al-Asad's tough speech drives for fast thought that the Syrians will not let Arafat or Junblat obstruct Syrian actions.[16]

On 12 April, President al-Asad, during a Ba`th party youth rally, violently attacked the LNM and the PLO, describing their leaders as 'criminals who buy and sell politics and revolution', before declaring his country's determination to intervene in Lebanon in order to 'defend every oppressed against every oppressor'. Already on 9 April, units of al-Sa`iqa had entered Lebanon and started to lift the siege of Zahleh – a siege that the pro-Syrian *fida'i* organisation had originally imposed – while tanks of the Syrian regular army appeared inside Lebanese territory in `Anjar, a few kilometres from the Syrian–Lebanese border and at Judaydat Yabus and Bayadir al-`Adas, further to the south. Brown 'assured' Junblat who inquired about these troop movements by telling him that the Syrians were on Lebanese territory in order to clear roads in the Biqa` and denied that their intervention constituted any form of 'occupation'. When it was brought to his attention that the clearing of roads did not require such a deployment of troops, Brown promised to inquire into the true size of the Syrian forces. In conclusion the envoy expressed the hope that Damascus would eventually control the Palestinians in Lebanon: 'If one makes allowances for plans in this imperfect world, it is not out of the question that the Syrians will "enforce" the Cairo agreement against the Palestinians.'[17]

On 21 April 1976, Israel's approval of the Syrian intervention was made public alongside its conditions. After reiterating its policy of non-intervention in Lebanese affairs, Israel made it clear that the Litani was a 'red line': any Syrian advance south of it would be regarded as a security threat to Israel. In fact, the 'red line' had shifted many kilometres southwards.

Thus, Syria and Israel were implicated in the Lebanese crisis and the Syrian–Israeli 'deterrence dialogue' on Lebanese territory was inaugurated.[18] Kissinger left no doubt about the convergence of the two regional powers. He wrote in his memoirs: 'We encouraged Israel to serve as arms supplier of the Christians even while Syria was acting – temporarily at least – as their protector.'[19] Furthermore, he had every reason to be happy with the 'astonishing reversal of fronts' he had helped create: Syria, the main advocate of the representation of the PLO in the peace talks (rejected by the US) was fighting the PLO or abstaining from doing so while Christian militias were besieging Palestinian camps. On the other hand, the Soviet Union, Syria's main ally, was turning against Damascus because of the military and political pressure it was exerting on the Palestinians. Ironically, 'moderate' Egypt was backing the 'radicals'.[20]

Brown disappeared just in time for the presidential elections to take place in his absence. But on the eve of his departure, the *Los Angeles Times* had already hinted that the US was backing Iliyas Sarkis. On 8 May, the MPs were accompagnied by Syrian soldiers to Villa Mansour, on the front line separating the two halves of the city, while LNM and PLO mortar fire failed to sabotage the election. Saudi Arabia and the CIA spent large sums of money to buy votes, and Sarkis was elected with the support of 66 votes. His rival Raymond Iddi boycotted the elections, as there was no guarantee that the vote would be free; he was followed by some twenty MPs from the parliamentary blocs of Junblat and Salam.

THE RACE BETWEEN ARAB MEDIATION AND MILITARY VICTORY

The eight months of fighting between spring and autumn 1976 were the longest continuous period of military operations of the war and constituted one of its most destructive and murderous phases. During this period, the LNM and the PLO had a double strategy: to liberate Tall al-Za`tar, besieged since mid-March by the Phalange of Amin Jumayil and Sham`un's *Numur*, and to impose military *faits accomplis* before the imminent massive intervention of the Syrian army.

In Beirut, fighting flared on two fronts. On 22 March 1976, as the fall of Holiday Inn ended the Battle of the Hotels and signalled the end of Phalange presence in West Beirut, the front was stabilised along the Beirut–Damascus road. More to the east, the Joint Forces of the LNM and the PLO deployed considerable efforts to open a breach in Phalange defences in the Shiyah-Sinn al-Fil-Galerie Sim`an area in the vain hope of relieving the siege of Tall al-Za`tar. But the main thrust of the Joint Forces' offensive aimed at breaking the defences of the Christian-held territories on three axes: the upper Kisrawan; the Upper Matn, where the localities of `Ayn Tura and Mutayn had fallen to the Joint Forces in early April while Bikfaya, fief of the Jumayil clan, was now within reach of their artillery; the `Alay-Kahhaleh front, overlooking Ba`abda and East Beirut, defended by a Lebanese army contingent, where the most deadly battles raged and the Lebanese and Palestinian fighters suffered heavy casualties (no less than a thousand) without being able to breach the defences of the other side.

On 1 June, President al-Asad, declaring that he was responding to a call for help by the inhabitants of the Maronite villages of Qubayat and `Andqit in `Akkar attacked by units of the ALA, announced in the presence of the Soviet prime minister on an official visit to Damascus, that he had ordered the entry of 6,000 Syrian soldiers into Lebanon. In a few days, Syrian troop numbers had reached 15,000 and had forked in three directions toward `Akkar in the north, Zahleh in the Biqa` and Sidon in the south. A meeting of the Arab League in Cairo decided to send an Arab Deterrence Force (ADF) to Lebanon, a preparation for granting Syrian military intervention pan-Arab cover and legitimacy.

The Joint Forces declared a general mobilisation and put their fighters under a unified military command to face the Syrian offensive. In Sawfar, on the Beirut–Damascus road, the first thrust of the Syrian forces was halted while in Sidon, Syrian tanks arriving from Jizzin met a ferocious resistance from Fatah fighters and had to retreat after having lost some twenty tanks – they were left charred and destroyed in the city's centre, an affront that the Syrian leadership qualified as a 'cowardly massacre' by President al-Asad himself. Meanwhile the Sa`iqa troops and militants of the pro-Syrian Ba`th were liquidated in the regions under the control of the Joint Forces. The Amal movement went underground, covered by the PLO. Sadr, definitively allied to Damascus and supporting its political and military initiatives, accused Junblat and the Left of being responsible for the war and of wanting to continue fighting Christians 'until the last Shi`i'. His positions in favour of Shi`i neutrality in the war earned him a promise by Pierre Jumayil to spare Nab`a, a promise that would not be kept. Shocked and distressed by the fall of the eastern suburb and the displacement of practically all of its 200,000 Muslims inhabitants, Sadr spent a good part of the next two years actively engaged in supporting the Iranian opposition.

In Beirut, Junblat formed a 'civil administration', which he hoped to transform into a shadow government by including in it a number of Muslim figures from outside the LNM. He was disappointed by the refusal of almost all of those invited to participate and had to put the civil administration in the hands of the LNM parties, headed by Albert Mansur, an independent deputy for the Biqa`. In a speech in Suhmur (the western Biqa`) in May 1976, Junblat accused the Arab regimes of opposing a 'progressive and democratic regime in Lebanon'. 'We are their mortal sin,' he concluded.[21] Short of an upheaval of the Arab masses to revolt against their rulers, the only recourse that remained was to seek an internal solution.

On 2 June 1976, Bashir Jumayil and Kamal Junblat met secretly at the apartment of Muhsin Dalloul, the vice-president of the Progressive Socialist Party, in West Beirut. The meeting was held upon the request of Jumayil, who wanted to present his condolences to Kamal on the assassination of his sister, Linda al-Atrash, in her apartment in East Beirut a few days earlier. Bashir made it a point to provide the head of the LNM with information on the identity of his sister's assassins, which was supposed to clear him of any responsibility for the murder. As for the subject of their encounter, the two men, equally opposed to a Syrian intervention, outdid each other in offering concessions. Junblat proposed that the president of the republic remain a Maronite Christian and insisted on a second chamber (the Senate) to represent the sects and counterbalance the non-sectarian Chamber of Deputies. Bashir, on the other hand, recited as an act of faith the complete secularisation of the state, including the abolition of political and administrative sectarianism. In return, he had only one request: the lifting of military pressure on the Christian regions, and particularly on his home town of Bikfaya, a request that Junblat took it upon himself to satisfy. Encouraged by this encounter, the LNM called for a 'peace of the brave' through direct negotiations between the armed protagonists, the LNM and the Lebanese Front, in order to reach an 'historic compromise' that would end the war. Only Bashir Jumayil answered the call, declaring that he was amenable to the LNM's programme of democratic reforms and that he accepted Palestinian presence in Lebanon as a *fait accompli*. He went on to attack the traditional political leaders (excluding Junblat and his own father) as well as the bourgeois of East Beirut who had fled the country with their capital. It was the poor who had defended the Holiday Inn, he said, though they had never set foot in the luxurious hotel.[22] But Bashir, at that time vice-commander of the Party's 'Regular Forces' but not a member of its politburo, was incapable of meeting his commitments: all members of the party leadership had come around to back the Syrian option.

In addition, the truce observed by the PLO and the LNM in support of a peaceful solution was shattered by the deterioration at the Tall al-Za`tar camp, upon which the military pressure of the Lebanese Front was becoming heavier and heavier. The following weeks witnessed a revolving door of Arab mediations: one by the Arab League, the other, an interminable mission of reconciliation between the LNM, the Lebanese Front and Syria by ʿAbd al-Salam Jallud, the number two man of the Libyan regime. The only result: a new cease-fire announced by ʿArafat and al-Asad on 29 July 1976, soon violated by the counter-offensive of the Phalange, which occupied Nabʿa on 6 August – expelling some 200,000 Shiʿa Muslims from East Beirut – before launching their final assault on Tall al-Zaʿtar. On 12 August, the Palestinian camp fell after six months of resistance. The devastated camp was 'the scene of one of the worst massacres of the war perpetrated by either side', wrote John Bulloch, correspondent of the London *Daily Telegraph*.[23] Hundreds of Palestinians (and Lebanese) were killed inside the camp and more still as they were trying to flee, not to speak of the kidnapped and disappeared.

On 23 September 1976, Sarkis replaced Franjiyeh as president as the Syrian forces launched their final offensive against the Joint Forces in the Mountain and Sidon and encircled Beirut. Meanwhile, Junblat had left West Beirut – besieged by Syrian troops who had occupied the airport and Israeli speedboats – by sea to Cyprus for an Arab tour that also took him to France. This was his last effort to balance the Syrian troops in the Arab Deterrent Forces (ADF) by contingents from the major Arab countries. In Cairo, Sadat refused any involvement of his troops in peacekeeping in Lebanon and advised the head of the LNM to mend fences with Syria. In Algeria, President Boumeddiene explained that the Riyadh/Cairo/Damascus axis controlled all decisions concerning Lebanon. In France, the Lebanese socialist leader was warmly welcomed, but his meetings with the French authorities and with the leaders of the Left opposition of Francois Mitterand convinced him that France would be unable to play any role in Lebanon as long as Syria and the US opposed it.

A few days later, on 16 October, the mini-Arab Summit at Riyad sealed the reconciliation between al-Asad and Sadat under the patronage of King Khalid of Saudi Arabia and declared a cease-fire in Lebanon as of 21 October. Syrian troops were rebaptised the Arab Deterrence Forces (ADF) with a symbolic participation of detachments from Saudi Arabia, the two Yemens and the United Arab Emirates. The Arab free hand accorded to Syria in Lebanon was ratified by the eighth Arab summit in Cairo a few days later. In mid-November, the ADF made an unopposed entry into West Beirut.

PARADOXES AND ILLUSIONS OF THE LNM–PLO ALLIANCE

The LNM–PLO alliance was based on common interests that intersected without becoming identical. The PLO's main concern was to pursue its military operations against Israel from Lebanese territory, its last refuge after the Jordanian drama of 1970. No doubt the PLO had benefited from the internal contradictions and divisions of Lebanese society and the weakness of the state to achieve this aim. For its part, the LNM, in addition to its support for PLO's right to pursue its liberation struggle from Lebanon, was mainly interested in investing the PLO's military weight to impose political reform, a goal toward which the PLO organisations held ambiguous if not contradictory positions. In any event, the mere presence of the Palestinian *fida'iyin* served as a substitute army vis-à-vis a Lebanese army increasingly subject to the command of the Maronite leadership. This PLO military force permitted the LNM to not only face the stronger right-wing militias but also move to the offensive in order to change the balance of power inside the country. On the other hand, armed Palestinian presence endowed the Lebanese conflicts with an additional weight that modified its very nature. What the LNM gained in terms of military strength, it lost in terms of popular support because of the sectarian division that this presence introduced into the Lebanese conflicts. This asymmetry of interests between two allies also expressed itself in the regional reactions toward the Lebanese crisis: there was no place in the positions of the different Arab regimes for a democratic secular Lebanon, but there still was some place for the PLO in the politics of an Arab world that was heading, with small steps and big divisions, toward a political solution of the Arab–Israeli conflict.

On the Palestinian side, the spectre of the Jordanian drama was still fresh in people's minds and produced different reactions. One was distrust for any involvement with one of the Lebanese protagonists against the other. The other was a desperate search for a stable anchorage in the Lebanese population by strengthening the PLO's alliance with the LNM. A conservative tendency, highly sensitive to the positions of the oil-producing Arab regimes, represented by Khalid al-Hasan, was against any involvement in the Lebanese war. The second tendency was represented by the left wing of Fatah, led by Nimr Salih (alias 'Abu Salih', a member of the triumvirate leadership of the `Asifa, the military wing of Fatah, with Arafat and Abu Jihad), Majid Abu Sharar, who headed the information department of the PLO, and a number of influential officers who controlled the 'regular' forces of Fatah, namely Abu Musa and Abu Khalid al-Amleh, who was a strong supporter of the alliance with the LNM. The Popular Front for the Liberation of Palestine (PFLP) of George Habash and

Nayif Hawatmeh's Democratic Front for the Liberation of Palestine (DFLP) held a similar position, though the DFLP later rallied to the Syrian stance. Between the two lay the 'centre' of the leading troika of `Arafat/Abu Jihad/Abu Iyad, although the latter leaned more toward the Left.

Fatah units in the Biqa` under the direct command of Abu Jihad did not oppose the Syrian advance, although the localities of `Anjar, Bayadir al-`Adas and especially the mountain pass of Dahr al-Baydar were ideal territory for such a resistance. Nevertheless, the Palestinian *fida'iyin* engaged Syrian troops at Sawfar-Bhamdun, under the leadership of Abu Jihad, most probably in order to impose the interposition of Arab troops in Lebanon and also as a manoeuvre to make Syria suffer the consequences of the spilled Palestinian blood. On the other hand, the biggest deployment of Lebanese and Palestinian fighters, concentrated in the high Matn under the command of Abu Khalid al-`Amleh, did not even engage in battle against the advancing Syrian troops in September.

The Lebanese Marxist Left played an important role in the elaboration of the LNM programme. From the results of the 1972 elections and the politicisation of the social movements of the prewar years it had drawn the conclusion that it had no chance to achieve any of its socio-economic reforms without prior political reforms. The principal tactics of the LNM were to impose a new superstructure on the Lebanese oligarchy – 'bourgeois', modern and non-sectarian instead of 'feudal', sectarian and 'underdeveloped'. Hassan `Awada, representing the Left in the National Dialogue Committee, insisted that the reform programme of the LNM involved simple democratic reforms 'within the context of the capitalist system'. It was also said that these reforms were destined to 'strengthen the [Lebanese political] system and enable it to respond to the requirements of the century'.[24] However, the imposition of bourgeois rationality was exercised by threatening bourgeois economic interests. By this the LNM hoped that the bourgeoisie, rather than see its economy destabilised, would put pressure on the Phalange and Franjiyeh to compromise on the issue of reforms. In fact, the bourgeoisie in its different components opted for the 'security' solution against reform; it sided with a strong government, namely a strong president of the republic. Nothing illustrated this dramatic choice more than the marginalisation of Raymond Iddi, the representative of a 'reformist bourgeois rationality'.

Be that as it may, the attempts to impose reforms through the force of arms were broken by the force of Syrian arms. At the end of 1976, Sarkis, crowned 'king of the Arabs' by the Arab heads of state, had under his command the 30,000 soldiers of the ADF. His government headed by Salim al-Huss – a respected economist who had served in the banking sector – started its activity by imposing press censorship and summoning the various militias to hand in their arms before 5 December.

As if to close the Two Years' War, its most notable protagonist Kamal Junblat was assassinated on his way from Mukhtara to Beirut on 16 March 1977, a punishment for venturing to change the Lebanese system and for his opposition to Syrian intervention in Lebanon.

Everything indicated that Lebanon was finally moving toward peace. It was but the beginning of a new phase of the war.

12
The Longest *coup d'etat* (1977–1982)

For the first time the Nation has taken charge of the State.
Bashir Jumayil, proposed inaugral address

When Bashir Jumayil was elected president of the Lebanese Republic in September 1982, Karim Pakradoni, one of his close collaborators, commented that it was the longest *coup d'etat* in the history of Lebanon. The second phase of the war can be seen as the story of the unfolding of that coup against the background of the developments of the Arab–Israeli peace process and the collapse of the tripartite alliance between Syria, President Sarkis and the Lebanese Front, ending in the propulsion of Bashir Jumayil to the presidency of Lebanon backed by the US and the tanks of the Israeli army occupying Lebanon.

BREAKUP OF THE TRIPARTITE ALLIANCE

Iliyas Sarkis took office as a partner in a tripartite alliance comprising Syria and the Lebanese Front. During the first years of his term, major events related to the American-brokered peace process between Egypt and Israel dissolved that alliance. On 19–21 November 1977, the Egyptian president made his spectacular visit to Jerusalem. Less than a year later, in September 1978, the Israeli-Egyptian accords were signed in Camp David under the patronage of President Carter, and in March 1979 Menahem Begin and Anwar al-Sadat signed the Israeli-Egyptian peace treaty. Three factors related to that process undermined the basis of the Sarkis regime: the contradictory Arab reactions to Camp David; the Israeli counter-offensive against the Syrian role and the Palestinian presence in Lebanon; and the shift in the Phalange alliance from Syria to Israel and the latter's decision to intervene directly in Lebanese affairs.

The immediate effect of the Camp David accords was a change in Damascus's priorities toward the PLO. `Abd al-Halim Khaddam, who boasted that he would disarm the Palestinians in Lebanon 'until the last kitchen knife', did not even achieve the much pressed-for application of the Cairo Accords, as Brown had hoped. The Syrian authorities needed to wean the PLO away from Sadat's fold to join al-Asad's strategic alliance. The Syrian leader's project was double-edged: it aimed at forming an Arab bloc to fill the gap left by Sadat's defection, but it could equally serve al-Asad to negotiate, from a position of force, a peace accord with the Hebrew state, in the name of three countries and four peoples (Syria, Lebanon, Jordan and the Palestinians). Arafat, having survived the Syrian onslaught, including the attempts to replace him at the head of Fatah and the PLO, found a reprieve in the Syrian advances. Paradoxically, it was during that phase of the Lebanese war that Arafat's mini-state was built on Lebanese territory in spite of the massive presence of the predominantly Syrian Arab Deterrent Forces.

On the other hand, the mounting Israeli offensive in Lebanon went hand in hand with the progress registered in the peace negotiations with Egypt, especially after the coming to power of Menahem Begin in 1977. In June 1976, Israel opened the 'good frontier' in the south and co-opted the dissidents of the units of the Lebanese army under Major Sa`d Haddad, who founded the Army of Free Lebanon (AFL). The Phalange used the southern militias to put pressure on Syria and the central government to abrogate the Cairo Accords, disarm the Palestinian organisations and redistribute the Palestinians of Lebanon among the Arab countries. The PLO, for its part, responded to the pressing demands for the deployment of the army in the south by posing two conditions: the closure of the 'good frontier' and a break in relations between the Lebanese Front and the Jewish state. Israel's offensive escalated with Operation Litani of March 1978, which led to the creation of the frontier zone under the control of Haddad's AFL, financed, armed and officered by the Israeli army. Rabin's warning to the US that the Israelis would occupy strategic positions on Lebanese territory 'as quietly as they can' had been put into practice. The interposition of the UNIFIL troops in Lebanon did not solve much of the thorny southern question, except that these troops served as a safety net to reinforce Israel's control over the border strip.

Meanwhile, talks between Damascus and its Phalange allies were becoming more and more a dialogue of the deaf. Damascus used the argument that its intervention had saved the Lebanese Front from inevitable defeat, in order to demand allegiance and the cutting of the LF's ties with Israel. Reinforced by these same Israeli ties, the LF demanded that Syria disarm the PLO.

THE SECURITY DREAM OF ILIYAS SARKIS

It has been written that Syria and the US, by electing Sarkis, had staged a *coup d'etat* to avert a revolution. The new president did all he could to implement that *coup d'etat*. He was practically the exact opposite of his mentor Fu'ad Shihab. True, the latter based his rule on the army and the security services. However, in order to achieve political stability and social control, he carried through a series of major economic, social, educational, administrative and political reforms. Whereas Shihab took seriously his own motto of 'no vanquished and no victor', his disciple believed the war had ended with a victory for the Lebanese Front and defeat for the PLO, the LNM and by extension, the Muslims.

Sarkis's first task was to consolidate his presidential prerogatives. Salim al-Huss had formed a government of technocrats and businessmen. But real power laid in the hands of the president's men: Fu'ad Butrus, Sarkis's alter ego and the only politician in the cabinet, who held the posts of foreign affairs and defence;[1] Faruq Abillama`, a personal friend, was named director of general security; Ahmad al-Hajj, a Shihabi officer, headed the Arab Deterrent Forces but failed to win over Syrian sympathy and was soon replaced by the more amenable Sami al-Khatib. Finally, Johnny `Abdu, an army officer of Palestinian origin known for his American sympathies, took over the rehabilitated Military Intelligence (the ex-Deuxième bureau). Sarkis had inherited a weak and divided army. `Abdu transformed a part of it into a strike force under his direct command.

In the economic and social fields, Sarkis's security fixation was expressed in his motto 'security before bread', a pretext for attributing socio-economic difficulties to the absence of security. His reconstruction policies revolved around the banking sector, increasingly subject to foreign capital, and he pursued the privatisation policies initiated under Franjiyeh.

The only relic of Shihabism that Sarkis preserved was a project to rebuild the political system on the basis of a Maronite–Druze alliance represented by Walid Junblat and Bashir Jumayil, but with a power relationship neatly tipped in favour of the latter. Johny `Abdu deployed considerable effort to dissociate the Druze chief from his partners in the LNM and the PLO, including dispatching booby-trapped cars to West Beirut.

One of the rare political initiatives of the president was a project for 'national concord' presented in 1980. All the parties to the conflict approved it, but the initiative was 'killed' by a veto from Pierre Jumayil. Less than a month later, in February of that year, Sarkis returned from the Arab summit at Ta'if, insisting on the priority of deploying the army over political reforms. Convinced that the Camp David peace process would not dissociate Lebanon from the Arab–Israeli conflict, Sarkis opted for the unity of presidential prerogatives, and for the exclusivity of Bashir Jumayil's political representation of the Christians. After a campaign against the duality of power between president and prime minister, he replaced Salim al-Huss by Shafiq Wazzan, a more conservative and malleable politician. Caught between the contradictory pressures of his two allies, Syria and the Phalange Party, and having to deal with two mini-states, the Marounistan of Bashir Jumayil – as the foreign press called the Phalange refuge – and the Fak'hani mini-state of Yasir `Arafat, Sarkis finally opted to help and protect the former. Incapable of fully executing his own *coup d'etat* himself, he decided to help prepare one by Bashir.

THE RESISTIBLE RISE OF BASHIR JUMAYIL

Bashir Jumayil began his rise to power when he succeeded William Hawi as chief of the Phalange's Security Council upon the latter's death during the siege of Tall al-Za`tar camp. Bashir, who had resigned from all his posts to object to the entry of Syrian troops into East Beirut and already enjoying firm Israeli backing, accepted a compromise brokered by his father. He was granted funds to build new military units and transform Karantina into a headquarters for his Security Council, which was baptised the Military Council. Thus was created the thousand-strong SKS (Section Kata'ib de sécurité), under Bashir's sole command, which he used to dominate local chiefs and establish his control over East Beirut. In 1977, Bashir had rallied to his side the party's Kisrawan section and besieged his older brother Amin's fief in the Matn.[2]

Two major factors contributed to Bashir's rise: first, the stabilisation of the military front in Beirut, pacified for a while by the ADF, which led to the withdrawal of each camp to its 'own' region; and second, the progressive crumbling of the tripartite alliance between Sarkis, Syria and the Phalange party. But the constituents of what became the Lebanese Forces had a deeper social meaning. They represented the rise of new social forces (youth, fighters, members of the professional middle class, members of subaltern families or villages, the salaried, etc.) all opposed in one way or another to the traditional Christian leaders, including the Phalange leadership itself.

Incapable of imposing himself directly on the family-run party, Bashir made a detour through the two weakest and most contested regions, the north and the Biqa`. In the north, a bitter conflict raged between the Phalange and the Franjiyeh clan. Sulayman Franjiyeh, faithful ally of Damascus, had left the Lebanese Front to protest at its Israeli connection. But the Phalange, well entrenched in the villages and 'farms' subordinated to the ruling families of Zgharta, presented a serious challenge to the authority of the Franjiyehs. In June 1978, a unit of some 200 Phalange militiamen under the command of Samir Ja`ja`, the party leader of Bisharri, attacked Sulayman Franjiyeh's villa in Ihdin. His son, Tony, Tony's wife and their small daughter were killed in the battle. Bashir, who justified the attack as retaliation for the assassination of the northern Phalange leader, Jud al-Bayi`, attributed to the Franjiyeh clan, denied having given the order to kill the family of the ex-president's son. He nevertheless qualified the military operation as an insurrection by 'farmers against injustice and feudalism'. Bashir's act divided the fighting Christian camp for the first time. With the advance of Syrian forces in the north, the control exercised by the Marada over Ihdin, Zgharta, `Akkar and parts of Batrun in the north of Mount Lebanon, and the control by the SNSP militia over the Matn town of Duhur al-Shuwayr, 'Marounistan' shrank to some 800 sq. km, a mere one-thirteenth of Lebanese territory.[3]

More importantly, the Ihdin killing triggered the first Syrian–Phalange confrontation in the summer and autumn of 1978. Syrian troops, still forbidden by the 'red lines' agreement to invade East Beirut and the Christian part of Mount Lebanon, subjected them to a deluge of artillery fire. However, the '100-days' battle' ended with the withdrawal of Syrian positions from East Beirut, and Bashir, emerging from the rubble of Ashrafiyeh as the champion of the 'Lebanese resistance', began imposing himself as sole leader of the Christian zone. In 1978 and 1979, the regular Phalangist forces and Sham`un's *Numur* gradually imposed their control over the militias of the Armenian parties in Beirut's eastern suburbs, blaming them for being neutral in the war and refusing to pay taxes and protection money. On 7 July 1980, Sham`un's *Numur* were overrun in their turn, in a bloodbath that left 150 to 200 victims, most of them civilians. Bashir also wanted to eliminate any competitor in his relationship with the Jewish state. Dany Sham`un left for exile while his father remained and adapted to the new situation. In the name of 'military unification within political pluralism', the Lebanese Forces (LF) were created, run by an executive committee of eight members headed by Bashir, with three representatives from the Phalange, now firmly under Bashir's control, two from the NLP, two from the Tanzim and one from the Guardians of the Cedars. The LF could mobilise 5,000 armed men, 4,000 of whom belonged to the Phalange militia. A few months later, the last armed enclave in the Matn, commanded by Amin Jumayil, fell under the control of the younger brother.

Economically, Bashir articulated his political power on the tertiary sector of the economy. He took over the fifth basin of Beirut port, organised a tax system on individuals and enterprises and administered the state's public services. With the help of Sarkis, the vital state administrations in West Beirut (the Central Bank, the Lebanese University, etc.) were duplicated in East Beirut.

In order to extend his control over Lebanon's Christian communities, the leader of the LF targeted Zahleh. Torn between its economic interests in the mainly Muslim Biqa` plain, its status as a Catholic city and its political sympathies, which drew it toward the Mountain, the political paralysis that hit the city in the absence of any real internal leadership allowed Bashir to take over the capital of the Biqa` at the end of 1980 with a few dozen LF fighters sent from Beirut. He thus managed to escape Syrian control over the Matn highlands and provide his Christian ghetto with some depth. In March 1981 Syrian troops reacted, encircling the city and pounding the LF's strongholds in Mount Sannin, demanding that the LF militiamen withdraw from the city and disengage the Beirut–Damascus road. As the conditions were rejected, Zahleh was besieged and bombarded. The battle of Zahleh allowed the LF to launch a successful campaign in the West against the danger of a 'genocide' that threatened the 'last Christian city in the Arab world'.

Bashir had hoped to implicate Israel in a confrontation with Damascus through the Zahleh crisis. The long 'missiles crisis' between Israel and Syria was provoked by an incident related to the Zahleh fighting, as two Syrian helicopters transporting troops to Mount Sannin were downed by Israeli fighter planes. Tel Aviv charged that the 'copters were on fighting missions, a breach of the 'red lines' agreement. Damascus said they were merely transporting troops and responded by introducing three batteries of Soviet-made Sam 3 surface-to-air missiles into the Biqa` and positioning a number of longer-ranged ones along the Syrian borders with Lebanon. Israel, feeling that the strategic balance between the two countries had been disrupted, demanded the immediate withdrawal of the missiles. The crisis was defused at the end of a long mediation by Philip Habib, a veteran diplomat of Lebanese origin, acting as personal envoy of President Reagan.

As for Zahleh, the LF fighters vacated the town but the Syrian troops were not allowed to take their place. Nevertheless, the 'red lines' had withstood the test and Bashir Jumayil was saved thanks to the intervention of Kuwaiti and Saudi emissaries who tried to convince him to sever his relations with Israel. Al-Asad had accepted that the commander of the LF entrust Sarkis with a letter pledging to comply with that demand. But the Zahleh crisis introduced Bashir to the US administration; invited to Washington, Bashir was to be groomed for the presidency. Ultimately, he did submit the famous letter, but it had no effect: the US and Israel were already preparing the invasion of Lebanon.

In March 1980, the LNM organised a military parade on the occasion of the third anniversary of the assassination of Kamal Junblat during which it launched a programme for 'the peace of the brave', which called for the reconstitution of national unity on the basis of political balance between the two warring camps. *al-`Amal* responded (on 20 March 1980) by insisting that there would never be Lebanese unity as long as half a million Palestinians were on Lebanese territory and demanded that priority be given to the deployment of the Lebanese army in the south. In October 1980, the Phalange daily went on the offensive: the partition of the country had taken place in West Beirut, which had fallen under the control of the 'Syrian Ba`thist, Palestinian, Communist and Arab Nationalist invasion' that sought to change Lebanon's identity in order to Arabise and Islamise the country. 'Real Lebanon' had been reduced to what is pejoratively called the 'Christian ghetto', concluded *al-`Amal*.

Secure inside his 'ghetto', Bashir set about preparing a military takeover in the country, with the help of Sarkis, as represented by Johny `Abdu. Whereas the Lebanese Front fought the 1975/76 war to defend the 'sacred Constitution' against any amendment or change, it was now preparing a military campaign to impose radical modifications to that same constitution to wipe out any trace of Muslim–Christian partnership in running the country's affairs and to establish decisive Christian control over the state.

'Study for seizure of power by Bashir' was the title of a plan drafted in September 1980 by Lieutenant-Colonel Michel `Awn and Antoine

Najm for the eventuality of a power vacuum on the expiration of Sarkis's term of office. `Awn – at the time commander of the army's 8th Brigade in Mount Lebanon – was the closest Lebanese army officer to the LF. Najm, a philosophy teacher and ideologue of the Phalange, who resigned from the party in 1976 to oppose Pierre Jumayil's soft line, was Bashir's closest adviser and the initiator of a federal plan that divided Lebanon into five regions. The plan ensured LF control over the largest and richest regions of Lebanon, all the while sharing power in the others. The 'study', assuming that the *putschists* would be quite weak facing Syrian and Palestinian opposition, suggested an immediate agreement with Israel, mutual recognition by the two countries and a defence treaty.[4] A second plan drafted in December 1980 by Karim Pakradoni and Joseph Abu Khalil expressly called for a 'federation, a new structure for Lebanon to replace the 1926 constitution'.[5] Delivered to Ba`thist Iraq by Elie Hubayqa and Zahi Bustani, the plan was welcomed by Tariq `Aziz, and the Iraqi leadership granted the LF generous aid in money, arms and ammunitions. Christian Lebanon was sold to the US ambassador as a second Israel with all the benefits for the USA of the first, minus its inconveniences (meaning that it would be accepted by the Arab world). As for the Saudis, they were promised a tripartite coalition between Lebanon, the US and Saudi Arabia against Communism and the Soviet Union's allies, Syria and the PLO. Bashir even discussed his projected *coup d'etat* with General Muhammad al-Khuli, commander of the Syrian Air Force and emissary of President al-Asad. In all these encounters, Bashir repeated 'I want the whole country' and insisted that Lebanon needed a 'strong President'. In early 1982, another plan for the military–LF takeover was drafted after Ariel Sharon had informed Bashir of the Israeli plan to invade Lebanon. Unsure of the support of the majority of the members of parliament for Bashir's election to the presidency, it was decided to attempt a military–LF takeover during the Israeli invasion. As the Israeli troops advanced, President Sarkis would dissolve parliament, suspend the constitution and appoint Bashir Jumayil to head a government, the main portfolios in which would will be held by LF leaders.[6]

LEBANON: SUBSTITUTE STATE OR BARGAINING CHIP?

During the Sarkis regime, the PLO was in control of the country's predominantly Muslim regions. Brandishing the threat of the Phalangist mini-state and the Phalangist–Israeli connection, the PLO refused to cede territories under its control to the army and proceeded to build its own mini-state, 'the Fak'hani canton', as it was called after the location of Arafat's Beirut headquarters.

During the 'Two Years' War', the Palestinian factor had been invested in the project to impose the reforms of the LNM. In this new phase of the war, Lebanese factors were mainly invested to serve a Palestinian strategy. Arafat faced the whole world with the following message: give us an independent state in Palestine in return for the dismantling of the temporary mini-state on Lebanese territory. Years had passed since the PLO had adopted the two-state solution and had been recognised as the sole representative of the Palestinian people by all the Arab countries and some twenty foreign states and accepted at the UN with observer status. Yet no progress had been achieved regarding its role in the Middle East peace process.

With their incursions across the Lebanese–Israeli border severely restricted by the establishment of the Israeli-controlled border strip, the Palestinian *fida'iyin* resorted to artillery or missile attacks against the settlements of the Upper Galilee. This development acquired a new political function, that of imposing the PLO as a belligerent in the Arab–Israeli conflict and partner in the peace process. For some time, it seemed that this tactic was bearing fruit. In July 1981, Israeli Prime Minister Menahem Begin, after a visit to the settlements of Upper Galilee, gave the green light for a cease-fire agreement with the PLO on the Lebanese border, negotiated by Habib and `Arafat. The cease-fire survived for almost one year, but it turned out to be a diversion to cover operation Peace for Galilee, whose goals involved destroying the PLO infrastructure and expelling the *fida'iyin* from Lebanon altogether.

For many Lebanese in the dominantly Muslim regions, the Palestinian mini-state was a buffer against the extension of Phalange domination over the whole Lebanese entity. But the price was high: the deterioration of life in West Beirut and the other areas under PLO control with concomitant exactions and suffering, especially among the inhabitants of south Lebanon who had been subjected for ten years to Israeli bombardment and incursions.

The LNM, having returned to the scene after the assassination of Kamal Junblat, provided itself with a more centralised structure under the presidency of Walid Junblat, with Muhsin Ibrahim, of the OCA, as executive secretary-general, and the general secretaries of the major parties and organisations as vice-presidents. But the LNM now presented a purely defensive programme. At the initiative of the LCP, seconded by the OCA, it had dropped from its reform programme the article concerning the voluntary civil personal status law, allegedly to reassure the Muslim 'street' and notables. Its discourse was progressively slipping toward an Arab nationalist one with sectarian themes, in which sects were divided between 'patriotic' and 'non-patriotic' ones.

Syria, for its part, incapable of disarming and controlling the PLO, contributed to the deterioration of the situation in the predominantly Muslim regions. A bitter struggle between Damascus and the PLO was launched to win over Walid Junblat and the LNM. Junblat opened up to Syria, in the hope that the sister country would oblige by backing the establishment, his own mini-state and the creation of 'local councils' to administer public affairs in the predominantly Muslim regions. But the battle for the 'local councils' did not take place. Strongly opposed by the Amal movement and the traditional Muslim leadership, it received the *coup de grâce* by Damascus. It was left to the Left and the LNM to serve as Lebanese cover for the Palestinian military presence.

The Amal movement, presided over by the lawyer Nabih Birri since 1980, took the lead in opposing the Palestinian mini-state, demanding the halt of *fida'iyin* operations from Lebanese territory and the return of Lebanese authorities to the south. The two years that preceded the Israeli invasion of June 1982 witnessed frequent clashes between Amal, on the one hand, and the Palestinian organisations and the LNM, on the other.

OPERATION 'PEACE FOR GALILEE'

In March 1980, an American spokesman invited Lebanon to join the Camp David accords, as the question of power in Lebanon was on the agenda in Israel. Sharon's vision for a new regional order envisaged a Christian Lebanon, under Bashir Jumayil, an Israeli West Bank and a Palestinian Jordan. On 6 June 1982, the Israeli army began its invasion of Lebanon to put that vision into effect.

On 20 June, as Israeli troops were encircling the Presidential Palace in Ba`abda, Sarkis, backed by Habib, convoked a six-man 'salvation committee' of representatives of the six major sects: Shafiq al-Wazzan, prime minister, Fu'ad Butrus, minister of foreign affairs, Bashir Jumayil, Walid Junblat, Nabih Birri and Nasri al-Ma`luf, a veteran Greek Catholic politician close to Sham`un. Sarkis congratulated himself for having finally succeeded in organising a meeting between

Bashir and Walid. But both Bashir and Walid were focusing elsewhere. Bashir was thinking of the Sunnis whom he exhorted to liberate themselves from Palestinian influence, or else 'there will never be a Sunni left to participate in government'. Junblat, for his part, was preoccupied by the Israeli occupation and Habib's *diktats* to the PLO, accusing him of 'preparing a genocide against the Palestinian people', not an 'honourable surrender' for the PLO fighters. As for Bashir, Junblat accused him of seeking to profit from the Israeli occupation, to which Bashir cynically replied, 'we can all profit from it'. Significantly, the Israeli occupation was not even on the agenda of the meeting. When Junblat mentioned the government's neutral stance vis-à-vis Israeli occupation, Butrus explained that the government had already submitted two complaints at the UN Security Council. Nevertheless, the point on the meeting's agenda was the formation of a restricted cabinet to negotiate the withdrawal, not of the Israeli troops but of the PLO. Not surprisingly, the committee members could not agree on aims or procedures. Nabih Birri suspended his participation, while Walid Junblat, refusing to 'deal the final blow to the Palestinians', resigned altogether from the committee and the government with minister Marwan Hamadeh.

23 DAYS OF AN ABORTED *COUP D'ETAT*

Philip Habib had the Israeli army at his disposal to wield pressure in his negotiations for the withdrawal of the Palestinian *fida'iyin* and the election of a new president. Sarkis had been chosen by Brown in accord with Syria and elected under the protection of the pro-Syrian *Sa`iqa* organisation as the Syrian army was extending its control over the country. Bashir, already promised the presidency by Begin, was confirmed in the post by Habib ('I'll make you President', he told him) and elected with the Israeli army occupying Lebanon.

On 23 August, West Beirut was bidding farewell to the last PLO *fida'iyin* under the supervision of a Multinational Force (MNF) composed of troops from the United States, France and Italy. Overlooking the capital, in an army barracks in Fayadhiyeh, Bashir Jumayil was elected President of the Lebanese Republic. The 'candidate of the Israeli tanks', as Walid Junblat described him, needed a quorum of 62 deputies. He got them by intimidation, terror and buying MPs' votes, his campaign directors acknowledged.[7]

The major event of the following days was the forced visit of the president-elect to Natania on 1 September 1982, to meet Begin who was spending his vacation in the Galilee. After reminding him of the efforts Israel made to 'save the Christians from extermination', the Israeli prime minister – addressing the president-elect as he always had done as 'my son' – asked Bashir to open immediate negotiations with the Jewish state to conclude a peace treaty between their two countries. Bashir, with strong American support and advised to win over the Lebanese Muslims and not alienate the Arabs, asked for a respite of six to nine months to establish his authority. Upon the insistence of Begin, he conceded to an agreement to 'normalise' relations between the two countries. Begin still wanted a peace treaty, or else, he threatened, the Israeli army would occupy a 40–50 kilometre strip deep inside Lebanese territory.[8] Lebanon's president-elect left the meeting humiliated. An intentional Israeli leak to the press added insult to injury as on the following day everyone concerned knew about Bashir's 'secret' visit.

Bashir's inaugural speech, published posthumously, reveals the key outlines of his vision for Lebanon. In a *pronunciamento* instituting a 'constitutional despotism' Bashir saw himself as the winner of a war rather than a parliamentary election. He made it clear that he was taking his constitutional oath in parliament for the six years to come after having 'delivered its content during eight years of resistance'. This is why the president did not feel he had to thank the MPs for their confidence; the obligation was on them: 'You have elected me, now help me!' he exhorted them. Moreover, the fundamentalist Christian nationalist president now saw himself as the incarnation of the nation embodied in the state: 'it is the first time that the Nation takes charge of the State', he affirmed. Having presented his election as the result of unanimity around his person, he felt that all of Lebanon's 'civilisation groups' (read: religious communities) should feel themselves associated to government by the mere fact of his election!

The first task of this *pronunciamento* was a new definition of the country. 'Lebanon is not a Christian country', Bashir announced, 'but a country of Lebanese Christians and Muslims.' Nevertheless, Lebanon was purged of any Arab identity, defined by its 'oriental belonging' and 'Arab links'.[9] No wonder that this muscular Libanity was alien to any form of pluralism or opposition: the state was a single whole. Legitimacy could not be opposed. No opposition to an institution of the state or an agency of the administration would be tolerated, threatened the president-elect, who said 'opposition stops at the borders of the policy of the State and cannot reach its institutions'.

On the other hand, Bashir invited 'all foreign forces' to withdraw from Lebanese territory and 'vacate the area, in favour of the Lebanese army and security forces'. As for the conflict, it was never a 'civil war' but a 'war against Lebanon', which formed part of the war of succession waged by the three monotheistic religions for the control of the Middle East. In this war, Lebanon was represented as the only Christian country that criticised the two other religions, one for seeking to bring it back to 'the time of the Caliphs' and the other to that of 'the Prophets'. Finally, Lebanon was defined as an integral part of the 'free world', which sought to become a 'partner' of that world instead of its victim.

According to his advisers Bashir had envisaged the creation of an office of vice-president to be occupied by a Maronite Christian, and considered naming Sulayman al-`Ali as prime minister. This was a highly significant choice, as Bashir's 'new Lebanon' was to be built by the victorious fighting Christians and the old marginalised conservative notables of political Islam.[10]

Bashir's socio-economic programme had already been presented in his May Day speech, a few weeks before his election; he proposed a social contract based on 'freedom and planning... production and equality of opportunities... participation... and... social justice and welfare'. This amalgam was the closest approximation to a fascistic vision that mixed a profession of faith in economic *laissez-faire* with the desire to purge dependent tertiary capitalism of its 'defects' and 'excesses', without proposing an alternative mode of socio-economic organisation. The programme further sought to liberate Lebanon from economic dependence on the outside by developing the country's productive sectors, as it was 'no longer permitted to leave our economy at the mercy on brokerage and speculation'. The idea of 'reducing envy and bringing classes together' reveals a corporatist function of the state, to which a moral role is attributed, that of 'purifying' the economic system of monopoly, brokerage, patronage and corruption. Employment and promotion in the public sector should be based on merit, competence and specialisation, not on the privileges of birth or on patronage. 'Tomorrow will end the era of favouritism and be the advent of the era of accountability,' promised the president-elect. Finally, the defence of the narrow socio-cultural privileges of sectarian origin was already manifest in the federation project. Bashir Jumayil answered the problem of the 'deprived regions' with a double rejection: he would not allow one region to absorb another or be parasitical on it. Regions under a federal system would finance their own development projects.[11]

In any case, Bashir did not have the opportunity to implement his project. On the night of 14 September 1982, barely one week before his inauguration, his body was unearthed from under the rubble of the Phalange party headquarters in Ashrafieh, destroyed by an explosive charge activated by remote control.

The next morning, Israeli troops entered West Beirut, which had resisted them for over three months, ostensibly 'in order to prevent a bloodbath'; in fact, they initiated one. On Wednesday the 15th and for the whole of Thursday the 16th and early Friday the 17th, hundreds of special security units of the LF, seconded by regular troops stationed at the airport, were mainly responsible for committing the massacre of more than a thousand Palestinians (and no less than a hundred Lebanese[12]) in the twin camps of Sabra and Shatila, not to speak of hundreds who disappeared. They were let in by the Israeli troops who were encircling the camps and helped by the hundreds of flares launched by these same troops. Ariel Sharon had visited Bikfaya the day before and informed the mourning Jumayils that Bashir had been killed by Palestinians.[13] George Shultz, then US Secretary of State, later recalled that on Friday 17 September 1982, Ariel Sharon informed Maurice Draper that he had asked the Lebanese army to enter the camp and 'clean them out'. He added: 'They can kill the terrorists. But if they don't we will.'[14] The Lebanese army failed to do so. On Wednesday 15th, units of the elite Israeli army 'reconnaissance' force, the Sayeret Mat`kal, which had already carried out the assassination of the three PLO leaders in Beirut, entered the camps with a mission to liquidate a selected number of Palestinian cadres. The next day, two units of killers were introduced into the camps, troops from Sa`d Haddad's Army of South Lebanon, attached to the Israeli forces in Beirut, and the LF security units of Elie Hobeika known as the Apaches, led by Marun Mash`alani, Michel Zuwayn and Georges Melko.

Presented as a reaction to the assassination of the LF leader, the massacre was rather a posthumous achievement of Bashir's 'radical solution' to the Palestinian presence in Lebanon, which he conceived as a 'people too many' in the region.[15] Commenting on the massacre, *Skira Hodechith*, the Israeli army's monthly journal, wrote that the LF hoped to provoke 'the general exodus of the Palestinian population, first from Beirut, then from all over Lebanon'. The monthly added: 'The Christians wanted thus to create a new demographic balance in Lebanon.'[16]

Be that as it may, Ariel Sharon was found 'indirectly responsible' for the massacre by the Israeli Kahan commission of inquiry and had to resign his post as minister of defence. The US administration's responsibility was considerable. The American peace-keeping force that oversaw the evacuation of the PLO was also assigned the task of guaranteeing the safety of 'law-abiding Palestinian non-combatants in Beirut, including the families of those who have departed'. However, the US administration withdrew the Marines detachment two weeks before the end of its 30 days mandate, forcing the French and the Italian forces to follow suit. George Shultz later confessed to the fact that the Marines of the MNF had been 'hurriedly withdrawn'.[17]

On 20 September, President Reagan recalled the MNF to Beirut.

13
The War Order (1983–1990)

> For war is a banker, its gold, human flesh.
> Aeschylus, *The Oresteian Trilogy*

AMIN JUMAYIL AND THE PHALANGIST STATE

Amin Jumayil was elected to the presidency to succeed his assassinated brother on 21 September 1982 in the same Lebanese army barracks in which Bashir had been elected under the protection of Israeli tanks. The next day, Ilyias Sarkis left the Presidential Palace in Ba`abda: a sad sortie for a grim and sad president. His mandate had started with the assassination of Kamal Junblat and the entry of Syrian troops to Beirut, and here he was terminating it with the assassination of Bashir Jumayil and the Israeli forces occupying his capital.

With Amin Jumayil's presidency the Phalange party came to power. This, at least, was the opinion of many Lebanese. Lebanon was being governed by the 'Somoza-type regime of the Jumayils', as Raymond Iddi put it: the country had two presidents of the republic – the father and the son – two commanders-in-chief of its armed forces, one commanding the regular army and the other the Lebanese Forces, both controlled by the Israeli army. The family ruled over a party that ruled over a part of the country and wielded both legitimacy and illegitimacy.[1] As if to confirm this bitter accusation, the first thing that the new president did was to visit the LF Military Council and vow to emulate his brother Bashir, even as far as offering the ultimate sacrifice. He used the presence of international troops to dominate his adversaries. Thomas Friedman remarked that Amin Jumayil, instead of using the US Marines as a crutch for the reconstruction of his country, used them as a club with which to beat his Muslim adversaries.[2] A number of Bashir's men held key posts in the administration while the economic posts were reserved for Amin's men.[3] Fadi Frem, the successor to Bashir at the head of the LF, launched his troops to the Shuf, under the cover of the Israeli troops, explaining that his militiamen had been installed there in order to 'dissipate any ambiguity concerning its identity', implying that that identity was Christian rather than mixed Druze and Christian.

During the first days of Amin's presidency, the Lebanese Forces and the army invaded West Beirut, implementing a plan prepared under Bashir, and kidnapped many hundreds of Palestinians and Lebanese Muslims whose whereabouts remain unknown at the time of publishing this book.[4] Beirut had its 'women in black', enquiring about the fate of a husband, a brother, son and demanding their return. Hardly a month later, Amin sent a police force, backed by bulldozers, to raze 'illegal squatters' areas in the poor shantytowns of Uza`i and Raml al-`Ali in the southern suburbs, on the pretext that they were too close to the airport and endangered international air travel. The gendarmes shot at the demonstrating inhabitants and left a number of dead and wounded. Finally, in August 1983, Amin ordered his army to occupy West Beirut and its southern suburb. After no more than one year in power, the Phalangist president had failed all those who hoped he would build a state and guide the country to a just and lasting peace. He had asked the protagonists to rally to his support and received a positive reaction only from Nabih Birri. After a brief entente with the president, the leader of Amal, shocked by the monopoly of power exercised by the Phalange, rallied to the opposition.[5]

SOME NEGOTIATE, OTHERS RESIST

On 24 September 1982, the Multinational Forces (MNF) were back in Beirut, driven by the anger of international public opinion at the massacres at Sabra and Shatila. Their mission was to help the Lebanese army restore sovereignty and authority in the capital.

On the eve of 1983, Lebanon was as a country divided into two parts: one resisted the Israeli occupation with arms and another negotiated a peace accord with Israel. To the first belonged the militants of the Lebanese National Resistance Front (LNRF) who since the first days of the occupation had been harassing the Israeli troops in the capital, Mount Lebanon and especially the south and the Biqa'. The LNRF, which was created on 16 September 1982 at the initiative of the Lebanese Communist Party (LCP), the Organisation for Communist Action (OCA) and the Socialist Arab Action Party (SAAP), served as an umbrella for the activities of the organisations and parties of the ex-LNM, including the SNSP and the Palestinian organisations still present and active in the Biqa`. Armed resistance to occupation was the determining factor that transformed the 'two-weeks stroll' that Ariel Sharon had promised Begin into a bloody adventure that would cost the Israeli army hundreds of soldiers killed and the bitter taste of the impotency of arms in front of a people's will to freedom. Ultimately this resistance contributed to isolate Begin in his depression, immobilised by the shocks and failures of his Lebanese venture as well as by the loss of his wife.

Increasingly embarrassed by the reactions to the Sabra and Shatila massacres and the escalation of armed operations against its troops, Israel executed a partial retreat from West Beirut on 27 September. It was 'Just in time', noted Robert Fisk in *The Times*, as the occupation army had been bogged down in a guerrilla war and assassinations targeting its soldiers 'at the rate of one operation every five hours'.[6] In other parts of the country, small groups of militants harassed the occupation forces: they threw grenades, planted landmines, attacked isolated soldiers, launched raids against posts, roadblocks and camps and organised ambushes against military convoys. They also succeeded in triggering massive civil resistance movements in villages in the south and among the thousands of prisoners in the Ansar camp in the Nabatiyeh region: there were women's demonstrations in front of the prison gates, hunger strikes by the prisoners, coordinated revolts in the whole camp by burning tents (of which the most violent were in September 1982 and August 1983), mass escapes, etc. In early 1983, an editorial in *Le Monde* was already talking of a Lebanon 'that was frightening its occupation forces'.[7]

As a year passed under occupation, the popular mood in the south and the Biqa` was turned upside down. Those who had entertained the illusion that Israeli troops would dislodge the Palestinian resistance and retreat behind the borders had realised by then that the occupation was there to stay. Cadres and rank-and-file of Amal in the south were mobilised and played a major role in the resistance. On the occasion of the first anniversary of the invasion, in June 1983, strikes and insurrections occurred in most towns and villages of the south and the western Biqa`, mobilising tens of thousands of men, while women played a role of prime importance. The courage and determination of the first resistance members had revealed that an Israeli army deprived of air cover and incapable of using its tanks and sophisticated armaments was no longer frightening. To civilian insurrections and military operations was now added the redoubtable suicide operations of Hizb Allah, recently created and operating under the banner of the 'Islamic Resistance'.

Meanwhile, Amin Jumayil, who in his inaugural address had given verbal concessions concerning Lebanon's Arab relations 'as a voluntarily choice', did not demand the withdrawal of Israeli forces. He and Sharon had agreed to conclude a peace treaty between the two countries. Negotiations started as the Phalange party insisted on the need for a Palestinian and Syrian withdrawal. In December 1983, Fadi Frem talked about a 'civilised dialogue' and 'special relations' among all the minorities of the Middle East. The peace accord with Israel, signed on 17 May 1983, stipulated the end of the state of war between Lebanon and Israel, confirmed Lebanese arrangements to ensure security on Israel's northern borders and the integration of Sa`d Haddad's SLA into the Lebanese Armed Forces in addition to restrictions on Lebanon's Arab and foreign relations. In return for all this, Israel committed itself to withdraw from Lebanon pending the withdrawal of the Syrian troops.

The accord, openly opposed by a minority of the Lebanese, met with reservations and mixed reactions from the majority. The initial position of the Syrian regime to go along with the negotiations helped this state of affairs. Ultimately, when the final text was published, President al-Asad described it to US Secretary of State Shultz as a 'pact of domination', highlighting the articles that gave Israel the right to oversee Lebanon's foreign policy and normalising relations between the two countries. But al-Asad's main objection was making the Israeli withdrawal dependent on Syrian withdrawal. Although parliament ratified the accord with 65 votes against only two and four abstentions, it was stillborn. Amin, eager not to antagonise Damascus, did not sign it and his government officially renounced it on 5 March 1984. This was the second Israeli setback in Lebanon, following the loss of Bashir Jumayil.

Meanwhile, the parties of the former LNM and the Palestinian organisations in addition to the Amal movement under Nabih Birri, Rashid Karami and the leader of Zgharta, Sulayman Franjiyeh, rallied to Damascus to launch a counter-offensive under the banner of the National Salvation Front (NSF). This was founded on 23 July 1983 to re-establish the equilibrium disrupted by the Israeli invasion. Hafiz al-Asad, believing that he had been duped by the Americans who, under the cover of an operation against the Palestinian infrastructure, encouraged Israel to strike humiliating blows against the Syrian army, was determined to return the situation in Lebanon to the *status quo ante*.

In early September 1983, the Israeli army withdrew from `Alay and the Shuf, in order to exert pressure on Jumayil to sign the peace accord and with the hope of attracting the sympathy of the Druze. The withdrawal spelled disaster for the LF in Mount Lebanon who had committed many killings and desecrated a number of Druze religious sites and figures. Thomas Friedman likened the Phalangists to 'tin soldiers' when deprived of the protection of the Israelis and the Lebanese army.[8] Under the leadership of Samir Ja`ja`, the LF troops were swept from `Alay and the Shuf within 48 hours, dragging with them thousands of Christian villagers to take refuge in Dayr al-Qamar, besieged by Walid Junblat's militia for long weeks between September and December 1983. The 'War of the Mountain' ended with massacres perpetrated by Junblat's militiamen in which no fewer than 1,500 Christian civilians were killed and 62 villages destroyed; the majority of the Christians of the Mixed Districts of Mount Lebanon simply left. An international campaign and long negotiations finally obtained the lifting of the siege and the evacuation of Ja`ja` and his troops to East Beirut.

A conference of the Lebanese belligerents convened in Geneva under the patronage of Syria and Saudi Arabia ended in failure. The determined duo of Junblat and Birri faced the irredentism of Sham`un and Pierre Jumayil. Amin Jumayil contributed to the sabotage of the agreed-upon reforms and the genuine representation of Muslims in political power. He explicitly rejected the abolition of sectarianism as a way of achieving equality between the Lebanese and insisted on the distinction between democracy and pluralism; he wrote later:

Applying the rules of simple democracy founded on the principle of 'one man one vote', would definitely not contribute to the salvation of Lebanese pluralism, as one component of the national collectivity would monopolise the totality of power.[9]

In his counter-offensive, al-Asad held many trump cards, prominent among which were military pressure on the Presidential Palace exerted by his allied Lebanese and Palestinian militias, keeping Jumayil in check, and the formidable range of kidnappings and executions manipulated by Hizb Allah commandos. Those factors combined to promote the withdrawal of the multinational forces and provide renewed legitimacy for the Syrian role in Lebanon. In early 1984, Junblat declared that the fighting would continue until the resignation of Jumayil's government 'even if this means the destruction of Lebanon'.[10] On 6 February 1984, Amin Jumayil, in an attempt to prevent the link-up of PSP militiamen in the Mountain with their Amal counterparts in Beirut's southern suburb, sent army units to take over West Beirut. The result was a new division of the army as the predominantly Shi`i units rallied to the rebels and West Beirut and its southern suburb fell under the control of the militias of Junblat and Birri.

Following this radical reversal in the balance of power, the MNF left Beirut, after having suffered heavy casualties in the October 1983 suicide attacks against the US and French contingents. Jumayil's rule held by a thin thread, besieged as he was in his Ba`abda Palace by Junblat's fighters and the Palestinian *fida'iyin* from Suq al-Gharb. He was protected only by loyal army units under General Michel `Awn and by the US aircraft carrier *New Jersey*, which subjected the country to the bombardment of its imposing artillery, the biggest naval fire force in the world.

In an attempt to save his floundering regime, in which he exercised mainly economic power, Jumayil decided to cede larger political participation to the traditional Muslim *za`im*s and militia leaders. Rashid Karami, designated prime minister after the Lausanne conference, formed a government of 'national unity' in which Walid Junblat and Nabih Birri participated. This inaugurated a short period of precarious coexistence between the Phalangist state and the militia forces.

On 17 February 1985, Israeli forces withdrew from Sidon and the area of the Beirut–Damascus road near the border strip, putting an end to the occupation resulting from the 1982 war, with the exception of the Jizzin region. Israel had lost some 500 soldiers in its Lebanese adventure. *Maariv*'s military correspondent spoke of an Israeli army that 'had suffered the unforgivable' at the hands of 'those who organized the Lebanese war'. He added that the big lesson to draw from this adventure was 'how Israel's military omnipotence could be transformed into impotence and precarious-ness'.[11] According to a tacit agreement mediated by the US, Israel left security in the south to the Amal movement; the price to be paid was its anti-Palestinian role in the war against the Palestinian camps during 1984–85. In the western Biqa`, the accord negotiated by US officials stipulated that Syrian troops would not enter the zones south of the Beirut–Damascus road, though Lebanese army units loyal to Damascus were tolerated, with the discreet participation of Syrian intelligence officers in them.

PROGRESSION OF THE SYRIAN COUNTER-OFFENSIVE

At the end of the year, the Syrian counter-offensive saw a new push in Lebanon. On 28 December 1985, a tripartite agreement was signed in Damascus by the three leading militia chieftains, Junblat, Birri and Elie Hubayqa. Hubayqa had taken over the leadership of the LF on 9 September 1985, in association with Samir Ja`ja`, the northern militia leader who was named commander-in-chief of the LF. Hubayqa – who consummated the break with Amin Jumayil and the Phalange – had tried to wash his hands of the Sabra and Shatila massacres and executed an about-face, in the direction of Damascus where he was embraced and his public image restored. This break signalled the first division inside the Christian camp, which had hitherto been united, at least vis-à-vis Syria. The signatories to the accord pledged to end the war and dissolve all of the militias within one year. Politically, it confirmed parity in sectarian representation between Christians and Muslims, the abolition of political sectarianism after a short transitional period and established a new balance in the prerogatives of the president of the republic, in favour of the prime minister and the cabinet.

In direct response to Bashir Jumayil's revisionism, the Tripartite Agreement document redefined Lebanon as an 'Arab country as regards its belonging and identity'. Provision was made for amending the electoral law in order to increase the number of deputies, reduce the voting age (from 21 to 18) and create a Senate – this body would be chosen along sectarian lines and rule on 'vital questions' regarding constitutional amendments, naturalisation, the declaration of war and peace, the signing of treaties with foreign parties and the like. Finally, the agreement provided for the signature of bilateral treaties between Syria and Lebanon to give concrete expression to the 'strategic complementarity' between the two countries. Economically, the accord stipulated close bilateral collaboration while respecting the difference between their respective economic systems. During the banquet to celebrate the event in Khaddam's office, the vice-president in charge of the Lebanese file reiterated the desire of Damascus to preserve Lebanon's economic system, and launched the idea that Syria could well become 'a consumer market for Lebanon'.

Amin Jumayil opposed the accord, despite the attempts to convince him to the contrary during his many meetings with President al-Asad; the final session, which marked the break between the two, was on 13–14 January 1986. Jumayil argued that the accord deprived the president of his role as an arbiter, replaced a 'truly complex democracy' by numerical democracy and responded to the call for the abolition of sectarianism by advocating complete secularisation. Damascus responded by organising a conference of the signatories, who declared war on the Phalangist government. Jumayil's reaction was not in the least weak. In February, he resorted to parliament to oppose the Tripartite Accord, while on 12 March 1986 he and Samir Ja`ja` engineered an armed coup that ousted Hubayqa from Marounistan with hundreds of his partisans. The Tripartite Accord thus met its end, to be resurrected after some years as the basis for the Ta'if accords.

THE ECONOMIC DEBACLE

Meanwhile, the country was on the verge of economic catastrophe. In 1984, 'war in a time of abundance' ended. Many factors contributed to this end: the withdrawal of PLO deposits in Lebanese banks and the cessation of PLO spending; the massive destruction caused by the Israeli invaders, part of which was intentional and involved economic objectives; the decrease in bank deposits (from $12 billion in 1982 to $3 billion in 1990); the increased subjection of the economy, and particularly the banks, to foreign capital and the flow of a good part of the deposits outside the country. The president's profiteering and that of his men accounted for much of this deterioration. Nicknamed Mr Two Percent at the beginning of the war for the percentages he levied on all transactions in East Beirut, Amin Jumayil saw his popular appellation rise to the rank of Mr Twenty Percent.

The end of the 'war in time of abundance' period was also the beginning of the dollarisation of the economy and the devaluation of the Lebanese lira. Indeed, the devaluation of the currency had a lot to do with the speculation on the dollar. Practised by the state (through the Central Bank) as well as the president's men and the militias, speculation was soon transformed into a national sport: there were no fewer than 200,000 bank accounts in US dollars in 1988. But a structural cause is frequently neglected when it comes to dollarisation: the country was practically producing nothing and importing practically everything.

Two effects of this crisis are worth mentioning. First, public debt rose from LL 7 billion in 1981 to LL 35 billion in 1985, partly owing to the decrease in state revenues because of spoliation by the militias and the increase in expenses and military spending. The

Jumayil government had agreed to arms purchases, especially from Washington, for $1.1 billion, paid in cash. A second effect was the soaring increase in the cost of living and the depreciation of incomes. The vital minimum income for a worker's family was estimated at LL 3,000 while an average worker's salary did not exceed LL 952.

RETURN OF THE SYRIAN FORCES

On 28 February 1987 Syrian troops returned to Beirut, invited by Muslim leaders. They were favourably welcomed by the capital's population as likely to put an end to the murderous infighting between Amal and the PSP. Once more, the 'red lines' had functioned. The confrontations between Amal and the PSP threatened to produce a PSP victory that would have rendered the PLO, still the single most important military force in West Beirut, masters of the city, thus overturning all of the 'achievements' of the June 1982 invasion. Damascus received the American 'green light' this time to prevent this eventuality and in the hope that Syrian troops would find a way to release Western hostages. Thus, al-Asad's counter-offensive did achieve a return to the pre-Israeli invasion situation of 5 June 1982.

Internally, the hegemony of the Phalange contributed to a situation in which an already marginalised state had to accommodate itself to a de facto partition of Lebanese territory among a number of armed sectarian cantons that were robbing it of much of its resources, revenues and political power. At times, history plays curious tricks on its actors. Encouraged by the progress of the US–Israeli offensive, the Phalange under Bashir abandoned regionalism in favour of a muscular domination over the whole country. Amin's attempts to implement this control triggered a process of disintegration in which cantonisation ran rampant across Lebanese territory. Bashir Jumayil bequeathed to his comrades in the Phalange and the LF a heavy inheritance, which divided them; however, he bequeathed to his 'enemy brothers', the other warlords, a poisoned gift: the desire to emulate his model of territorial mini-states. This was a time of proliferation in mini-states whose justifications were the defence of their regions against the expansionism of the Phalangist mini-state and the fall of the 'central' state under Phalangist domination.

Seventeen sects, a dozen cantons, some twenty ports and dozens of armed organisations – this was the Lebanese scene after 1983.

THE REPRODUCTION OF ARMED SECTS

The war, partially the result of sectarian conflicts, was to become the crucible in which those sects were reproduced.

The marginalisation of the Sunni community is a hallmark of the post-1983 period. A combination of factors contributed to this development, such as the impact of the Palestinian withdrawal; the disappearance of prestigious leaders (Sa'ib Salam in voluntary exile, and Rashid Karami and Mufti Sheikh Hasan Khalid assassinated); and the political disappearance of the only militia that represented the Sunni community, the *Murabitun* of Ibrahim Qulaylat, liquidated by the joint efforts of Amal and the PSP, presumably upon Syrian request. The LNM, dissolved by its President Walid Junblat, progressively ceded the arena to an increased sectarianisation of Muslim political forces.

Musa al-Sadr's 'disappearance', the failure of the reformist programme of the LNM, the outbreak of the Islamic revolution in Iran and the combined effects of the Israeli occupation and the dismantling of the Palestinian mini-state gave a new configuration to political *shi`ism*, and posed new challenges. With the As`ad leadership marginalised, Husayn al-Husayni, elected president of Amal after the disappearance of Imam Sadr, attempted to renew Shi`i leadership by parliamentary and political means. Husayni resigned two years later in favour of Nabih Birri, refusing to compromise himself in an armed conflict against the Palestinians.

Three currents were fighting for the heritage of Imam Musa Sadr. Sheikh Muhammad Mahdi Shams al-Din, vice-president of the Higher Islamic Shiite Council (HISC), supported a political solution that would reveal the numerical weight of the Shi`a, better to take place in time of peace than in time of war. At the opposite extreme was leading Shi`i *mujtahid* of Lebanon, Sayid Muhammad Husayn Fadl Allah. Unconvinced by Khumayni's 'governance of the jurisprudent' (*Wilayat al-Faqih*) and hesitant to recognise the authority of Qum and the Iranian mullahs at the expense of the Najaf in Iraq, Fadl Allah was nevertheless the spiritual guide of Hizb Allah, which advocated the Islamic Republic. Though present in the south and Beirut's southern suburb, Hizb Allah's bastion was in the Biqa`. As Amal was progressively subjected to the interests of the parvenu bourgeoisie, especially those who made their fortunes in Africa, the middle classes and the intelligentsia claimed by public service,

Hizb Allah's radicalism attracted the more deprived and the younger segments of the population.

Another bone of contention between the two organisations concerned the anti-Israeli resistance and the Palestinian presence in Lebanon. After the Israeli withdrawal of 1985, Amal was content to suspend most of its resistance activities, while Hizb Allah's role progressed at the expense of the other organisations, especially on the Left. The new force was soon to become the sole resistance movement, strongly backed by the Syrian authorities, which deployed all available efforts to block the participation of the Communists in the resistance. On the other hand, Hizb Allah had publicly disavowed Amal's 'war of the camps', a war encouraged and armed by Damascus and backed by a parliamentary vote abrogating the Cairo Accords.

Amal, in both discourse and practice, held an intermediary position between the two poles of the community, the 'legalist' and the 'radical'. Birri's contribution can be likened to that of Bashir Jumayil. Like the LF commander in rebellion against the image of the Christian/businessman/pacifist who always turned the other cheek, Birri represented the rebellion against the traditional image of the Shi`a as millenarian oppositionists, permanent victims and scapegoats of Muslim history. Representing a political and armed brand of Shi`ism, Birri was intent on eliminating this historical image in favour of a positive image of a community claiming its share of political power.

On the Druze side, a slow but steady radical revision of Kamal Junblat's democratic and secular project was taking shape. The 'Battle of the Mountain' figured in the speeches of Walid Junblat as revenge by the Druze against a Maronite 'expansionism' that had been perpetuating itself for centuries. Its climax, the occupation of Bashir Shihab's palace in Bayt al-Din, was the occasion for the reversal of roles among the three Bashirs. Bashir Jumayil was associated with Bashir Shihab II, seen as the emir who reversed power in the Mountain in favour of the Christians after he had Bashir Junblat assassinated in 1825. Bashir Junblat was thus promoted to the rank of mythical ancestor of the Druze community and rehabilitated by an act of historical revenge executed by one of his descendants more than a century and a half later. Thus, Walid Junblat could finally declare: 'The only Bashir we recognize is Bashir Junblat'!

But, as always, sectarian distinction cannot function without its class component. For the historical reversal to be completed, the historical identification had to be pushed to its ultimate logic. A popular poem by the Druze poet Tali` Hamdan, celebrating his community's victory in the War of the Mountain, identified the Druze community with its feudal status and reduced its adversaries to their former status as commoners and peasants. The Christians found themselves attacked in Hamdan's poem as peasants, share-croppers and servants whom 'we brought to our [Druze] region' but revealed their ungrateful nature as 'venomous serpents' who turned against their benefactors.

In contrast to Junblat's socio-sectarian model of the *muqata`ji* sect, the superior aristocratic/tribal community that was condescending toward those who ploughed the earth and engaged in manual labour, Nabih Birri's sect was primarily defined by its populist, anti-feudalist connotations. In the Lebanon of the second half of the twentieth century, Amal's war against 'political feudalism', represented primarily by the As`ad clan, interpellated the bourgeois parvenus and the intellectuals – blocked in their social mobility – to occupy the place they deserved in the political and economic system.

It is of course highly significant that militia legitimacy began to erode as the militia took over control of its own 'territory'. In the relative absence of 'external' enemies to frighten their subjects with, militia violence was 'internalised' in order to control its 'subjects' inside the communitarian ghettos carved out and cloistered by violence. In the ambient chaos, Lebanon between 1985 and 1990 lived under the domination of associated armed mafias that had renounced fighting each other, respected their mutual borders and entertained close ties between themselves for a better spoliation and control of everything Lebanese.

THE POLITICAL ECONOMY OF MILITIA CONTROL

It has been said that wars have no sense but functions. In fulfilling a series of extra-military functions, the Lebanese civil war created its own order, an order that was a monstrous mutation of its prewar political and economic system: the autonomy of the sects mutated into armed control and 'sectarian cleansing', while the wild *laissez-faire* economy transformed into mafia predation. This new order was a new form of war: the war waged by the militias against the state and its citizens.

Political and military power became the principal means of extracting the economic surplus and the constitution of new economic interests and social relations. The tribute-collecting and tax-farming role of the warlords achieved the supreme capitalist phantasm – the generation of revenues and profits without capital investment – through the militias' parasitical politico-military levy on practically all economic activities.[12]

Cantons and ports: a new configuration of space

Beirut's central and centralising role – in the economic, political and administrative fields – was dissipated in favour of no less than ten militia-controlled cantons mostly built around a number of 'illegal' ports. Similarly, the central market towns of the interior lost their function or were replaced by new ones. Catholic Zahleh ceded its monopoly position as the economic and administrative capital of the Biqa` to a number of localities, among them Ba`albak (Shi`i), while Maronite Dayr al-Qamar, in the Shuf, lost much of its role to Ba`aqlin (Druze).

The first illegal ports on the Lebanese coast emerged at the beginning of the war and were used to smuggle arms. Later they became economic enterprises in their own right and controlled foreign trade. In the extreme north, the small port of al-`Abdeh was primarily engaged in imports destined for the Syrian market. The port of Tripoli was still run by the Lebanese government but with Syrian control and 'protection'. Businessman Tariq Fakhr al-Din on behalf of the fundamentalist Islamist organisation *al-Tawhid* administered *al-Mahdi* port. Shikka's port primarily exported the products of its cement factories, under the protection of Franjiyeh's Marada, the SNSP and other pro-Syrian groups. Juniyeh port imported foodstuffs for Marounistan and ran a regular ferry to Cyprus. The port of Beirut's fifth basin was under the control of the Phalange party and the Lebanese Forces. Uza`i, south of Beirut, was run by Amal militia beginning in 1984, while the neighbouring ports of Khaldeh and Jiyeh were operated by Junblat's PSP as outlets for the Druze canton in the Shuf. Users of the port of Sidon had to pay duties twice, to the government authorities and to Mustafa Sa`d's Popular Nasserite Organisation. A part of the port's revenues was also paid to the South Lebanese Army (SLA) of dissident General Lahd as the port was within reach of SLA artillery. The port of Zahrani, under the control of Birri's Amal, was mainly used to import fuel oil. Its revenues were divided between Amal and the Lebanese government, and a share also went as 'protection money' to General Lahd. The port at Naqura, on the Lebanese–Israeli border, had since 1978 been managed by the SLA and the Israeli army. It imported goods for the Israeli-controlled southern strip.

Marginalisation of the state

Robbed of its monopoly of violence, its army divided along sectarian lines and the Lebanese state – whose power was at times reduced to the parameters of the Presidential Palace in Ba`bda – had to coexist, as the weaker partner in a true duality of power with the militias, which were the effective rulers of the greater part of Lebanese territory. Militias took over most of the state's income-generating functions, especially those that provided the bulk of state revenues – customs duties and indirect taxes. At least a quarter of the state's revenues were thus reverted to militia funds. Further, the state's monopoly over the audio-visual media was shattered as a number of militia-owned TV stations and FM radios went on the air.

Sectarian division and purification

When the militias finally 'cleansed' their territories and came to control 'their own people' and run their affairs, pressure on the individual to define himself/herself in terms of a unique social and cultural sectarian identity reached its climax. Militia power not only practised ethnic, sectarian and political 'cleansing' of territories but also committed what Juan Goytisolo has aptly called 'memoricide', the eradication of all memories of coexistence and common interests between Lebanese. Instead, they imposed their discourse of 'protection' on their own 'people': the 'other' wants to kill you, but we are here to save your lives.

Paradoxically, however, when the sectarian system achieved its paramount goal – self-rule of each community on its own territory – the contradictions inherent in the system exploded in the most violent forms. War shifted from inter-sectarian fighting to a bitter struggle for power and control inside each community. The notion of a unique political and military representation of the community, undertaken for a brief period under Bashir Jumayil, became the dream of each and every militia leader. This period witnessed the bloodiest confrontations of the war: the 'war of the camps' between Amal and the Palestinian organisations (in West Beirut and southern Lebanon), periodic fighting between Amal and the Socialist Progressive Party of Walid Junblat and the parties of the ex-Lebanese National movement (for control over West Beirut), bitter and prolonged fighting between Amal and Hizb Allah (in Beirut, the Biqa` and the south) for the monopoly of representation of the Shi`a, etc. On the other hand, fighting erupted regularly inside the Christian camp between the Phalange party and the Lebanese Forces, and between different factions of the Lebanese Forces themselves (Ja`ja` and Hubayqa), and culminated in two destructive wars between the Lebanese Forces and the Army of General Michel `Awn.

Pillage, piracy and plunder

Difficult as it is to calculate the sums involved in the arms traffic during the Lebanese wars,[13] a large surplus of arms and ammunitions existed throughout the war to turn the PLO organisations and the warring Lebanese into international arms dealers. Afghan guerrillas, Yemeni tribes and the protagonists of the war in the former Yugoslavia were among their many customers.

Drug trafficking was the economic activity in which all militias collaborated. During the war period, the area devoted to *hashish* cultivation doubled and came to occupy more than 40 per cent of the cultivable land in the Biqa`. More importantly, opium culture was introduced for the first time, its production estimated at a dozen tons of heroin processed in a number of clandestine laboratories that even processed Colombian cocaine. The estimated value of narcotics produced in Lebanon was around $6 billion and their market value reached as high as $150 billion.[14] The yearly tributes accruing to the various parties that controlled the traffic have been estimated at between $500 million and $1 billion.[15]

The Lebanese war was the scene of the most famous thievery of recent times: the pillage of the Port of Beirut by the Phalangist party (estimated at $1 billion) and the robbery by a Palestinian organisation of the British Bank of the Middle East, which entered *The Guinness Book of Records* as the biggest bank robbery of all time (estimated at £20–50 million). To these we should add the regular practice of stealing cars, which became a lucrative trade in itself throughout the war. According to police files, during only eight months in 1985–86, a total of 1,945 cars were registered as stolen, the majority in Beirut.

Georges Corm has estimated the total revenue accruing from pillage and robbery during the Lebanese civil war at $5–7 billion.[16]

The illegal ports engaged in smuggling cigarettes, drugs and arms; they also moved contraband commercial goods and livestock. It has been calculated that the value of goods smuggled into Syria, Israel and Cyprus through Lebanon amounted to LL 21 billion in 1986.

A modern form of piracy took on an exaggerated importance during the Lebanese war as merchants' ships along the Lebanese coast were diverted from their course, their merchandise sequestrated and the ships sunk or returned to service under a different name, registration and flag. The LF mainly carried out this activity, allegedly in collaboration with the Italian Mafia. Between 1986 and 1989, 140 ships en route to the Indian Ocean disappeared along the Lebanese coast. By 1989, British insurance companies had paid no less than £120 million in compensation for ship owners who had suffered from piracy on the Lebanese coast.

Militia-controlled ports were also engaged in the import of toxic waste from Europe, dumped inland in return for large sums of money.[17]

Tribute and protection money

The first aspect of the new configuration of space were the armed checkpoints and passageways on the 'borders' between the different cantons, which had the dual function of controlling entry and exit to the zone under militia control and serving as customs posts. The various militias imposed their tolls on passengers, vehicles and merchandise. Passengers paid 'per head' while cars were taxed on the estimated value of the goods transported and the nature of the vehicle itself (tourist car, van or truck). At the LF checkpoints, goods were taxed at 2 per cent of their estimated value. On the road to south Lebanon, one had to pass the checkpoint of the PNO on the outskirts of Sidon, further on; one would find Amal militiamen imposing a fixed tax on trucks leaving the IPC refinery at Zahrani. Further south, the five checkpoints of the SLA were designed to seal off the Israeli-occupied zone economically from the rest of Lebanon and help divert its economy toward northern Israel.

Most militias levied a head tax. Protection money and income taxes were imposed on economic activities: agricultural enterprises, commercial and industrial firms, the liberal professions, and so on. A direct lump sum tax of $30 per month was imposed on all industrial or commercial enterprises. Thereafter, enterprises were taxed according to their importance. Tourist centres and beaches, for example, were taxed at the rate of LL 350–550/m^2 of the centre's installations and cottages at the rate of LL 2,500–5,000/m^2. Sand extraction along the coast was taxed per cubic metre likewise by the LF and Amal. This activity turned out to be so profitable that Amal created its own company for sand extraction in partnership with migrant capital.

The bulk of the revenues of the northern canton of the Marada came from protection money imposed on the cement plants of Shikka, taxed at the rate of $3–5 per tonne. Most big companies, like Middle East Airlines and the *Régie*, paid enormous sums in protection money to almost all of the militias. In the agricultural areas of the south, the Amal militia levied a tax on land ownership at the rate of $2/dunum. Consumer goods were equally taxed: for example, cigarettes (5 per cent of the price), cigars ($3 per cigar box), cinema and theatre tickets (3 per cent of the price) and restaurant bills (5 per cent of the sum).

Another important source of militia fiscal revenues was taxes and dues levied on administrative formalities previously gathered by the state: this included registration of transfers of landed property, registration of cars, building permits, work permits and residence permits for foreigners. The decrease in state revenues led to an increase in public debt, which doubled five times in five years from LL 7 billion in 1981 to LL 35 billion in 1985. It has been estimated that the militias expropriated at least 20 per cent of the state's revenues.[18]

MILITIAS AS BUSINESS ENTERPRISES

In addition to robbing the state's revenues and heavily taxing their 'own' communities, the militias in power articulated their economic activities around the dominant and more profitable services and commercial economic sectors. After 1983, the main militias took control of a large part of the import trade and all distribution of fuel and flour. In addition to their monopoly control over those vital products, they imposed high taxes on their consumption and reaped enormous profits from speculation on the differences in the prices of those commodities between different Lebanese regions.

Practically all foreign trade was in militia hands. The newly created ports had become militia-owned enterprises. The Phalange and LF managed to buy the majority of the shares in the company that ran the port of Beirut. Containers were taxed at the rate of $800 per unit. Imported cars were taxed at the rate of 20 per cent of their price. In Naqura, Lebanese businessman Samir al-Hajj engaged in the reexport business: Israeli merchandise destined for Arab markets, camouflaged as Lebanese products. He paid $15 million in yearly protection money to the SLA, which gives an idea of the volume of his trade.

Cooperation between the militias in the narcotics traffic and in the distribution rackets laid the foundation for future cooperation in other fields. The same militia representatives who would sit on joint 'security' committees, as representatives of belligerents at war, would, perhaps in the same day, reconvene as members of the board of directors of companies that they now collectively controlled – TMA, the national air transport company, for one – or meet to divide their revenues from the distribution of butane gas. Strange bedfellows such as the general secretary of the pro-Syrian Ba`th party and the sons of the Christian right-wing leader Kamil Sham`un were partners in the lottery business, which held monopoly rights over all Lebanese territory.

Not only did militias 'exchange services' with sections of the bourgeoisie (protection money in return for import and export quotas or sheer profiteering), but they soon became large business enterprises in their own right and an integral part of that class, entering into close business partnerships with many of its members, especially in the flour and fuel trade. And as war neared its final phase, the warlords had 'laundered' a part of their capital into privately owned companies.

One other important function of the 'informal' militia economy was the development of a black market for imports to Syria, which involved a number of ports and the central Biqa` region.

WAR AND SOCIAL MOBILITY

How were the revenues of these enormous enterprises distributed? One part was invested in the war effort. Another became the personal fortune of the warlords, deposited in Swiss banks or invested abroad. Yet another part was reinvested in a number of 'holding companies' duly registered in Lebanon, the three main ones being under the control of the Lebanese Forces, the Amal movement and the Progressive Socialist Party of Walid Junblat. A striking aspect of sectarianism in business, these Maronite, Shi`i and Druze holdings came to own a number of companies operating in all economic sectors: private ports, import–export trade, cement factories, tourism, real estate agencies, FM radios, television companies, newspapers and publishing houses, to name but a few.

In the early phase of the war the sacking of the Port of Beirut and the city centre were orgiastic forms of redistribution of wealth. Later on, redistribution became more stratified as the 'masses' withdrew gradually from the stage. Although the above-mentioned forms of income redistribution by military and political means were not

238 The Wars of Lebanon

restricted to the warlords, the amounts that trickled down to the rank-and-file militiamen are more difficult to identify, especially since social mobility related to emigration cannot be easily differentiated from that arising from the war itself. We can safely say that mafism in Lebanon, the highest stage of clientelism, follows the same logic as any other form of clientelism, that of 'uneven exchange' and 'uneven distribution' between patrons and clients, except for the fact that the main role of clients in war was to die for their patrons.

WAR AS DEMOGRAPHIC PURGE

Wars, civil or regular, share a common anthropological function, that of the expulsion of human surplus and the establishment of demographic equilibrium.

It has been estimated that the bloody fifteen-year purge in Lebanon resulted in 71,328 killed and 97,184 injured. The expulsion of the human surplus in Lebanon took three basic forms.

The first, sectarian 'cleansing' of the community's territory of 'strangers' (mainly Shi`i Muslims in the 'Christian' enclave and Christians in the 'Druze' Mountain) led to some 670,000 displaced among the Christians and 157,500 among the Muslims.[19] This sectarian 'cleansing' was coupled with a political one, the expulsion of political 'strangers' and those members of the community who did not comply with the policies or dictates of the dominant militia.

Second, there was the expulsion of 'foreigners' or 'intruders', which in this case refers mainly to the Palestinians. Bashir Jumayil had a famous phrase for the Palestinians as 'a people too many in the Middle East'. The massacres of Sabra–Shatila and the wars of Amal against the Palestinian camps, not to speak of Israeli military operations and the two outright invasions of 1978 and 1982, can be seen as military procedures to get rid of that 'people too many'.

Third was migration: nearly a third of Lebanon's population (estimated by Labaki and Abou Rjeili at 894,717 people) was driven out of the country. The economic and social consequences of this massive outflow of the working population, mainly the young, have been enormous: a majority of the Lebanese workforce has become employed outside their country; the balance of power among the sectors of the economy has tipped even more in favour of tertiary and rentier activities at the expense of productive sectors (which suffered most from the destruction); the extroverted character of the economy has been intensified as has been the specific logic of capital investment directed toward speculation in property and foreign currency.

However, it still can be said that the war did its job in establishing a new demographic equilibrium by the double means of death and emigration.

Postscript
Ambiguities and contradictions
of the Ta'if Agreement

The Ta'if Agreement, signed on 22 October 1989 in Saudi Arabia by the Lebanese parliamentarians, inaugurated a process that put an end to the Lebanese civil war and set the country on the path to peace and reconstruction. A year later, a Syrian–American rapprochement, in preparation for negotiations on peace in the Middle East, reinforced by the participation of Syrian troops in the operation Desert Shield, in October 1990, allowed Damascus to launch a final assault to dislodge General Michel 'Awn from the Presidential Palace in Ba'abda and put an end to two years of dissidence and to 'dual legitimacy'. General 'Awn, took refuge in the French embassy, and after long deliberations between the French and Lebanese governments, he was allowed to leave for France as an exile, in August 1991.

'Awn's dissidence had started in October 1988 when Amin Jumayil's term of office ended without the election of a new president, as most of the concerned factions had rejected Mikha'il al-Dhahir, a compromise candidate agreed upon by Syria and the United States. Jumayil named army commander-in-chief Michel 'Awn as prime minister, an appointment immediately contested by Muslim politicians. Salim al-Huss, who had resigned as prime minister went back on his decision and declared himself the legitimate holder of the post. Thus Lebanon lived for two years with a vacant presidency and a duality of power between two competing prime ministers.

Michel `Awn could well be called Bashir II, as his policies, in more than one sense, were echoes of Bashir Jumayil's: in his quest to monopolise Christian representation, his military methods and his identification of 'Lebanese' with 'Christian'. All is said in the title of a brochure by one of his advisers, 'The Army is the Solution'. But whereas Bashir sought to integrate the army in his project for taking over power by the LF, `Awn, while calling for the end of all militias, eventually sought to suppress the LF and integrate it into the army's project to take over power. In his quest for regional and international 'legitimacy', `Awn received massive aid from Saddam Hussein's Iraq, yet he opened negotiations with Damascus on his candidacy for the

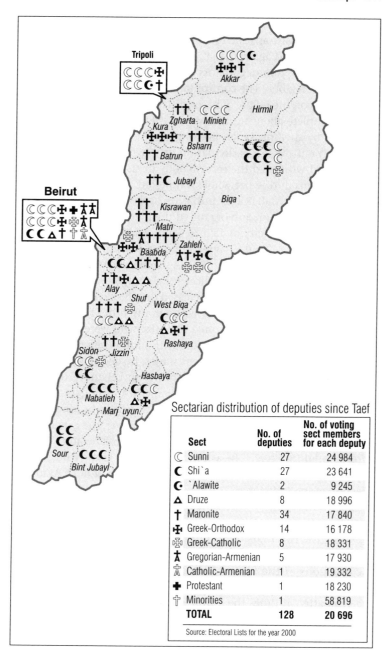

Sectarian distribution of deputies since Taef

Sect		No. of deputies	No. of voting sect members for each deputy
☾	Sunni	27	24 984
☾	Shi`a	27	23 641
☾	`Alawite	2	9 245
△	Druze	8	18 996
†	Maronite	34	17 840
✚	Greek-Orthodox	14	16 178
✥	Greek-Catholic	8	18 331
✝	Gregorian-Armenian	5	17 930
✝	Catholic-Armenian	1	19 332
✚	Protestant	1	18 230
†	Minorities	1	58 819
	TOTAL	**128**	**20 696**

Source: Electoral Lists for the year 2000

Map 6   Sectarian representation of parliamentary seats since Ta'if

presidency. Earlier on, he had helped the LF of Samir Ja'ja' eliminate Amin Jumayil's partisans and establish full control over Marounistan. But he soon turned against Ja'ja', in February 1989, most probably to prove to his Syrian negotiators that he was the sole authority in the Christian regions. The confrontation between the two ended in stalemate. Upon the failure of his negotiations with Damascus, `Awn made a complete about-turn in March 1989 and launched his 'war liberation' by shelling Syrian positions in West Beirut; the ensuing war, which enlisted LF participation on 'Awn's side, lasted for six months, and witnessed the most bloody duels of artillery between the two regions during the whole war period.

Meanwhile, an Arab League initiative, backed by the US, brokered a cease-fire in Lebanon and organised the meeting of Lebanese parliamentarians in the city of Ta'if in Saudi Arabia. After a month of deliberations, the deputies agreed upon a Document of National Understanding, known as the Ta'if Agreement. 'Awn rejected the agreement because it did not allow for a complete Syrian military withdrawal from Lebanon, and decreased the president's prerogatives in favour of the prime minister, without any other reforms of the political system. `Awn summoned the MPs, who were stationed in Paris, to come and discuss the accord with him. When they refused, suggesting negotiations through emissaries, he declared himself, in September 1989, sole legitimate authority in Lebanon, dismissed prime minister Huss and dissolved parliament, accusing its members of being 'warlords' and promising to substitute them by 'new leaders elected on the basis of their programmes'. However, the general gave himself the right to delay 'other reforms' until after 'liberation': 'What reforms would we have', he asked, 'if we do not know whether the Biqa' and the South are going to remain in Lebanon or not?' As for his rejection of the Syrian mandate, it went much beyond his opposition to the Syrian regime, as the general could not imagine his country ruled by a 'society that lives in the Middle Ages'.[1]

During the two years of his disputed rule, General 'Awn enjoyed undeniable popularity among the Christian public, exasperated by the exactions of the LF and the corruption under Amin Jumayil, and easily mobilised against Syrian presence. He even attracted the sympathy, at times the enthusiastic support, of many Muslims who suffered from the militias, the Syrian mandate and looked up to the army as a symbol of the country's unity. But the populism that animated him was quite reductionist and one-sided. After one of his enthralling rallies around the Presidential Palace – in which

'Awn became the object of a new cult; huge posters representing him as Saint George slaying the dragon – his official organ, *l'Eveil* (Consciousness) declared: 'The people was only born sixty days ago. But it is not participating in the fighting against the LF.' Not only does the general substitute himself and his army for the 'people', but the country is also reduced to a 'liberated Christian nucleus' and the Lebanese to the 'Christian people': '[The General] relies first on the people itself', explained *L'Eveil*, 'then on the Muslim groups when they acquire the capacity to express themselves freely'.[2]

Entrenched in his Presidential Palace in Ba'abda, 'Awn refused to recognise President René Mu'awad, when the latter was elected on 5 November 1989 at an air force base in the north of the country. And when Mu'awad was killed in a car bomb on Independence Day (22 November), 'Awn persisted in refusing to recognise his successor, the deputy for Zahleh, Iliyas Harawi.

The general's final war was launched against the LF of Ja'ja', to punish the latter for his positive attitude toward the Ta'if Accord, and in a last bid for exclusive control of the Christian enclave. The war for 'unifying the guns', as it was called, transformed East Beirut and the heart of the Christian region from January to May 1990 into a real battlefield, severely divided the Christians and dealt a heavy blow to their position in the country's sectarian balance of power. The general's wars incurred great losses: 1,500 killed and 3,500 wounded; 25,000 destroyed apartments; the decline of the Lebanese pound from LL 550 to LL 1,100 per $1, and more than 100,000 Lebanese, mostly Christians, emigrating to Canada, the USA and Australia. Capital flight reacting to the fighting inside the Christian camp had been estimated at $1 billion.

With 'Awn in exile, Iliyas Harawi started exercising his powers over the entire country and designated `Umar Karami as prime minister. The militias disbanded with the help of the Syrian forces and handed in their arms to the Lebanese authorities. Many of the militiamen were incorporated into the army, the security services and the administration. Armed Palestinians were disarmed and driven back into the camps. Only Hizb Allah was allowed to keep its weapons, in recognition of its role in the armed resistance against Israeli occupation. Simultaneously, the legitimate army, reorganised under General Emile Lahud, accomplished its deployment across the entire country, except the border enclave. In May 1991, presidents Harawi and al-Asad signed a Brotherhood, Cooperation and Coordination Agreement, ratified by the Lebanese parliament six months later, which was followed, on 1 September 1991, by a Common Defence and Security Agreement.

On 21 September of that year, parliament voted a constitutional law to incorporate the reforms of Ta'if into a new constitution designed to put an end to the old duality of constitution/National Pact. Its preamble proposed a new compromise on the country's identity, defining Lebanon as 'Arab in its belonging' and 'the final homeland for the Lebanese'. The finality of Lebanon, meaning that it would never enter any union with any other state, namely Syria, had been a major demand by Christians since the formulation of the National Pact of 1943. On the other hand, Lebanon's Arab identity was upgraded from the 'Arab character' in the National Pact to 'Arab belonging'. The preamble also included general lines of economic policy: the decisive adoption of the 'system of free enterprise' linked to the equitable and concerted development of all Lebanese regions and to social justice.[3]

The Document of National Accord adopted in Ta'if had envisaged a solution to the Lebanese crisis in two periods. The Second Republic to which it gave birth was conceived as leading to a Third Republic in which political sectarianism would be abolished. Article 95 was modified to commit the first elected parliament to create a special council for that purpose, without a time limit. The Third Republic, liberated from political sectarianism, would be inaugurated by the election of a non-sectarian parliament. The sects would be represented in a Senate similar to that of the 1926 constitution, which would have a decisive vote on issues of a national character. However, the council for the abolition of sectarianism was stillborn, encountering open opposition from Christian leaders and tacit opposition from other sectarian leaders.

In practical terms, the Ta'if regime reproduced the sectarian system, but with a sizeable modification in the balance of power between its constituents. To begin with, parity replaced the previous 6/5 ratio in the distribution of parliamentary seats, which were increased to 128, and of cabinet portfolios. On the other hand, sectarian quotas were abolished in civil service posts, the judiciary, the army and the police, with the exception of Degree One posts, that is, general directors of ministries, where parity and rotation were to be applied, meaning that no Degree One post would be reserved to a fixed sect.

More importantly, the prerogatives of the president of the republic were severely curtailed in favour of the prime minister, the cabinet, the parliament and its speaker, all confirmed in their representation of the Maronite, Shi'i and Sunni sects respectively. Though he remained head of state, symbol of the country's unity and guardian of the constitution, the president had practically lost most of his executive powers. He would attend cabinet meetings but without the right to vote, compared to the previous situation in which he would preside over cabinet meetings and cabinet could not issue decrees in his absence. The prime minister, previously appointed by the president of the republic, would henceforth be designated by 'obligatory consultations' that the president carried out with the MPs, and he was bound by the decision of the majority (modified article 53). In addition, the right to dissolve parliament passed from the president to the cabinet (article 55 modified), and the decrees he previously signed with the minister concerned required henceforth the additional signature of the prime minister (article 54 modified).

This ruling troika arrangement created one of the most unstable power relations imaginable. In that sense, the Ta'if Accord merely created another system of discord. Conflicts between the holders of the three top posts became endemic. But this time, there was an arbiter: President al-Asad in Damascus. Thus, in the best tribal manner, mediation in conflicts, and what we now call 'conflict resolution', became in itself a potent lever of Syrian power over Lebanon and the Lebanese.

But there was much more than that to the Syrian role in Lebanon. Postwar Lebanon had been entrusted to Damascus as a mandatory power by the US and Europe. Although the Ta'if Agreement had Syria and Saudi Arabia as regional patrons, the decisive role was taken over by Damascus, especially as its Saudi partner got increasingly bogged down in the Gulf crisis. The withdrawal of Syrian troops to the Biqa`, supposed to take place before September 1992, did not materialise and the designation by Syria of 40 new deputies in the transitional parliament greatly influenced the coming elections and the advent of a legislature with a pro-Syrian majority. That imbalance was aggravated by a massive decision by the major Christian forces to boycott the 1992 elections.

On the eve of the publication of the Fraternity Agreement, General Ghazi Kan'an, security chief of the Syrian troops stationed in Lebanon, made a revealing declaration to the Lebanese press:

You Lebanese, you are shrewd, creative and successful merchants. Soon, you are going to have 12 million neighbours coming toward you. Create light industries.

Engage in trade and commerce. Indulge in light media, which does not affect security. Shine all over the world by your inventiveness, and leave politics to us. Each has his domain in Lebanon: yours is trade; ours, politics and security.[4]

Therein lies a comprehensive programme. Not only was security entrusted to Syria's officials and troops in Lebanon, but the whole Lebanese state also. As for the linkage between media and security, it was not the product of some professional deformation from which Kan`an suffered. Freedom of the press in Lebanon was dealt with as a security matter in the Defence and Security Agreement between the two countries, submitting it to the decades-long phobias of Syrian rulers vis-à-vis the role of the Lebanese press in affecting political change in the sister country. All this assumed that Syrian officials in Lebanon and in Syria would respect the division of labour that allotted the economy to the 'creative and successful merchants', and leave 'light industry', 'trade and commerce' and 'light media' in the hands of the Lebanese. This, of course, had not been the case at all during the war and it would not be the case in the postwar period. But that is another story.

With its ambiguities and contradictions Ta'if nevertheless managed to put an end to the armed conflicts. A new period in the history of Lebanon had begun.

Chronology

634–641	Arab Muslim conquest of Syria. Mount Lebanon and the Coast (Tripoli to Sayda) are part of the *Jund* of Damascus
663	Umayyads settle Persians in Jabal, Kisrawan and Tripoli and Yemeni tribes (Tanukhs and Arsalans) in western Mount Lebanon to defend coast against Byzantine attacks
	Islamisation of southern Lebanon tribes while northern tribes remain Melchite Christians (believers in dual nature of Christ), including Maronites, followers of the hermit Mar Maroun (4th to 5th centuries) in the Hums region
680–681	Maronites split from Byzantine Church; elect Yuhanna Maroun as their patriarch. Seat in `Assi (Orontes) valley, where they remain for three centuries
750–1258	The Abbassid Caliphate
759–760	Revolt of 'King Bandar' (Christian) in Jubbat al-Munaytira (Jubayl highlands)
765	Death of Imam Ja`far al-Sadiq initiates Shi'i split between Imamists (Twelvers) and Isma`ilis
874	*Ghayba* of Imam Muhammad bin al-Husayn, twelfth Imam for the Twelver Shi`as
	Spread of Shi'ism in Lebanese territories
901–922	Qarmates in Syria: besiege Damascus, destroy Hums, control Biqa` and parts of Mount Lebanon
908	Qarmates defeated by Fatimides in `Assi valley
969	Byzantines invade northern Syria. Migration of Maronites from `Assi valley to Mount Lebanon, fleeing Byzantine advance
	Fatimids overthrow Akhshidi rule in Egypt
977	The Fatimids in Syria. Defeat Qarmates
	Tyre rebels against Fatimids under Amir `Ullaqa
1000	Maronites move into northern Mount Lebanon
1017	Beginning of Druze *Da`wa* in Cairo: Anshiktin Darazi calls for deification of Fatimid ruler, Al-Hakim bi Amr Illah. He is killed by Fatimids. Hamza bin `Ali organises Druze as *Muwahiddin* sect. Druzism spreads in Syria

1019	Fatimids in Syria. Control Mediterranean trade between Syrian coast and Italian city-states
	Tripoli (under the Bani `ammar) and Tyre affluent enough to attain self-rule
1058	Seljuks in Syria, fight weakened Byzantine and Abbassid empires
1086	Seljuks achieve control of Syria and Mediterranean trade
	Fatimids raid Syria and reconquer coastal cities, except Beirut
1096–99	Pope Urbanus II launches First Crusade against Islam (and Byzantine heteredoxy)
	Crusaders take Constantinople and Antioch and march toward al-Quds
1110–24	Cities of the Syrian coast fall to Crusaders
	Crusaders open al-Quds; Muslim influence reduced to Damascus and Aleppo
1110–1282	Maronites divided on alliance with Crusaders: Maronites of coast, loyal to Crusaders; Maronites under Patriarch Gregorius al-Halati (1130–41) vow allegience to Rome; highlanders in Jubbat Bisharri, Jubayl and Batrun refuse allegiance
1110–1230	Civil war between Maronite factions
1282	Continued schism inside Maronite community leads to election of two separate patriarchs; divisions remain until departure of Crusaders; rise of *muqaddams* benefiting from Church weakness
1516	Ottoman rule
1523–1697	The Ma`n dynasty in Mount Lebanon
1590–1635	Reign of Fakhr al-Din Ma`n II
1697–1841	The Shihab dynasty
1697–1707	Reign of Bachir I
1707–32	Reign of Haydar Chihab
1711	Final victory of *Qaysis* over *Yamanis* in `Ayn Dara battle
	Druze internal strife for succession
1750–75	Dahir al-`Umar in Acre
1775–1804	Ahmad Pasha al-Jazzar in Acre
1788–1840	Reign of Bachir Shihab II
1820–21	Antiliyas-Lihfid commoners' revolt crushed by joint forces of Bashir Shihab and Bashir Junblat

1825	Assassination of Bashir Junblat
1831–40	Ibrahim Pasha in Syria
1838	Druze revolt against Bashir Shihab and Ibrahim Pasha
1840	Revolt against Bashir and Egyptians; military intervention of foreign powers in Mount Lebanon ends Egyptian rule; Bashir II banished to Malta
1841	Civil strife in Mount Lebanon
1842	13 January: Ottomans declare end of Emirate of Mount Lebanon
1843	Double Qaimaqamate; Mount Lebanon divided into a Christian region and a Druze region
1845	Renewed civil strife in Mount Lebanon
1858–61	Kisrawan commoners' revolt
1860	Civil war in mixed regions of Mount Lebanon and massacre of Christians in Damascus
1861–1915	The *Mutassarrifiya* of Mount Lebanon
1915	Ottomans abolish *Mutasarrifiya*; appoint Ottoman governor
1916	Famine hits Beirut and Mount Lebanon
1918	French armies in Lebanon
1920	San Remo conference grants France mandate over Syria and Lebanon
	24 July: Battle of Maysaloun; French troops overthrow Arab rule in Damascus
	31 August and 1 September. Declaration of Greater Lebanon
1926	Lebanese Constitution
1936	French–Lebanese Independence Treaty
1943	November crisis: Lebanese parliament terminates French mandate
	French delegate Hellu dissolves Lebanese Parliament, arrests President Khuri, Prime Minister Sulh and ministers Ussayran and Taqla.
	22 November: Khuri and companions released; official date of Lebanese independence
1947	25 May: rigged parliamentary elections (Black May)
1948	15 May: Palestine war
1949	March: Husni Za`im's *coup d'etat* in Syria
	June: renewal of Khuri's mandate
	9 June: SSNP armed rebellion; Sa'adeh flies to Damascus

	6–7 July: SSNP leader Antun Sa`adeh delivered by Syrian authorities; executed 8 July

6–7 July: SSNP leader Antun Sa`adeh delivered by Syrian authorities; executed 8 July

Lebanese–Israeli truce treaty

1950   Breakup of Syrian–Lebanese customs union

1951   April: general elections give sizeable representation to anti-Khuri opposition

16 July: assassination of Riad Sulh in Amman airport by SSNP commando

21 October: Lebanon officially asked to join ME Military United Command; Khuri rejects offer

1952   23 July: Free Officer's coup in Egypt

17 September: general political strike forces resignation of Bishara al-Khuri

23 September: Kamil Sham`un elected president of Lebanese republic

1953   Summer: parliamentary elections; women granted right to vote

1954   24 February: Iraq and Turkey sign 'Baghdad pact'

1956   26 July: nationalisation of Suez Canal; 30 October, Suez War; November: Arab Summit in Beirut

1957   March: Lebanon joins Eisenhower Doctrine

May–June: parliamentary elections; major Muslim leaders fail to be reelected

1958   8/22 February: declaration of United Arab Republic (UAR)

9 March: Nasser in Damascus; massive popular Lebanese delegation to greet him

May: armed revolt against Kamil Sham`un

6 June: UN Security Council sends observers to Lebanon

14 July: republican coup in Baghdad

15 July: US marines land in Lebanon

31 July: election of Fu'ad Shihab president of Lebanese republic

23 September: Shihab appoints Rashid Karami prime minister; Phalange party declares 'counter-revolution'

mid-end October: four-man ministry under Karami ends 'counter-revolution'; US marines leave Lebanon

1959   Shihab–Nasir meeting on Syrian–Lebanese borders

1960   June/July: general elections for a 99-seat parliament

1961   28 September: breakup of UAR

1961–62	New Year's eve: SNSP failed *coup d'etat*
1963	8 March: military *coup d'etat* by Ba`thists and Arab Nationalists in Syria
1964	Charles Hilu elected president of republic
1965	Intra Bank crash
1967	June: Arab–Israeli war Tripartite Alliance between Jumayil, Sham`un and Iddi, against 'Arabism, Zionism and Communism'
1968	First Palestinian commandos enter Lebanese territory 28 December: Israeli raid on Beirut International Airport
1969	23 April: massive demonstration in support of PLO; security forces open fire; many killed and wounded 3 November: Cairo Agreement between Lebanese government and PLO 26 November: Karami forms Government of National Union
1970	September: 'Black September' in Jordan September: election of Sulayman Franjiyeh president of republic November: corrective move in Syria puts Hafiz al-Assad in power
1973	May: fighting erupts between Lebanese army and *fida'iyin*; Syria closes its borders with Lebanon Pierre Jumayil visits Damascus at head of Phalange delegation October war
1975	7 January: President Assad visits Lebanon, declares Syria ready for military support to Lebanon in case of Israeli aggression March: assassination of Ma`ruf Sa`d in Sayda 13 April: `Ayn al-Rummana incident. Beginning of civil war 23 May: Franjiyeh appoints military cabinet, survives for three days 6 July: Karami forms six-man cabinet excluding Junblat and Phalange August: Lebanese National Movement (LNM) launches 'Transitional Programme for Democratic Reforms' August: fourth and fifth rounds of fighting in Zahleh and Zgharta Committee for National Dialogue

6 December: Jumayil in Damascus; Black Saturday in East Beirut, at least 200 Muslims killed; LNM reacts by launching 'Battle of Hotels'

1976   13 January: fall of Dbayyeh Palestinian camp; Quarantine and Maslakh quarters besieged by Phalangists; LNM–PLO besiege Damour; 20 January, fall of Quarantine and Maslakh; 22 January, fall of Damour

23 January: new Syrian mediation and cease-fire

7 February: President Franjiyeh, in accord with President al-Asad, declares Constitutional Document

11 March: *coup d'etat* of Brigadier Ahdab; 68 MPs demand resignation of Franjiyeh; Franjiyeh refuses, backed by Damascus

22 March: fall of Holiday Inn hotel; Phalange lose last stronghold in West Beirut

25 March: Ba`abda Presidential Palace shelled; Franjiyeh takes refuge in East Beirut

March: 7-hour al-Asad–Junblat meeting ends with discord

1 April: US emissary Bean Brown in Beirut

11 April: Syria–PLO agreement on restoring order in Beirut

13 March: al-Asad's speech attacking LNM

8 May: Ilyas Sarkis elected president

end May: Syrian troops enter Lebanon

June: Israel opens 'Good Frontier' in south; defection of Major Sa`d Hadad and formation of Army of Free Lebanon (AFL)

12 August: fall of Tall al-Za`tar Palestinan camp and predominantly Shi´i Nab`a suburb in eastern Beirut

23 September: end of Franjiyeh term of office; Iliyas Sarkis elected president

16 October: six-man Arab summit in Riyad declares cease-fire in Lebanon starting 21 October; 25 October, Arab summit in Cairo confirms Riyad decisions; Syrian troops named Arab Deterrent Force (ADF)

mid-November: ADF enter Beirut

December: government of technocrats under Salim al-Huss

1977   16 March: assassination of Kamal Junblat

19–21 November: Sadat's visit to Jerusalem

1978	February: Syrian–Phalangist fighting in Ashrafieh
	14–15 March: Operation Litani: Israeli army invades south Lebanon and establishes buffer zone under Haddad; UN creates UNIFIL
	June: Tony Franjiyeh, his wife and daughters killed during a Phalange raid in Ihdin led by Samir Ja'ja'
	Summer–September: Camp David Accord between Egypt and Israel; 100 days' battle between Syrian troops and Phalanges in East Beirut
1979	January: Islamic revolution in Iran overthrows Shah regime
	March: Sadat and Begin sign peace treaty in Washington
1980	March: battle of Zahleh; Israeli–Syrian 'missile crisis' defused by US envoy Philip Habib
	7 July: Bashir Jumayil eliminates PNL 'Tigers'; creation of Lebanese Forces (LF) under his command
1982	4–6 June: Israeli invasion of Lebanon. Beirut besieged; Syrian troops retreat to northern Lebanon and the Biqa`
	23 August: Bashir Jumayil elected president; evacuation of PLO troops by US-led Multinational Force (MNF)
	14 September: assassination of Bashir Jumayil
	15 September: Israeli troops enter Beirut; 15–17, Sabra and Shatilla massacres
	16 September: Left parties launch Front for Lebanese National Resistance (FLNR)
	21 September: Amin Jumayil elected president
1983	17 May: Lebanese–Israeli treaty
	'War of the Mountain' by Junblat's Druze forces; massacres and displacement of majority of Christians from southern parts of Mount Lebanon
	Lauzanne Conference between warring Lebanese factions
1984	Amal militia controls West Beirut; MNF leave Beirut
	Official declaration of the creation of Hizb Allah, Party of the Islamic Revolution, already active in the resistance against Israeli occupation since 1982
1985	Tripartite agreement between Junblat's Progressive Socialist Party (PSP), Nabih Birri's Amal movement and the Lebanese Forces (LF), commanded by Elie Hubayqa, under Syrian auspices

January, *coup d'etat* by Samir Ja`ja` against Tripartite Agreement; Elie Hubayka and his partisans ousted from East Beirut

'War of the Camps' launched by Amal militia against Palestinian camps in Beirut and the south

1986   Trade unions lead civil society demonstrations in opposition to the war

1987   Syrian troops return to Beirut after devastating fighting between Amal and PSP militias

1988   Amin Jumayil, at the end of his presidential term, appoints General Michel `Awn interim prime minister. Post of president of republic vacant; two prime ministers, Salim al-Huss and Michel `Awn, compete for recognition

1989   February: first confrontation between army units loyal to `Awn and Lebanese Forces militia

March: `Awn bombards West Beirut; declares 'Liberation War' against Syrian troops

22 October: Lebanese parliament convened in Ta'if (Saudi Arabia) issues Charter of National Concord

5 November: parliament, meeting at Qulay`at military base, approves Ta'if Accord and elects Rene Mu`awad president

22 November: Mu`awad assassinated by bomb

Iliyas Hrawi elected president

1990   Second round of `Awn–LF fighting

Iraq invades Kuwait; Syria joins US-led coalition, given green light to pacify Lebanon

October: Syrian troops assault Ba`abda Presidential Palace; Michel `Awn takes refuge in French embassy; allowed to depart to exile in France in August 1991

1991   Syrian troops begin disarming Lebanese militias

Glossary

`Abaya: traditional Arab dress for upper classes and tribal chiefs

`amma: commoners, all inhabitants of Mount Lebanon who do not hold a noble title

`ammiya: commoners' movement or revolt

`Araq: popular alcoholic drink made of alcohol distilled from grapes and tempered with aniseed

Bilad al-Sham: natural Syria

Beyk: initially the title of a *Sanjak* ruler, came to be a title in itself

Caza: subdivision of a *Sanjak*

Diwan: administrative council

Emir liwa': ruler of a Sanjak or *liwa'*

fida'iyin: Palestinian commandos

Gharadiya (or *Ismiya*): partisan allegiance of commoners to their lords

Hawch: seigneurial closure in nineteenth-century Mount Lebanon

Intifada: uprising

Iqta` (or *Iltizam*): Ottoman tax-farming and land tenure concession

Jizya: protection tax for the 'people of the Book', according to the millet system

Manasib: *Muqata`ji* orders: Emirs, Sheikhs and *Muqaddams*

millet system: a two-tier hierarchy in the Ottoman Empire between a higher community, made up of Muslims, and a lower 'protected' community, made up of the 'people of the Book', Christians and Jews. The latter enjoyed a measure of freedom of religious belief and religious rites in return for the payment of a protection tax, the *Jizya*

Mudabbir: secretary to a *Muqata`ji*, usually Christian

Muqasama (and *Mugharasa*): form of tenant farming in which the share-cropper comes to own a plot of the land after having cultivated it for a number of years, usually between six and ten

Muqata`ji: holder of a tax-farming concession

Musha`: village commons

Nahie: subdivision of a *Caza*

Qa'im maqamiya: division of Mount Lebanon into two political and administrative units each governed by a *qa'im maqam* (1842–61)

Qaysi/Yamani: political factionalism prevalent in *Bilad al-Sham* until the late eighteenth century between tribes claiming descent from northern Arabia and tribes claiming descent from Yemen

Sanjak or *liwa'*: subdivision of a *Wilaya*, ruled by an *Emir liwa'* or a *Sanjakbey*

Sharaka (partnership): share-cropping

Sheikh-shabab: local leaders of the commoners' revolts. Under the *Mutasarrifiya* (1861–1915), elected representatives of Mount Lebanon villages and towns who formed the electoral college for the election of the Administrative Council

Tanzimat: Ottoman centralising and modernising reforms, 1839 and 1856

`Uhda*: *Muqata`ji estate

Wakil: elected village representative during the commoners' revolts in Mount Lebanon

Waqf: non-commercialised properties donated to religious institutions for pious and charitable purposes

Wilaya: main Ottoman administrative unit, ruled by a *wali*. The *Wilaya* is divided into a number of *Sanjaks* and the latter into a number of *nahies*

Za`im: political boss

Zajaliya: popular poem in colloquial Arabic

Notes

CHAPTER 1

1. The principal Ottoman political/administrative divisions were the *wilaya* (ruled by a *wali*), divided into a number of *sanjak*s or *liwa*`s (ruled by an *emir liwa*`), and the *sanjak*, subdivided into *caza*s and the *caza*s into *nahie*s.
2. For the entire Ma`n period, see: `Abd al-Rahim abu-Husayn, *Provincial Leadership in Syria, 1575–1660* (Beirut: American University of Beirut, 1985) and *Lubnan wa-l-Imara al-Durziya fi-l-`Ahd al-`Uthmani* (Beirut: Dar al-Nahar, 2005).
3. Abu-Husayn, *Provincial Leadership in Syria*, pp. 114–21.
4. Husayn Ghadhban Abu Shaqra and Yusuf Khattar Abu Shaqra, *Al-Harakat fi Lubnan ila `Ahd al-Mutasarrifiya* (Beirut: Matba`at al-Ittihad, 1952), p. 157.
5. William Polk, *The Opening of South Lebanon, 1788–1840* (Cambridge, MA: Harvard University Press, 1963), pp. 63–81.
6. Iliya Harik, *Politics and Change in a Traditional Society: Lebanon, 1711–1845* (Princeton: Princeton University Press, 1968) pp. 167–99.
7. The contract signed by the villagers of the village of Bshi`li well illustrates this function – 'united as one man and speaking with one voice – ready to share equally the losses and sacrifices that might result from their adventure, the [undersigned] delegate to one of them the task of representing them and vow to obey him and fight under his command as long as he acts "according to his conscience" and remains faithful to "our interests and public interest"', Harik, *Politics and Change*, pp. 213–14.
8. *Ibid.*, pp. 290–5.
9. David Urquhart, *The Lebanon: A History and a Diary*, 2 vols (London, 1860), p. 252.
10. Jacques Weulersse, *Paysans de Syrie et du Proche-Orient* (Paris, 1946).
11. Mikha'il Mashaqqa, *Kitab Mashhad al-A`yan bi-Hawadith Suriya wa Lubnan* (Cairo, 1908), p. 13.
12. Mas`ud Dhahir, *Al-Judhur al-Tarikhiyya li-l-Mas'ala al – Zira`iyya al-Lubaniyya, 1900–1950* (Beirut: Dar al-Farabi, 1981).
13. Urquhart, *The Lebanon*, pp. 117–18; Eugène Poujade, *Le Liban et la Syrie, 1845–1860* (Paris, 1867), pp. 166 ff.
14. Leila Fawaz, 'Zahleh and Dayr al-Qamar: The Market Towns of Mount Lebanon During the Civil War of 1860', in Nadim Shehadi and Dana Haffar Mills (eds), *Lebanon: A History of Consensus and Conflict* (Oxford and New York: Centre for Lebanese Studies and I.B. Tauris, 1988), pp. 49–63; see also her *An Ocasion for War: Civil Conflict in Lebanon and Damascus in 1860* (London and New York: I.B. Tauris, 1994).
15. Témoin oculaire, *Souvenirs de Syrie: Expédition française de 1860* (Paris: Librairie Plon, 1903), pp. 58–9.

16. Cf. `Issa Iskandar al-Ma`luf, *Tarikh Zahla*, 2nd edn (Zahla: Zahla al-Fatat Editions, 1977) and Alixa Naff, 'A Social History of Zahle, the Principal Market Town in Nineteenth Century Lebanon' (unpublished Ph.D. thesis, Los Angeles: University of California, 1972).
17. John Bowring, *Report on the Commercial Statistics of Syria* (London: HMSO, 1840), p. 118.
18. Cf. Leila Tarazi Fawaz: *Merchants and Migrants in Nineteenthth Century Beirut* (Cambridge, MA and London: Harvard University Press, 1982), pp. 31–61, and Ratib al-Husamy, 'The Commerce of Beirut and the Bayhum Merchant House some 100 Years ago, 1828–1856' (unpublished M.A. thesis, American University of Beirut, January 1942).
19. This double dependence is well expressed by the pathetic testimony of a Druze sheikh who complained to a British trader that British ships now arrived full of textiles and left with the captain's cabin full of gold. 'In the past, we used to sell you tobacco and our silk, and make our own clothes ourselves, says he, and now we buy all our clothing from you, except the `abayas*, and you do not buy any of our products.' Urquhart, *The Lebanon*, p. 38.
20. Dhahir, *Intifadat*, pp. 131–72.

CHAPTER 2

1. The Abi-l-Lamas, Druze emirs of the Matn, followed the majority of their Maronite subjects and converted to Christianity.
2. Colonel Charles Churchill, *The Druzes and the Maronites under Turkish Rule from 1840 to 1860* (London: Bernard Quarick, 1982), p. 75.
3. Poujade, *Le Liban et la Syrie, 1845–1860*, pp. 245–6.
4. Harik, *Politics and Change in a Traditional Society*, p. 249.
5. Cf. `Isa Iskandar al-Ma`luf, *Tarikh Zahla*.
6. Témoin oculaire, *Souvenirs de Syrie*, p. 26.
7. Both parties were arming themselves at a rapid rate. Marwan Buheiry's research into the Belgian archives revealed that no less than 14,325 firearms had been sold to Lebanon in 1855 from Belgium alone; two years later, the figure had reached 21,225. Marwan Buheiry, 'The Peasant Revolt of 1858 in Mount Lebanon: Rising Expectations, Economic Malaise and the Incentive to Arm', in Tarif Khalidy, (ed.), *Land Tenure and Social Transformation in the Middle East* (Beirut: American University of Beirut, 1984), p. 299.
8. Cited in Ussama Makdisi, *The Culture of Sectarianism: Community, History and Violence in Nineteenth-Century Ottoman Lebanon* (Berkeley: University of California Press, 2000), p. 135.
9. Cf. Dominique Chevalier: *La Société du Mont-Liban à l'époque de la révolution industrielle en Europe* (Paris: Librairie Orientaliste Paul Geuthner, 1971); and 'Que possédait un cheikh maronite en 1859?', *Arabica*, vol. 7 (1960), p. 77.
10. Gérard De Nerval, *Le Voyage en Orient* (Paris: Flammarion, 1980).
11. Cf. Yehoshua Porath, 'The Peasant Revolt of 1858–1861 in Kisrawan', *Asian and African Studies*, vol. 2 (1966), pp. 77–157.

12. Cf. Issam Khalifa, 'La révolution française et les révoltes sociales au Mont-Liban, 1820–1859', in Mouvement Culturel-Liban et Mouvement Culturel-France: *La Révolution française et l'Orient, 1789–1989* (Paris: Cariscript, 1989).

13. Antun Dahir al-`Aqiqi, *Thawra wa Fitna fi Jabal Lubnan*, ed. Yusuf Ibrahim Yazbak (Beirut, 1938), p. 60.

14. *Nubdha Mukhtasara fi Hawadith Lubnan wa-l-Sham, 1840–1862*, ed. Louis Shaykhou (Beirut: Al-Matba`a al-Kathulikiya, 1927), p. 7. Shaykhou attributes the testimony to Antoun Khanjiyan, chaplin of the Armenian Catholic community in Beirut.

15. al-Aqiqi, *Thawra wa Fitna*, p. 194.

16. Chevalier, 'Que possédait un cheikh maronite en 1858?', pp. 72–84.

17. al-Aqiqi, *Thawra wa Fitna*, p. 208.

18. Karam was born in Ihdin in 1823 and grew up in a house accustomed to receiving French tourists en route to the Cedars. He pretended to be the godson of the French crown prince. An ardent Maronite, he distinguished himself in the 'witch hunt' against the 'heretical' Protestants. Though an unconditional supporter of Bkirki – his slogan was 'our Sultan is the Patriarch' – he had not backed Mas`ad for the patriarchal seat, preferring a northern candidate.

19. Bentivoglio reported to his government that the patriarch and his bishops were 'losing all influence on the inhabitants, incapable of inspiring them with the necessary trust for the exercise of any form of authority'. Adel Ismail, *Histoire du Liban du XVIIème siècle à nos jours. Tome IV: Redressement et déclin du féodalisme Libanais, 1840–1861* (Beyrouth, 1958), p. 329. Furthermore, Father Bulus al-Ashqar relates how coming to collect the church tax from the inhabitants of Zuq Mikayil, he was expelled from the town by the delegate Elias Habalin, at the head of armed men, who told him: 'Let the one who appointed you in this village pay you, we do not owe you anything.' Khalifa, *La révolution française*, pp. 53–4.

20. Yusuf Karam was stopped en route, seemingly by joint pressure from the European consuls and the Abi-l-Lama`s. The latter were too eager to take their revenge from the town that had expelled them and expropriated their properties. As for the consuls, they were too respectful of the 'red lines', as Zahleh lay outside the confines of the *qa'im maqamiya*, that is, in purely Ottoman territory.

21. By that time, the Christians of Damascus had surpassed their Jewish competitors, which explains why the latter were spared during the riots.

22. Unpublished lecture and private communication to the author. Worthy of note is the fact that the rioters did not include any textile workers or artisans, which damages the hypothesis that the riots were mainly a reaction to the invasion of imported European textiles and the collapse of local textile production.

23. Marcel Emerit, 'La crise syrienne et l'expansion économique française en 1860', *Revue Historique*, vol. 207 (1952), pp. 211–32.

24. Iskandar Ya`qub Abqarius, *Nawadir al-Zaman fi Waqa'i` Jabal Lubnaan* (London: Riad el-Rayyes Books, 1987), p. 144.

CHAPTER 3

1. The electoral constituencies were: Batrun and Kisrawan, with one Maronite councillor each; Jizzin, with three councillors: a Maronite, a Druze and a Sunni; the Matn with four councillors: a Greek Orthodox, a Shi`i and a Druze and Zahleh, reintegrated into Mount Lebanon at the demand of its inhabitants, represented by one Greek Catholic councillor.

2. The project was initiated by the French consul in Cairo in 1841, then relaunched by a French journalist in the 1850s and finally championed by a Prussian countess in 1860 to save Lebanon's Christians. Mir`i al-Dahdah, a rich Lebanese merchant in Marseilles and friend of Karam, was among its supporters and enlisted his friend's help. A variety of economic and political arguments were proposed in favour of the transfer project: Maronite settlers would be cheaper to install in Algeria than European *colons*, their skills would encourage the development of sericulture and cotton production, or alternatively, they would be used to create a commercial network in favour of French interests. Finally, the Maronites, Arab and Christian, speaking both Arabic and French, would be ideal intermediaries between the colonial administration and the native population. However, the Quai d'Orsay was opposed to the project from the start, arguing that the Maronites were France's most loyal allies in the Orient and the basis of its colonial policy, and should therefore remain in their territory to counter the Druze, heavily supported by the British.

3. Boutrus Labaki, *Introduction a l'histoire économique du Liban: Soie et commerce extérieur en fin de période ottomane, 1840–1914* (Beyrouth: Publications de l'Université libanaise, 1984), pp. 210–14.

4. Between 1783 and 1860, the population of Mount Lebanon increased from 120,000 to 200,000, a 67 per cent growth in 77 years, yet it doubled in only three decades between 1880 and 1913 (200,000 to 414,000). See Akram Khater, *Inventing Home: Emigration, Gender and the Making of the Lebanese Middle Class, 1861–1921* (Berkeley: University of California Press, 2001).

5. Elie Safa, *L'émigration libanaise* (Beyrouth: Publications de l'Université St Joseph, 1960), pp. 187–90.

6. Paul Jouplain, *La question du Liban. Etude d'histoire diplomatique et de droit international* (Paris, 1908), p. 573.

7. Ferdinand Tyan, *France et Liban: Défense des intérets francais en Syrie* (Paris, 1917), p. 84.

8. These are the population statistics for the *Mutasarrifiya* in 1865 and 1895.

	1865	1895
Maronites	171,800	229,680
Greek Orthodox	29,326	54,208
Druze	28,560	49,812
Catholics	19,370	34,472
Shiites	9,820	16,846
Sunnis	7,611	13,576
Total	266,487	398,594

Source: John Spagnolo, *France and Ottoman Lebanon* (London: Ithaca Press, 1977), p. 24.

9. Hani Faris, *Al-Niza`at al-Ta'ifiya fi Tarikh Lubnan al-Hadith* (Beirut: Al-Ahliya li-l-Nashr wa-l-Tawzi`, 1980), p. 81.

10. 'Feudal' families held 23 (62%) of the 37 district governors under the *Mutasarrifiya*, and 260 (77%) of the 337 sub-district governors. Toufic Touma, *Paysans et institutions féodales chez les druzes et les maronites du Liban du XVIIIème siècle à 1914*, 2 vols (Beyrouth: Publications de l'Université libanaise, 1971), p. 338.

11. Engin Akarli, *The Long Peace: Ottoman Lebanon, 1861–1920* (Los Angeles: University of California Press, 1993), pp. 416–17.

12. Spagnolo, *France and Ottoman Lebanon*, pp. 163–4.

13. *Ibid.*, pp. 290–1.

14. Yusuf al-Sawda, *Fi Sabil al-Istiqlal, vol. 1, 1906–1922* (Beirut, 1967), pp. 50–63.

15. Spagnolo, *France and Ottoman Lebanon*, p. 276 and passim.

CHAPTER 4

1. Marwan Buheiry, 'British Official Sources and the Economic History of Lebanon: 1835–1914', in Lawrence I. Conrad (ed.), *The Formation and Perception of the Modern Arab World: Studies by Marwan R. Buheiry* (Princeton: The Darwin Press), 1989, p. 492.

2. Jacques Thobie, *Intérêts et impérialisme français dans l'empire ottoman, 1895–1914* (Paris: Publications de la Sorbonne, 1977), p. 164.

3. Salim al-Bustani, *Al-A`mal al-Majhula*, ed. Michel Giha (London and Beirut: Riad al-Rayyes Books, 1990), pp. 183–6.

4. See Mas`ud Dhahir, *Al-Judhur al-Tarikhiyah li-l-Mas'ala al-Ta'ifiya al-Lubnaniya* (Beirut: Ma`had al-Inma' al-`Arabi, 1981).

5. See Fawaz, Leila Tarazi, *Merchants and Migrants in Nineteenth Century Lebanon* (Cambridge, MA and London: Harvard University Press, 1982).

6. *L'Indicateur Libano-Syrien, 1922* (Beyrouth: Société Syrienne de publicité, 1922).

7. As early as 1850, Bustros Cousins distributed Manchester-manufactured products, while another branch of the family, Mussa Bustrus and Nephews, was the agent of European transport companies (the British Liverpool Steamers among others). The Trads, backers of Emir Fakhr al-Din II, specialised in finance. The Tuwaynis started their career under Al-Jazzar. Lutfallah Tuwayni arrived in Beirut after having amassed a large fortune in Sidon from olive oil presses, soap manufacture and commerce. Girgis Tuwayni was a commercial partner of the Sursuqs (Sursock). These latter were undoubtedly the wealthiest and most prestigious of the Beiruti families. Dimitri Sursuq was moneylender for Khedive Isma`il of Egypt, who granted him the title of Pasha and repaid his debts in the form of shares in the Compagnie du Canal de Suez. Nicolas Sursuq's annual income was estimated at £60,000 and he was a major shareholder in the DHP and the Port Company.

8. Gaston Ducousso, *L'industrie de la Soie en Syrie et au Liban* (Beyrouth, 1913).

9. *Al-Janna, al-Junayna and al-Jinan* are variations on the word 'garden' in Arabic and synonyms of *'bustan'*, hence the family name *'bustani'* (gardener).

10. Ahmad Faris al-Shidyaq, *Al-Saq `Ala-l-Saq Fi Ma Huwa al-Fariyaq*, first published Paris, 1855 (Beirut: Dar Maktabat al-Hayat, 1966), pp. 188 and 194.

11. `Adil Al-Sulh, *Sutur Min al-Risala* (Beirut, 1966), pp. 124–5.

12. al-Khuri, Antun Yammin, *Lubnan Ba`d al-Harb, 1914–1919* (Beirut: al-Matba`ah al-Adabiya, 1919), pp. 121–4.

CHAPTER 5

1. 'His Majesty's Government view with favour the establishment in Palestine of a national home for the Jewish people, and will use their best endeavours to facilitate the achievement of this object, it being clearly understood that nothing shall be done which may prejudice the civil and religious rights of existing non-Jewish communities in Palestine, or the rights and political status enjoyed by Jews in any other country.'

2. Akarli, *The Long Peace*, p. 474.

3. Tyan, *France et Liban*, p. 84.

4. Spagnolo, *France and Ottoman Lebanon*, p. 304.

5. Al-Sawda, *Fi Sabil al-Istiqlal*, pp. 72–3.

6. Auguste Adib, *Lubnan Ba`d al-Harb* (Cairo, 1919), pp. 109–17.

7. Al-Sawda, *Fi Sabil al-Istiqlal*, pp. 204–5.

8. Marwan Buheiry, 'The Role of Beirut in the Political Economy of the French Mandate, 1919–1939', in *Lebanon Papers* (Oxford: Centre for Lebanese Studies, 1986), p. 589.

9. Akarli, *The Long Peace*, pp. 181–2.

10. Its administrative bureau was composed of fifteen members among whom were Jean de Freij (Latin), president; Na`um Bakhus, vice-president; Emile Iddi, secretary; Emile Kachou`, director of the Banque de Syrie, treasurer; members: Bishara al-Khuri, Shukri Qirdahi, Alfred Naqqash, Yusuf Jumayil (Maronites), Salim Asfar, Michel Chiha, Emile `Arab and Alphonse Zayni (Greek Catholics).

11. In a satirical poem addressed to the Maronites, Shibl Dammus (Greek Catholic deputy for Zahla) related the inversely proportional relationship between Greater Lebanon and Maronite 'greatness':

> Sons of Marun…/
> You thought that Lebanon's 'Greatness' would do you honour…/
> By God, your fate resides in the menu/
> By enlarging Lebanon, you have reduced Marun!

12. Meir Zamir, *The Formation of Modern Lebanon* (London and Sydney: Croom Helm, 1985), p. 113.

13. 20 August 1920, *Archives of Ministry of Foreign Affairs*, vol. 32, pp. 188–9.

14. Gérard D. Khouri, *La France et l'Orient Arabe: Naissance du Liban Moderne, 1914–1920* (Paris: Armand Colin, 1993), p. 396.

15. Zamir, *The Formation of Modern Lebanon*, pp. 75–7, 90.

16. Most proponents of an enlarged Lebanon adopted the map drawn by the French military command in the years 1860–61 as their reference for Lebanon's borders. That map defined Lebanon's southern borders just south of the Litani river as it exited into the Mediterranean south of Sidon and included the Hula plain but excluded Tyre and Jabal Amil. Only Bulus Nujaym and Auguste Adib had included the latter two regions in their Greater Lebanon. Adib was the only advocate of a Greater Lebanon to put the Lebanese–Palestinian frontiers at Naqura, the actual southern border of Lebanon with Palestine. See `Isam Khalifa, *Al-Hudud al-Junubiya li-Lubnan* (Beirut, 1985).

17. Samir Kassir and Farouk Mardam-Bey, *Itinéraires de Paris à Jérusalem: La France et le conflit israélo-arabe*, 2 vols (Washington and Paris: Les livres de la Revue d'études palestiniennes, 1992 and 1993), pp. 51–2.

CHAPTER 6

1. Al-Batriyark Antun`Arida, *Lubnan wa Faransa*, ed. Mas`ud Dhahir (Beirut: Dar al-Farabi, 1987), p. 22.

2. Michel Van Leew, 'Un cas particulier de nationalisme: Emile Edde', *Cahiers du GREMAMO*, no. 7 (1990), pp. 9–10, 18–19.

3. The 1932 census showed a slight Christian majority of 402,000 to 383,000 for the Muslims. The population distribution by sects was as follows: 226,000 Maronites (28%), 76,000 Greek Orthodox (10%), 46,000 Greek Catholics (6%), 53,500 Other Christians (7%), 176,000 Sunnis (22%), 154,000 Shi'is (20%) and 53,000 Druzes (7%).

4. The Common Interests for Syria and Lebanon were: Administration generale des Douanes; Société du chemin de fer de Damas, Hamah et Prolongements (DHP); Société des Tramways et Éclairage de Beyrouth; and the Compagnie des eaux de Beyrouth. The main franchise-holding companies were: Banque de Syrie et du Liban (BSL); Crédit foncier d'Algérie et de Tunisie; Banque française de Syrie; Crédit foncier de Syrie; Compagnie du port, des quais et entrepôts de Beyrouth; Société des Grands Hôtels du Levant; Compagnie générale du Levant; la Régie co-intéressée libano-syrienne des tabacs et des tombacs and Radio Orient.

5. Roger Owen, 'The Political Economy of the Great Lebanon, 1920–1970', in Owen, ed., *Essays on the Crisis in Lebanon* (London: Ithaca Press, 1976), p. 24.

6. Amin al-Rihani, *Qalb Lubnan* (Beirut: Dar al-Rihani, 1965), p. 99.

7. `Arida, *Lubnan wa Faransa*, p. 63.

8. In May 1936, as the Palestinian rebellion was in full swing, Iddi addressed a message to the Orient Fair in Tel Aviv, recalling the traditional friendship between the two countries, 'always turned toward each other', and promised greater cooperation between Lebanon and Palestine. Nevertheless, the fair was boycotted by the majority of Lebanon's businessmen. For his part, Bishara al-Khuri declared his support for the Palestinian rebellion and criticised the indifference of the Lebanese government toward it.

9. Kazim Al-Sulh, *Mushkilat al-Ittisal wa-l-Infisal fi Lubnan* (Beirut, March 1936).
10. *Ibid.*
11. Whatever the case, Christian independentists did not limit themselves to the positions of Khuri's Constitutionalist Bloc. Jibran Tuwayni, founder and editor of the daily *Al-Nahar*, gave priority to independence over the return to the constitution, and insisted on the creation of an independent national Lebanese army. More importantly, Tuwayni demanded the opening of direct negotiations between Syria and Lebanon to conclude a treaty that would define their economic and social relations and establish a unified institution to administer the Common Interests. Similarly, the National Front of Yusuf al-Sawda and Amin Taqi al-Din called for the conclusion of a treaty with France on the basis of Lebanon's sovereignty and the strengthening of economic and social ties with Syria.
12. Significantly, clause 14 of decree no. 60 L.R. of 1936 envisaged the etablishment of common-law communities (*communautés de droit commun*) not bound by the religious and sectarian personal status codes. This clause was never applied, although it laid the foundation for a voluntary civil code for personal status.
13. Nicolas Ziadeh, *Syria and Lebanon* (London: Ernest Benn, 1957), p. 195.
14. *Taqrir wa Muqarrarat al-Mu'tamar al-Watani al-Dimuqrati fi Lubnan* (Beirut, 27 November 1938).
15. It was not surprising that the conservative *Le Jour* of Michel Chiha supported the transport strikes of 1931 and 1935 against the TEB. The Kettaneh family, a major funder of the paper, was the agent for American truck companies and owner of a large truck transport company for the whole Middle East (including Iran). They made no bones about their desire to privatise transport and buy the DHP.
16. The wartime French restrictions were considerable: prior permission was required from the Mandatory Control Service for any transfer of capital transfer outside the franc and sterling zones; an official rate of currency exchange was imposed; import and export licences were made obligatory, and so on. This excessive control encouraged the development of an extensive black market, which accounted for 40–50 per cent of imports financed by foreign currency for the years 1944–46. That same market was also responsible for handling the remittances of émigrés and the currencies arising from transit and reexport trade that illegally entered the country. This money was offered by non-authorised brokers to importers looking for foreign currency and unable to obtain it through the Office des Changes. Cf. Samir Makdisi, 'Post-War Lebanese Foreign Trade', unpublished M.A. thesis (American University of Beirut, June 1955), and Carolyn Gates, *The Merchant Republic of Lebanon: Rise of an Open Economy* (Oxford and New York: Centre for Lebanese Studies and I.B. Tauris, 1989).
17. *General Spears' Papers*, Oxford, Middle East Centre, St Antony's College, Box III/2.
18. Iddi's acceptance to serve as front man for the dying French mandate cost him dearly: he was deprived of his parliamentary mandate by a vote in the Chamber of Deputies and retired from politics. He died in 1949.

CHAPTER 7

1. Although the Lebanese constitution does not openly provide for a state religion, article 9 introduces the Divinity into political and civil life: 'Freedom of belief is absolute. The State – in performing its obligations of reverence to God almighty – respects all religions and all sects and guarantees [*takfal*] the freedom of practice of religious rites under its protection, provided that this does not disturb public order, and [the State] also insures [*tadmann*] the respect of the system of personal status and religious interests for all the subjects [*Ahlin*] in their diverse sects.'
2. Nawaf Salam, *Mythes et politiques au Liban* (Beirut: Editions FMA, 1987), p. 69.
3. Edmond Rabbath, *La formation historique du Liban politique et constitutionnel: Essai de synthèse* (Beyrouth: Publications de l'Université Libanaise, 1973), p. 173.
4. Karami and Pharaon's alliance was sealed in 1944 by the creation of *Hizb al-Hurriya*, the Freedom Party.
5. Spears was replaced in December 1944, blamed for being too hosile to the French, and his protégé Kamil Sham`un was sent, in response to French pressure, as ambassador to the court of Saint James.
6. The movement of goods in its port increased from 301,500 tons in 1946 to 1,051,400 in 1950 and 1,887,000 in 1955. In 1955, the volume of transit trade passing through Beirut port had risen 27 times from the beginning of the Arab–Israeli war of 1948 (from 21,000 tons in 1947 to 574,100 tons in 1955).
7. According to Wilbor Eveland, ex-CIA operative in the Middle East, Miles Copeland, major CIA operative in the Middle East, and Stephen Mead, assistant military attaché at the US embassy in Damascus, were largely responsible for engineering Za`im's coup in order to drive Syria to sign an agreement with TAPLINE, the US company that built and operated the pipeline carrying Saudi oil to the Mediterranean. The Syrian parliament had found the transit fees too low and refused to ratify the agreement. See Irene Gendzier's interview with Eveland in *Notes from the Minefield: United States Intervention in Lebanon and the Middle East, 1945–1958* (New York: Columbia University Press, 1997), p. 98 and Douglas Little, 'Cold War and Covert Action: The US and Syria, 1945–1958', *Middle East Journal*, vol. 44, no. 1 (Winter, 1990), p. 55.

    Husni al-Za`im, ruled for 137 days during which he signed the TAPLINE agreement and the Syrian–Israeli Armistice Agreement before being overthrown and killed by a military coup led by Colonel Hinnawi on 14 August 1949.
8. Data on the consortium has been computed from a variety of sources, both written and oral. Among them should be cited two reports by the Foreign Service of the United States of America (FSOUSA), Declassified Material: (i) Lane to Department of State: *Memorandum of an interview with Prime Minister of Lebanon prepared by the Commercial attache*, no. 1048, secret, Beirut, 17 December 1945; (ii) *The Political Control Exercised by the Commercial Class in Lebanon*, despatch no. 372, 21 January 1952, by Harold B. Minor. Minor's exceptional report is based on information

supplied by a number of Lebanese and foreign businessmen, politicians and high state functionaries. It contains information on 25 members of the 'commerical class' including those whom Minor calls the 'President's clique': Husayn al-`Uwayni, Fu'ad Khuri, Michel Doumit, Jean Fattal, the Kettaneh brothers and Sheikh Khalil al-Khuri, the president's son. Minor's list served as a basis for further research for the present work.

9. Michael Johnson, *Class and Client in Beirut: The Sunni Muslim Community and the Lebanese State, 1840–1985* (London: Ithaca Press, 1986), p. 4.
10. Among these banks were Banque Misr-Syrie-Lebanon; Arab Bank; Trad – Crédit Lyonnais; Sabbagh – Banque d'Indochine; Pharaon-Chiha: Banque Commerciale Italia; Al-Ahli (Salim, Sahnawi, Doumit, Karam, Salha, Fattal and Kettaneh).
11. When family firms were recycled into joint-stock companies in the 1960s and 1970s, the consortium families still held a position of command and control in the main sectors of the economy.
12. See Michael Hudson, *The Precarious Republic: Political Modernisation in Lebanon* (New York: Random House, 1968).
13. In 1951–53, 50% of imports came from the US dollar zone, 22% from the sterling bloc, 11% from the franc bloc and 17% from Syria; 37% of exports were destined for the stering zone, 34% to the dollar zone, 21% to Syria and only 8% to the franc zone. Revenues from transit trade (including the transit of oil) exceeded the value of imports, exports and reexports combined in 1951–52. Jibra'il Munassa, *Fi Sabil Nahda Iqtisadiya Lubnaniya Yusahim Fiha Lubnan al-Mughtarib* (Beirut, 1950), pp. 40, 56.
14. 'Transmitting a Survey of the Economic Problems of Lebanon', address delivered by Naim Amiouné, assistant director of the Lebanese Ministry of National Economy, at American Junior College, FSOUSA, no. 1258, Beirut, 3 July 1946.
15. *L'Orient*, 18 March 1950.
16. See Mlle Durand, 'La rupture de l'union syro-libanasie', in *Mélanges Proche Orientaux d'Economie Politique* (Beyrouth: Faculté de Droit, Université St Joseph, 1956), pp. 293–358.
17. Michel Chiha, *Propos d'économie libanaise* (Beyrouth: Editions du Trident, 1965), pp. 126, 136, 162.
18. Ziadeh, *Syria and Lebanon*, p. 111.
19. A typical example of the financial scandals under Khuri was related to the construction of Beirut Airport. The scandal was revealed in a dispatch by the commercial attaché of the US embassy in Beirut, who relied on information largely furnished by Gabriel al-Murr, an engineer, deputy and government minister. The minister of public works at that time was southern *za`im* Ahmad al-As`ad and the main contractors were the Kettanehs. Four different teams of American experts had decided that the project should not cost more than LL 24 million. In 1952, it had already cost LL 45 million and was still incomplete. Government expenditure on land expropriation, estimated at LL 5,500,000 in 1948, had reached LL 13 million in 1952 and was not terminated. A big beneficiary of these indemnities was Sa'ib Salam, owner of the al-Ghadir area on which the airport was being built. The costs of excavations and sand extraction were estimated at 110 piastres/cubic metre and the contract was fixed at

170 for the *Régie des Travaux* owned by Michel Doumit, Alfred Kettaneh and the Sabbaghs, all belonging to the 'president's men'. The cement contract was awarded exclusively to the Shikka plant of Fu'ad al-Khuri, the president's brother and a member of the governmental commission that supervised the construction of the Beirut International Airport. The Shikka plant delivered cement at a higher price than that of imported cement from the USA, which included transport costs and customs duties. 'The Political Control Exercised by the Commercial Class in Lebanon', FSOUSA, despatch no. 372, 21 January 1952, by Harold B. Minor.

20. Ziadeh, *Syria and Lebanon*, pp. 118–19.
21. Michel Chiha, *Politique Interieure* (Beyrouth: Editions du Trident, 1957), p. 234.
22. As early as 1945, when the French troops departed, Charles Malik, spokesman for the Lebanese delegation in Washington established contacts with the State Department to ensure US political and military engagement on the side of Lebanon. Lebanon, about to be 'detached' from France, could not survive without the presence or support of the leader of the 'free world', he argued. Malik went back to the State Department to propose a military alliance in 1947 and 1949. During this last visit, the ambassador emphasised Lebanon's need for American protection to ward off the threat of the nascent state of Israel. In May 1949, Francis Kettaneh proposed to the State Department the establishment of US military bases in Lebanon in return for the sum of $5 million, which was the estimated loss incurred by the Lebanese economy in the event of the breakup of economic union with Syria. Both Malik and Kettaneh expressed Michel Chiha's belief that the new power in the world that should protect Lebanon was the US and not Britain. While Charles Malik pursued his Washington contacts, Riad al-Sulh spent most of 1948–49 in France and England, trying to convince its leaders to sign bilateral agreements for the defence of Lebanon without it having to join the Western military pacts.
23. Upon the advice of Chiha, the deputies of the '*Le Jour* group', Pharaon, de Freige and Abi Shahla, voted for Sham'un.

CHAPTER 8

1. For the Sham'un era, consult the painstaking and rich work of Irene Gendzier, *Notes from the Minefield.*
2. Camille Chamoun, *Crise au Moyen Orient* (Paris: Gallimard, 1963), p. 248.
3. *L'Orient*, 17 June 1956, cited in Hudson, *The Precarious Republic*, who himself spoke of the Sham'un's 'dictatorial' tendencies, p. 290.
4. Irene L. Gendzier: 'The Declassified Lebanon, 1948–1958: Elements of Continuity and Contrast in US Policy Toward Lebanon', in Halim Barakat (ed.), *Toward a Viable Lebanon* (London and Sydney, Croom Helm, 1988), pp. 178–209.
5. The main operative of the CIA in Beirut also revealed that the Company paid $25,000 to help Charles Malik become deputy for the Kura district. A similar sum was paid to Sham'un to 'convince' the rival candidate

to step down in favour of Malik. W.C. Eveland, *Ropes of Sand: America's Failure in the Middle East* (London and New York: W.W. Norton, 1980), pp. 252, 266.

6. Gendzier, *Notes from the Minefield*, p. 237.
7. Notable examples are the sugar refinery in the Biqa` and the second cement plant in Shikka whose licence had been granted to the Dumit family, related by marriage to Michel Chiha and President Khuri's wife, and associated with German capital. For this Kamal Junblat accused Sham`un of receiving 1,640 shares for the net value of LL 1 million as the 'price' of the Shikka plant licence. Junblat himself had applied in 1947 for a licence for a second cement factory in Siblin (Iqlim al-Kharrub) but his application had been blocked by Khuri to preserve the monopoly of the Shikka plant, owned by Khuri's brother Fuad and his in-laws, the Haddads. Under Sham`un, Junblat found himself deprived of that licence again. Ironically, Junblat's lawyer in that affair, under Khuri's term of office, was none other than Kamil Sham`un himself! See Junblat's press conference, *Al-Muharrir*, 7 September 1973.
8. Georges Naccache, 'A l'heure de Mme. Afaf', *L'Orient*, 17 January 1958.
9. The military capability of the rebels, estimated at 12,000 men, was superior to that of the army. See Adel Freiha, *L'armée et l'Etat au Lebanon, 1945–1980* (Paris: Librairie générale de droit et de jurisprudence, 1980).
10. Gendzier, *Notes from the Minefield*, p. 203.
11. Sham`un received Jordanian and Iraqi military units that were stationed to defend the airport.
12. Gendzier, *Notes from the Minefield*, pp. 297–9. See also Ben Fenton, 'Macmillan backed Syria assassination plot: Documents show White House and No. 10 conspired over oil-fuelled invasion plan', *Guardian*, 27 September 2003.
13. Sham`un's adherence to the Eisenhower doctrine did not help him much, as the doctrine only provided for American military intervention in the case of aggression by a 'country under the domination of international communism'. The official justification for the Marines' intervention was to 'defend American citizens' and counter the UAR's 'indirect aggression against Lebanon's independence'.

CHAPTER 9

1. Hudson, *The Precarious Republic*, p. 174.
2. Kamal Salibi, 'Lebanon under Fuad Chehab, 1958–1964', *Middle East Studies*, vol. 2, no. 3 (April 1966), p. 210.
3. The two notable exceptions were the textile factories strike in the summer of 1963, broken when the workers were threatened with layoffs, and the 1,600-strong Post, Telegraph and Telephone employees' strike of 1964, during which the army took over the installations and maintained service until the employees were forced back to work.
4. Waddah Sharara, *Al-Silm al-Ahli al-Barid: Lubnan al-Mujtama` wa-l-Dawla, 1964–1967*, 2 vols (Beirut: Ma`had al-Inma' al-`Arabi, 1980), p. 19.

5. See Malcolm H. Kerr, *The Arab Cold War: Gamal `Abd al-Nasir and his Rivals, 1958–1970* (London: Oxford University Press, 1971).
6. Hudson, *The Precarious Republic*, p. 328.
7. The popular housing projects were never built and the building of the LU university campus was only completed in the autumn of 2005!
8. In addition to `Uwayni himself, the cabinet included businessmen `Ali `Arab, a rich Shi`i émigré from Africa, Antoine Sahnawi, a member of the consortium, and Najib Saliha, the business partner of `Uwayni from Saudi days and a major shareholder in the Intra Group.
9. In 1965, 800 villages planted tobacco in the south, Jubayl and Batrun; the peasants and farmers in that sector numbered around 30,000. In addition, the *Régie* employed 600 functionaries and 3,000 workers, and ruled the destinies of 15,000 licensed retailers.
10. Among the demands were lowering of electricity and cold storage charges; the direct import by the state of fertilisers and insecticides to break the power of the monopolies; an Arab common market; the development of exchanges of agricultural products between Lebanon and the socialist countries; and finally, the creation of a federation for Lebanese farmers.
11. The massive naturalisation of Palestinians, mainly Christians, was carried under Sham`oun.
12. Sharara, *Al-Silm al-Ahli*, footnote to pp. 740–1.
13. *Al-`Amal*, 8 October 1966. Maysalun and Wadi al-Harir are on the Syrian side of the Lebanese–Syrian borders.
14. *Lisan al-Hal*, 9 October 1966.
15. *Al-Nahar*, 19 October 1966.
16. *Al-Nahar*, 16 December 1966.
17. *Al-Nahar*, 29 January 1967.
18. *Al-Nahar*, special annual edition, 1966.
19. *Le Monde*, 16–17 November 1969.

CHAPTER 10

1. Claude Dubar and Salim Nasr, *Les Classes sociales au Liban* (Paris: Fondation nationale des sciences politiques, 1976), p. 68.
2. Cf. Zuhayr Hawwari, *Al-Ijtiyah al-Iqtisadi al-Isra'ili li-Lubnan* (Beirut: Al Mu'assasa al `Arabiyya lil-Dirasat wa-l-Nashr, 1985), pp. 118–19.
3. Cf. Selim Nasr, 'Bayrut al-Kubra 1975: Hudud al Indimaj al Ijtima`i', *Al Waqi`*, no. 3 (1981), pp. 69–110.
4. Lebanese Communist Party, 'Report of the Central Committee to the 4th National Congress', *Al-Tariq*, no. 4 (August 1979), p. 15.
5. *Ibid.*, pp. 8–16, 272–80.
6. Labaki, cited in Dubar and Nasr, *Les Classes sociales au Liban*.
7. *Ibid.*, p. 357.
8. *Ibid.*, p. 322.
9. *Ibid.*, p. 297.
10. David Gordon, *Lebanon: The Fragmented Nation* (London: Croom Helm, 1980), pp. 136–7.
11. Grégoire Haddad, 'Primum vivere', *L'Orient – Le Jour*, 15 July 1975.

12. Gordon, *Fragmented Nation*.
13. A. el-Amine and N. Wehbi, *Système d'enseignement et division sociale au Liban* (Paris: Éditions le Sycomore, 1980), pp. 43 ff.
14. Yusef Sayegh, *Entrepreneurs of Lebanon* (Cambridge, MA: Harvard University Press, 1962), pp. 69 ff.
15. Boutros Labaki, 'L'économie politique du Liban indépendant, 1943–1975', in Nadim Shehadi and Dana Haffar Mills (eds), *Lebanon: A History of Consensus and Conflict* (Oxford and New York: Centre for Lebanon Studies and I.B. Tauris, 1988), pp. 166 ff.
16. *Ibid.*
17. Cf. Ahmad Beydoun, *Le Liban: itinéraires d'une guerre incivile* (Paris: éditions Karthala, 1993), pp. 103–25.
18. Gordon, *Fragmented Nation*.
19. *Al Nahar*, 23 April 1974.
20. In 1970, at the initiative of Labour Minister Jamil Lahhud, the General Workers' Union in Lebanon (GWUL) was unified; it was comprised of ten trade union federations (and 126 trade unions) run by an executive committee of 37 members presided over by Gabriel Khouri, and had a total membership of 54,070 workers.
21. USADOS, *Annual Labour Report, 1972–73*, 20 July 1973, E.O. 11652: GDS.
22. *al-Safa*, 7 February 1973.
23. *Le Monde*, 16 February 1972.
24. *Le Monde*, 26 April 1972.
25. Antoine Massarra, *La Structure sociale du Parlement libanais de 1920 à 1973* (Beyrouth: Publications de l'Université St Joseph, 1975).
26. *Le Monde*, 30 May 1972.
27. Kamal Salibi: *Cross-Roads to Civil War: Lebanon, 1958–1976* (New York: Caravan Books, 1976), p. 57.
28. Jonathan Randall, *Going All the Way: Christian Warlords, Israeli Adventurers and the War in Lebanon* (New York: Random House, 1984), p. 164.
29. *Le Monde*, 2 September 1972.
30. Robert Solé, 'Le Liban, bastion chrétien?', *Le Monde*, 5–7 December 1972.
31. Haddad, 'Primum vivere'.
32. Fuad Ajami, *The Vanished Imam: Musa al Sadr and the Shia of Lebanon* (Ithaca, NY and London: Cornell University Press, 1986), p. 112.
33. *Ibid.*, pp. 48–9.
34. *Ibid.*, p. 189.
35. *al `Amal*, 20 February 1973.
36. On 18 October 1973, a commando unit of the Revolutionary Socialist Organisation occupied the local branch of the Bank of America, took a number of hostages and demanded the liberation of one of their imprisoned comrades, a $10 million ransom and their safe departure to Algeria. Police stormed the bank the next day after the kidnappers had executed the first hostage, an American employee of the bank. The operation ended with four killed, including a policeman and the leader of the commando unit, Ali Shu`ayb.

CHAPTER 11

1. The Lebanese Front, successor to the Front of Liberty and Man, was led by Sulayman Franjiyeh, Sharbil Qassis (president of the Maronite Brotherhoods), Pierre Jumayil, Kamil Sham`un, Charles Malik, Edward Hunayn (MP and secretary-general of the Front) and Fu'ad Bustani (historian and ex-president of the Lebanese University). The immobilism advocated by the Lebanese Front is best expressed in the following statement addressed to the French envoy Couve de Murville: 'The New Lebanon the Lebanese Front wants is the original and millenial Lebanon with its 6,000 years' continuous heritage... and including its miraculous achievements'.

2. The Lebanese National Movement, headed by Kamal Junblat and his Progressive Socialist Party, represented an alliance of Leftist and Nationalist parties: the Lebanese Communist Party (general secretary Nicolas Shawi, later George Hawi), the radical leftist Organisation for Communist Action in Lebanon (general secretary Muhsin Ibrahim, later the LNM's executive secretary), the SNSP (represented by `Abd Allah Sa`adeh and In`am Ra`d), the Independent Nasserite Movement (*al-Murabitun*, headed by Ibrahim Qulaylat), the Popular Nasserite Organisation of Mustafa Sa`d, the Nasserite Arab Socialist Union of `Abd al-Rahim Murad and a number of independent figures including Albert Mansur, Usama Fakhuri and Samir Franjiyeh.

3. *L'Orient-Le Jour*, 8, 13 June 1975.

4. A Lebanese Front memorandum said it clearly: 'the Muslim majority is oppressive *nolens*, *volens*, which constitutes a danger for the sheer existence of the Christians in all of Lebanon' (*al-Nahar*, 20 December 1977).

5. See the complete minutes of the CDN sessions in *Al-Tariq*, nos 1–8 (January–August 1976), pp. 97–321.

6. Interview on Radio France International, reported in *Al-Safir*, 9 August 1975.

7. Acronym for *Afwaj al-Muqawama al-Lubnaniya* (Battalions of Lebanese Resistance).

8. Declaration of the Phalange Politbureau, 10 January 1976.

9. Randall, *Going All the Way*, p. 96.

10. Henry Kissinger, *Years of Renewal* (New York: Diane Pub. Co., 1999), p. 1045.

11. In a secret memorandum to French emissary Maurice Couve de Murville, revealed to the public by the leftist weekly *al-Hurriya*, the Kaslik monks called for a return to a Christian 'Little Lebanon'. In fact, special French envoy Georges Gorse was in Beirut during Brown's mission with a message from President François Mitterand expressing France's willingness to form a joint French–Syrian military intervention force to end the Lebanese war, a proposal that was sabotaged by the Americans.

12. Alain Ménargues, *Les Secrets de la guerre du Liban* (Paris: Albin Michel, 2004), pp. 73–4.

13. Abu Khalil, *Qissat al-Mawarina fi-l-Harb*.

14. 'For Secretary from Brown', 1 April 1976, *FSOUSA* (Secret), Beirut, no. 02866.
15. Department of State Telegram, Beirut, no. 02935 041901Z, *FSOUSA*, 4 April 1976.
16. 'For Secretary from Brown', *FSOUSA* (Secret), Beirut, no. 3266, 13 April 1976.
17. *Ibid.*, no. 3545, 21 April 1976.
18. Cf. Y. Evron, *War and Intervention in Lebanon: The Israeli-Syrian Deterrence Dialogue* (London: Croom Helm, 1987).
19. Kissinger, *Years of Renewal*, p. 1042.
20. *Ibid.*, p. 1048.
21. *al-Hurriya*, no. 773, 17 June 1976. See also Abou Iyad, *Palestinien sans patrie* (Paris: Fayrolle, 1978).
22. *al-Hurriya*, no. 775, 30 June 1976.
23. John Bulloch, *Death of a Country: The Civil War in Lebanon* (London: Weidenfeld & Nicolson, 1977), p. 180.
24. Cf. Pierre Vallaud, *Le Liban au bout du fusil* (Paris: Hachette, 1976), pp. 96–8.

CHAPTER 12

1. He was succeeded to this post by the commander-in-chief of the army General Victor Khuri, who had replaced General Hanna Su`ayd, known to be too close to the rebel troops in the south.
2. Percy Kemp, 'La stratégie de Bachir Gemayel, *Hérodote*, nos 29/30 (1983), pp. 55–82.
3. Bashir confessed to the American TV journalist Barbara Newman that he had received an Israeli 'green light' for executing the Ihdin operation. Barbara Newman, *The Covenant: Love and Death in Beirut* (New York: Crown Publishers, 1989), pp. 140–1.
4. See the full text in Ménargues, *Les Secrets de la guerre du Liban*, annex no. 1, pp. 501–5.
5. *Ibid.*, p. 508.
6. *Ibid.*, p. 198.
7. The opposition to Bashir, incapable of preventing the elections proper, worked to sabotage the quorum. There was an attempt made on the life of a Sunni deputy for Ba`albak with the intention of reducing the quorum, while his Catholic partner had to flee East Beirut to escape Phalange threats on his life. Joseph Skaff, the political boss of Zahleh, was transported to Beirut by private plane from his Paris hospital, where he was due to undergo surgery, to vote for Bashir.
8. Ménargues, *Les Secrets de la guerre du Liban*, pp. 422–31.
9. Quoting his father Pierre, Bashir said: 'Without us, the Orient would not have been the Orient, its peoples would have been reduced [by one people] and it would have been deprived of the Renaissance and lost their contact with God.' The speech was prepared for Bashir by one of his close collaborators, Sij`an Qazzi. See the full text in *Al-Nahar*, 15 September 1992.

10. See the confessions of As`ad Shaftary, LF intelligence chief, in *al-Hayat*, 14, 15 and 16 February 2002. The conservative 'feudal' *beyk* of `Akkar seemed to be the favourite of organisers of *coup d'etats*. He had already been designated as prime minister by the organisers of the failed *coup d'etat* of the SNSP against Shihab in 1962!
11. Cf. Fawaz Traboulsi, 'al-Fashiya fi-l-Iqtisad', *Bayrut al-Masa'*, 8 May 1982.
12. Thomas Friedman has estimated that a quarter of those killed in the camps were Lebanese: cited in Noam Chomsky, *The Fateful Triangle: The United States, Israel and the Palestinians* (Cambridge, MA: South End Press, 1999), p. 370.
13. Associated Press Report, 15 September 1982.
14. Alexander Cockburn, as cited in Chomsky, *The Fateful Triangle*, p. 389. See also George Shultz, *Turmoil and Triumph: My Years as Secretary of State* (New York: Charles Scribner's Sons, 1993), p. 105.
15. During the siege of West Beirut, in a discussion on the situation after the departure of the Palestinian *fida'iyin*, Bachir mentioned to Sharon his intention to introduce bulldozers into West Beirut, erase the Palestinian camps and transform them into a 'vast zoo' or 'tennis courts'. Shimon Shiffer, *Opération Boule de Neige: Les secrets de l'intervention israélienne au Liban* (Paris: J.C. Lattes, 1984), pp. 172–3; and Ménargues, *Les Secrets de la guerre du Liban*, p. 487.
16. Randall, *Going All the Way*, p. 15.
17. Shultz, *Turmoil and Triumph*, pp. 106–9.

CHAPTER 13

1. *Le Monde*, 14 September 1983.
2. Thomas Friedman, *From Beirut to Jerusalem*. (New York: Farrar Straus Giroux, 1989), p. 194.
3. Zahi Bustani, Bashir's political adviser, was named director of general security; a close collaborator of Amin, `Abdalla Abu Habib, became ambassador in Washington, while Elie Salem, AUB professor and legal counsellor to Bashir during the negotiations with the Israelis, was appointed minister of foreign affairs. See 'La mainmise phalangiste sur les rouages de l'État', *Le Monde Diplomatique* (October 1983).
4. On 7 July 1982, a Phalange officer revealed the plan to the Parisian daily *Le Matin*. 'After the withdrawal of the PLO', he said, 'the Lebanese army would enter Beirut and we will enter with them and there will be excesses by the middle cadres and the rank and file as we have bloody accounts to settle. We will try to evade a bloodbath, but it will be difficult to prevent an explosion of hatred which will be brief and limited.'
5. A number of the Amal partisans in the Biqa` split under the leadership of Husayn al-Musawi, who reproached Birri for being too soft vis-à-vis Israeli occupation, and founded Islamic Amal, linked to Iran.
6. Robert Fisk, *The Times*, 27 September 1982.
7. *Le Monde*, 10 January 1983.
8. Friedman, *From Beirut to Jerusalem*, p. 220.

9. Amine Gemayel, L'Offense et le pardon (Paris: Gallimard, 1988), p. 200.
10. *al-Safir*, 23 January 1984.
11. *International Herald Tribune*, 21 May 1985.
12. Data concerning the militias has been compounded from many private testimonies and published sources among which are: David Hirst, 'Jumhuriyat al-Milishiyat', *al-Qabas*, nos 98–100 (26–28 August 1985); 'L'argent des milices', *Les Cahiers de l'Orient*, no. 10 (Paris, 1988); an *al-Hayat* series of articles on the Lebanese militias, their administration and revenues (31 December 1990–9 February 1991); 'Le Livre Noir des Forces Libanaises', in *L'Eveil*, Centre Libanais d'Information (CLI), no. 2 (17 May 1990); Ph. de V., 'Les ports de l'angoisse... et des Pirates', *L'Evénément du Jeudi*, no. 233 (Paris, 20–26 April 1989); Georges Corm, 'Liban: hégémonie milicienne et problème du rétablissement de l'Etat', *Maghreb–Machreq*, no. 131 (January–March 1991), pp. 13–25.
13. At the beginning of the war, when observers still made estimates of arms contracts by Lebanese belligerents, Sampson put those contracts at between $200 million and $600 million and named two arms dealers: Sarkis Soghanalian, representative of Colt Industries, and Dany, son of ex-President Kamil Sham'un, considered by the author as the biggest arms dealer on the Christian side. David Hirst estimated the cost of one day of artillery duels at LL 25 million, while an Arab source put the cost of one day of fighting with light weaponry at between $150,000 and $500,000. This should give an idea of the sums consumed in more than 5,000 days of war and a very rough estimate of the profits made from arms sales. A. Sampson, *The Arms Bazaar*, 5th edn (London: Hodder & Stoughton, 1985), p. 21.
14. Denis Eisenberg, *The World and I Magazine* (June 1990).
15. Newman, *The Covenant*, p. 212.
16. Corm, 'Liban: hégémonie milicienne', p. 14.
17. In June 1988, reports were issued of 200 barrels containing toxic waste from Italy imported by sea and dumped in the LF-controlled canton. Though Italian experts admitted they contained chemicals used in the making of chemical arms during World War II, the Italian government refused to take back the goods on the grounds that the deal was made between private companies and did not engage the Italian state. The importer, identified as Armand Nassar, was a close collaborator of the Lebanese Forces. Based in Cyprus, he fled the island in due time to escape an international arrest warrant upon request of the Lebanese government. The affair of dumped toxic waste re-emerged in 1994–95 after a ministry for the environment was created. Two revelations were made: (i) new dumping locations for toxic waste and thousands of barrels discovered all over the country, some of them constituting an imminent threat to water resources; (ii) top officials of that ministry were believed to be implicated in the import of toxic waste in militia days. Despite serious accusations against the ministry, the affair was hushed up.
18. Hirst, 'Jumhuriyat al-Milishiyat'.
19. Boutros Labaki and Khalil Abou Rjeili, *Bilan des guerres libanaises* (Paris: Editions l'Harmattan, 1994), pp. 256 ff.

POSTSCRIPT

1. Council for Lebanese American Organisations (CLAO), *Policy Statement and Analysis of the Lebanese Situation* (July 1991), appendix C, p. 5.
2. Weekly published by `Awn partisans in the Centre Libanais d'Information (CLI), no. 3 (24 May 1990), p. 14.
3. For comprehension of the Ta'if accords and their application, see Albert Mansur, *Al-Inqilab `Ala-l-Ta'if* (Beirut: Dar al-Jadid, 1993) and Farid Al-Khazin, *The Communal Pact of National Identities: the Making and Politics of the 1943 National Pact* (Oxford: Centre for Lebanese Studies, 1991).
4. *Arabies*, Paris, no. 54 (June 1991).

Bibliography

PRIMARY SOURCES

Brochures, guides and memos

Mémorandum de Protestation, Présenté par les Habitants des Territoires Annexés Illégalement au Sandjak Autonome du Mont Liban (Beyrouth, n.d.).

Le Bequaa aux Libanais! Mémoire présenté aux gouvernements des Grandes Puissances, protectrices du Liban, par les Conseils Municipaux de la ville de Zahlé et du Mont-Liban (Zahleh, March 1913).

Chambre de Commerce de Marseille, *Congrès français de la Syrie – Séances des Travaux* (Marseille, 1919).

L'Indicateur Libano-Syrien 1922 (Beyrouth: Société Syrienne de Publicité, 1922).

L'Indicateur Libano-Syrien 1928–1929 (Beyrouth: Société Syrienne de Publicité, 1929).

Crédit Foncier d'Algérie et de Tunisie, *Répertoire economique et financier de la Syrie et du Liban* (Paris, 1932).

Direction Centrale de la Statistique, Ministère du Plan, *Population active au Liban* (Beirut, 1972).

Archives

The Foreign Service of the United States of America (FSOUSA), The State Department Declassified Lebanon, USA.

General Spears' Papers, Middle East Centre, St Antony's College, Oxford.

Newspapers and journals

Al-`Amal (Beirut)
Les Cahiers de l'Orient (Paris)
The Economist (London)
L'Eveil (Beirut)
L'évenement du jeudi (Paris)
Foreign Affairs (Washington)
Al-Hayat (London and Beirut)
The International Herald Tribune (New York)
Le Jour (Beirut)
Lisan al-Hal (Beirut)
Los Angeles Times (Los Angeles)
Maghreb–Machreq (Paris)
Le Monde (Paris)
Le Monde Diplomatique (Paris)
Al-Nahar (Beirut)
L'Orient-Le Jour (Beirut)
Al-Qabas (Kuwait)
Al-Safa (Beirut)

Al-Safir (Beirut)
Al-Sahafi al-Ta'ih (Beirut)
The Times (London)

Unpublished works

al-Husamy, Ratib, 'The Commerce of Beirut and the Bayhum Merchant House some 100 Years ago, 1828–1856', Unpublished M.A. thesis (American University of Beirut, January 1942).

Makdisi, Samir, 'Post-War Lebanese Foreign Trade', unpublished M.A. thesis (American University of Beirut, June 1955).

Naff, Alixa, 'A Social History of Zahle, the Principal Market Town in Nineteenth Century Lebanon', unpublished Ph. D. thesis (Los Angeles: University of California, 1972).

Nasr, S. and M., 'Remarques sur la composition structurelle du secteur industriel au Liban' (Beyrouth, 1971).

—— 'Les travailleurs de la grande industrie dans la banlieue-Est de Beyrouth' (Beyrouth, 1974).

Salam, Nawaf, 'L'insurrection de 1958 au Liban' (Paris: Université de Paris-Sorbonne, 1979).

Sassine, Fares, Le Libanisme maronite: Contribution à l'étude d'un discours Politique', Thèse de doctorat de 3ème cycle en philosophie (Paris: Université Paris V-Sorbonne, 1979).

SECONDARY SOURCES

Abqarius, Iskandar Ya`qub, *Nawadir al-Zaman fi Waqa'i` Jabal Lubnan* (London: Riad al-Rayyes Books, 1987).

Abou el-Rousse Slim, Souad, *Le métayage et l'impot au Mont-Liban, XVIIIe et XIXe siecle* (Beyrouth: Dar el-Machreq, 1987).

Abu Husayn, `Abd al-Rahim, *Provincial Leadership in Syria, 1575–1660* (Beirut: American University of Beirut, 1985).

—— *Lubnan wa-l-Imara al-Durziya fi-l-`Ahd al-`Uthmani* (Beirut: Dar al-Nahar, 2005).

Abu Shaqra, Husayn Ghadhban and Yusuf Khattar Abu Shaqra, *Al-Harakat fi Lubnan ila `Had al-Mutasarrifiya* (Beirut: Matba`at al-Ittihad, 1952).

Adib, Auguste, *Lubnan Ba`d al Harb* (Cairo, 1919).

Ageron, Charles-Robert, 'Abd el-Kader, souverain d'un royaume arabe d'Orient', *Revue de l'Occident musulman et de la Méditerranée* (1970), pp. 15–30.

Ajami, Fuad, *The Vanished Imam: Musa al Sadr and the Shia of Lebanon* (Ithaca, NY and London: Cornell University Press, 1986).

Akarli, Engin, *The Long Peace: Ottoman Lebanon, 1861–1920* (Los Angeles: University of California Press, 1993).

El-Amine, A. and N. Wehbi, *Système d'enseignement et division sociale au Liban* (Paris: Editions le Sycomore, 1980).

'L'argent des milices', *Les Cahiers de l'Orient*, no. 10 (Paris, 1988).

Al-`Aqiqi, Antun Dahir, *Thawra wa Fitna fi Jabal Lubnan*, ed. Yusuf Ibrahim Yazbak (Beirut, 1938).

`Arida, Al-Batriyark Antun, *Lubnan wa Faransa*, ed. Mas`ud Dhahir (Beirut: Dar al-Farabi, 1987).

`Ata Alla, M. and Y. Sayigh, *Nazhra Thaniya fi-l-Iqtisad al-Lubnani* (Beirut, Dar al-Tali`a, 1966).

Al-Bacha, Constantin, *Tarikh Usrat Al-Fir`awn* (Harissa-Lebanon, 1932).

Al-Bustani, Salim, *Al-A`mal al-Majhula*, ed. Michel Giha (London and Beirut: Riad al-Rayyes Books, 1990).

Balibar, E. and I. Wallerstein, *Race, nation, classe: les identités ambiguës* (Paris: La Découverte, 1988).

Bakhit, Muhammad, *The Ottoman Province of Damascus in the Sixteenth Century* (Beirut: Librairie du Liban, 1982).

Barakat, Halim (ed.), *Toward a Viable Lebanon* (London and Sydney: Croom Helm, 1988).

Benassar, *Anatomie d'une guerre et d'une occupation: Evénements du Liban de 1975 à 1978* (Paris: Editions Galilée, 1978).

Beydoun, Ahmad, *Identité confessionnelle et temps social chez les historiens libanais contemporains* (Beyrouth: Publications de l'Université Libanaise, 1984).

—— *Le Liban: itinéraires d'une guerre incivile* (Paris: éditions Karthala, 1993).

Binder, Leonard (ed.), *Politics in Lebanon* (New York: Wiley, 1968).

Bowring, John, *Report on the Commercial Statistics of Syria* (London: HMSO, 1840).

Buheiry, Marwan, *Beirut's Role in the Political Economy of the French Mandate, 1919–1939* (Oxford: Centre for Lebanese Studies, 1986).

Bulloch, John, *Death of a Country: The Civil War in Lebanon* (London: Weidenfeld & Nicolson, 1977).

CERMOC, *Etat et perspectives de l'industrie au Liban* (Beyrouth: Centre d'Etudes et de Recherches sur le Moyen Orient, 1978).

Chamoun, Camille, *Crise au Moyen Orient* (Paris: Gallimard, 1963).

—— *Crise au Liban* (Beyrouth, 1977).

Chevalier, Dominique, 'Aspects sociaux de la Question d'Orient: Aux origines des troubles agraires libanais en 1858', *Les Annales: Economies, Sociétés, Civilisations*, Year 1, no. 1 (January–March 1959).

—— 'Lyon et la Syrie en 1919, les bases d'une intervention', *Revue Historique*, vol. 224 (1960), pp. 275–320.

—— 'Que possédait un cheikh maronite en 1858?', *Arabica*, vol. 7 (1960).

—— *La Société du Mont-Liban à l'époque de la révolution industrielle en Europe* (Paris: Librairie Orientaliste Paul Geuthner, 1971).

Chiha, Michel, *Le Liban Aujourd'hui* (Beyrouth: Editions du Trident, 1949).

—— *Politique Intérieure* (Beyrouth: Editions du Trident, 1957).

—— *Visage et présence du Liban* (Beyrouth: Les Conférences du Cénacle Libanais, XVIIIe année, nos 9–12, 1964).

—— *Propos d'économie libanaise* (Beyrouth: Editions du Trident, 1965).

—— *Palestine*, 2nd edn (Beyrouth: Editions du Trident, 1967).

Chomsky, Noam, *The Fateful Triangle: The United States, Israel and the Palestinians*, foreword by Edward Said (Cambridge, MA: South End Press, 1999).

Churchill, Colonel Charles, *The Druzes and the Maronites Under Turkish Rule, from 1840 to 1860* (London: Bernard Quaritch, 1982).

Comité Central Syrien, *La question syrienne exposée par les Syriens* (Paris, 1919).

Conrad, Lawrence I. (ed.), *The Formation and Perception of the Modern Arab World: Studies by Marwan R. Buheiry* (Princeton: The Darwin Press, 1989).

Corm, Georges, *Géopolitique du conflit libanais* (Paris: La Découverte, 1986).

—— 'Liban: hégémonie milicienne et problème du rétablissement de l'Etat', *Maghreb Machreq*, no. 131 (January–March 1991), pp. 13–25.

—— *Le Liban Contemporain. Historie et Société* (Paris: La Découverte, 2003).

Couland, Jacques, *Le mouvement syndical au Liban, 1919–1946* (Paris: Editions Sociales, 1970).

De Nerval, Gérard, *Le Voyage en Orient*, 2 vols (Paris: Flammarion, 1980).

Dhahir, Mas`ud, *Al-Judhur al-Tarikhiyah li-l-Mas'ala al-Ta'ifiya al-Lubnaniya* (Beirut: Ma`had al-Inma' al-`Arabi, 1981).

—— *Al-Judhur al-Tarikhiya li-l-Mas'ala al-Zira`iya al-Lubaniya, 1900–1950* (Beirut: Dar al-Farabi, 1981).

—— *Al-Intifadat al-Lubnaniya dhidd al-Nizam al-Muqata`ji* (Beirut: Dar al-Farabi, 1988).

Dib, Kamal, *Warlords and Merchants: The Lebanese Business and Political Establishment* (Reading: Ithaca Press, 2004).

Dubar, C. and S. Nasr, *Les Classes sociales au Liban* (Paris: Fondation nationales des sciences politiques, 1976).

—— 'Lubnan: al-Sidamat al-Ta'ifiya, al-Qadiya al-Wataniya wa al-Sira`at al-Tabaqiya', *Al-Tariq*, nos 1–8 (January–August 1976), pp. 69–79.

Ducousso, Gaston, *L'industrie de la Soie en Syrie et au Liban* (Beyrouth, 1913).

Ducruet, Jean, *Les capitaux européens au Proche Orient* (Paris, 1963).

Durand, Mlle, 'La rupture de l'union syro-libanaise', in *Mélanges Proche Orientaux d'Economie Politique* (Beyrouth: Faculté de Droit, Université St Joseph, 1956), pp. 293–358.

Eisenberg, Denis, *The World and I Magazine* (June 1990).

Eisenberg, Laura Zittrain, *My Enemy's Enemy: Lebanon in the Early Zionist Imagination, 1900–1948* (Detroit: Wayne State University Press, 1994).

Emerit, Marcel, 'La crise syrienne et l'expansion économique française en 1860', *Revue Historique* , vol. 207 (1952), pp. 211–32.

Eveland, W.C., *Ropes of Sand: America's Failure in the Middle East* (London and New York: W.W. Norton, 1980).

Evron, Yair, *War and Intervention in Lebanon: the Israeli–Syrian Deterrence Dialogue* (London: Croom Helm, 1987).

Faris, Hani, *Al-Niza`at al-Ta'ifiya fi Tarikh Lubnan al-Hadith* (Beirut: Al-Ahliya li-l-Nashr wa-l-Tawzi`, 1980).

Fawaz, Leila Tarazi, *Merchants and Migrants in Nineteenth Century Lebanon* (Cambridge, MA and London: Harvard University Press, 1982).

—— 'Zahleh and Dayr al-Qamar: The Market Towns of Mount Lebanon During the Civil War of 1860', in Nadim Shehadi and Dana Haffar Mills (eds), *Lebanon: A History of Consensus and Conflict* (Oxford and New York: Centre for Lebanese Studies and I.B. Tauris, 1988), pp. 49–63.

—— *An Ocasion for War: Civil Conflict in Lebanon and Damascus in 1860* (London and New York: I.B. Tauris, 1994).

Fisk, Robert, *Pity the Nation* (Oxford: Oxford University Press, 1991).

Freiha, Adel, *L'armée et l'Etat au Liban, 1945–1980* (Paris: Librairie générale de droit et de jurisprudence, 1980).

Friedman, Thomas, *From Beirut to Jerusalem* (New York: Farrar Straus Giroux, 1989).

Gates, Carolyn, *The Merchant Republic of Lebanon: Rise of an Open Economy* (Oxford and New York: Centre for Lebanese Studies and I.B. Tauris, 1989).

Gemayel, Amine, *L'Offense et le pardon* (Paris: Gallimard, 1988).

Gendzier, Irene, *Notes from the Minefield: United States Intervention in Lebanon and the Middle East, 1945–1958* (New York: Columbia University Press, 1997).

Ghorayeb, Amal S., *Hizb'ullah, Politics and Religion* (London: Pluto, 2001).

Gilsenan, Michael, *Lords of the Lebanese Marches: Violence and Narrative in an Arab Society* (Berkeley: University of California Press, 1996).

Gordon, David, *Lebanon: The Fragmented Nation* (London: Croom Helm, 1980).

Guys, Henri, *Esquisse de l'état politique et commercial de la Syrie* (Paris, 1862).

Haley, P. Edward and Lewis S. Snider (eds), *Lebanon in Crisis: Participants and Issues* (Syracuse and New York: Syracuse University Press, 1979).

Hamdan, Kamal, *Le conflit libanais: Communatés religieuses, classes sociales et identité nationale* (Paris: Garnet, 1997).

Hanf, Theodor, *Coexistence in Wartime Lebanon: Decline of a State and Rise of a Nation* (London and New York: Centre for Lebanese Studies and I.B. Tauris, 1996).

Hannoyer, Jean (ed.), *Guerres civiles: Economies de la violence, dimensions de la civilité* (Paris: CERMOC/Karthala, 1999).

Haqqi, Isma`il, *Lubnan, Mabahith `Ilmiyyah wa Ijtima`iya*, 2nd edn (Beyrouth: Publications de l'Université libanaise, 1970).

Harik, Iliya, *Politics and Change in a Traditional Society: Lebanon, 1711–1845* (Princeton: Princeton University Press, 1968).

——— *Man Yahkum Lubnan?* (Beirut: Dar al-Nahar, 1972).

Harik, Judith, 'The Public and Social Services of the Lebanese Militias', *Papers on Lebanon*, no. 14 (Oxford: Centre for Lebanese Studies, 1994).

Harris, William W., *Faces of Lebanon: Sects, Wars – and Global Extensions* (Princeton: Markus, Weiner, 1997).

Hawwari, Zuhayr, *Al-Ijityah al-Iqtisadi al-Isra`ili li-Lubnan* (Beirut: Al Mu'assasa al `Arabiyya lil-Dirasat wa-l-Nashr, 1985).

Al-Hayat (31 December 1990–9 February 1991): a series of articles on the Lebanese militias.

Hilu, Charles, *Muzakkarati, 1964–1965* (Beirut: al-Matba`a al-Kathulikiya, 1984).

——— *Hayat fi Zikrayat* (Beirut: Dar al-Nahar, 1995).

Hirst, David, 'Jumhuriyat al-Milishiyat', *al-Qabas*, nos 98–100 (26–28 August 1985).

Hitti, Philip, *Lebanon in History: From the Earliest Times to the Present* (London: Macmillan, 1957).

Hourani, Albert, *Arabic Thought in the Liberal Age, 1798–1939* (Cambridge: Cambridge University Press, 1983).

—— *Political Society in Lebanon – A Historical Introduction* (Oxford: Centre for Lebanese Studies, 1986).

Hudson, Michael, *The Precarious Republic: Political Modernisation in Lebanon* (New York: Random House, 1968).

Huvelin, Paul, *Que vaut la Syrie?* (Paris: Honoré Champion et Edouard Champion, 1919).

IRFED, *Besoins et possibilités du Liban* (Beyrouth: Ministère du Plan, 1962).

`Isawi, Charles (ed.), *The Economic History of the Middle East, 1800–1914* (Chicago: University of Chicago Press, 1966).

Ismail, Adel, *Histoire du Liban du XVIIème siècle à nos jours*, vols 1 and 4 (Paris, 1955; Beyrouth, 1958).

Iyad, Abou, *Palestinien sans partie* (Paris: Fayrolle, 1978).

Jabir, Mundhir, *Al-Sharit al-Janubi al-Muhtal* (Beirut: Institute of Palestine Studies, 1999).

Johnson, Michael, *Class and Client in Beirut: The Sunni Muslim Community and the Lebanese State, 1840–1985* (London: Ithaca Press, 1986).

—— *All Honourable Men: The Social Origins of War in Lebanon* (London and New York: Centre for Lebanese Studies and I.B. Tauris, 2001).

Jouplain, P. (Bulus Nujaym), *La question du Liban: Etude d'histoire diplomatique et de droit international* (Paris, 1908).

Junblat, Kamal, *Haqiqat al-Thawrah al-Lubnniyah* (Beirut, 1959).

—— *I Speak for Lebanon* (London: Zed Press, 1982).

Kapeliouk, Amnon, *Sabra et Chatila: enquête sur un massacre* (Paris: éditions du Seuil, 1982).

Kassir, Samir, *La guerre du Liban de la dissension nationale au conflit régional, 1975–1982* (Paris and Beirut: Karthala-CERMOC, 1994).

—— *Histoire de Beyrouth* (Paris: Fayard, 2003).

Kassir, S. and Mardam-Bey, F., *Itinéraires de Paris à Jérusalem: La France et le conflit israélo-arabe*, 2 vols (Washington and Paris: Les livres de la Revue d'études palestiniennes, 1992 and 1993).

Kawtharani, Wajih, *Al-Ittijahat al-Ijtima`iya wa-l-Siyasiya fi Jabal Lubnan wa-l-Machriq al-`Arabi, 1860–1920* (Beirut: Ma`had al-Inma' al-`Arabi, 1982).

Kemp, Percy, 'La stratégie de Bachir Gemayel', *Hérodote*, nos 29/30 (1983), pp. 55–82.

Kerr, Malcolm, *The Arab Cold War: Gamal `Abd al-Nasir and his Rivals, 1958–1970* (London: Oxford University Press, 1971).

Khalaf, Samir, *Persistence and Change in 19th Century Lebanon* (Beirut: Khayat, 1979).

—— *Lebanon's Predicament* (New York: Columbia University Press, 1987).

—— *Civil and Uncivil Violence in Lebanon: A History of the Internationalisation of Communal Conflict* (New York: Columbia University Press, 2002).

Khalifa, Issam, 'La révolution française et les révoltes sociales au Mont-Liban, 1820–1859', in Mouvement Culturel-Liben et Mouvement Culturel-France, *La Révolution française et l'Orient, 1789–1989* (Paris: Cariscript, 1989).

Khalidy, Tarif (ed.), *Land Tenure and Social Transformation in the Middle East* (Beirut: American University of Beirut, 1984).

Khalidy, Walid, *Conflict and Violence in Lebanon: Confrontation in the Middle East* (Cambridge, MA: Harvard Center for International Affairs, 1976).

Khalifa, `Isam, *Abhath fi Tarikh Lubnan al-Mu`asir* (Beirut: Dar al-Jil, 1985).

—— *Al-Hudud al-Janubiya li-Lubnan* (Beirut, 1985).

Khater, Akram, *Inventing Home: Emigration, Gender and the Making of the Lebanese Middle Class, 1861–1921* (Berkeley: University of California Press, 2001).

Al-Khazin, *The Communal Pact of National Identities: the Making and Politics of the 1943 National Pact* (Oxford: Centre for Lebanese Studies, 1991).

—— *The Breakdown of the State in Lebanon, 1967–1976* (London: I.B. Tauris, 2000).

Khouri, Gérard D., *La France et l'Orient Arabe: Naissance du Liban Moderne, 1914–1920* (Paris: Armand Colin, 1993).

Al-Khuri, Bishara, *Majmu`at Khutab, Septembre 1943–Decembre 1951* (Beirut, 1951).

—— *Haqa'iq Lubnniya* (Beirut, 1960).

Al-Khuri, Shakir, *Majma` al-Masarrat*, 2nd edn (Beirut: Dar Lahd Khatir, 1985).

Khuri, Fuad, *From Village to Suburb: Order and Change in Greater Beirut* (Chicago: University of Chicago Press, 1975).

Al-Khuri, Antun Yammin, *Lubnan Ba`d al-Harb, 1914–1919* (Beirut: al Matba`ah al-Adabiya, 1919).

Kissinger, Henry, *Years of Renewal* (New York: Diane Pub. Co., 1999).

Labaki, Boutros, *Introduction à l'histoire économique du Liban: Soie et commerce extérieur en fin de période ottomane, 1840–1914* (Beyrouth: Publications de l'Université libanaise, 1984).

—— 'L'économie politique du Liban independent, 1943–1975', in Nadim Shehadi and Dana Haffar Mills (eds), *Lebanon: A History of Consensus and Conflict* (Oxford and New York: Centre for Lebanese Studies and I.B. Tauris, 1988).

Labaki, B. and K. Abou Rjeili, *Bilan des guerres libanaises* (Paris: Editions l'Harmattan, 1994).

Laurens, Henri, *Le Royaume Impossible: La France et la genèse du monde arabe* (Paris: Armand Colin, 1990).

'Le Livre Noir des Forces Libanaises', in *L'Eveil*, Centre Libanais d'Information, no. 2 (17 May 1990).

Little, Douglas, 'Cold War and Covert Action: The US and Syria, 1945–1958', *Middle East Journal*, vol. 44, no. 1 (Winter, 1990).

Longrigg, Stephen, *Syria and Lebanon under French Mandate* (London: Oxford University Press, 1958).

Makdisi, Samir, *The Lessons of Lebanon: The Economics of War and Development* (London and New York: I.B. Tauris, 2004).

Makdisi, Ussama, *The Culture of Sectarianism: Community, History and Violence in Nineteenth-Century Ottoman Lebanon* (Berkeley: University of California Press, 2000).

Makki, Muhammad `Ali, *Lubnan min al-Fath al-`Araba ila-l-Fath al-`Uthmani* (Beirut, 1977).

Al-Ma`luf, `Issa Iskandar, *Tarikh al-Amir Fakhr al-Din al-Ma`ni al-Thani*, 2nd edn (Beirut: Al-Matba`a al-Kathulikiya, 1966).

—— *Tarikh Zahla*, 2nd edn (Zahla: Manshurat Zahla al-Fatat, 1977).

Mansur, Albert, *Al-Inqilab `Ala-l-Ta'if* (Beirut: Dar al-Jadid, 1993).

Mashaqqa, Mikha'il, *Kitab Mashhad al-A`yan bi-Hawadith Suriya wa Lubnan* (Cairo, 1908).

Massarra, Antoine, *La Structure sociale du Parlement libanais de 1920 à 1973* (Beyrouth: Publications de l'Université St Joseph, 1975).

Ménargues, Alain, *Les Secrets de la guerre du Liban* (Paris: Albin Michel, 2004).

Mouvement Culturel-Liben et Mouvement Culturel-France, *La Révolution française et l'Orient, 1789–1989* (Paris: Cariscript, 1989).

Munassa, Jibra'il, *Fi Sabil Nahda Iqtisadiya Lubnaniya Yusahim Fiha Lubnan al-Mughtarib* (Beirut, 1950).

Naji, Amin (Antoine Najm), *Shur`a Min Ajl Mithaq Watani Jadid* (Beirut: Afaq Mashriqiya, 1979).

—— *Dawlat al-Tanmiya wa al-Musawat wa-l-`Adala wa-l-`Aych al-Mushtarak* (Beirut: Afaq Mashriqiya, 1992).

Nasr, Selim, 'Pour éclairer la guerre civile au Liban', *Liban–Palestine: promesses et mensonges de l'Occident* (Paris: L'Harmattan, 1977).

—— 'The Crisis of Lebanese Capitalism', *MERIP–Middle East Reports*, no. 73 (1978).

—— 'Bayrut al-Kubra, 1975: Hudud al Indimaj al Ijtima`i', *Al Waqi`*, no. 3 (1981), pp. 69–110.

—— 'La transition des chi`ites vers Beyrouth: mutations sociales et mobilisation communautaire à la veille de 1975', in CERMOC, *Mouvements communautaires et espaces urbains au Machreq* (Beirut, 1985), pp. 86–116.

—— 'Roots of the Shi`i Movement in Lebanon', *MERIP–Middle East Reports*, no. 15:5 (1985).

Newman, Barbara, *The Covenant: Love and Death in Beirut* (New York: Crown Publishers, 1989).

Norton, Augustus Richard, *Amal and the Shi`a: Struggle for the Soul of Lebanon* (Austin: University of Texas Press, 1989).

Nubdha Mukhtasara fi Hawadith Lubnan wa-l-Sham, 1840–1862, ed. Louis Shaykhou (Beirut: Al-Matba`a al-Kathulikiya, 1927).

Owen, Roger (ed.), *Essays on the Crisis in Lebanon* (London: Ithaca Press, 1976).

—— *The Middle East in the World Economy, 1800–1914* (London: Methuen, 1981).

Petran, Thabita, *The Struggle Over Lebanon* (New York: Monthly Review Press, 1987).

Picard, Elizabeth, *Liban, état de discorde, des fondations à la guerre civile* (Paris: Flammarion, 1988).

Polk, William, *The Opening of South Lebanon, 1788–1840* (Cambridge, MA: Harvard University Press, 1963).

Porath, Yehoshua, 'The Peasant Revolt of 1858–1861 in Kisrawan', *Asian and African Studies*, vol. 2 (1966), pp. 77–157.

Poujade, Eugène, *Le Liban et la Syrie, 1845–1860* (Paris, 1867).

Poujoulat, Baptistin, *La vérité sur la Syrie* (Beyrouth: éditions Lahd Khater, 1986) [first published, 1861].

Rabbath, Edmond, *La formation historique du Liban politique et constitutionnel: Essai de synthèse* (Beyrouth: Publications de l'Université Libanaise, 1973).

Rabinovich, Itamar, *The War for Lebanon, 1970–1985* (Ithaca and London: Cornell University Press, 1984).

Rafik, M. and M. Bahjat, *Wilayat Bayrut*, 2 vols (Beyrouth: Imprimerie al-Iqbal, 1914 and 1917).

Randall, Jonathan, *Going All the Way: Christian Warlords, Israeli Adventurers and the War in Lebanon* (New York: Random House, 1984).

Al-Rihani, Amin, *Qalb Lubnan* (Beiurt: Dar al-Rihani, 1965).

Al-Riyashi, Iskandar, *Qabl Wa-Ba`d, 1918–1941* (Beirut, 1953).

—— *Al-Ayyam al-Lubnaniya* (Beirut, 1959).

—— *Ru'asa' Lubnan Kama `Ariftuhum* (Beirut: al-Maktab al-Tijari, 1961).

Saadé, Joseph, *Victime et Bourreau: Une vie racontée par F. Brunquell et F. Couderc* (Paris: Calmann-Levy, 1989).

Sadaki, L. and N. Salam, *Civil War in Lebanon since 1975* (Beirut: American University of Beirut, 1987).

Safa, Elie, *L'émigration libanaise* (Beyrouth: Publications de l'Université St Joseph, 1960).

Salam, Nawaf, *Mythes et politiques au Liban* (Beirut: Editions FMA, 1987).

Salamé, Ghassane, *Lebanon's Injured Identities: Who Represents Whom During A Civil War?* (Oxford: Centre for Lebanese Studies, 1986).

Salibi, Kamal, *The Modern History of Lebanon* (New York: Praeger, 1964).

—— 'Lebanon under Fuad Chehab, 1958–1964', *Middle Eastern Studies* vol. 2, no. 3 (April 1966).

—— *Crossroads to Civil War: Lebanon 1959–1976* (New York: Caravan Books, 1976).

—— *Muntalaq Tarikh Lubnan* (Beirut, 1979).

—— *A House of Many Mansions: The History of Lebanon Reconsidered* (Berkeley: University of California Press, 1988).

Salim, Yusuf, *Khamsun Sana Ma`a al-Nas* (Beirut: Dar al-Nahar, 1975).

Samné, Georges, *La Syrie* (Paris, 1920).

Sampson, A., *The Arms Bazaar*, 5th edn (London: Hodder & Stoughton, 1985).

Al-Sawda, Yusuf, *Fi Sabil al-Istiqlal, vol. 1, 1906–1922* (Beirut, 1967).

Sayegh, Rosemary, *Too Many Enemies: The Palestinian Experience in Lebanon* (London and New Jersey: Zed Books, 1994).

Sayegh, Yusef, *Entrepreneurs of Lebanon* (Cambridge, MA: Harvard University Press, 1962).

Schiff, Z. and E. Ya`ari, *Israel's Lebanese War* (London: Allen & Unwin, 1986).

Schultze, Kirsten, *Israel's Covert Diplomacy* (Oxford: Oxford University Press, 2001).

Sfer, Abdallah, *Le Mandat français et les traditions françaises en Syrie et au Liban* (Paris, 1922).

Sharara, Waddah, *Transformations d'une manifestation religieuse dans un village du Liban-Sud-`Ashura* (Beyrouth: Université Libanaise, Institut des sciences sociales, 1968).

—— *Fi Usul Lubnan al-Ta'ifi, Khatt al-Yamin al-Jamahiri* (Beirut: Dar al-Tali`a, 1975).

—— *Hurub al-Istitba`: Lubnan al-Harb al-Ahliya al-Da'ima* (Beirut: Dar al-Tali`a, 1979).

—— *Al-Silm al-Ahli al-Barid: Lubnan al-Mujtama` wa-l-Dawla, 1964–1967*, 2 vols (Beirut: Ma`had al-Inma' al-`Arabi, 1980).

Shehadi, Nadim, *The Idea of Lebanon: Economy and State in the Cénacle Libanais, 1946–1954* (Oxford: Centre for Lebanese Studies, 1987).

Shehadi, Nadim and Dana Haffar Mills (eds), *Lebanon: A History of Consensus and Conflict* (Oxford and New York: Centre for Lebanese Studies and I.B. Tauris, 1988).

al-Shidyaq, Ahmad Faris, *Al-Saq `Ala-l-Saq Fi Ma Huwa-l-Fariyaq* (Beirut: Dar Maktabat al-Hayat, 1966) [first published, Paris, 1855].

Shiffer, Shimon, *Opération Boule de Neige: Les secrets de l'intervention israélienne au Liban* (Paris: J.C. Lattès, 1984).

Shultz, George P., *Turmoil and Triumph: My Years as Secretary of State* (New York: Charles Scribner's Sons, 1993).

Smilianskaya, I., *Al-Harakat al-Fallahiya fi Lubnan Khilal al-Nisf al-Akhir min al-Qarn al-Tasi` `Achar* (Beirut: Dar al-Farabi, 1972).

Spagnolo, John, *France and Ottoman Lebanon* (London: Ithaca Press, 1977).

Stoakes, Frank, 'The Supervigilantes: The Lebanese Kata'eb Party as a Builder, Surrogate and Defender of the State', *Middle East Studies*, vol. 11, no. 3 (1975), pp. 215–36.

Al-Sulh, `Adil, *Sutur min al-Risala: Tarikh Haraka Istiqlaliya Qamat fi al-Machriq al-`Arabi Sanat 1877* (Beirut, 1966).

Al-Sulh, Kazim, *Mushkilat al-Ittisal wa-l-Infisal fi Lubnan* (Beirut, March 1936).

Taqrir wa Muqarrarat al-Mu'tamar al-Watani al-Dimuqrati fi Lubnan (Beirut, 27 November 1938).

Témoin oculaire, *Souvenirs de Syrie: Expédition française de 1860* (Paris: Librairie Plon, 1903).

Thobie, Jacques, *Intérêts et impérialisme français dans l'empire ottoman, 1895–1914* (Paris: Publications de la Sorbonne, 1977).

—— *Ali et les quarante voleurs: Impérialismes et Moyen-Orient de 1914 à nos jours* (Paris: Editions Messidor, 1985).

Touma, Toufic, *Paysans et institutions féodales chez les druzes et les maronites du Liban du XVIIIème siècle à 1914*, 2 vols (Beyrouth: Publications de l'Université libanaise, 1971).

Tueni, Ghassan, *Une guerre pour les autres* (Paris: J.C. Lattès, 1985).

Tyan, Ferdinand, *France et Liban: Défense des intérêts français en Syrie* (Paris, 1917).

Al-`Umari, Subhi, *Awraq al-Thawra al-`Arabiya*, 3 vols (London: Riad el-Rayyes Books, 1991).

Urquhart, David, *The Lebanon: A History and a Diary*, 2 vols (London: Thomas Cautley Newby, 1860).

V., Ph. de, 'Les ports de l'angoisse … et des Pirates', *L'Evénément du Jeudi*, no. 233 (Paris, 20–26 April 1989).

Vallaud, Pierre, *Le Liban au bout du fusil* (Paris: Hachette, 1976).

Van Leew, Michel, 'Un cas particulier de nationalisme: Emile Edde', *Cahiers du GREMAMO*, no. 7 (1990).

Watha'iq al-Haraka al-Wataniya al-Lubnaniya, 1975–1981 (Beirut, n.d.).

Weinberger, Naomi, *Syrian Intervention in Lebanon* (New York: Oxford University Press, 1986).

Weulersse, Jacques, *Paysans de Syrie et du Proche Orient* (Paris, 1946).

Yammin, al-Khuri Antun, *Lubnan Ba`d al-Harb, 1914–1919* (Beirut: al-Matba`ah al-Adabiya, 1919).

Yver, Georges, 'Les maronites et l'Algérie', in Y. Moubarac (ed.), *Pentalogie antiochienne/domaine Maronite*, tome I, vol. 2 (Beirut, 1984), pp. 981–1010.

Zamir, Meir, *The Formation of Modern Lebanon* (London and Sydney: Croom Helm, 1985).

—— *Lebanon's Quest: The Road to Statehood, 1926–1939* (London: I.B. Tauris, 2000).

Al-Zayn, `Ali, *Fusul Min Tarikh al-Shi`a fi Lubnan* (Beirut: Dar al-Kalima, 1979).

—— *Li-l-Bahth `an Tarikhina fi Lubnan* (Beirut, 1973).

Ziadeh, Nicolas, *Syria and Lebanon* (London: Ernest Benn, 1957).

Zisser, Eyal, *Lebanon: The Challenge of Independence* (Oxford and New York: I.B. Tauris, 2000).

Index

Compiled by Auriol Griffith-Jones

Crane, Charles 78, *see also*
King–Crane Commission
culture: Beirut as centre of 61–3; *al-Nahda* cultural renaissance 63–7
currency 122; Law on (1963) 140–1
customs 121, 122; revenues 50–1,
70

Dabbas, Charles 90
Dahdah, Edward 82
al-Dahdah, Mir'i 260n
Dalloul, Muhsin, PSP 200
Damascus 11, 19, 52, 112;
'autonomous state' 80, 89 (map);
riots (1860) 35–6, 37–8; road to
Beirut 21–2, 54
Dammus, Shibl, poet 89, 262n
Damur, besieged (1976) 192–3
Da'uq, 'Umar 89
Da'uq family 58
Dawud Pasha, governor 44, 45
Dayr al-Qamar 20, 27, 28, 232; Abu
Nakad lords of 9, 13, 20, 28;
besieged (1983) 224; massacre
(1860) 34
de Caix, Robert 86, 88
de Gaulle, Gen. Charles 104, 105,
108, 112
Democratic Front for the Liberation
of Palestine (DFLP) 203
Democratic Party 172
Democratic Socialist Party 179
Dentz, General 104
Dhahir al-'Umar, Emir 9
d'Hautpoul, General Beaufort 37
al-Din al-Rifa, Brig.-Gen. Nur 188
disease, epidemics 72
Draper, Maurice 218
drug trafficking 234, 236
Druze 4, 5, 8, 9, 15; and civil war
224, 230–1; decline in status of
25–6, 43, 48; and 'events of 1860'
(southern regions) 33–5; girls'
school 60; and revolt against
Egyptian rule (1838) 12–14; tax
privileges of 16, 25; War of the
Mountain 224, 231, *see also*
Muslims

Dulles, John Foster, US Secretary of
State 130, 134
Duwayhi, Father Sim'an, MP 148

economy 41, 47, 72, 128, 155; black
market 237; collapse (1984–5)
227–8; colonial trade 45–50; cost
of living 160, 167; crafts 4, 17;
detachment from Syria 120–3;
effect of civil war on 231–7;
effect of creation of Israel on
113; French interests 91, 96, 99,
118–19; and independence
118–20; and Intra Bank crash
149–52; monopolistic 'laissez-faire' 156–9; prosperity (1950s)
128; Salam's attempts at reform
172–3; Shihab's reforms 140–1;
viability of Greater Lebanon
85–6, 91–3, 94–7, *see also*
agriculture; industry; merchants;
oil; silk; trade
education: middle classes and
163–4; reforms (1958–70) 141;
schools 60–1, 64, 94; teachers'
strikes 146, 169–70
Egypt 68–9, 98, 126; armistice with
Israel (1949) 113; and Baghdad
Pact 130–1; defeat in 1967 War
152, 153; and Lebanese civil war
198, 201; and Lebanese
independence 105, 108; relations
with Lebanon 12–13, 144–5;
United Arab Republic with Syria
133, 136, *see also* al-Nasir, Jamal
'Abd, President
Eisenhower, Dwight, US President
132, 135
elections: legislative (1937) 103;
Nabatiyeh by-elections (1974)
180; national (1943) 106;
national (1957) 132; national
(1964) 143–4; national (1969)
153; national (1972) 171–2;
presidential (1936) 98;
presidential (1976) 198;
presidential (1989) 243
bin-Elezier (Fuad), Col. Benyamin
196

189; and civil war 187, 189, 193,
196; Kata'ib Party 102, 137, 144;
minister of interior 148, 154; and
presence of Palestinians 182–3;
and Taqi al-Sulh administration
181
Junblat, 'Ali, Druze uprising (1860)
34
Junblat, Bashir 9, 10, 11
Junblat, Kamal 123, 124, 132, 143,
168; and 1958 insurrection
133–4, 135; and agrarian protests
147; and Arab mediation 201;
assassination (1977) 204, 213;
civil administration in Beirut
199; meeting with Bashir Jumayil
200; minister of interior 154–5;
opposition to Baghdad Pact 131;
and President Asad 194;
Progressive Socialist Party 125,
128–9, 143, 182, 271n; proposal
on PLO presence 176; relations
with Salam 171; and Taqi al-Sulh
administration 181
Junblat, Sa'id, Druze leader 18, 27,
35
Junblat, Sa'id Bey (d.1861) 48
Junblat tribe 5, 6, 9, 16, 48; expelled
from Jizzin 13–14, 20
Junblat, Walid 225, 229, 230;
alliance with Bashir Jumayil 207,
213–14; and peace negotiations
214–15; siege of Dayr al-Qamar
224; and tripartite agreement
(1985) 226
June 1967 War 19, 152–3
Juniyeh, port of 19, 51, 196, 232

Kan'an, General Ghazi 245–6
Kan'an, Sulayman 84
Karam, Georges, Busson Group 118
Karam, Yusuf 33, 34, 39, 44–5, 68,
259nn
Karami, 'Abd al-Hamid, Prime
Minister 99, 107, 111
Karami, Rashid 133, 189, 223;
assassination 229; as Prime
Minister 137, 140, 144, 150,
153–4, 225

Kata'ib (Phalange) Party 102, 107
Kettaneh, Alfred 119
Kettaneh family 116, 264n
Khabbaz, Gabriel 94
Khaddam, 'Abd al-Halim 189, 205
Khairallah, K.T. 49, 50–1, 83–4
Khaldeh, port 232
Khalid, King, of Saudi Arabia 201
Khalid, Mufti Sheikh Hasan,
assassination 229
Khalifa, Marcel 180
al-Khalil clan 177
Khalil, Joseph Abu, Phalange party
196, 212
Khanjar, Adham, rebel leader (1920)
77
al-Khatib, Col. Ahmad 193
al-Khatib, Anwar 125
al-Khatib, Sami 207
Khattar, Michel, Busson Group 118
al-Khawaja, Fatima 168
Khayr, Antoine 109
al-Khazin, Farid 82
Khazin family (Maronites), of
Kisrawan 6, 16, 28, 29–30, 32
Khudr, George, Greek Orthodox
bishop 177
Khumayni, Ayatollah 229
al-Khuri, Abu 'Assaf Rizq Allah 18
al-Khuri, Abu Shakir 18
al-Khuri, Bichara Khalil 49
al-Khuri, Bishara 51, 84, 85, 91, 98;
and Arab League 112;
Constitutional Bloc 93, 103;
downfall of 123–7; and
independence accords (1942)
105–6; and independence
negotiations (1936–9) 103; and
National Pact 109; as president
106, 107, 123; rivalry with Iddi
93–5
al-Khuri, Butrus 117
Khuri, Emile, Arab federalist 82
al-Khuri, Fu'ad 92, 94, 119
al-Khuri, Ilias Dhyb 77
Khuri, Khalil, *Hadiqat al-Akhbar* 62
al-Khuri, Salim 123
al-Khuri, Sheikh Khalil 124
al-Khuri family 9, 18, 19, 116